CRITICAL POLITICAL THEORY AND
RADICAL PRACTICE

Mainstream political theory has been experiencing an identity crisis for as long as I can remember. From even a cursory glance at the major journals, it still seems preoccupied either with textual exegesis of a conservatively construed canon, fashionable postmodern forms of deconstruction, or the reduction of ideas to the context in which they were formulated and the prejudices of the author. Usually written in esoteric style and intended only for disciplinary experts, political theory has lost both its critical character and its concern for political practice. Behaviorist and positivist political "scientists" tend to view it as a branch of philosophical metaphysics or as akin to literary criticism. They are not completely wrong. There is currently no venue that highlights the practical implications of theory or its connections with the larger world. I was subsequently delighted when Palgrave Macmillan offered me the opportunity of editing Critical Political Theory and Radical Practice.

When I was a graduate student at the University of California: Berkeley during the 1970s, critical theory was virtually unknown in the United States. The academic mainstream was late in catching up and, when it finally did during the late 1980s, it predictably embraced the more metaphysical and subjectivist trends of critical theory. Traditionalists had little use for an approach in which critique of a position or analysis of an event was predicated on positive ideals and practical political aims. In this vein, like liberalism, socialism was a dirty word and knowledge of its various tendencies and traditions was virtually non-existent. Today, however, the situation is somewhat different. Strident right-wing politicians have openly condemned "critical thinking" particularly as it pertains to cultural pluralism and American history. Such parochial validations of tradition have implications for practical politics. And, if only for this reason, it is necessary to confront them. A new generation of academics is becoming engaged with immanent critique, interdisciplinary work, actual political problems, and more broadly the link between theory and practice. Critical Political Theory and Radical Practice offers them a new home for their intellectual labors.

The series introduces new authors, unorthodox themes, critical interpretations of the classics and salient works by older and more established thinkers. Each after his or her fashion will explore the ways in which political theory can enrich our understanding of the arts and social sciences. Criminal justice, psychology, sociology, theatre and a host of other disciplines come into play for a critical political theory. The series also opens new avenues by engaging alternative traditions, animal rights, Islamic politics, mass movements, sovereignty, and the institutional problems of power. Critical Political Theory and Radical Practice thus fills an important niche. Innovatively blending tradition and experimentation, this intellectual enterprise with a political intent will, I hope, help reinvigorate what is fast becoming a petrified field of study and perhaps provide a bit of inspiration for future scholars and activists.

STEPHEN ERIC BRONNER

Published by Palgrave Macmillan:

Subterranean Politics and Freud's Legacy: Critical Theory and Society
Amy Buzby

Politics and Theatre in Twentieth-Century Europe: Imagination and Resistance
Margot Morgan

Rosa Luxemburg: Her Life and Legacy
Edited by Jason Schulman

Hannah Arendt and the Specter of Totalitarianism
Marilyn LaFay

The Radical Humanism of Erich Fromm
Kieran Durkin

Decolonizing Time: Work, Leisure, and Freedom
Nichole Marie Shippen

The Politics of Total Liberation: Revolution for the 21st Century
Steven Best

The Political World of Bob Dylan: Freedom and Justice, Power and Sin
Jeff Taylor and Chad Israelson

The Political World of Bob Dylan

Freedom and Justice, Power and Sin

Jeff Taylor and Chad Israelson

THE POLITICAL WORLD OF BOB DYLAN
Copyright © Jeff Taylor and Chad Israelson, 2015.

All rights reserved.

Portions of Chapter 4 are adapted from "Bob Dylan and Antithetical Engagement with Culture" by Jeff Taylor, *Pro Rege* 41:4 (June 2013) © Pro Rege (Dordt College), 2013. Used by arrangement with the publisher.

Small portions of Chapter 1 (Anglo-Celtic folk music) and Chapter 7 (agrarianism) are adapted from *Politics on a Human Scale: The American Tradition of Decentralism* © Lexington Books, 2013. Used by arrangement with the publisher.

Dylan concert raps (1979–80) are from *Saved!: The Gospel Speeches of Bob Dylan* © Clinton Heylin, 1987–88, 1990. Used by arrangement with the editor.

Scripture quotations are from Revised Standard Version of the Bible © 1946, 1952, and 1971 National Council of the Churches of Christ in the United States of America. Used by permission. All rights reserved.

All quotations, including lyrics, are for review, study, or critical purposes only.

First published in 2015 by
PALGRAVE MACMILLAN®
in the United States—a division of St. Martin's Press LLC,
175 Fifth Avenue, New York, NY 10010.

Where this book is distributed in the UK, Europe and the rest of the world, this is by Palgrave Macmillan, a division of Macmillan Publishers Limited, registered in England, company number 785998, of Houndmills, Basingstoke, Hampshire RG21 6XS.

Palgrave Macmillan is the global academic imprint of the above companies and has companies and representatives throughout the world.

Palgrave® and Macmillan® are registered trademarks in the United States, the United Kingdom, Europe and other countries.

ISBN: 978–1–137–48234–1

Library of Congress Cataloging-in-Publication Data

Taylor, Jeff, 1961– author.
    The political world of Bob Dylan : freedom and justice, power and sin / by Jeff Taylor and Chad Israelson.
       pages cm. —(Critical political theory and radical practice)
    Includes bibliographical references and index.
    ISBN 978–1–137–48234–1 (hardback)
       1. Dylan, Bob, 1941– Political and social views. I. Israelson, Chad, author. II. Title.

ML420.D98T39 2015
782.42164092—dc23
                                                 2015001197

A catalogue record of the book is available from the British Library.

Design by Newgen Knowledge Works (P) Ltd., Chennai, India.

First edition: July 2015

10 9 8 7 6 5 4 3 2 1

Contents

Preface — vii
Acknowledgments — xi

Chapter 1 Bob Dylan's Roots and Traditional World — 1
Chapter 2 Voice of a Generation — 43
Chapter 3 Freedom and Justice — 93
Chapter 4 Conversion and Culture — 127
Chapter 5 Christian Anarchism — 151
Chapter 6 Dylan and the Jesus People — 173
Chapter 7 Dylanesque Politics in the Real World — 201

Notes — 235
Selected Bibliography — 281
Index — 289

Preface

According to Bob Dylan, we live in what his 1989 song calls a "Political World." He is correct. But what does this mean? And what is Dylan's relation to this world?

As an artist, a public figure, and a man, Dylan has at once been typical and exceptional. An examination of his songs, interviews, and pronouncements indicates that he defies easy categorization. He is identified as one of the most iconic figures of the 1960s, yet he felt virtually no connection with the decade's mythos. Dylan was accorded prophetic status while he criticized American society and idealized many of its traditions. Additionally, he has been an unwilling voice of a generation and a willing corporate spokesperson. He has held devout religious convictions while partaking in a libertine lifestyle.

In the 1970s, Dylan sometimes attributed this dualistic quality to being a Gemini. Astrology aside, he shares a trait that many successful politicians possess: the ability to be projected upon by audiences. People see characteristics in Dylan that they want him to embody, whether that belief conforms to reality or not. When Jack Nicholson introduced Dylan for the Lifetime Achievement Award at the 1991 Grammy Awards, the actor said that he searched the dictionary for a word to describe Dylan and all of them applied.

Dylan once sang that everybody wants him to be just like them. He has fought against being defined by outside expectations his whole career. Liberal audiences asserted that Dylan belonged to them. In later years, claims to Dylan's conservatism have been staked. Jews, Christians, nonsectarian spiritualists, and atheists have all assumed, sometimes simultaneously, that his beliefs and theirs are the same. To borrow a religious term, fans and critics have turned Dylan into a totem. He has become a symbolic representation, a projected image—good or bad, with adulation or antipathy.

On multiple occasions, fans have turned on Dylan, labeling him a traitor and a sellout. This happened in the mid-1960s when he went electric, in the late 1960s during his rural family man retreat to upstate New York, in the late 1970s after his conversion to Christianity, and in the 2000s when he began lending his music and image for commercials. People were confused and reacted as if an interloper had taken the place of the "real" Dylan. Robbie Robertson, a member of the Band and Dylan collaborator, has said, "People have a fictitious past in mind about him."[1]

One of the tasks for anyone writing about Bob Dylan is sifting through the layers erected to keep the world at bay and discerning what is real and what is not. This speaks to the difficulty of understanding Dylan. Dave Kelly, Dylan's personal assistant in 1979–80, says, "I'm not sure anybody really knows him."[2] In Kelly's opinion, this intrigue is a key component of Dylan's success. To make any definitive assessment, an assumption must be made that most of what Dylan puts out is not directly contrary to himself—and if a theme occurs frequently enough, it carries some likelihood of being true. Within the enigmatic man, there are core beliefs. This book will address the forces that acted upon Dylan and to which he reacted, the world that he influenced and that influenced him. From this comes an understanding that while there may be many Bob Dylans, there is a single life that they encompass. Today, he can play "Blowin' in the Wind," "Like a Rolling Stone," "If Not for You," and "Gotta Serve Somebody," and it is all water from the same fountain.

Sometimes in interviews Dylan has engaged in deliberate obfuscation, other times he reveals annoyance at being asked questions that have no answer. Dave Kelly watched this process during an interview with the BBC: "He turned into another guy. It was brilliant to watch. He just came up with all these riddles and he had them jumping through hoops and he took them on a merry dance... It was like theatre. And they lapped it up. And then they left and he went back to being regular old Bob like it'd never happened."[3] For these reasons, not all of Dylan's statements can be taken at face value, though oftentimes writers take one and ignore the rest. We have attempted to base our conclusions on themes that have repeated themselves in his songs, interviews, and pronouncements and apply them to broader historical, political, and religious concepts.

This is a book about the politics of Bob Dylan—not only his personal politics but his influence on the wider world. The political themes most commonly appearing in Dylan's work are freedom, suspicion of power, belief in universal sacred truths, and justice for the vulnerable. He understands that to be free is to be empowered and the downtrodden enjoy very little of either. Power is at the heart of politics and Dylan distrusts both the exertion of power and the ability of human beings to utilize it to correct the wrongs of society. This work is not an attempt to analyze Bob Dylan's music per se, or to provide a complete biography of him, but rather we are trying to place his politics in historical context and examine the political ramifications of his art. In a sense, this book is similar to an LP. Any one of the chapters could essentially stand on its own as a self-contained essay, just as one can put the needle down on a record and listen to a song. However, the book's meaning is best understood when taken as a whole. Dylan fans familiar with *Bringing It All Back Home*, containing an electric side A and an acoustic side B, may appreciate our approach as two authors. The first and second halves of the book are distinct, yet the chapters build on one another and transitions will make the connections explicit.

The first half of the book, written primarily by Chad Israelson, provides the foundation and origins of freedom, justice, and power, as they appeared in Dylan's life and work. The second portion of the book, with Jeff Taylor serving as primary author, focuses on Dylan's conversion to Christianity and the manner his newfound faith interacted with the aforementioned themes while adding a fourth value (salvation). The subtitle of the book refers to two sides of Dylan's politics: freedom and justice, power and sin—the idealistic and the realistic, the inspirational and the theological.

The entire book contains history and ideas as we examine the political world of Bob Dylan. Yet each half has a somewhat different feel. Chad the historian emphasizes events and the cultural, while Jeff the political scientist emphasizes theory and the institutional. The former has more zeitgeist, the latter more time-transcendence. The first half deals more with Dylan's biography and musical evolution, the second more with his conversion and theological perspective. Chad concentrates on the first half of Dylan's life, Jeff on the second half.

In contrast to many Dylan analysts, we are lifelong Americans, which might give us some insights that are less accessible to those who are not. More specifically, like Dylan, we are both sons of the Upper Midwest. Chad's roots are in Minnesota, where he lives today. Jeff was born and raised in northern Iowa—30 miles from Minnesota—and he spent a dozen years living in the North Star State. Most of our lives have been spent in the Minnesota-Wisconsin-Iowa-Nebraska-Dakotas region.

Chapters 4 through 7 include many endnotes that are not only source citations but also carriers of information. If you find something of particular interest in the text of these chapters, you may wish to consult the notes for additional information.

The second half of the book contains Christian theology and Bible verses. This is necessary since these chapters mostly deal with Dylan during the post-1978 period. The reader may or may not share Dylan's Christian worldview and interpretation of Scripture, but it is important to take his thoughts and actions seriously, and in the way they have been intended. In an oversimplified nutshell, we could say that Bob Dylan's political philosophy since 1979 has been that of Woody Guthrie supplemented by the gospels of the New Testament, of C. Wright Mills supplemented by the prophet Isaiah, of *Merchants of Death* supplemented by the book of Revelation. This being the case, ideology and theology are naturally intertwined.

Fifty-one years after interviewing the singer for the *Freewheelin'* liner notes, Nat Hentoff called Bob Dylan a "singular person."[4] Dylan is a singular person, but he embodies some important values that we would all do well to consider. If Dylan were totally sui generis, listening to him might be fascinating but of little practical value because we could not hope to learn from his example or find a real connection to the things that he is saying. Every human being is unique and perhaps geniuses are even more so, but Dylan lives within a context and exemplifies certain thoughts and tendencies, even as he puts his own stamp on them. Intentionally or not, Dylan has something to teach us about politics. He is more a conduit than an idol, more a servant than a leader. His power comes from truth. One of the truths Dylan shares is the danger of power.

Acknowledgments

This was an unexpected, fast-moving, lifetime-dream book. It is special to be able to write at length about someone we admire and about songs that have affected our lives deeply over the years.

In addition to the multitude of books, articles, and webpages we have used, there are a handful of helpful reference sources that deserve mention, including Michael Gray's *Bob Dylan Encyclopedia* and Clinton Heylin's *Bob Dylan: A Life in Stolen Moments, Day by Day* and *Bob Dylan: The Recording Sessions*. Olof Björner's *Still on the Road* website of concert setlists has been useful. Karl Erik Andersen's *Expecting Rain* website continues to be a great source of daily information about Dylan.

Nat Hentoff is a legendary music critic. Born in Boston, he later moved to New York City. He became famous writing about jazz and then branched out into other genres. A self-described Jewish atheist, Hentoff became friends with Duke Ellington and Malcolm X, among many other talented individuals, over the years. Bob Dylan was also a friend. Hentoff first interviewed Dylan in 1963 when he wrote the liner notes for his second album, *The Freewheelin' Bob Dylan*. Hentoff subsequently conducted important interviews with Dylan for *The New Yorker* (1964) and for *Playboy* (1966). He interviewed Joan Baez and Allen Ginsberg when writing a story about the Rolling Thunder Revue for *Rolling Stone* (1975–76). A half-century after he met Dylan, we asked Hentoff for his impressions of the young man, and Hentoff agreed to write the foreword to our book. Unfortunately, circumstances prevented the foreword-writing, but it was an honor to speak with Mr. Hentoff on several occasions and we appreciate his encouragement.

We want to thank those who agreed to be interviewed and with whom we had conversations and email exchanges: Charles Evers, Dave Kelly, Jerry Waldman, Charles Norman, Wendell Berry, Robert Dean Lurie, Michelle Werner, Alberta Cooley McCrory, Suzanne Duscha, Ralph Nader, Matt

Zawisky, Allen Flemming, and Bill Batchelder (and his father, Speaker William Batchelder III).

We also want to thank Cindy Lee Berryhill (widow of Paul Williams), Daniel Mark Epstein, Stephen Webb, Clinton Heylin, Jesse Walker, and Bill Kauffman for their assistance and encouragement.

We are grateful to Palgrave Macmillan acquisitions editor Brian O'Connor, to editorial assistants Nicole Hitner and Elaine Fan, and to Abby Oladipo, Chelsea Morgan, Deepa John, and the entire production team.

Thanks to the anonymous peer reviewer who provided support and suggestions.

A special thank-you goes to our friend—and fellow Dylan fan—Jon Benson. He has once again used his computer program to assist with the indexing of the book.

* * *

Chad would like to thank:

Beth, Addison, and Garrison for your love, support, hard work, and sacrifice. There is no way I could have done it without you three. What you mean to me cannot be expressed in words, certainly not in the space allowed—our family is what it is all about.

Kit and Isaac, my parents, who provided my foundation, bought me cassettes, LPs, and CDs; influenced my musical tastes and passions; and aided and loved me always.

Jeff, who gave me this opportunity, believed in my own ability, and enlightened me with conversations over the years.

My friends from La Crescent, UW-L, and UN. You contributed to this more than you know.

Zobin, I really appreciate your pep talks.

The Hogans, who, among other things, lent me those Dylan albums back in 1987, and lifelong friends who value music (Pat, Frank, Boohan, and Russ).

The professors who inspired me: Vettes, Pemberton, Hollenback, Miller, and Rader.

The RCTC library staff and faculty: Diane, Gwenn, Sandy, Teddy, Gretchen, and the student workers who helped me get materials and answered my questions.

Rochester Public Library, especially Brian Lind for his assistance.

Cheryl at the Hibbing Public Library for her help.

Those at RCTC who read chapters and gave me their comments: Atef, Barry, Richard, Ruth, Scannell, especially Mark Schnaedter (Dylanologist is a real word) who put in so much time, and all my friends and colleagues at RCTC for their encouragement during the fall of 2014.

Anyone else—family or friend—who I may have missed due to space constraints, but who contributed to the project.

* * *

Jeff would like to thank:

Nat Hentoff for being so kind when we spoke. As a civil libertarian, consistent prolife advocate, and biographer of A. J. Muste, you have long been a hero of mine.

Steve Wandro for talking to me about Dylan and letting me listen to your *Greatest Hits* albums at a time when I was only familiar with the Dylan of *Slow Train Coming* (July 10, 1980).

Fellow Dylan fans over the years, including Sally Flake Pitlyk, Kelly DeBrine, Tim Carter, and Karen Carlson.

Dordt colleagues Neal DeRoo, Jake Van Wyk, and Charles and Pam Adams in connection with the Popular Culture Conference on campus, which inspired me to write what became the foundation of this book (chapter 4).

Mary Dengler for wanting to publish that conference paper in *Pro Rege*, and Cal Seerveld for noticing the journal article and expressing thanks, and Gabe Eliserio for your e-mail.

Matt Drissell for cover design advice.

Peter Haworth for creating the Ciceronian Society panel at APSA that sparked Brian O'Connor's interest in my planned Reagan paper. The paper wasn't presented and was already a chapter in my previous book, but Brian's query led to a Bob Dylan book instead.

Chad, who was a kindred spirit at RCTC, has been my compatriot in political perspective, and is into Dylan as much as I am. You made the writing of this book not only easier but possible.

My older brother Greg shaped my taste in music—the Beatles coming first and then later moving into other manifestations of power pop. Your Byrds and Hollies albums were a gateway to Dylan.

Of course, I am indebted to my parents, Jim and Judy Taylor, for all you have given me over the years. I first heard Dylan songs on albums in your record collection. They were covers by Peter, Paul and Mary (*In the Wind*—1963), the Dillards (*Live!!!! Almost!!!!*—1964), and Johnny Cash (*Orange Blossom Special*—1965; *At San Quentin*—1969).

This book is dedicated to my wife, Shirley, and to my children, William, Jane, and David.

אלוהים תודה לך על בוב דילן

CHAPTER 1

Bob Dylan's Roots and Traditional World

From a purely statistical standpoint, Bob Dylan—Jewish and hailing from Minnesota's Iron Range—should reliably vote Democratic. Loath to have labels put upon him, his political outlook cannot be reduced to statistics. Dylan's political world has proved too broad and independent to be classified simply as left or right, conservative or liberal, though he has often been assumed to be decidedly leftist. His political outlook is partly derived from the atmosphere of his home state and partly from his religious upbringing. Placed into those two cultures by birth, Dylan melded what he learned from them with traditional American ideals and roots music. His appreciation for the ideals of an America rooted in the past, a powerful sense of the sacred, and identification with the underdog coalesced into a belief system that transcended contemporary politics. This combination intermingled in the fertile and artistic mind of a sensitive young man and reappeared consistently over the years.

Upon his arrival in New York in January of 1961, Bob Dylan created a persona separate from his actual background. Whether that meant emulating Woody Guthrie, changing his name, or creating a false adventure-filled past, he desired to fulfill a vision of greatness that existed within him from a very early age. However, a pseudonym, a phony back story, and misleading comments in an interview did not divorce Dylan from the culture that shaped him. One of his great talents as a songwriter has been the ability to apply his influences. In nearly every biography or interview about Dylan, someone who knew him in Greenwich Village refers to him as a "sponge" due to his ability to absorb the culture around him. They use the term to explain Dylan's immersion in the culture and music of the folk scene, but he had already begun the process of assimilating nearly everything around him. Though his career began in New York, it was neither Dylan's home nor his background. Bob Dylan's roots lie to the north and west, in a small Minnesota mining town with an even smaller Jewish community.

Political Culture

The culture of Dylan's home state still retains the influences of its early European settlers. In the 1850s, when Minnesota achieved statehood, the greatest number of white immigrants came from New York and New England. These immigrants were referred to as Old Stock Americans, Yankees, or Yorkers. They transmitted to Minnesota their Puritan heritage, which originated in Massachusetts. David Hackett Fischer and Daniel J. Elazar, among others, have noted the strong cultural connection between Minnesota and New England. Fischer's *Albion's Seed* lays out four cultural ways prevalent in the United States, all tracing their roots to a group of seventeenth- and eighteenth-century British Isles immigrants: Puritans, Cavaliers, Quakers, and Backcountry. According to Fischer, even though new groups moved in, merged with and influenced American culture, these four remained dominant and spread across the nation. Although Fischer has received criticism for painting with too broad a brush, nonetheless his analysis has merit.

The Puritan culture mandated a lifestyle built on a sober, hardworking citizenry. "Yankee idealism," a notion that expressed faith in government as an instrument of protecting the public good, was transmitted across the northern tier of America.[1] These Yankees advocated participatory politics and placed an emphasis on education. The Puritan influence in Minnesota remains present today in leftover Blue Law restrictions that mandate, for example, that liquor stores stay closed on Sunday.

In political scientist Daniel Elazar's analysis, the dominant political cultures in states such as Minnesota and Massachusetts are identified as "moralistic." States or regions that embody this type of political culture cling to a sense that power should be used for society's improvement. Thus, when political power is exerted, it should be for the purpose of pursuing justice, civic betterment, or similar activities. Elazar linked the moralistic culture to areas populated by large numbers of Yankees, Scotch, Dutch, Scandinavians, and Jews.[2] The desire for community enhancement makes Minnesotans acutely attuned to human shortcomings, and in their attempt to overcome them, Minnesotans are prone to "issuing jeremiads...commentaries on the weakness of their society."[3] Dylan has denied repeatedly that he is any sort of political figure and that politics can affect real change in the world. Although he has never claimed to have answers, frequently in both songs and interviews he has pointed out the failings manifest in society. Less a crusading reformer or political activist than a social critic, Dylan's pronouncements have the ring of an individual raised in a region accustomed to striving for civic improvement.

Puritans stressed hard work, humility, and a strict adherence to biblical law. During the English Civil War, they generally pitted themselves against the landed gentry. The Puritans came to America as one of the most egalitarian groups of colonists and were "suspicious of inherited privilege and the conspicuous display of wealth."[4] Dylan consistently acknowledged the corrupting influence that the concentration of economic power brought and despite his vast wealth, seemed to grapple internally with reconciling the two.

The Puritan sense of freedom and justice originated in their religious beliefs and obedience to God's will via the Covenant. They emphasized predestination, adherence to Old Testament laws, and the concept of original sin. In New England, the Puritans sought to make a "city on the hill" or a "New Israel" as a model for a sinful world. Dylan consistently paralleled this discontent with a society he viewed as corrupt, wayward, or empty. His 1989 song "Everything Is Broken" addressed a variation of a world gone wrong—which also happened to be the title of his 1993 folk covers album.

To the Puritans, allowing heretical beliefs such as witchcraft to exist among them threatened to incite God's wrath on the entire community. This notion of collective guilt caused early New Englanders to fear the potentially damaging consequences of "otherness."[5] That created an atmosphere that exerted pressure to conform and fostered suspicion of outsiders. That attitude found its way into Minnesota, a state known both for its "niceness" and for its stoic aloofness, which is notoriously hard for newcomers to penetrate.

In Minnesota, the population centers of Minneapolis and St. Paul dominate the attention and often the politics of the state. In the Minnesotan lexicon, Minneapolis and St. Paul along with their suburbs are called "the Cities." Everything outside this metro region is considered "outstate," and just about anything north of the Twin Cities is "up north." Bob Dylan did not just come from "up north"; he was raised on the ore-rich Iron Range. This is a distinct region within the state and stands apart geographically and culturally from Minnesota's seat of power. "The Range," as it is commonly known, has produced billions of dollars worth of iron ore that has benefitted the entire state. Despite its essential contributions to Minnesota's economy, the Iron Range has been overlooked politically and has only seen one of its politicians ascend to the governorship—Hibbing's Rudy Perpich. The region's uniqueness has been summed up as a "frontier melting pot mixed with the fierce pride of the people [which] has brewed a certain mystique on the Iron Range that has always been difficult for outsiders—even fellow Minnesotans—to understand."[6]

During the twentieth century, Minnesota's largest three immigrant groups—Swedes, Norwegians, and Germans—comprised the majority of the ethnicities found in the state. For most of the state's history, the Iron Range and Duluth, a harbor city roughly an hour from Hibbing, encompassed Minnesota's most diverse locale outside the Twin Cities. The Range's population consisted of Italians, Irish, Poles, Finns, and a variety of Eastern Europeans—to which Dylan and his relatives belonged. All told, thirty-five "sufficient sized" ethnic groups and a few members "from a handful more" found a home on the Iron Range.[7]

In the late nineteenth century, Jews from Eastern Europe arrived in Duluth and the Iron Range. Overall, the state's religious distribution remained nearly as homogenous as its ethnic groupings. The vast majority of Scandinavians and many of the Germans were Lutherans, though a sizable number of Germans practiced Catholicism. Other Protestant denominations were represented across the state as well. Minnesota housed a small Jewish contingent, less than 1 percent of the state's population, generally clustered in the Twin Cities, Duluth, and the Iron Range.[8] During the early to mid-twentieth century, the Iron Range housed four synagogues, one of them in Hibbing. Especially as he grew older, Dylan has acknowledged the degree to which his experiences growing up on the Iron Range impacted him.

Throughout its history, Minnesota's political tradition has boasted a strong independent streak and voters have expressed their willingness to diverge from major parties. In the late nineteenth century, the People's ("Populist") Party garnered strong support among farmers, workers, and those who sympathized with them in Minnesota and other Midwestern states. Primarily a reaction against economic hardship and corporate power, populism concerned itself with the plight of the "little guy" oppressed by a system rigged against him.

During the last decade of the nineteenth century, populism's strength reached its pinnacle. The presidential election of 1892 was the high-water mark for the Populist Party on a national scale and its candidate, James Weaver, finished second in Minnesota behind Republican Benjamin Harrison. Ignatius Donnelly of Minnesota wrote the preamble to the Populist Party's platform. In 1912, former Republican President Theodore Roosevelt, who ran as a Progressive, won the state over both Woodrow Wilson and President William Howard Taft. In addition, Socialist candidate Eugene V. Debs received the most popular votes from two of Minnesota's northern counties. In 1924, Independent candidate Robert La Follette, from neighboring Wisconsin and a torchbearer of populist sentiment, finished second to Republican Calvin Coolidge, but received roughly six times the votes of Democratic candidate John Davis.[9]

Minnesota's populist heritage, its independent streak, and the country's economic woes converged in the 1930s. When the Great Depression hit, a new political force formed, the Farmer-Labor Party. It was similar in scope and sentiment to North Dakota's Nonpartisan League and other independent or populist organizations. In Minnesota, the Farmer-Labor Party combined the Populist Party's base of agriculture with the mining and manufacturing workers of the Twin Cities and Iron Range. The Farmer-Labor Party won gubernatorial races in 1930, 1934, and 1936 when their dominance seemed so complete that the Democratic Party did not even run a candidate. By the 1940s, the third party's profile was high, but its electoral success waned and it merged with the Democrats. This created an entity unique to Minnesota, a party called the Democratic-Farmer-Labor (DFL).[10]

Minnesota voters' willingness to support candidates outside of Democrats and Republicans sustained throughout the second half of the twentieth century and into the twenty-first. In 1998, Minnesota gained national attention by again sending a third-party candidate to the governor's mansion. In this case, former professional wrestler Jesse Ventura, who ran as a member of the Reform Party, won the office. In national elections, third-party candidates such as John Anderson (1980), Ross Perot (1992 and 1996) and Ralph Nader (1996, 2000, and 2004) did better in Minnesota than their national averages (roughly two percentage points higher for Anderson and Nader's 2000 bid and five points for Perot in 1992).

The economic realities of the Iron Range helped to shape its political leanings as well. Not exactly urban, it is different from typical rural areas also. General attitudes on the Range demonstrate a population somewhat socially conservative but economically liberal, and who tends to vote overwhelmingly Democratic. Iron Range political stances have been branded a "quasi Libertarian brand of Democrat."[11] In every presidential election since World War II, essentially when Dylan's family moved to Hibbing, Democratic candidates far outpolled Republicans—generally by a two-to-one margin. Even in contests that were national blowouts, such as 1972 when Richard Nixon defeated George McGovern, St. Louis County (which includes Duluth and much of the Mesabi Range) turned out for the Democrat 3:2. Incidentally, in that same election, perennial Communist candidate and Iron Range native Gus Hall received his highest vote total in the entire state from St. Louis County at 138. That number proved two votes higher than he got from Hennepin County, home of Minneapolis, with roughly two and half times more voters. Continuing to the present, in elections for state and national offices, Iron Range voters remain one of Minnesota's most reliable Democratic strongholds.[12] Though the Range retains elements that are "Minnesotan," the culture and political leanings of its residents have been shaped by ethnic, geographic, and economic factors that make it unique within the state.

Hibbing, Minnesota

Robert Zimmerman (Bob Dylan) was born in Duluth, a picturesque city on the shore of Lake Superior in northern Minnesota. When he was six, his family moved from Duluth to Hibbing about 75 miles to the northwest. Despite having a history of radical political activity, Hibbing in the 1940s and 1950s may have seemed dreary to a youngster. Margaret Stark, who knew Dylan in high school, says, "He was treated as an outcast as he was growing up. He was odd, and different."[13] Thus, Dylan, both Jewish and socially unconventional, experienced some element of being "the other" among the dominant culture of his hometown. Although Hibbing's social norms could be stifling, the town also provided enough freedom and lack of distraction for Dylan's personality to emerge—a situation that was not exactly oppressive, not completely fulfilling, and requiring the development of a self-reliant streak. Reminiscing about a youth he called neither "happy nor unhappy," Dylan remembers Hibbing as a place where he had the "whole town to roam."[14] He graduated from Hibbing High School in 1959, and that fall he attended the University of Minnesota. Within roughly a year, he left school and headed to New York City to pursue a career in music.

Those who live on the Iron Range venerate hard work and have a proud heritage of union support. Organized labor helped create a sense of camaraderie among residents who "learned to stand together for working men and women during collective bargaining strikes."[15] Whether in time of strike or in difficulties inflicted by the harshness of the climate, cooperation potentially meant survival. In addition, the economy's volatility created a leveling effect on Range attitudes. Dylan speaks of his experience growing up in Hibbing: "Being poor when I was young didn't have a terrific influence on me. Where I came from, everyone was the same, so you didn't know you were poor, because you had nothing to compare with."[16] According to a lifelong Ranger, "It's more of a stigma to be rich here than it is to be poor."[17] In his autobiographical book *Chronicles*, Dylan explains that growing up on the Iron Range, "mine owners were more to be feared, more of an enemy," than communists.[18] Dylan's distrust of those in power began in his formative years and never wavered.

Dylan's father, Abraham Zimmerman, worked with two of his brothers, Paul and Maurice, at their appliance/furniture store. The Zimmerman family was comfortable, but very few people in town could be said to be well off. According to close high school friends, working with Abe helped to shape Dylan's empathy for those down on their luck. Echo Helstrom, his high school girlfriend, relates that Dylan had to accompany his father to repossess items when miners missed their payments to the Zimmermans' store. Helstrom thinks that this was when "Bob first started feeling sorry for poor people." She adds that when Dylan had to help load the truck with the repossessed item, he "hated that—used to dread it more than anything."[19] John Bucklen, a good friend from Hibbing and fellow music enthusiast, reiterates the young Dylan's feelings in an *A&E Biography* episode on the singer.[20] Abe Zimmerman told the *Saturday Evening Post* that he used to make Bob obtain payments from poor residents. Even though he knew that his son would not be able to collect, Abe Zimmerman wanted to show him "another side of life." He also imparted to Bob that some of them made as much money as the Zimmermans did, but they could not "manage it."[21]

Many stories relate Dylan's quiet beneficence to family and friends, though not all acquaintances claim to have experienced his generosity. Whether or not this sentiment stemmed from sympathies he developed as a young person, Dylan frequently espoused support for those on the fringes. According to Joan Baez, he "seldom reached out to anticipate another's needs, though occasionally he would exhibit a sudden concern for another outlaw, hitchhiker, or bum, and go out of his way to see them looked after."[22] Baez uses the phrase "another outlaw," implying that Dylan was some sort of outlaw or at least identified with them. He certainly saw himself as an outsider in Hibbing, and he continued to resist being "one of them," a notion he voiced several times in the *No Direction Home* documentary. Dylan says that his friends, as a teenager, were those "who couldn't make it as the high-school football halfback" or "Junior Chamber of Commerce leader."[23] Friends and teachers note that Dylan preferred individual or small group pursuits and avoided "organized activities."[24] The Iron Range shaped the young Dylan's sense of being an outsider and most likely caused him to identify with kindred spirits and underdogs.

The societal pressure to not stand out stemmed, in part, from the Iron Range's economic situation and its abundance of nationalities. Although the ethnic groups maintained their own foods and customs, they faced external expectations to assimilate.[25] Linda Fidler, a Hibbing native, says that residents were raised with few expectations except to be like everyone else.[26] Dewey Collyard, an old Dylan acquaintance, sums up the mood in Hibbing: "The demand for conformity here is strong"; even if a person was "talented and successful," that "talent and success should never stand in the way of being just like everyone else."[27] A local historian, Pat Mestek, confirms the same sentiment. She stated that her mother taught her not to "stick your head above the herd. You'll get it chopped off."[28] When the Hibbing Historical Society explored honoring Dylan, "he did not cooperate with us in any way," Mestek says. Dylan indicated through family channels that "he did not want any notoriety about him here."[29]

It may seem hard to believe that someone who is as internationally famous as Dylan would have reservations about success, especially when he willingly chose a career in the spotlight and, even as a youngster, dreamt of making it big. Considering the accolades heaped on Dylan and the dizzying level of fame he achieved, his roots sustained him to a remarkable degree and he never escaped Hibbing's influence. He frequently displayed the humility his northern Minnesota upbringing demanded. In a 2004 interview conducted with Ed Bradley, which aired on CBS's *60 Minutes*, Bradley informed Dylan that 12 of his songs were placed in *Rolling Stone*'s top 500. Bradley pressed Dylan to express how gratifying that type of critical acclaim must have felt. Dylan seemingly unimpressed by the accolade and knowing well the fleeting nature of critical adulation responded laconically, "Maybe this week." Bradley prodded him for a more enthusiastic response. Dylan, unwilling to take the bait, simply repeated the answer.[30]

The amalgamation of pressure to conform and Dylan's individualistic drive put him socially at odds with many in his hometown and certainly helped to form his sympathetic views toward those he saw as fellow outsiders. In the 1960s, the population of Hibbing was relatively small with one public high school. It seems reasonable that in 1964 most Hibbing residents would have known all about their most famous former citizen. However, that year, the *Hibbing Daily Tribune* ran articles on Dylan's exploits and introduced him as the "son of Mr. and Mrs. Abe Zimmerman."[31] This was after stories about him had appeared in *Newsweek*, the *New York Times*, and *Life*, among other publications, and after Dylan had made multiple television appearances. Apparently in the Hibbing of 1964, Bob Dylan remained more easily identifiable as the son of Abe and Beatty Zimmerman than as the composer of "Blowin' in the Wind." Charles Miller, a social studies teacher in Hibbing, noted that Dylan's political music "shook the hell out of the community. They were protest songs."[32]

Early in his career, Bob Dylan created a colorful past for himself, spinning a number of tall tales about working carnivals, playing music with old bluesmen, being orphaned, or running away from home. Some have interpreted this as an attempt by Dylan to deny his background as a Jewish Minnesotan who maintained a good relationship with his family. In late

1963, *Newsweek* ran a story that exposed Dylan's fabrications concerning his personal history, parental relationship, and last name. Dylan was furious about the *Newsweek* piece, which in addition to shedding light on his past contained an unsubstantiated claim that he stole "Blowin' in the Wind."[33]

Dylan probably believed his upbringing in Hibbing lacked a certain cachet among the Greenwich Village folkies and may have sought to shield his family from investigation. During his ascent to fame, he alternately dismissed and spoke openly of his northern Minnesota roots. Other than briefly in 1979–80, Dylan has rarely called attention to his religious beliefs or other personal details of his life. In his *60 Minutes* interview, when questioned about choosing the name Dylan, he responded that in the land of the free, a person can call himself whatever he wants.[34]

Dylan's refusal to divulge personal information, and/or his delight in confounding the press, was evident in 1964 when a writer for a Minneapolis newspaper asked him what he considered to be his hometown. Dylan responded first that it was Hibbing, then Fargo, insinuated Denver, and "some place in Michigan."[35] In written pieces such as "My Life in a Stolen Moment" (1963), he referred to Hibbing as "a good ol' town," perhaps in the manner of Sinclair Lewis's Gopher Prairie, and conversely in "11 Outlined Epitaphs" (1964) as desolate and dying. Both descriptions contain truth and need not be considered mutually exclusive. He was unequivocal about his need to leave it and keep "runnin.'"[36]

Dylan's stated impressions of his hometown have varied over the years, but his need to break out from its limitations remained constant. He said in 1965, "I left where I'm from because there's nothing there. I come from Minnesota, there was nothing there." He added, "when I left there, man, I knew one thing: I had to get out of there and not come back."[37] In 2004, he described needing to get away from Hibbing and going to a place that had more to offer.[38] Despite his desire to leave, the truth is Bobby Zimmerman probably had a better chance of becoming Bob Dylan growing up in Hibbing than in some other little Minnesota town, or anywhere else in America for that matter. For the man who continually charted his own path, he began the practice of running counter to a dominant culture in Hibbing. As he ran, he carried the lessons he learned from the region with him.

As Dylan advanced in his career, he became less evasive about his childhood and willingly acknowledged the impact that northern Minnesota had on him. In 1978, the only interview Dylan granted in the Upper Midwest was with *High Times*, the Hibbing High School newspaper. Prior to a concert in St. Paul, he told the paper's student editor that he was "proud to be from Hibbing." He also said that hailing from northern Minnesota "gave me a sense of simplicity."[39] In 2009, he spoke wistfully of the region's beauty and the way in which it remained partially frozen in time.[40] Dylan's observations in the twenty-first century express a fondness not only for the Hibbing of his boyhood, but for a society "before supermarkets, malls and multiplexes."[41] In large part, Dylan's political views reflect his yearning for a bucolic, lost America.

Economic Populism

The Iron Range's place in Minnesota's history stems from its geography as well as its demography. The whole region is often called the Range, though there are technically three different ranges: the Cuyuna, Vermillion, and Mesabi. Historically, the Mesabi Range has been the most profitable and is also where Hibbing is located. The Iron Range rests on a natural resource that provided the economic impetus for the area's late-nineteenth-century settlement when iron was first discovered. The prospect of work brought an influx of immigrants to the region. Despite its far northern location and unforgiving cold weather that Dylan claims "equalizes everything," Iron Range towns flourished.[42]

Hibbing is remote but it is not precisely a rural setting; rather it is a part of an industrial corridor that runs approximately 100 miles through northern Minnesota. This stretch of individual towns cuts through forests, lakes, and iron pits. Among places such as Babbitt, Virginia, and Eveleth, Hibbing grew to be the largest town on the Range and became the "unofficial capital" of the region. It was where the mine executives lived, and it housed the best retail stores.[43] It also boasts a spectacularly constructed high school. Built in the 1920s, it remains a remarkable testament to mining dollars and the region's civic commitment to education.

An economy reliant on a single natural resource is at the mercy of that commodity's availability and demand. The causal relationship was evident: as the iron ore mining declined, the economic well-being of the Range faltered. Discovered in the late nineteenth century, iron ore proved a timely find in a relatively new, sparsely settled state. Minnesota's ore became essential for the burgeoning Industrial Revolution. East Coast investors quickly purchased rights and soon owned much of the region's most valuable land. Financial titans Andrew Carnegie and John D. Rockefeller, among others, had a financial stake in Minnesota mines and railroads. When mining companies began operating, immigrants in search of work moved into the area. Laborers endured miserable conditions but without the mines, there was little other employment, and the threat of immense hardship constantly loomed for the entire population.

In the early twentieth century, local Range governments took on mining interests. The mining companies shipped their freight through the middle of town, blasts from their mines shook and damaged homes, yet the companies contributed little to nothing for civic improvements. In addition, to be employed in the mines meant experiencing dirty, difficult, and dangerous conditions. Worker and citizen discontent developed and soon challenged the status quo. The emergence of a fiery populist sentiment on the Iron Range was the outgrowth of these realities. Politicians who pushed back against the mine companies attracted a following. The archetype of a feisty underdog willing to stand up and fight the moneyed interests resonated with many Rangers.[44]

Politicians who were considered "for the people" influenced the development of a radical heritage in northern Minnesota. During the early twentieth century, it would have been common to hear communist, socialist, and anarchist speakers in numerous towns across the Range. In 1907, the Western Federation of Miners (WFM) went to the Iron Range to organize. The Industrial Workers of the World (IWW) used the Socialist Opera House in Virginia, Minnesota, as a headquarters. The labor organizations hosted rallies and 17,000 strikers eventually walked the picket line. On both sides of the struggle, out-of-state strikebreakers and supportive socialists such as Mother Jones arrived.[45] In 1916, a second and much more violent strike occurred. Hibbing hosted an IWW parade and the city's Workers' Hall served as a planning center for the strikers.[46]

By the 1940s and 1950s, some of the workers from this earlier contentious period remained in the area. Many of their children, who would have had the lessons from the strikes instilled in them, continued to live on the Iron Range in towns such as Hibbing. Their memories, resentments, and alliances helped to create the local political culture. Iron Range historian Marvin G. Lamppa notes that in every town, "there remained those who didn't forget. To them, there were two Mesabi ranges, the Mesabi of 'company men' and the Mesabi of the 'worker.'"[47]

Dylan's introduction to protest did not originate in New York's Greenwich Village. Minnesota's political heritage, and in particular that found on the Iron Range, exhibited a long history of dissent. According to Minnesota historian G. Theodore Mitau, "Voices of agrarian and urban protest, often discordant and intense, have risen from the mining pits of the Mesabi Range...to find expression in the platforms and conventions of Minnesota's third and minor parties."[48] He also notes that the Range's "tradition of protest has continued to exert pressure on state politics." Bob Dylan or anyone else growing up in the state received exposure to "the fervor for social justice and economic opportunity [that] has long had organizational expression in Minnesota."[49] That influence was reflected in the songs he wrote throughout his career. Bob Dylan may not have been the politically radical "King of Protest" in the manner that the media portrayed him. However, radical was a relative term and reporters, critics, and those who grew up in northern Minnesota interpreted it in different ways.

The centrality of the iron mines to the economy of the region cannot be overstated. The finances of the Iron Range revolved around the mines, the only game in town. Even before the United States entered World War II, iron ore production boomed due to the United States' support of the allies. Steel production tripled between 1938 and 1943.[50] With the end of World War II, when Dylan lived in Hibbing, mining declined rapidly and the region experienced a recession. In the late 1940s, the miners on the Range participated in nationwide steelworker strikes. McCarthyism and the Red Scare helped to weaken unions in the next decade.[51] The 1950s may have been the start of a decline for American labor, but the populist and prounion attitudes that developed during the previous 50 years in northern Minnesota thrived.

Dylan's youth in Hibbing allowed him firsthand knowledge of the vagaries unleashed by power concentrated in the hands of a few businesses. Enormous holes, opened in the earth in pursuit of ore, served as a constant reminder of this. Dylan also would have known that a few decades before he lived there, the houses and buildings of his hometown were uprooted and moved a few miles south to accommodate the mining interests. When output declined, the impact reverberated across the region and all businesses suffered. In a 1964 interview with *Life*, Dylan described Hibbing's economic situation as being like "death" all around him. "I was raised in a town that was dying. There weren't no need for that town to die. It was a perfectly valid town."[52] The economic distress to families made a lasting impression on the young Dylan.

In "North Country Blues" from his third album, *The Times They Are A-Changin'*, Bob Dylan offers his most direct statement about his home and the financial hardship caused by mining corporations. The song invokes Dylan's roots on the Iron Range and chronicles the social ramifications of sagging production. It begins in the vein of a Great Depression era folk song, inviting listeners to "gather 'round." Dylan then proceeds to describe when the "pits ran plenty" and the miners enjoyed a full "lunch bucket."[53] This prosperity did not last and, as the song unfolds, the harsh reality is laid bare.

As a songwriter, Dylan possessed an uncanny ability—especially for a young man only 22 years old—to delve deeper than his contemporaries. "North Country Blues" represents not merely a lament that "times were tough" but describes the numerous social ravages that an economic downturn unleashed. For example, he addresses alcohol abuse and a room that smelled "heavy from drinking" where out-of-work men passed the time. Job loss often led to family abandonment, and Dylan wrote "North Country Blues" from the perspective of a woman whose husband left her to care alone for three children.[54]

Also apparent in "North Country Blues" is the influence of Minnesota and the Iron Range's populist political sentiment. Populists often indicted eastern bankers as the root of their troubles. Populist icon and three-time Democratic presidential candidate William Jennings Bryan envisioned "a union between the producers of the South and West against the predatory corporations that dominate the politics of the Northeast."[55] In his song, Dylan explains that "in the East" owners thought Mesabi Range miners were paid too much. Using Easterners to represent banking interests and mine owners, Dylan taps into a suspicion that had long percolated in Northern Minnesota. Iron Range educator and author Aaron Brown reflects that sentiment: "Those of us who grew up here weren't taught we were radical. We were taught that people…probably wearing suits, were coming to get us, and that we needed to be prepared to defend ourselves."[56] Denizens of the Iron Range often view those from outside with suspicion and they tend to "distrust a shirt and tie much more than a greasy pair of overalls."[57]

Dylan's song recognized the rising impact of globalization before widespread use of the term entered the language. He witnessed mining jobs shifting to South America where miners worked more cheaply than their US counterparts. "North Country Blues" also identified a disheartening trend rampant in late-twentieth- and early-twenty-first-century rural and small-town America. Due to virtually nonexistent employment opportunities or the promise of only low-end jobs, many of these areas experienced a population stagnation or decline. Dylan captured the desperation brought on by the closed storefronts and a people forced to leave their homes. "North Country Blues" appeared during his so-called protest period and Dylan continued to write and speak about the plight of the American worker throughout his career.

In 1983, Dylan put out *Infidels*, an album that contained the song "Union Sundown," something of an updated "North Country Blues." Released during Ronald Reagan's first term, the original lyrics contained a line criticizing the president who had busted the air traffic controllers' union.[58] To start the song, Dylan lists a variety of items he owns that were made outside of the United States. At first glance, "Union Sundown" claims that the victims are American laborers put out of work by globalization. However, they are not blameless because very little of what they themselves own was "made in the USA." Dylan, a singer and not an economist, oversimplifies the hypocrisy of Americans buying foreign products and then complaining about being out of work. Nevertheless, he makes a point concerning cheap goods, a lure that has led to a materialistic culture and the working class undermining its own economic self-interest. He indicts an overly monetized society, observing that with capitalism, nothing counts "unless it sells."[59] What Dylan describes in "Union Sundown" is a world without values, other than value determined by cash. This notion harkens back to his mid-1960s classic "It's Alright Ma (I'm Only Bleeding)," in which he attacks excessive consumerism by declaring that it taints the culture until very little is sacred.

Addressing globalization, Dylan leaves it open-ended whether workers in South America who make 30 cents per day—a considerable amount to them—are exploited, lucky to make even that, or both. Dylan refers to capitalism as "above the law" and makes clear that it steamrolls workers on both continents. This should not be understood as Dylan's expression of Marxist rhetoric, although those ideas did flourish on the Iron Range of the early twentieth century. Rather, the populist in Dylan recognizes a need to call attention to the inimical effects of unbridled capitalism on people around the world. In his 1984 *Rolling Stone* interview with Kurt Loder, Dylan pointed out that people only recently started to work for "slave wages" and that the current situation was "just colonization." He continued by connecting the example of South America to Hibbing's fate of having lost jobs due to the quest for profit.[60]

Dylan slammed the corruption of union leaders by calling their organization "big business too."[61] The intent of that line is not to judge whether unions are inherently good or bad, but rather to level a criticism against any organization preceded by the adjective "big." Dylan saw big business, big government, and big labor as self-serving and therefore contemptible. In the late 1980s, he observed that individuals "who work for big companies, that's their religion. That's not a word that has any holiness to it."[62] The views Dylan expressed indicated belief that unfettered capitalism's power results only in damaging effects. This did not preclude Dylan from earning a tremendous amount of money in his professional career or working with corporations. He may have been able to compartmentalize or rationalize the competing instincts from his background and professional reality. Still, Dylan always regarded corporatized interests with suspicion because they exerted power over individuals.

At one point in "Union Sundown," Dylan envisions a scenario when the collusion of big business and government might declare a family's home garden illegal. Though such a line may appear overly paranoid, it articulates a concern that consolidated finances could reduce the populace to a state of serfdom. With the balance of power tipped too greatly in favor of big business, the free market would cease to create freedom and people would lose the ability to sustain themselves independently. Dylan makes clear that moneyed interests seek greater control and political organizations do their bidding. His understanding of the unholy alliance between financial and political powers can be traced back to Jeffersonian and Jacksonian advocacy of a decentralized political and economic system. Dylan observes, toward the end of the song, what he believes to be an insidious reality: violence rather than democracy rules the world.

The word "Union" in "Union Sundown" clearly applies to organized labor, but it can also be understood as the United States itself. The song implies that the middle class' erosion will lead to the country's demise. Once "greed got in the way" it subverted owners, union bosses, workers, and American values.[63] Sometimes interpreted as a patriotic, even a jingoistic declaration that advocates consumers buy only American made products, "Union Sundown" consists of more than simply that.

In 2003, Dylan released a feature film, *Masked and Anonymous*, which he cowrote with Larry Charles. The movie, set in a near-future, postrevolutionary United States, starred Dylan as Jack Fate, an imprisoned and out-of-vogue singer. John Goodman's character, Uncle Sweetheart, needs to raise money and stage a benefit concert in order to get out from under a mafia-type loan shark. The film is a commentary on politics, greed, popular culture, and what seem to be Dylan's personal experiences with fame. His distaste for political organizations and the damaging influence of big business is evident throughout. Early in the film, Uncle Sweetheart refers to the "dark princes, Republicans and Democrats," and states that money is the mother's milk of politics. Not an earth-shattering revelation but indicative of Dylan's general contempt for the business of politics and the politics of business.

Masked and Anonymous features a host of quirky characters, and one of the most off-kilter is an indigent man, played by Val Kilmer, who keeps a variety of animals. Some of the dialogue conveys messages that Dylan has expressed in song or interviews. In a scene with Jack Fate, Kilmer delivers a monologue essentially concerned with human depravity and observes that big corporations sacrifice humans in a manner reminiscent of the Aztecs. Later in the film, a stagehand played by Christian Slater comments that humans are comprised of only two races, workers and bosses.[64]

Dylan has frequently expressed his antipathy for authority figures and the notion of bosses. When asked about Bruce Springsteen, Dylan acknowledged the New Jersey singer's *Nebraska* album, which featured several hardscrabble, down-and-out song stories. He also found humor in Springsteen's moniker, "the Boss." Dylan commented that typically, "the boss was a dreaded figure" who made workers endure dangerous conditions, and perpetually kept them "under his thumb."[65] On "It Takes a Lot to Laugh, It

Takes a Train to Cry" from *Highway 61 Revisited*, Dylan sings to a potential love interest that he does not want to be her boss. He revisits the phrase "boss" in "Are You Ready?" from his gospel album *Saved*. Dylan asks himself whether he has submitted to God, or whether he is still "acting like the boss."[66] He rarely displayed a willingness to surrender to authority until his conversion, but in this case Dylan mocks the notion of an earthly boss, who thinks himself in charge while ignoring the true power of the supernatural "commander-in-chief," a title he later conferred upon God.

Separated by another two decades from "Union Sundown," Dylan included "Workingman's Blues #2" on his 2006 album *Modern Times*. The title could be interpreted as a commentary on the new millennium's first decade, as well as a nod to Charlie Chaplin's critique of industrialization in the film of the same name. Considerably less of a screed than "Union Sundown," Dylan borrows the title of the song from one that Merle Haggard wrote and recorded, "Workin' Man Blues." Dylan once again broaches the subject of globalization when he observes that wages are kept low by the need for businesses to compete overseas. Singing from the perspective of a worker exhausted and pushed to the margins, Dylan adds that the proletariat's purchasing power has declined and that this has resulted in a hunger creeping "into my gut." He welcomes sleep as "a temporary death," the only time he escapes the shattered life around him. In the song, Dylan evokes the melancholy of a lost world many Rustbelt laborers have experienced. In the postindustrial present, he deems the old life he once knew as a "sweet memory."[67]

At the song's end, more wistful than bitter, Dylan sings that some people have never done an honest day's labor and are unaware of "what work even means."[68] Siding with the victims of the consuming drive for profit, he turns his scorn on owners who closed businesses. He articulated a reminiscent train of thought in a 1963 interview to the leftist *National Guardian*. As he did later in "Workingman's Blues #2," Dylan targeted the ruling and managerial classes. He addressed the damage inflicted upon Hibbing by corporate mining interests and personified the group of owners as "he." "You should'a seen what he did to the town I was raised in—seen how he left it. He sucked up my town." Dylan indicated that in his hometown, it was "too late now for the people—they're lost." He also wondered when it would be "too late for him?" Dylan connected the businesses that drained the ore on the Range to the military industrial complex—"The same guy who sucked up my town wants to bomb Cuba, but he don't want to do it himself—send the kids." Dylan asked the question many exploited workers wondered themselves and that he echoed over 40 years later on "Working Man's Blues #2: "He made all this money, but what does he do to earn it?" Dylan characterized "him" as "a criminal, a crook, a murderer."[69] "He" could be thought of as "The Man."

Iron Rangers value authenticity from their politicians. Dylan has generally dismissed politicians as phony and rarely in his songs has he portrayed them in a positive light. For example, in his early song "I Shall Be Free," he mocks a politician who, in an attempt to appeal to "all kinds of people," eats bagels, pizza, and chitlins. Though it did not appear on the recorded version, the printed lyrics add that the politician ate "bullshit."[70] Five albums later, "I Want You" conjures a "drunken politician," and a senator who hands out tickets to his son's wedding comes across as unaware and self-serving in "Stuck Inside of Mobile."[71] On 2009's "It's All Good," written with Robert Hunter, a "big politician, telling lies" is mentioned in the same context as a kitchen in a restaurant "full of flies."[72] In a song that "belittles all those arrogant narcissists," politicians are at the front of the line.[73] In "I Pay in Blood" on Dylan's 2012 album *Tempest*, he sings of a "politician pumping out the piss." Politicians either as a group or as individuals do not make frequent appearances in Dylan songs, but when they do they are usually described as inauthentic.

One of Minnesota's most liberal and most genuine political figures was the late Senator Paul Wellstone, a firebrand who enjoyed great popularity on the Iron Range. Even though the region was, and still is, a DFL stronghold, ultra-left politicians have not always played well there. According to an Iron Range writer who summed up Wellstone's appeal, "The Range will forgive political differences if people perceive the politician's motives as sincere and if the candidate visits often and listens well. So Wellstone thrived here while other liberals have not."[74] Dylan shared that appreciation for the senator who represented his home state. Wellstone died in a plane crash near Eveleth, on the Range, in October 2002. A few nights later, Dylan performed a concert in the Twin Cities. He played "Forever Young," which had been used at the Wellstone memorial service. Dylan also performed "The Times They Are A-Changin'" and dedicated it to Wellstone, saying, "That song was for my man, who came to the end of the road in Eveleth."[75] Other than to introduce the band, Dylan rarely addresses the audience in concert. His statement about Wellstone should be taken as an acknowledgment of Dylan's genuine respect and admiration for the man.

Jewish Heritage

Dylan's grandparents left Tsarist Russia in the late nineteenth and early twentieth centuries to escape pogroms, and they settled in the area around Lake Superior. Their new country was about to witness an upsurge of anti-Semitism. In the 1920s, the Ku Klux Klan expanded their scope of hatred to include immigrants, Catholics, and Jews. The difficulties brought on by the Great Depression made competition for jobs more acute and heightened existing animosities. During the first half of the twentieth century, anti-Semitic attitudes ran high in the nation and state. Newspapers in Minnesota printed employment classifieds that included the phrase "gentiles preferred."[76] In 1930, Minnesota elected Farmer-Labor Party candidate Floyd Olson as governor. Olson grew up among Jewish families on Minneapolis's North Side, and when elected, he opened the doors of government that had previously been shut to Jews in Minnesota. Despite this amelioration, Minneapolis continued to have a reputation for virulent anti-Semitism. The Silver Shirts, a fascist and primarily anti-Semitic hate group, maintained a membership in the state of roughly 6,000 members.[77]

Nationally, the New Deal era saw American Jews move solidly to the Democratic Party. In the election of 1944, over 90 percent of Jewish voters cast their ballots for Franklin Roosevelt. Only 20 years earlier, Jewish partisan support had been roughly split. Starting with Roosevelt's presidency, Jews became for decades the Democratic Party's most reliable white voting bloc.[78] Historian Jonathan Sarna describes the postwar period as a time when American Jews found increasing social acceptance, indeed many experienced a renewal of faith, and the country became the "cultural center of world Jewry."[79] Nonetheless, anti-Semitism remained an undercurrent in the nation and in Minnesota in the immediate post–World War II years. Jerry Waldman, who grew up in St. Paul during the 1940s and 1950s, recalls his family waiting for a seat at a restaurant for nearly an hour and leaving when it became apparent that they were not going to be served. He adds that country clubs routinely excluded Jews, and neighborhood bullies provoked fistfights with the Jewish children.[80]

The profundity of the Holocaust reverberated through American Jewish communities in varying degrees. The term "Holocaust" did not come into widespread usage until the 1960s, and many American Jews did not fully grasp the tragedy's magnitude until that time.[81] Some individuals sought to compartmentalize the event and downplay their identification with Judaism. For others, the Holocaust sparked a renewal of faith and desire to reconnect to their religious roots. Regardless of when individuals or communities came to terms with the significance of the Holocaust, one of the general effects was an increased awareness of injustice and discrimination. For Jews, a sense emerged that they could never again let something similar happen. As Waldman explains, that feeling of self-determination led, when dealing with bigotry, to an attitude of "enough of this shit."[82]

In 1953, historian and writer Rufus Learsi wrote a remembrance that was distributed nationally through a variety of Jewish organizations and newspapers. It was intended to be read at Passover Seders, and one of the lines wished for a time "when justice and brotherhood would reign among men."[83] Coming to terms with the Holocaust, an increasing number of Jewish Americans engaged in movements that promoted social justice. For many Americans who had faced discrimination, the 1950s marked a time when their voices emerged. The clearest example was the fight against one of the United States' great moral injustices—the lack of civil rights for African Americans. Among the various political movements of the 1960s, the only one Dylan unequivocally supported was civil rights.

American Jews had always been socially active on an individual basis, but after World War II, Jewish organizations became increasingly involved in social issues.[84] In 1963, Rabbi Joachim Prinz spoke at the March on Washington and equated the plight of African Americans to Jews in Hitler's Germany. Theologian and philosopher Rabbi Abraham Heschel marched with Martin Luther King Jr. and asserted that civil rights were part of the prophetic tradition and a mitzvah, or something that was considered an obligation.[85] College students volunteered for civil rights organizations, and two young Jewish men, Michael Schwerner and Andrew Goodman, were murdered in Mississippi on a voter registration drive. Though civil rights had many Jewish supporters, this connection does not prove that *because* Bob Dylan grew up in a Jewish home, he became predisposed to supporting civil rights. Yet the fact remains that he supported racial equality and did so from an early age. Because of, or in addition to, his roots, Dylan felt a bond with the dispossessed—a tie that complemented his populist economic leanings.

Several biographers have tried to answer whether Dylan sought to hide from his Jewish heritage. When *Playboy* interviewer Ron Rosenbaum asked him whether he thought about being Jewish growing up, Dylan responded that he "never felt Jewish." It is difficult to discern whether this is a case of willful obfuscation or an actual sentiment. When he added that he did not "have much of a Jewish background," Dylan was not being forthright. Typically, Dylan resisted any type of classification, because in the same interview he professed his faith in God, just not a certain creed.[86] As a boy, he could not have been unaware of his connection to Hibbing's Jewish community as his parents were leaders in the local Hadassah (a women's Zionist organization) and B'nai B'rith.

The young Bob Dylan spent some of his boyhood summers near Webster, Wisconsin, attending Herzl Camp, a Jewish summer camp with a Zionist focus. Waldman, who shared a cabin with Dylan and continues to work for the camp, describes the Herzl experience in the 1950s. Activities included simulating the difficulties of being an Israeli settler, waking at 3:30 a.m. to build a site, learning Jewish folk songs and dances, and connecting with other young people of a shared faith. Waldman explains that campers lived as minorities in their home communities and now were surrounded by 150 other Jewish kids—an experience he maintains "had to have some impact on you." He also notes that Herzl Camp is "where I learned to be Jewish in a fun way."[87] At the camp, a quote from Theodore Herzl was posted on a large sign and read, "If you will it, it is no dream."[88] There is no telling if that inspired the young Dylan, but it easily could have served as a slogan for his musical career.

Moreover, it is possible that Iron Range pressures to blend in caused him to shrink from identifying his ethnic/religious background. Helstrom, Dylan's high school girlfriend, said she was unaware that he was Jewish until she asked him. According to her, Dylan remained silent, and friend John Bucklen told her later not to mention it again, because he did not like the topic.[89] His desire to avoid having his inner world penetrated by outsiders proved consistent throughout his life. The attempt by some biographers to use his name change from Zimmerman to Dylan as proof that he was trying to deny his Jewish background, spurn his past, or distance himself from his family adds an unnecessary layer of psychodrama and does not coincide with hard evidence. Bob Dylan is a deeply private public figure, and religious belief, even that of people who publicly profess their faith, is ultimately an internal affair.

Dylan's catalog is filled with songs that employ biblical references, and he certainly had intimate knowledge of the Judeo-Christian canon; still one could not necessarily surmise from his songs or political statements that he was Jewish. For each time Dylan retold Abraham's near sacrifice of Isaac, he offered an admonishment that Jesus would not forgive the sins of the "Masters of War." There were references to Cain and Abel, Leviticus and Deuteronomy, but also St. Augustine and John the Baptist. The letter "L" from "the Law" was capitalized in "She Belongs to Me," indicating Mosaic Law rather than the American legal system.[90] Whether it was talking about God and the law, or living outside it, the law made a number of appearances in Dylan songs. These references are open to interpretation, and that constitutes one of Dylan's great appeals.

The purpose is not to prove Dylan's Jewishness—that question is not in doubt—but rather to understand how his ethnic and religious experience may have shaped his political worldview. It would perhaps be too convenient to assume that Dylan's attitudes about freedom or justice were simply a result of a familiarity with Exodus, or inspired by commemoration of the

Maccabean Revolt. At the same time, biblical stories and religious community informed how he understood the world.[91]

Since immigrants poured into the Iron Range in the late 1800s, numerous ethnicities and religions have called it home. Most denizens would have been well aware of what ethnic and religious groups their fellow residents belonged to. Though an undercurrent of anti-Semitism certainly existed on the Range, as it did elsewhere in Minnesota and America, it appeared to be minimal. In the 1980s, Dylan's mother Beatty commented that she had not experienced anti-Semitism and had many non-Jewish friends.[92] In an industrial town like Hibbing, men of all nationalities and faiths would have needed to be ready to walk a picket line and know that everyone would stick to it. The remoteness of the Range created an independent population, interdependent on each other. Jewish women on the Iron Range formed Sunshine Groups for visiting the sick, as well as other charitable activities that assisted Jews and non-Jews alike.[93] For example, when John Bucklen's father was hurt in a mining accident, some of the Jewish women in town took their sewing to his mother so she could earn a little extra money. Among those participating was Beatty Zimmerman.[94] Hibbing's tenuous economy and brutal winters contributed to a sense of interdependence. When a car would not start in thirty-degree-below-zero weather, the ethnicity or religion of the person who assisted did not matter. A Jewish businessman from Hibbing confirms that what existed was "a melting pot here in this town. We always had to get along."[95]

One constant in Dylan's career has been his willingness to play benefit concerts. He was introduced to the idea of extending a hand to the less fortunate during his boyhood. This attitude did not necessarily come from a single source, such as biblical injunctions found in Amos or Jeremiah calling for just treatment of the needy. In the *No Direction Home* documentary, Dylan notes that being on the side of people who are struggling does not make one political.[96] Instead, it was both Hibbing's economic atmosphere and the Jewish religious community that reinforced the young Dylan's sense of charity and support of underdogs.

Although it is hard to determine the degree to which growing up Jewish in northern Minnesota affected Dylan's outlook, it appears evident that he drew on it for his appreciation of the sacred. In the same way that Dylan transcends typical political labels, he refuses to be defined by religious categorization. According to his mother, Bob "has always been religious," and during the late 1960s, he frequently read the Bible. Beatty Zimmerman also commented that "as a child, Bob attended *all* the churches around Hibbing; he was very interested in religion, and *all* religions, by no means just his own."[97] Noel Stookey, "Paul" of Peter, Paul, and Mary, confirmed Dylan's advocacy of biblical study. Stookey said he visited Dylan at Woodstock in 1967, and Dylan urged him to read the Bible.[98] During the 1980s, when asked about the origins of his interest in spirituality, Dylan said it developed "before I was born" and that he began reading the Bible in grade school.[99]

From his earliest songwriting, Dylan has produced work of powerful spiritual quality. "Lay Down Your Weary Tune" is a hymn-like celebration of natural splendor and a paean to the beauty of creation. Dylan called his 1967 release, *John Wesley Harding*, rock and roll's first biblical album.[100] Some critics and Dylanologists have claimed that the LP contained over 60 biblical references.[101] The album coincided with a transformation of Dylan's public persona and private life. By 1967, Dylan was married and starting to raise children. For the next eight years, he retreated from all but a few public appearances. *New Morning*, from 1970, closed with the brief but intense "Father of Night." The song praises God, the father of wheat, rivers, and night among other natural occurrences.

Beginning in the late 1960s, Dylan placed a greater emphasis on the eternal and traditional in his music rather than the surreal and contemporary. Dylan's late 1960s and early 1970s work represents his most effusive expression of domestic contentment. The albums *Nashville Skyline* and *New Morning* in particular contain songs such as "Tonight I'll Be Staying Here With You" and "To Be Alone With You." Dylan seems to have unlocked the key to happiness on *New Morning*'s "Sign on the Window," in which he pines to build a cabin, get married, catch fish, and "have a bunch of kids" who call him "Pa." A life spent doting on his family, Dylan sings, "must be what it's all about."[102] He filled the album with songs that celebrate the pleasures of family life and hint at a traditionalist worldview that many fans had not associated with Dylan. The aforementioned "Father of Night," as well as love songs such as "If Not for You" and "The Man in Me," were not written simply *because* of his heritage. However, at this time Dylan drew upon his interconnected religious and familial roots and demonstrated a Dylan less wary of the external world.

In 1974, he released a beautiful elegy for his children, "Forever Young," which appeared on *Planet Waves*. The opening lines of the song echo Numbers 6:24–26. The biblical passage reads, "The Lord bless you and keep you; the Lord make his face to shine upon you, and be gracious to you."[103] "Precious Angel," a song from after Dylan's late 1970s conversion to Christianity, contains a declaration that "our forefathers were slaves." It is likely that he addressed the line to Mary Alice Artes, an African American background singer and love interest. Additionally, Dylan sings a line about getting "out of Egypt," a reference to Exodus.[104] The lines represent Dylan's most direct acknowledgment of his Jewish heritage in song. Prior to becoming Christian, Dylan had already made enough religious references to reveal he was well-versed specifically in his Jewish spiritual background as well as in general Judeo-Christian themes.

In 1975, a few years before his conversion, Dylan spoke to *People* about "the Bob Dylan myth," something that was, he claimed, "given to me—by God."[105] The singer took pains to separate his political image from his desire to access something more mystical. Dylan maintained that his work should be understood artistically, "not politically or philosophically." He alluded to a divine mission of making music: "I'm doin' God's work. That's all I know."[106] In another interview about a year later, Dylan was asked how he imagined God. He laughed and turned the question around: "How come nobody ever asks Kris Kristofferson questions like that?" Using words that he echoed half a decade later in "Every Grain of Sand," Dylan stated, "I can see God in a daisy. I can see God at night in the wind and rain. I see creation just about everywhere. The highest form of song is prayer."[107] Over the years, Dylan never wavered from his concept of a divine presence in the world. He told *Rolling Stone*, "I see God's hand in everything. Every person, place, and thing, every situation." At the same time, he eluded the question of his own faith by asking rhetorically, "Who's to say that I even have any faith or what kind?"[108]

Innumerable times a journalist, critic, or fan has hailed Dylan as a prophet. He never claimed, sought, or accepted responsibility for the pressures that accompany such a distinction. The political implications of that designation, which is surely one of the main reasons why he denied it, were tremendous. The expectations as "Voice of a Generation" must have been like a lead weight for Dylan, but the notion that he spoke for God had to have been ten times worse. In 2004, Dylan told *60 Minutes* that despite what people called him, he never saw himself as a prophet or savior but could have envisioned himself being Elvis.[109] Rabbi Abraham Heschel describes the role of prophet as "poet, preacher, patriot, statesmen, social critic, moralist."[110] Aside from "statesman," every one of Heschel's descriptions has been applied to Dylan. Heschel also discusses the prophet's elusive nature: "The most assured way of missing the goal is an approach carried on with the preconceived certainty of being able to explain him."[111] These words could also serve as the opening line of a Dylan biography. One of Dylan's most famous attributes is ineffability, and several of the books about him have titles that suggest his hidden personality.

A designation as a prophet typically suggests an individual capable of predicting a calamitous future event. However, the significance of biblical prophets was not just in their forecast; instead their significance was delivery of an urgent message. In their time, they occupied a role as social critics, political commentators, and moral judges channeling God's Will—and were often not well received by society. Some Dylan commentators have drawn a connection between him and Jeremiah, another young man delivering messages warning a corrupt society to change its ways. In Jeremiah 1:10, God told him to "pull down, to destroy and to overthrow, to build and to plant." The theme of destruction of the old and growth of the new echoes the sentiment found in "The Times They Are A-Changin.'" While bestowing a divinely inspired insight upon Dylan stretches credulity, to say that he has served as a social herald or issuer of jeremiads does not. When pressed to explain how he creates his songs, Dylan often claims not to know and answers that they are given by God, magic, or an unknown source. Dylan's greatest skill is that what he creates contains messages that few could express as eloquently. Creativity has often been equated with divinity, and the adulation surrounding Dylan intensifies that connection.

Though not overtly religious and oftentimes described as political, colossal, or apocalyptic, "A Hard Rain's A-Gonna Fall" appeared on his second album, *Freewheelin' Bob Dylan*. When the handwritten manuscript of "A Hard Rain's A-Gonna Fall" went up for auction in 2014, we learned that Dylan wrote part of a verse from the book of Jeremiah at the very top of the first page: "Before I formed you in the womb, I knew and approved of you" (Jer. 1:5).[112] The verse ends with God telling him, "I appointed you a prophet to the nations." The very next verse describes Jeremiah resisting his divine calling by claiming, "Truly I do not know how to speak, for I am only a boy." Maybe these lines showed Dylan having fun with his burgeoning reputation as spokesman/prophet, or he sensed the power and uniqueness of the song he was writing and felt intimidated by it. Perhaps he felt that he was channeling the Divine when he wrote and had little choice in the matter.

Often misrepresented as an antinuclear song, "A Hard Rain's A-Gonna Fall" contains lyrics that left a great deal open to interpretation. It has also mistakenly been described as about the Cuban Missile Crisis but was actually written prior to that event. When Dylan introduced it in concert, now found on *Bootleg Series 7*, he said that the title meant "something is going to happen."[113] The song is not explicit, the something could have been war but the mood more than suggests something forbidding. What is certain is that Dylan created a song like no other of the time. The surreal images he conjured defied the standards of 1962's songwriting style and foreshadowed the type of work that defined his mid-1960s output. Dylan asked questions of his "blue-eyed son": "Where have you been?" "What have you seen?" and the answers—blood dripping from branches, oceans that are dead, and women who are burning—provided little comfort.[114] In the Dylan canon,

"Hard Rain" has few peers and is a prime example of a "political" song that contains no specific political message.

Similar to Dylan's questioning in "Hard Rain," God twice asks Jeremiah, "What do you see?" Though Dylan's song certainly shares a more direct connection to the Scottish ballad "Lord Randal," enlisting more than one influence in a song of such impact would not be surprising. Speculating on the meaning of Dylan lyrics is a rabbit's hole that rarely can be navigated with certainty. Though it could be debated endlessly, ultimately there *was* a reason Dylan chose to write that particular biblical passage on the top of the page. He may not have called much attention to his religious roots, but he was never separated from them and he often drew upon them for inspiration.

Dylan biographers and followers often search for indicators about what he thought at a given point in his life. Some believe that in the late 1960s, Dylan reconnected with Judaism after his father's death and may have considered moving to a kibbutz.[115] The 1975 *People* magazine article asserted he "unquestionably returned to his Jewish roots, or at least to a generalized spiritualism." In a 1978 interview with *Playboy*, he attributed the problems the country faced to a spiritual crisis.[116] In the early 1980s, rumors swirled that Dylan had "returned" to Judaism. Around the same time reports circulated that he was associating himself with the Lubavitchers, an ultra-Orthodox Hasidic group. Rabbi Kasriel Kastel said Dylan was "a confused Jew" and that he was "coming back."[117] Any time he observed Jewish rites and holidays (which he seemed to frequently) or delivered an indication of his religious beliefs, divination of what it meant immediately proceeded. Whether none, some, or all of the instances are accurately portrayed ultimately is Dylan's business and changes very little concerning the message of his music—the influences of his Jewish roots were already in place.

In 1983, Dylan demonstrated both his desire to avoid any classification as well as his suspicion of just about anything organized. Reaffirming his contempt for corporatization, Dylan noted that Coca-Cola, oil, and steel were all religions. "You can turn anything into a religious context. Religion is a dirty word."[118] This should not be understood as Dylan's repudiation of Judaism, or any religious belief, but rather a confirmation of the individualistic approach that he applied to so many areas of his life.

Ironically perhaps, Pastor Paul Esmond from the Vineyard Church, which is the congregation Dylan attended when he accepted Christianity, may have most accurately identified Dylan's postconversion relationship to Judaism. Esmond stated that Dylan never left his Jewish roots because he understood that the two religions worked in conjunction with one another.[119] Setting the ethnic quality of Judaism aside, the religious aspect had always influenced Dylan. As much as Dylan's views cannot be described in conventional political terms, his religious attitudes are equally as broad. The oldest and deepest roots in his life are his religious ones and Dylan absorbed these influences and as a result they informed his views and the songs he wrote. His attitudes toward freedom, power, and the workings of the world within a religious context were influenced first by Judaism, later by Christianity, and then continually by both. Dylan's religious beliefs, when he expressed them as an adult, generally transcended typical classifications. What he consistently demonstrated was a spiritual understanding that was individualistic and went to the Source. As Dylan said in his 2004 interview with *60 Minutes*, "God's the judge. The only person you have to think about lying twice to is either yourself or to God." He also spoke of making a "deal" with the "Chief Commander." Ed Bradley asked him whether that commander was on this earth. Dylan replied, "On this earth and the one we can't see."[120]

Southern Musical Roots

Beyond his own Hebraic culture, Bob Dylan is indebted to several musical traditions with deep roots in America: Anglo-Celtic folk; popular, old-time country; and Delta blues. One of the salutary cultural contributions of the South has been its preservation of English, Scottish, and Irish traditional and popular ballads—sometimes known as "Child Ballads" after compiler Francis James Child—that were brought from the British Isles to colonial America. Settlers in the Shenandoah Valley, Appalachia, and Ozarks were largely responsible for passing these songs on to later generations, thereby serving as the foundation for early folk music and country ("hillbilly") music.[121]

The South also produced the African American genre of Delta blues, coming out of slavery and spirituals. Dylan has been an important transmitter of these largely lost traditions in an era of trendy, commercial entertainment. This is surprising because Dylan has neither Anglo-Celtic nor African heritage and is just a third-generation American with all four of his grandparents having been born in the Russian Empire.

Ramblin' Jack Elliott is an American folk singer who was influenced by Woody Guthrie. Elliott, in turn, influenced Dylan. Born Elliot Adnopoz in Brooklyn, Elliot is Jewish. Robert Dean Lurie points out that Elliott adopted a cowboy persona despite his lack of roots in the tradition.[122] Why would a twentieth-century person of Jewish descent become immersed in American tradition? One possibility is so that he might better fit into the dominant culture. A second possibility is that he has the zeal of a convert.

A third possibility is that he sees value in things that other Americans take for granted.

Jesus told a group of Galileans in the synagogue, "A prophet is not without honor, except in his own country, and among his own kin, and in his own house."[123] Why is a prophet without honor in his own land? He has grown up among these people. They cannot see his specialness. They take him for granted. A prophetic or special tradition has the same problem. A middle-American who has grown used to folk stories and songs—or worse, to the Disneyfication of such cultural treasures—will not recognize their value. It takes new eyes to see them for what they are. It may take the eyes of the grandson of immigrants to strip off the layers of dust and commercialization, to recover things that have fallen victim to the syndrome of familiarity breeding contempt. This was one of the achievements of young Robert-Zimmerman-turned-Bob-Dylan.

Dylan's immersion in and reliance on the deep roots of American music—folk and blues—is a cliché because it is true. The recounting of this immersion and reliance is a much-traveled road. Greil Marcus has referred to this aspect of Dylan's music as his debt to the "old, weird America." But such a country and its music are weird only to modern ears that have lost their connection to the past as they have bowed to the false gods of progress and fashion. Michael Gray has analyzed the influence of traditional songs—especially their lyrics—on Dylan. With vast knowledge of old-time music, Gray has connected dots...at times even if Dylan did not consciously do so himself when writing a song.[124] Dylan is a genius but he has lived and worked within a stream of culture and history. His use of southern musical roots is second nature for him as he has near-encyclopedic yet heartfelt familiarity with folk, bluegrass, honky-tonk, gospel, and blues songs.

The historical touchstone for American roots music is the *Anthology of American Folk Music*. Assembled by Harry Smith, it is a multialbum compilation of folk, country, gospel, and blues songs recorded in 1926–34 and first released in 1952.[125] Throughout the years, Dylan has repeatedly drawn from these traditional songs in creating his own, from "Hard Times in New York Town" (1961—"Down on Penny's Farm") to "Tempest" (2012—"When That Great Ship Went Down").

As an acoustic performer, Dylan wrote a number of talkin' blues songs. In the mid-1960s, when Dylan went electric, he was backed by members of the Paul Butterfield Blues Band. Dylan has made use of electric blues for many songs since the 1960s. His new recordings during the past decade have routinely contained one or two blues-rock songs (sometimes to a tiresome degree since little lyrical and arrangement creativity is necessary for such songs). Traditional acoustic folk/blues songs also continue to influence

Dylan's writing. For instance, the opening lines of "If You Ever Go to Houston" (2009) are borrowed from "Midnight Special."[126]

The folk-country tradition is predominantly white music, but Dylan is also indebted to black music. One of Dylan's earliest musical heroes, in the late 1950s, was Little Richard. Blues music had early acoustic origins and a later electric development. The first is known as Delta, Rural, or Country Blues. The second is known as Urban Blues. Dylan's first professional gigs were at Gerde's Folk City in New York in early 1961 supporting John Lee Hooker.[127]

Dylan's fame resulted partly from his civil rights anthems. By the mid-1960s, he no longer had to write an entire song about civil rights to convey a message of racial equality. In "Outlaw Blues," Dylan sang that he loved a "brown skinned woman."[128] Whether he actually was romantically involved with an African American woman at the time is beside the point. This line provided one of rock and roll's first open comments on interracial romance. Three years later, Van Morrison released "Brown Eyed Girl," with the girl changed to "brown eyed" from the original "brown skinned," most likely to avoid controversy. Once again, Dylan exemplified attitudes of equality as his identification with African American culture has been both musical and personal. In the 1970s and 1980s, Dylan often used black backup singers. On a personal level, Dylan has had many African American friends, including girlfriends, and his second wife (1986–92), Carolyn Dennis, is African American.[129]

Musically, there has been a lot of crossover between white folk and black blues. Woody Guthrie and Huddie Ledbetter were good friends, and the genres intermingled, with Guthrie using talking blues and "Leadbelly" singing folk. Dylan has been very open through the years in talking about his reliance on blues and country "old-timey records," as well as live renditions of traditional folk songs. The same names come up repeatedly: Hank Williams, Bill Monroe, Muddy Waters, Robert Johnson, Sonny Terry, Stanley Brothers, Big Bill Broonzy, Woody Guthrie, Jimmie Rodgers.[130] In 1991, Dylan said that he keeps returning to Elizabethan folk ballads for melodies. Speaking to Robert Hilburn in 2004, Dylan explained, "I'm not a melodist... My songs are either based on old Protestant hymns or Carter Family songs or variations of the blues form."[131]

Dylan's reliance on folk and blues music has sociopolitical implications. It is liberal because it recognizes the value of the common people, of the poor and powerless, of the despised and discriminated-against. It is conservative because it recognizes the value of tradition, of the old and spiritual, of the familiar and time-tested.

Traditional Values

The songs Dylan produced in the mid-1960s changed the rules of popular music and, for many listeners, represented everything countercultural. Despite this, he maintained time and again that he felt little in common with the era. He wrote in *Chronicles* that the events of the decade imprisoned his soul and nauseated him.[132] Although Dylan pointed out injustices and critiqued society, he offered little in the way of solutions. He sought less to remake society than to remind people that it had taken a wrong turn. His political outlook did not consist of partisan arguments or sophisticated theory, but rather of a simple approach and of desire to see America's ideals realized. Dylan wrote in *Chronicles*, "Being born and raised in America, the country of freedom and independence, I had always cherished the values and ideals of equality and liberty. I was determined to raise my children with those ideals."[133] His sense of tradition ran deep, and he frequently invoked an America both real and mythologized. A conservative aspect underlies this type of worldview, but that label too proves inadequate when describing Dylan. He may have possessed traits that are similar to conservative thinking but calling Dylan a traditionalist is more accurate. He pulled together influences from all around him, including reaching back and connecting to ideas from American history. In retrospect, Dylan wrote that his songs did not "conform to modern ideas."[134] Stookey confirmed Dylan's affinity for traditional values when he commented that "Bobby discovered that so many things are timeless."[135] American roots music, lessons from history, and his religious background intermingled to help produce Dylan's traditionalist thinking.

The assumption that Dylan's folk/protest music or his anarchic rock and roll innovations symbolized a rejection of America and its ideals demonstrates a partial and one-dimensional understanding. Dylan's patriotism has been undervalued or dismissed because he is so closely associated with the 1960s, and because the leftist political movements of the decade have been portrayed as un-American. This interpretation is muddled for two reasons. First, Dylan himself identified very little with the times. Second, what happened during the decade was not a rejection of American values but rather an affirmation of their importance and an attempt to make them a reality. Both the Left and Right employed language that advocated freedom, justice, and equality.

Greil Marcus, whose writing about Dylan has been among the best known and most prolific, noted in 1970 that "there is no theme richer for the American artist than the spirit and the themes of the country and the country's history." He added that Dylan's "impulses seem to take him back into the forgotten parts of our history."[136] Marcus tagged this lost America as an "Invisible Republic." In *Chronicles*, Dylan refers to the republic he uncovered via traditional American music as "different" and "liberated." He added that he was not against popular culture or looking to tear down anything, but he found "mainstream culture as lame as hell and a big trick."[137]

Dylan, a worldwide phenomenon today, had just begun to break through in foreign markets during the 1960s. Dylan's early interviews in particular have to be approached with some skepticism since he was in the habit of creating a persona for himself. Nonetheless, visiting Great Britain in late 1962, Dylan asserted his affinity for the United States, its music, and to an extent its mythology. He claimed, "I don't like singing to anybody but Americans. My songs say things. I sing them for people who know what I'm saying."[138] Three years later, during his controversial electric tour of Europe, he commented, "England is OK, but I prefer America. America is what I know. It's all there for me."[139] Frequently heckled during concerts, Dylan provocatively informed the crowd that he was playing American, not British, music, and he often performed with a huge American flag hanging in the background.[140]

Music critic Ralph Gleason noted that "Dylan's songs are carved from the reality of the American dream contrasted to the unreality of how it is. And Dylan sings them out of his own experience."[141] The assumption that equality and individual freedom should be linked abounded in the movements of the 1960s, as well as some of the ideas Dylan expressed in his songs. Despite inconsistencies between these principles and their application in American history, they are at the heart of the country's political ideals. From America's inception, those with a social conscience have noted the discrepancy between the country's promise and reality.

Dylan's professed desire for the simplicity of an earlier time drew a connection to a Jeffersonian decentralized America. In the early 1800s, Jeffersonian liberalism championed a virtuous nation of individual liberty and small government. This vision celebrated the country's yeoman farmers and artisans, and their success was equated with the nation's well-being. A Jeffersonian notion of natural aristocracy meant that an individual (white and male at that time) theoretically could rise to the level of his abilities. In an 1825 letter, Jefferson expressed his disdain for those who "look to a single and splendid Government of an aristocracy founded on banking institutions and moneyed corporations, under the guise and cloak of their favoured branches of manufactures, commerce and navigation, riding and ruling over the plundered ploughman and beggared yeomanry."[142] Jefferson's ideals were in contrast to what Alexander Hamilton envisioned: a United States that featured larger centralized political, economic, and commercial interests.

The latter version ultimately won out in the United States, and it is exactly what Dylan has criticized so frequently.

In the bicentennial year of 1976, many Americans were disillusioned more than usual with politics, and at the same time were inundated with a celebration of the country's origins. Dylan told *TV Guide*, "I'd like to see Thomas Jefferson, Benjamin Franklin and a few of those other guys come back. If they did, I'd go out and vote. They knew what was happening."[143] A few years later, Dylan invoked Jefferson in the song "Slow Train" from the album *Slow Train Coming*. The first LP released after his conversion to Christianity, *Slow Train Coming*, featured both personal religious numbers and songs that served as a jeremiad for a society gone astray. "Slow Train" fell into the latter group. The global economy once more served as the focus of Dylan's scorn when he lambasted "foreign oil" and its control of "American soil." Channeling a growing popular sentiment, he fretted that the country's fortunes were being decided in European capitals. Multinational corporations and America's economic dependency on foreign markets are antithetical to a Jeffersonian worldview. That is why Dylan surmises in "Slow Train" that present conditions would have Thomas Jefferson rolling over in his grave.[144]

Dylan's identification with Jeffersonian principles may have been done unconsciously, but he certainly reflected and espoused them. When Thomas Jefferson utilized the phrase "the pursuit of happiness" in the Declaration of Independence, he "tied the new nation's star to an open-ended, democratic process whereby individuals develop their own potential and seek to realize their own life goals."[145] The arc of Dylan's professional career embodied this sentiment. Dylan's fierce independent streak and individualism became evident early in his life. His mother, Beatty, remembered that he was "forever the individual; always had to do it his way, and by himself."[146] Historian Douglas Brinkley writes that Dylan criticized "anything that cheapens the spirit of the individual."[147] Speaking to *60 Minutes*, Dylan describes feeling that destiny has propelled him. Whether it has been changing his name or repudiating the expectations others set for him, Bob Dylan embodies the great American myth of the self-made man.

The Antebellum Era, with the desire for social reform and spiritual awakening, allows for an easy comparison to the 1960s. The 1830s and 1840s witnessed the formation of groups working to abolish slavery and establish women's rights. The Second Great Awakening lit a renewal of religious fervor and utopian communal societies offered a vision of a perfected future. The religious, political, and market transformations reinforced the development of individualism. Hailing from New England, inheritors of the Puritan tradition of jeremiads, Transcendentalists represented America's most visible intellectual development of the time.

The Transcendentalist approach voiced by Ralph Waldo Emerson and Henry David Thoreau, among others, preceded the political and social movements of the 1960s by more than a century. In the nineteenth century, Emerson and Thoreau criticized the United States' provocation of the Mexican-American War and its inability to extend equality to blacks and women; both men, moreover, developed an interest in Eastern religion. Such similarities may be superficial but when understood in the context of a moralizing political culture, the connection strengthens. Emerson and his compatriots envisioned an America fulfilling its ideals, which made the reality of its shortcomings more acute. In essence, the Transcendentalists advocated for an American society that ought to be. Sharing Dylan's distrust of the political process, Emerson asserted that "politics is a deleterious profession." Looking back decades later, Emerson wrote that the "ancient manners were giving way." Andrews Norton, a Unitarian minister defending his religious beliefs against Transcendentalist nonconformity, feared that their way of thinking posed a threat. He referred to them as "the prophets and priests of a new future, in which all is changed, all opinions done away, and all present forms of society abolished." Evidently, the times they were a-changin' in Antebellum America.[148]

In *Chronicles*, Dylan describes his fascination with the Antebellum Era—an interest expressed in reading newspapers on microfilm in the New York Public Library. He found the virulence of that era remarkable and noted the "mysterious and traditional way" the period resembled his own age. Dylan added that it became "the all-encompassing template behind everything I would write."[149] Though that statement is perhaps hyperbolic, finding traditional America in his work is by no means difficult. Specifically, Dylan noted that a biography of Thaddeus Stevens particularly inspired him. Stevens, a Pennsylvania Radical Republican known as "The Great Commoner," despised slavery and sought to punish the former Confederacy after the Civil War. What impressed Dylan was Stevens's "white-hot hatred for the bloated aristocrats of his day."[150] It is noteworthy that of all the things Dylan could have chosen to comment on, he picked Stevens and his disgust with the excesses of wealth and privilege. Party alignment meant little to Dylan; instead, his views were influenced by traditional, timeless American principles. Grounded in a common sense approach that he would have experienced on the Iron Range, Dylan described his outlook as "primitive" and that he preferred a style of politics he called "country fair."[151] Fellow Greenwich Village folk singer Dave Van Ronk called Dylan's political views "naive" at the time but later admitted that Dylan's understanding probably contained a sophistication missing from those more active and doctrinaire.[152]

After the Civil War, the US Army began the removal of the Plains Indians to make way for white settlers, an episode Dylan references in "With God on Our Side." In the song, Dylan anachronistically refers to the Midwest as "the country" he came from—terminology commonly used in pre–Civil War America. In the late 1800s, farmers from that region were saddled with debt and were at the mercy of banking interests. Tapping into that discontent, the Populist Party emerged and espoused ideas derived from the "physiocratic tradition and from the democracy of Jefferson, Jackson, and Lincoln."[153] Rooted in a philosophy defined as "egalitarian radical," Populists feared the encroachment of an economic form of slavery and sought to recalibrate the nation's direction.[154] After the Populists were essentially annexed by the Democratic Party, the crusading torch passed to the Progressives. In the early twentieth century, progressivism, socialism, and other movements maintained the tradition of societal improvement. World War I interrupted the reform movement, and in the 1920s politicians and citizens routinely venerated business interests.

According to numerous profiles of Dylan, he has read extensively about the Civil War. Assessing the event, he posited that it crucified and resurrected the country. This rebirth, however, did not cleanse the nation of its sins. In *Chronicles*, Dylan stated the war would haunt the country in perpetuity: "the suffering is endless, and the punishment is going to be forever."[155] In 2012, he told *Rolling Stone* that the violence necessary to root out slavery had left a country "just too fucked up about color." Dylan deemed the lingering racial animosity from slavery the "height of insanity" and something that continued to hold the nation back.[156]

Dylan's powerful ode to a bluesman, "Blind Willie McTell," also evokes slavery, its cruelty, and the Civil War—all in one stanza. In 2003, Dylan contributed "'Cross the Green Mountain" to the Civil War film *Gods and Generals* by Ronald Maxwell. An epic, poignant song, "the death-dream of Stonewall Jackson" captures the sadness of loss and a sense of the war's futility. Bill Kauffman writes, "Bob Dylan's haunting ''Cross the Green Mountain'... [sounds] like Appalachia by way of Hibbing, Minnesota, as abolitionist folkie meets Jewish Confederate in the great song that is America."[157] One of the arguments for Dylan as a traditionalist is his uncanny ability to conjure a bygone America. As Kauffman notes, Dylan is capable of writing a song that *is* America.

On his 2001 album *Love and Theft*, "Floater (Too Much to Ask)" sounds as if it were written in the 1920s. "Floater," as the title suggests, drifts like a summer day in rural pre–World War II America. The lyrics evoke a setting in a Mason-Dixon border state, a land of ring-dance Christmas carols, and fishing for bullheads. The song follows no linear track but a traditional world is conjured throughout. Dylan evokes a long-gone time as he sings about his grandparents who eked out a living by sewing their own clothes and catching ducks with nets and ropes. Dylan surmises that they must not have had any "dreams or hopes."[158] With one line, Dylan encapsulates a mindset and reflects a lifestyle of a lost time before mass media and the age of celebrity. This America, not necessarily an "Old Weird" one, was a land where people worked hard, practiced self-reliance, and had few touchstones to imagine a life outside their own experience. They dreamt not of fame and fortune, but faced the tasks at hand. He echoes the same sentiment in his *60 Minutes* interview when he explains that his parents never went anywhere and thought the capital of the world was wherever they were. Dylan has imbibed the music, newspapers, and books of traditional America and that allows him to so ably portray its characteristics. His songs become a sort of historical fiction.

Dylan has employed virtually every turn-of-the-twentieth-century American musical format. Folk music's roots reach back the furthest. Blues music—performed by Charley Patton, Blind Willie McTell, and Robert Johnson, among many others—and nascent country-and-western recordings emerged during the time before World War II. In a 2010 book about Dylan, Ian Bell refers to the singer as an avant-garde conservative. Bell explains that the pattern Dylan followed was moving forward by reaching back.[159] As a teenager in the 1950s, rock and roll captivated Dylan, but he gave it up as the first wave of rockers disappeared from the scene and teen idols and girl groups dominated the market. In the 1960s, he then adopted folk, a musical world of tradition and one he described as containing "archaic principles and values."[160] Within a few years he began performing blues-based rock music and then songs that contained country influences. Starting in the 1970s and continuing until the present, his repertoire expanded to include jazz, gospel, blues, Tex-Mex, vaudevillian shuffles, World War II Era pop standards, rockabilly, and even a rap on Kurtis Blow's "Street Rock." With each musical transformation or experimentation, Dylan has harkened back to something else within America's musical history. He has innovated while drawing inspiration from traditional sources.

Dylan has often lamented the loss of an earlier world, not due to a political wrong turn but because of the usurpation of a simpler life. Beginning in 1967, often considered the quintessential psychedelic year, Dylan began to implement a country influence in his work. To some fans, country music represented something more authentic. In 1968, *Rolling Stone*'s Jann Wenner wrote an article that praised the country and rock fusion and identified *John Wesley Harding* as the genre's "most significant" contribution. Presaging Bell's sentiment by roughly four decades, Wenner thought that

Dylan's country sound was "a natural and logical move: not a step forward, not a step backwards, but part of a circular pattern."[161]

John Wesley Harding, Nashville Skyline, Self Portrait, and *New Morning* constitute albums from what is often deemed Dylan's "rural family man" period. The four records hang together because of a similar country influence, odes to domestic bliss, and chronology. The third, *Self Portrait,* remains the most misunderstood and reviled of his catalog. When he reviewed the album in *Rolling Stone,* Greil Marcus issued his oft-quoted "What is this shit?" line.[162] *Self Portrait* contains Old West references, traditional songs, and pieces such as "Copper Kettle," which recalls Whiskey Rebellion protests. In the tumult of 1970, very few members of Dylan's fan base wanted an album that recalled an older America in the manner of *Self Portrait.* It proved the first truly polarizing album Dylan released, but not the last. He felt the backlash again when he participated in "an American cultural ritual called giving oneself up to Christ."[163] The concerts and albums from the late 1970s and early 1980s proved incongruent with the image many fans had of Dylan. Every time he moved in a new direction by reaching back, he upset listeners.

By the mid-1960s, a substantial number of rock fans considered country and western the music of reactionaries who they associated with racism and discrimination. *Rolling Stone*'s Bill Reed savaged the country-sounding songs Dylan recorded in Nashville, many of which now appear on *Bootleg Series 10.* To Reed, Dylan's new music constituted heresy, much in the same way folk fans derided his electric output. Reed concocted a hypothetical car ride in "the vast wasteland of Shitcake, Georgia" where two friends heard Dylan's version of "Blue Moon" without knowing he was the singer and decided they were in "Hicksville." Finding no redeeming value in Dylan's exploration of country culture, Reed railed against his appearance on the *Johnny Cash Show,* exaggerating the impact by calling it "controversial" and the show itself a "Marcusean nightmare." Reed recounted seeing a friend storm out of the room, enraged when he heard Dylan's "Blue Moon."[164] By exploring a classic American musical style he himself enjoyed, Dylan distanced himself too much from the 1960s countercultural icon many listeners demanded of him. The implication—though they were essentially apolitical songs—was that Dylan had switched sides in the period's cultural conflict. Aside from donning a Nixon button, Dylan could have done little more to dumbfound his fans during a time of great political turmoil than release *Self Portrait.* Nevertheless, no evidence suggests that Dylan's forays into traditional-themed music garnered him a new right-wing following.

The most obvious conservative touchstone in Dylan's career came with his conversion to Christianity in the late 1970s, but that will be analyzed in later chapters. His 1980s output represented an artist in transition, but with an uncertain direction. The early 1990s foreshadowed the path that Dylan eventually took. Having hit a creative roadblock, he reconnected to his roots and released two albums of traditional folk music, *Good as I Been to You* and *World Gone Wrong*. The latter's title reflected an attitude Dylan repeatedly expressed. In 1997, he underwent one of rock music's greatest resurgences. It began with the Grammy-winning *Time Out of Mind*. The albums that followed—*Love and Theft*, *Modern Times*, *Together Through Life*, and *Tempest*—drew from a deep well of musical tradition. In 1997, Dylan expressed his feeling of being out of step with the times to *Newsweek*. Discussing his career-revitalizing *Time Out of Mind*, he said that he felt "spooky" and not "in tune with anything."[165] The music Dylan made in the late twentieth and early twenty-first centuries, coupled with his onstage wardrobe, projected the image of a troubadour from an earlier period of American history—a roots revivalist personified whose voice rang with the "blood of the land."[166] Socially, culturally, and musically, Bob Dylan has had his eyes on the past, and at the same time he has continued to break new ground.

The New Right

During the Great Depression, Franklin Roosevelt's New Deal created a liberal consensus that became America's prevailing power base. For 20 years, Roosevelt and his successor, Harry Truman, occupied the White House. After the country elected Dwight Eisenhower as president, he pursued a moderate Republican path and refused to dismantle Social Security and other programs created by his predecessors. Beginning in the 1950s, a conservative backlash emerged against the period of liberal dominance. Russell Kirk and William F. Buckley garnered national reputations as the intellectual founders of the New Right. Their works—*The Conservative Mind* (Kirk) and *God and Man at Yale* (Buckley)—along with Buckley's magazine *National Review* inspired a movement that grew quietly but steadily during the decade.[167]

In the 1940s, Republican Senator Robert Taft had espoused a noninterventionist brand of conservatism ("Old Right"). While anticommunist, he subscribed to a Jeffersonian disdain of entangling alliances and voted against US entry into NATO. Fearful of the US abandoning its republican principles, he believed that Roosevelt's actions regarding World War II had imperialistic intent. For the same reasons, Taft opposed entry into Korea and involvement in Vietnam.[168] Though he nearly won the Republican nomination for president in 1952, his republican values opposing both economic and military imperialism increasingly put him outside the conventional wisdom of both parties. His death in 1953 created a void in conservative leadership that more hawkish individuals such as Buckley stepped into.

The nascent New Right gathered momentum throughout the decade but remained an outlying political force. Even further removed from the conventional politics of the late 1950s was Robert Welch, who founded the John Birch Society. Over the years, the hard-line anticommunist organization criticized Eisenhower and Richard Nixon, among others, for being either socialist dupes or not sufficiently vigilant against the ideology. Welch offered a string of conspiracy theories that caused more respectable conservatives such as Buckley to disown him.

Despite a degree of factionalism that inevitably exists within any political movement, the New Right formulated a basic conservative ideology. At its core, the conservative cause professed strong anticommunism; desire for small government; advocacy of individual liberty; adherence to free market values; and a disdain for unions. Some aspects like anticommunism were assumed by mainstream politicians of both parties. Others, namely the support of individual liberty, have a broad enough appeal that virtually anyone ascribes to them. When taken in total and understood within the context of the times, the New Right's rise was essentially a protest movement against the mainstream of both parties.

Though given less attention, Young Americans for Freedom (YAF) was as much a part of the decade as Students for a Democratic Society (SDS) on the Left. Meeting in September 1960 at Buckley's residence in Sharon, Connecticut, YAF produced the Sharon Statement, the document that outlined their belief system. The statement asserted the organization's youthfulness, an important characteristic in the 1960s.

The Sharon Statement affirmed the existence of "certain eternal truths" and "foremost among the transcendent values is the individual's use of his God-given free will, whence derives his right to be free from the restrictions of arbitrary force." Young Americans for Freedom argued that "liberty is indivisible" and the government's role is the protection of freedoms and the administration of justice. The document addressed the necessity of the free market, an anticommunist stance, and a foreign policy based on a just self-interest.[169] Similarly, Dylan's religious background and sense of the sacred clearly support the notion that he believed in perpetual truths. His desire for freedom will be discussed in a future chapter, and the strength of his individualism fueled his career choices. A magazine profile on Dylan in 1963 noted that he possessed "a strong desire to run his own world" and that he denounced those who attempted to "run it for him, whether they hide behind a KKK hood or a stock market ticker."[170] During that decade,

Dylan plainly deviated from a young conservative economic viewpoint—in particular he never proclaimed unyielding faith in the free market—and did not express a strong fear of communism. Dylan remained suspicious of institutions and even though he has benefited immensely from capitalism, he has never praised unrestrained business.

The New Right picked up momentum among young conservatives, business owners, and others in the early 1960s. In 1964, Arizona Senator Barry Goldwater's successful pursuit of the Republican nomination represented the apex of the New Right movement. Goldwater's principled and honest-to-a-fault approach, as well as his propensity for speaking gaffes, made him an easy target for President Lyndon Johnson's forces, and he lost the election overwhelmingly. The senator's opponents painted him as an extremist reactionary, and he had difficulty articulating the nuances of his beliefs. Though some at the time predicted the election meant the end of conservatism in America, in reality it created an atmosphere that allowed the ideology to flourish in the 1970s and claim electoral validation with Ronald Reagan's 1980 victory.

Dylan surprised readers by divulging in *Chronicles* that Goldwater was his "favorite politician" of the 1960s. At the time, Dylan himself found "there wasn't any way to explain that to anybody."[171] Some have wondered whether this statement means that Dylan is a closet Republican or is now finally able to announce his true conservative self. As Robert Dean Lurie in *The American Conservative* notes, "This is probably a case of wishful thinking."[172] The notion that Bob Dylan is more sympathetic to the Right than to the Left reaches too far. Dylan's political worldview aligned only a little with the New Right, a bit more with the New Left, and was an amalgamation of traditional concepts that defied easy classification. A subsequent chapter will deal with Dylan's relationship to the New Left.

Although in interviews Dylan is often evasive and at times less than forthright, his statement about Goldwater can most likely be taken at face value. That Dylan would find the Arizona senator's straightforwardness and image as an outsider appealing is perfectly consistent with Dylan's political views. Iron Rangers appreciated authenticity from their politicians, and Goldwater possessed it, even to the detriment of his candidacy. When Dylan has portrayed politicians in songs and interviews, he has generally taken them to task for phoniness or self-interest. In the 1970s, Dylan called Harry Truman his favorite president because he had "common sense" and a "common quality."[173] Dylan may well have appreciated Goldwater's advocacy of personal freedom and, as time went on, his acceptance speech, which asserted the senator's determination to "return to proven ways—not because they are old, but because they are true."[174] Goldwater's line echoed conservative intellectuals such as Richard Weaver and Russell Kirk who articulated their convictions of universal truths and tradition.[175]

Although Dylan may have admired Goldwater's integrity, the singer never articulated a specific political ideology and the two had little in common from a policy standpoint. In songs such as "Motorpsycho Nightmare" and "Talkin' John Birch Paranoid Blues," Dylan mocked the hysterical anticommunism many conservatives possessed. Although Dylan wrote a line that dismissed organized labor in "Union Sundown," he has never voiced the antiunionism of the New Right. In fact, the line can easily be turned around to be interpreted as a radical critique of union leaders bought off by "the System" and self-satisfied workers, happy with a pay raise now and again.[176]

Goldwater opposed segregation but he also did not believe that the federal government should intervene and he voted against the 1964 Civil Rights Act. In his 2012 *Rolling Stone* interview, Dylan revealed that he did not buy the states' rights argument of the southern elite in the buildup to the Civil War, and it is highly unlikely that he would have bought it when it came to civil rights. Even though Dylan generally preferred a decentralized approach, he sided with those who were struggling for freedom. Goldwater held on to his principles of liberty and small government over his concern for equality, and that is another point of divergence between the two. Dylan's political worldview, as best as it can be understood, was that the individual liberties of African Americans trumped concerns about government intervention. He would not have engaged in debates about the nuances of federalism or parsed the constitutionality of desegregation. Dylan simply saw a wrong to be fixed. In 1963, he wrote a piece titled "For Dave Glover," and in it, he asked how Jesus's "love thy neighbor" had become "I'll guard the school door with my body said by Governor Wallace."[177]

Goldwater had an appeal that transcended purely partisan views and resonated with many who advocated liberty for all. In the early 1960s, Karl Hess served as Goldwater's chief speechwriter. Later in the decade, Hess resigned from the senator's staff and joined the New Left. Kauffman tells Hess's story, which did not replicate Dylan's experience, but it contains some similarity. Hess, "reckoning that the best qualities of the Right of his boyhood—its cranky individualism, quasi-pacifist isolationism, and Main Street decentralism—had been purged, he rushed headlong—heedlessly, perhaps—into the New Left." In *Ramparts* magazine, Hess wrote an open letter to Goldwater, calling him "the most essentially honest and potentially radical major American political figure" and urging him to join SDS. Goldwater declined but did tell a young University of Arizona crowd in 1968 that he had "much in common with the anarchist wing of SDS," including opposition to the military draft and suspicion of large institutions.[178] Though leery of the political system, Dylan possessed a similar set of values that defied easy classification on the left/right continuum. Political ideologies contain a wraparound quality, and as Hess moved from Right to Left he did not travel as far as conventional wisdom would have it.

Conservatives pushed back against what they perceived to be the excesses of social change in the 1960s. Movements that opposed *Roe v. Wade*, the Equal Rights Amendment, busing, and gay liberation became political rallying points. Dylan's public statements on some of these issues will be discussed in a later chapter. Examining his 1970s work, one finds songs supporting victims of injustice, traditional and religious songs, and in-and-out-of love songs, but no topical song that supports a strictly conservative viewpoint. As an artist who followed his own muse, had Dylan possessed deep-rooted conservative beliefs, at some point he would have written songs that expressed them. He had no trouble conveying his newfound Christian convictions on vinyl and in concert. Ultimately, Dylan's political views transformed some over time. He remained economically liberal, at times socially conservative, but tending more toward libertarianism. In fact, very similar to the description of typical Iron Range beliefs earlier in the chapter.

The notion of Dylan as a left-wing herald has lost momentum, but attempts to backfill that with the idea that he was a conservative fall short as well. Dylan maintains a strong vein of traditionalism, but he cannot be tied to a movement. Although he may have liked Goldwater's personality, he subscribed to the senator's politics no more than he did to the liberalism of his fellow Minnesotan, Hubert Humphrey. If anything, Dylan viewed the world in terms of truths deeper than Left/Right on the contemporary American political spectrum. He is a Jeffersonian small "d" democrat rather than an LBJ Great Society Democrat. No matter the president, Dylan has expressed a suspicion of those in power. In 1963, Dylan told the *National Guardian* that he thought President Kennedy was "all right, but he's a phoney [sic], pretending all the time." He added that he did not bother voting because there was "nobody to vote for."[179] Dylan told *Playboy* 15 years later, "I have always considered politics just part of the illusion. I don't get involved much in politics. I don't know what the system runs on."[180]

In 1983, Dylan wrote an ode to Julius and Ethel Rosenberg, a husband and wife who were convicted of spying during the 1950s and sentenced to death. The song does not appear in any of the three official Dylan lyric books and has never been released by the singer. The Rosenbergs' execution proved somewhat controversial since the case against Ethel was never definitively proven. Dylan addressed that lack of certainty, the stifling of dissent during the time, and the Cold War hysteria of the McCarthy years. He also returned to the notion of fear being used to manipulate and control the population. Although the song's subject matter was not timely during the 1980s, Dylan may have meant it as a parable between the 1950s and the Reagan era. Whatever the case, it is unlikely that a conservative Cold Warrior would have written a song like "Julius and Ethel."

Into the 2000s, Dylan's refusal to ally himself with easily defined partisan labels confounded followers who wanted him to be like them. In interviews with *Rolling Stone*, he refused to criticize George W. Bush or praise Barack Obama. Dylan articulated his general distrust of the political game in 2009, and again in 2012, when interviewers asked him to comment on the right's harsh reaction toward Obama. Dylan surmised that it was essentially the same as Bush, Clinton, and Carter received. He dismissed the Far Right criticisms of Eisenhower and Nixon as un-American and socialist adding "look what they did to Kennedy."[181]

In a June 2008 interview with the *London Times*, Dylan spoke effusively about the prospect of an Obama presidency because the then senator represented a new type of politician.[182] In Minneapolis, on election night of that year, Dylan issued a rare onstage address. When he received news of Obama's election, he declared, "It looks like things are going to change now."[183] Four years later, and speaking to *Rolling Stone*, Dylan reverted to a familiar, wary stance concerning change on a systemic level. Despite Mikal Gilmore's best efforts to have Dylan say something definitive about the Obama presidency, the singer would not budge.[184]

In a 1986 conversation, *Rolling Stone*'s Gilmore asked Dylan if it bothered him that so many preachers equated being a Christian with adhering to political conservatism. Dylan, combining his populist background and Christian beliefs, answered, "Conservative? Well, don't forget, Jesus said that it's harder for a rich man to enter the kingdom of heaven than it is for a camel to enter the eye of a needle. I mean is *that* conservative?" Gilmore also prodded Dylan to respond to the charge that he moved to the right on songs such as "Slow Train" and "Union Sundown." Dylan followed with perhaps the most succinct summation of his political beliefs: "Look in the Bible, you don't see nothing about right or left."[185] Dylan disclosed very little about his thoughts concerning contemporary politicians, other than his lack of faith in them. He has remained mostly detached from desiring political solutions to social ills, though he frequently called attention to the existence of society's shortcomings.

Though he has shared certain characteristics with conservatives and traditionalists, Dylan's "Voice of a Generation" title came from his contributions to causes associated with the New Left. He has never accepted the designation and never bridged the gulf that separated left and right. Dylan told *60 Minutes* that the titles the media hung around his neck made him feel like an imposter.

CHAPTER 2

Voice of a Generation

Over a long and remarkable career, Bob Dylan expressed populist, traditionalist, and egalitarian beliefs. What Dylan called the "finger-pointin'" songs from his early 1960s folk style fostered an image that he was a protest singer. His artistic output during this period dovetailed with the emergence of a group of politically active young people often called the New Left. This convergence gave added potency to his civil rights, antiwar, and other social justice-minded anthems and created an impression of a synchronistic mass movement that drafted Dylan to be its musical spokesman.

In the mid-1960s, when Dylan changed his musical style from acoustic to electric and left behind "topical songs," his significance grew exponentially. Fans, critics, and scholars pored over his obscure lyrics to divine deep philosophical or political meanings from his new songs. Rather than becoming disassociated with politics, Dylan became further tethered to a movement he never joined. Though much admired by the Counterculture, Bob Dylan could be said to have been on the periphery of the movement at most. On numerous occasions, he distanced himself from the notion that he belonged to it. He told *Rolling Stone* in 2012, "I couldn't really identify with what was happening."[1] Labels that Dylan was the "Voice of a Generation" or "Leader of the Counterculture" were founded in hype, myth, or error. Even during his "protest period," which proved short-lived, Dylan wrote and recorded numerous songs that did not contain political themes at all. Though his reputation certainly helped to further Dylan's career, he never found it a comfortable fit. Maria Muldaur, Dylan's friend and fellow folk performer from the early 1960s, was one of many around Dylan who confirmed that he never wanted to be a spokesperson.[2]

By the end of the 1960s, Dylan had retreated to upstate New York and adopted a new persona after having children. He had little to do with political writing or public performances. In the 1970s, he dabbled in a few causes, got divorced, and converted to Christianity. All the while, critics and fans waited for him to return to the early 1960s political activism with which they associated him. The 1980s have often been portrayed as Dylan's artistic nadir, but he continued to perform charity benefits and released songs, a few of which addressed current issues. A new generation of fans began following Dylan and his mythology grew, especially as Boomer nostalgia kicked in. By that time, the music industry, as well as the social and political landscape, had changed enough so that a Dylan song no longer carried the weight it once did. Nevertheless, Dylan remained locked, in many people's minds, into a specific role.

Born in 1941, Bob Dylan and his peers who entered college in the late 1950s and early 1960s ignited a new era of political activism. No other age group has been as self-aware, nor possessed a tagline as easily identifiable, as the Baby Boomers. People such as Dylan and those engaged in the first wave of the student movement are lumped in together with the Boomer Generation, though they are a few years older. Among musicians of the era, only the Beatles occupied a position as rarified as Bob Dylan. And not even the Beatles earned the distinction, however ill-fitting it proved for Dylan, as the "Voice of a Generation." Even if one subscribes to the notion that Dylan "spoke" for anyone other than himself, the idea that he did it for an entire generation crumbles quickly. An age group's shared cultural experiences (movies, TV, etc.) span maybe ten years rather than twenty, and the idea that Dylan's "generation" existed as a political monolith overlooks racial, class, gender, and geographic differences.

In the years following World War II, Americans exuded a substantial degree of optimism. The mood created by the country's military and economic strength spilled over into many facets of society. The comfort and satisfaction found in the purchase of consumer goods and new technologies caused many Americans to anticipate an even brighter tomorrow. This postwar affluence, new forms of mass media, and the sheer amount of Boomers combined to create a youth culture that had not previously been possible. The great contradiction is that the nagging threats of nuclear holocaust and the elimination of their rosy future created an "Age of Anxiety" for the youth who practiced hiding under school desks. The resulting level of fear, Dylan later wrote, robbed "a child of his spirit."[3]

The dual factors of economy and demographics also opened higher education to numbers previously unimaginable. Prior to World War II, less than 1.5 million students went to college; by the mid-1950s, that number grew to 2.7 million; and in 1968, more than 7 million young people attended. Postsecondary schooling was no longer considered the domain of the elite. In addition, this meant that a large number of young people lived in close proximity with each other on campuses and somewhat separated from the rest of society.[4] By 1965, 41 percent of the country was under 20 years of age—a number that represented the largest such group in US history.[5] Many citizens came to the realization that in a country that espoused liberty, a sizable portion of Americans were systematically blocked from achieving the material comfort and political participation afforded to the rest. This discrepancy created a vocal, politically orientated youth.

The New Left

The New Left, which emerged in America at roughly the same time Dylan began his artistic career, pushed for civil rights, protested the Vietnam War, and railed against a society they saw as corrupt and inauthentic. They viewed these issues primarily in terms of a generational divide, although geography and class defined them as well. The older generation had led society astray, while the younger provided the solutions and desire to reorient it. The New Left movement consisted of both political and cultural revolt, though the emphasis of one or the other depended on the individual. Whatever the mixture, activists expressed their discontent by positing the issues as moral rather than as merely social.[6]

Age, rather than race or any other factor, proved to be the critical delineation for new political organizations. In the early stages, these young people were far more radical politically than they were culturally.[7] Their commitment to civil rights and the antiwar movement captured the imaginations of many and as time passed, the cultural pushback equaled political disgruntlement. In February 1960, four African American students engaged in a protest by sitting at a segregated lunch counter in Greensboro, North Carolina. Two months later, the Student Nonviolent Coordinating Committee (SNCC) was formed. Begun in 1959, the Student Peace Union (SPU) soon became the biggest student organization in the country.[8]

Created in 1960 and influenced by sociologist C. Wright Mills, Students for a Democratic Society (SDS) served as the "epicenter" of the New Left.[9] In 1962, "The Port Huron Statement" appeared, written primarily by Tom Hayden. It provided the first declaration of leftist political intent by a mostly white, middle class, and male organization. Adopted at the University of Michigan, "Port Huron" outlined the philosophical template for the New Left. It hinted at the growing alienation these students felt, and it questioned America's dominant institutions. The opening line, a warning of what was to come, proclaimed them a generation "raised in moderate comfort...looking uncomfortably to the world" they inherited.[10] Their affluence allowed them to attend universities, but they also found much of it stultifying and hollow.

"The Port Huron Statement" identified two primary issues that were, as its authors saw it, "too troubling to dismiss."[11] The first, the civil rights struggle, exposed society's hypocrisy. The second, the threat of nuclear annihilation, demonstrated the establishment's insanity. This dual disconnect created a moral indignation that prompted many New Leftists to question the "ruling myths," including those issued by the government, and the value of education. It claimed that universities had not "brought us moral enlightenment." Finding higher education lacking, "The Port Huron Statement" also bemoaned the fact that "there are few new prophets" to lead the fight.[12] Whether rooted in truth or merely in the impressions of their own minds, this subsection of a generation understood itself as having a special mission to enlighten society.

What flourished was an atmosphere, on predominantly northern campuses, that questioned authority, tested boundaries, and rejected tradition for tradition's sake. The University of Michigan's chapter of SDS proved the most active and worked with SNCC during the Freedom Rides.[13] Politically, the University of California-Berkeley campus heated up in May 1960 with a protest against the House Un-American Activities Committee (HUAC) and culminated with the creation of the Free Speech Movement in 1964.[14] The SDS document "America and New Era" stated, "In a growing number of localities a new discontent, a new anger is groping towards a politics of insurgent protest." They believed that this movement was a "demand for freedom," which necessitated a "demand for a new society."[15]

Desirous of transcending a culture they found stifling or hypocritical, many activists sought deeper, often spiritual connections. Personalism, a combination of Catholic social justice theory, pacifism, and anarchism, constituted another activist position. It acknowledged the God-given or (nonreligious) universal worth of all human beings. Personalists concerned themselves with people on society's margins, championing the poor and downtrodden. They remained "suspicious of systems," the bureaucracies and institutions that depersonalized human beings. Furthermore, they distrusted the capitalist market, which created injustice, and the state, which often abused power. In their view, large-scale structural and political change became possible when people could be incited to action. Personalists differed from postwar mainstream liberals in several key ways. First, liberals maintained faith in capitalism, while personalists were distrustful of consumerism. Second, liberalism invested faith in the current political system and the managerial state. Personalists advocated participatory rather than representational politics, and a decentralized system. Third, most liberals drew a hard-line anticommunist stance while personalists and their New Left counterparts could be classified as something closer to "anti anti-communist."[16] Though not all aspects of personalist thought can be applied to Dylan, a significant amount of the philosophy mirrors his outlook.

The growing lifestyle choices open to young people often promoted nonconformity and stressed the importance of individual freedom. New Leftists believed that "the economic system and the social institutions" threatened their liberation. These two entities defined people and limited "self-realization, self-expression and control over one's own life." The early social movements, based on direct action, focused on separate issues such as civil rights, antiwar, or antipoverty. Later, this approach transformed into the idea that American society was a "system" that denied freedom, equality, and authenticity. This interpretation centered less on partisan politics and more on wholesale change. The New Left rejected the political Right and, ultimately, the corporate liberalism of John Kennedy and, more so, Lyndon Johnson.[17] In 1963, Bob Dylan told the leftist magazine *National Guardian* that the US political system was filled with "phoneys [sic] and lies."[18]

Because many young people and left-leaning political activists adopted Dylan's music to their causes, by extension he became melded to those politics. He wrote songs about civil rights, peace, and antimilitarism from a youthful perspective. Despite being portrayed as the darling of the left-leaning Counterculture, Dylan never formally joined any movement. Too nuanced to be categorized as left or right, he chose not to venture into party politics, openly endorse candidates, or join protest marches. Folk music great Pete Seeger understood Dylan's reluctance: "Bob is determined to be independent."[19] When he did participate in political events, it was as a performer. While his history of playing benefits is long, he rarely made political pronouncements from the stage and he has seemed remarkably unimpressed with the power of his celebrity. Though he presumably mocks mainstream liberal attitudes, Dylan's line in the jokey "I Shall Be Free No. 10" that he was "liberal to a degree" and that he wanted everyone "to be free" is probably as close to a coherent description of his politics as anything.[20]

To the leftist movement Dylan allegedly represented, he remained an outsider and broke from it rather early in his career. From his interviews and actions, it is apparent that Dylan did not put as much faith in the group decision-making process as SDS and others did. As a songwriter, he addressed issues of freedom, justice, and the corrupt nature of society, but remained mostly detached from the idea of joining a movement. In her autobiography *A Voice to Sing With*, Joan Baez commented on Dylan's lack of overall political involvement. She stated that his participation in political activism or change began and ended with songwriting: "To my knowledge, he never went on a march. He certainly never did any civil disobedience, at least that I knew about. I've always felt that he just didn't want the responsibility."[21] According to Victor Maymudes, a longtime friend and tour manager, Dylan went to at least one march—one of the famous Selma to Montgomery protests in Alabama—with a ticket paid for by folk singer/actor, Theodore Bikel.[22]

Joan Baez articulated a sentiment that many left-leaning fans from the 1960s felt when she noted that "we would lose Bob to other things, but before the first official bullet was fired, he had filled our arsenals with song." She listed "A Hard Rain's A-Gonna Fall," "Masters of War," "The Times They Are A-Changin,'" "With God on Our Side," and "Blowin' in the Wind." Baez confirmed that the songs linked him with the movements of the 1960s, "whether he liked it or not, and I gather he doesn't much care one way or the other."[23] Despite these contributions, Dylan remained dubious about the efficacy of protest music. In 1965, he reiterated a sentiment expressed earlier when he told *Newsweek*: "I've never written a political song. Songs can't save the world.[24]

As groups such as SDS and others on the New Left rejected the authority of so many older political and educational figureheads, they sought leaders of their own generation. According to the attitudes espoused by SDS, a "new left must consist of younger people."[25] These leaders created essays such as "The Port Huron Statement," organized protests, and participated in sit-ins and teach-ins. Music served as one means to communicate their messages and united like-minded people in a cause. Though Dylan questioned the importance of song as a means of social change, others disagreed. Martin Luther King Jr. said, "The freedom songs are playing a strong and vital role in our struggle." The civil rights leader added that the songs "give the people new courage and a sense of unity." Activist Charles Jones concurred: "There could have been no Albany Movement without music." He stressed the importance it played in transmitting ideas: "We could not have communicated with the masses of people without music. They could not have communicated with us without music."[26]

Despite never having volunteered, Dylan was assumed to be a de facto leader of this growing but loosely defined movement. In the minds of many politically engaged young people, folk music and (later in the1960s) rock music became the best conduit to convey messages and Bob Dylan became their messenger. Dylan's Midwestern, middle-class background and disenchantment with the university setting made him, on the surface, a New Left prototype. There is no doubt that he shared much with members of groups such as SDS. However, the Dylan mythology exaggerates his degree of association with and commitment to political groups of any sort.

Bob Dylan's professional career began in 1960 when the emergent youth culture began to come of age. Upon his arrival in New York, Dylan quickly immersed himself in the folk scene around Greenwich Village. In the 1950s, hypervigilant Cold Warriors drew the conclusion that folk musicians were communists or at least fellow travelers. The John Birch Society's official publication, *American Opinion*, stated that folk songs were the tools of communists.[27] The folk community of the early 1960s certainly had Far Left roots, as well as some current or former Communist Party members. The scene was comprised of the children of radicals—the Red Diaper Babies—and essentially reflected the politics of the New Left. At this time, their leftist political worldview was not widely represented in mainstream American society.

Peace and Anti-anticommunism

Late winter and spring of 1962 proved to be the launching point for Dylan's songwriting and an especially fecund period for his politically themed work.[28] Throughout that year, he wrote songs that appeared on the album *The Freewheelin' Bob Dylan* and several additional ones that did not. In that time, he gained a standing as an inventive if not wholly original songwriter, and he became the darling of the folk crowd. Despite his growing reputation, Dylan's sound did not fit into the Top 40 mold. Among the most popular songs in April 1962, when he debuted "Blowin' in the Wind," were "Don't Break the Heart That Loves You" by Connie Francis, Shelley Fabares's "Johnny Angel," and "Good Luck Charm" by Elvis.[29] All of them were a far cry from the acoustic folk that Dylan recorded. According to Joan Baez, some foresaw Dylan's potential as a songwriter and believed that he would be bigger than Elvis.[30] But for most, the idea that a rough-voiced folkie from Greenwich Village would become arguably the most significant individual performer of rock history was unimaginable.

For a young folk singer like Bob Dylan, *Broadside*, a magazine that began publication in February 1962, provided a vital opportunity to gain exposure for his songs. *Broadside* aimed to publish topical songs that could eventually join the folk canon. Its editors claimed that they "may never publish a song that could be called a 'folk song.' But...many of our best folk songs were topical songs at their inception."[31] Five issues in, they noted, "If our songwriters reflect the mood of the country, the number one concern of Americans today is the problem of peace and the deadly nuclear arms race."[32] Cold War issues certainly occupied a position in the forefront of people's minds.

Fear of communist aggression reflected the concern of many, if not most, Americans not reading *Broadside*.

Songwriters who had their work published in *Broadside* offered songs on "the theme of peace—and related subjects such as renewed atomic bomb testing and fallout shelters." The editors noted that these topics made up the greatest percentage of songs submitted to the magazine and added that John Birch Society songs were second most submitted. The article then referenced John Birch–related songs by both Tom Paxton and the Chad Mitchell Trio.[33] Dylan's "Talkin' John Birch Paranoid Blues" appeared in *Broadside*'s first issue, and two weeks later the magazine published Malvina Reynolds's "The Birch Society."[34] *Broadside* editors noted that the Chad Mitchell Trio song, despite threatening phone calls to radio station WNEW, was "sort of a hit in New York City."[35]

Having emerged out of a scene that at the very least retained some Far Left influence, many young folk singers found Cold War fears to be overblown. This sentiment mirrored the New Left's. SDS's first president, Alan Haber, claimed that "anti-communism has become the chief ideological weapon of defenders of the status quo." In his opinion, the Red Scare was utilized both at home and abroad to further the ruling elite's economic and political control. Haber called for a rejection of fear-mongering and an embrace of "anti anti-communism."[36]

Dylan's "Talkin' John Birch Paranoid Blues" humorously captured Haber's sentiment about fear run amok. The live recording found on *Bootleg Series Volumes 1–3* contains slightly different lyrics than those that appear in *Broadside* and the *Witmark Demos: Bootleg Series 9*. The latter versions offer a stanza that attacks the Birch Society's anti-Semitic reputation, claiming that Birchers agreed with Hitler even though "he killed six million Jews."[37] In the *Bootleg Series 1–3* live recording, Dylan also references Pete Seeger's blacklisting by ABC from its television program *Hootenanny* because of his political views. In May 1963, Dylan refused to play the *Ed Sullivan Show* rather than sing a different song after CBS deemed "Talkin' John Birch" too controversial. Since the Sullivan Show was one of the most popular on the air, this action earned Dylan increased credibility among the folk crowd, but also represented a bold rejection of an opportunity to appeal to a wider audience. In 2009, Dylan reflected on the event with *Rolling Stone* and described it as a turning point in his professional life.[38]

When Dylan's career began, the American presence in Vietnam consisted of "advisors" and very few Americans could have imagined where it ultimately would lead the nation. Mainstream liberals took a hard-line anticommunist stance partly out of fear of being labeled soft on the issue and partly because they shared the imperial assumptions of bipartisan Cold

War foreign policy. John Kennedy's antagonistic Cuba policy and escalation in Vietnam are examples of how Democrats responded to domestic politics and their global perspective. The New Left tended to be suspicious of those in positions of power around the globe, regardless of their political affiliation. Many young leftist activists saw communist oppression as similar to what they witnessed in American society. This represented a break from some of the Old Left who overlooked or justified communist atrocities. Though not supportive of communism, the New Left lacked the hostility and fear of those ideologies that many mainstream liberals possessed. Although there were differences of opinion concerning the actual threat of communism, the specter of a nuclear disaster caused consternation for nearly everyone.

The threat of nuclear war, and antiwar attitudes in general, provided a major piece of the New Left platform. Young people concerned with these issues joined organizations such as the National Committee for a Sane Nuclear Policy (SANE), formed in Chicago in 1959, and the SPU.[39] The bomb shelter craze of the early 1960s proved profitable for some entrepreneurs but also provided song material for Bob Dylan. "Let Me Die in My Footsteps" jabbed at those who built fallout shelters in the hopes of surviving a nuclear war. Dylan, in his autobiographical *Chronicles*, describes the sentiment of the song as not "radical at all." He claims that in Hibbing, common sense and common decency influenced residents to eschew such projects.[40] Reminding listeners of the life they were missing when they worried about dying, "Footsteps" celebrated the natural beauty of the mountains, waters, and meadows of the United States—a "This Land is Your Land" for the Cold War era.

In 1962, "Footsteps" appeared in *Broadside* under the title "I Will Not Go Down Under the Ground." It also contained a stanza that does not appear on the *Bootleg Series Volumes 1–3*. In the missing portion, Dylan says that he wishes to purchase all weapons in the world and toss them into the ocean.[41] The recorded version does not suffer from the stanza's absence. Agnes Friesen's slightly satirical and class-conscious "Shelter Diggers" appeared in *Broadside*'s next edition. Dylan's "Let Me Die in My Footsteps" retains the hallmark of his best work—a song that works on more than one level.[42] "Footsteps" displays a defiant Dylan who claims that he would rather die experiencing his life than preserve it by cowering inside a shelter.

On another level, the song offers a critique of how Americans are manipulated by fear. As Dylan explains it, the powerful employ "rumors of war" as scare tactics that keep people isolated. He distrusts those who attempt to pull "the wool over" his eyes.[43] This atmosphere of alarm, Dylan claims, creates a public preoccupied with death rather than life. Not only does this fear-mongering have political ramifications as a means of social control, it also causes people to spend their money on this questionable precaution.

In January 1961, outgoing President Dwight Eisenhower warned the nation against the dangers of linking the economy too closely to war and the production of war materials. The next year, Dylan wrote "Masters of War," a biting polemic against the Military Industrial Complex. Dylan has denied that the song contains an antiwar theme but also calls it "pretty self-explanatory." If it does not outright oppose war, the song at least takes to task those responsible for starting and providing the equipment for violence. Although Dylan may have left the door open for justly fought wars, the song clearly reiterates the concept of a generational divide previously discussed.

New Left students believed their worldview to be more sane and humane than that of their older counterparts. In "Masters of War," Dylan acknowledges his youth and lack of education but did not shy away from challenging those in authority. He serves the role of gadfly, questioning authority and revealing their true motives. As the song unfolds, he maintains that despite his youth, he knows that Jesus would not forgive their greed and disregard for human life. In several of his songs, young Dylan condemned social ills by juxtaposing Christianity with the hypocrisy and corruption found in America.

New Left members believed that corporate capitalism fueled the war in Vietnam for the sake of profit. They also voiced concerns about the depersonalizing effects of technology.[44] SDS leader Todd Gitlin captured this sentiment when he called the political and economic free markets "illusory... largely *because* the economic model is a fraud. The dual engines of industrialization and war have created a tightly planned corporate complex that dominates the economy."[45] Gitlin's words are reminiscent of Dylan's, who often described the political system or modern culture as an "illusion." Three years after "Masters of War," Dylan sang of a "rovin' gambler" who wished to start "the next world war" and enlisted a promoter to help.[46] It is a single line from "Highway 61 Revisited" and does not possess the sheer intensity of "Masters of War," but it suggests the idea that wars are manufactured for the benefit of corporate interests or, on "Highway 61," for amusement. In 1980, in an interview with Robert Hilburn, Dylan said, "There are certain people who make a lot of money off of war the same way people make money off blue jeans. To say it was something else always irritated me."[47]

Dylan has occasionally distanced himself from "Masters of War," yet also played it at times and in styles that may have intentionally augmented the song's political ramifications. He has been notoriously evasive and/or annoyed in interviews that contain questions about the meaning of his work. When asked in a 1986 interview with Christopher Sykes, Dylan claimed not to know which of his songs were political. When Sykes suggested that "Masters of War" was a political song, Dylan replied that he was not sure if he agreed. Dylan asked, "Politics of *what*? If there is such a thing as politics, what is it politics of?" He continued, "Left, right, rebel...Afghanistan are rebels, but they're ok. Nicaragua's got rebels and they're ok. Their rebels are all right. But in El Salvador the rebels are the bad guys." He concluded, "If you listen to that stuff you go crazy. You don't even know who *you* are anymore."[48]

Dylan also expressed his disdain for ideological battles in the movie he cowrote, *Masked and Anonymous*. After getting out of prison, Jack Fate, Dylan's character, boards a bus and sits next to a young man who explains the morphing political situation in the postrevolutionary version of America. He tells Fate that he enlisted in an antigovernment rebel group, but they were as corrupt as the government, so he joined the counterrevolutionaries but left them and went over to the government. He claims the government actually supports what he believes, but ultimately they led him into a situation where he assisted in wiping out his own village. The absurdity of the situation mirrors Dylan's belief in the pointlessness of political solutions to eternal problems.

Never one to latch onto ideology, Dylan once commented to Joan Baez that when audience members requested "Masters of War," "They think I'm something I ain't." According to Baez's autobiography, she asked Dylan how he came up with "Masters of War," and he replied that "he knew it would sell." She refuted Dylan's claim, stating she could never "buy his answer."[49] In 1990, he played the song at West Point and at the Grammy telecast where he received a Lifetime Achievement Award. The latter performance took place at the time of the Persian Gulf War. Dylan played the song blisteringly fast—to the point of being virtually unintelligible. Some understood it to be a subversive political statement, others a sign of Dylan's eccentricity.

The song "John Brown" could have perhaps been titled "Only a Pawn in the Game of the Masters of War." Dylan did not officially release "John Brown" until his MTV Unplugged concert in 1995. In 1964, the song was recorded for a *Broadside Smithsonian* compilation and published in the magazine. In the song, the central character, John Brown, is shipped off to an unnamed foreign conflict. Brown's mother exudes pride as she prepares her son for war. When he returns badly mangled and unrecognizable even to her, she expresses shock at what has happened to him. Brown chastises his mother for living vicariously through him. He tells her that he, alone, had to face the horrors of war and the realization that his "enemy" was another young man the same as him.[50]

Reminiscent of the excitement prior to World War I, Brown's mother was thrilled by the prospect of her son achieving military glory and returning a hero. She stayed at home while John Brown fought and suffered. The song juxtaposed the glory and horror of war seen through lenses separated by a generation. Phil Ochs also captured this sentiment in "I Ain't Marching" when he wrote that it was the old who started wars and sent the young to die in them. Though his reputation at this time was as a "topical" writer, one of Dylan's great talents was his ability to write songs of a timeless quality. Though written prior to full-scale US involvement in Vietnam, "John Brown" could be set during any American conflict since the Spanish-American War.

Dylan did not necessarily possess a deeper understanding of the world than his contemporaries. He simply had the ability to express his ideas more deftly in songs. Joan Baez concurs, calling the bulk of the protest music "stupid." She notes that they lack strength and "beauty," but Dylan's songs are "powerful as poetry and they're powerful as music." Baez concludes by adding that other songwriters "are just trying desperately to say something, but they don't know how to say it. But Bob is expressing what all these kids want to say."[51] This is just one example of how Dylan became saddled with unreasonable expectations and why his every utterance was thought to be laden with political or philosophical meaning.

Dylan's greatest songs express multiple concepts and leave themselves open to various interpretations. "With God on Our Side" questions blind nationalism, American historical mythology taught in schools, and the invocation of God for political purposes. In an interview with *Life*, Dylan reflected upon the American educational experience. He said, "The teachers in school taught me everything was fine." Despite this message appearing in textbooks, Dylan asserted that it did not match reality and that things were not alright: "There are so many lies that have been told, so many things that are kept back." He asserted that young people felt like him, "but they ain't hearin' it no place." He again expressed the belief that fear kept young people in place, but added that he was not afraid.[52]

Dylan examines American imperialism and its world wars through a historical lens in "With God on Our Side." He begins the song acknowledging that his identity and age are inconsequential. He adopts the natural role of a youthful herald revealing the sins of previous generations. Starting with the Civil War, Dylan lists several examples of American military involvement, including the Plains Indian Wars. These conflicts, he notes with irony, ended successfully for the United States because God had chosen its side.

As "With God on Our Side" unfolds, Dylan admits his confusion about the reasons the United States entered World War I. He can overlook these questions, secure in the knowledge that as long as Americans believe that God chooses their side, the country will continue winning wars. The song continues to blast away at the jingoistic notion that God favors America in all conflicts. Dylan calls attention to the arbitrariness of this line of reasoning when he questions why the Holocaust occurred and only a few years later God now favors the (West) German allies of the United States.

It also offers a popular New Left theme, critique of the nuclear weapons build up, as well as the hope that God would avert the next war. Also, having been taught to "hate the Russians" his whole life added to Dylan's bewilderment. While most listeners at the time probably were unaware that Dylan's grandparents emigrated from Russia, the line must have carried extra weight for him considering his uncles had been born there.[53] In *Chronicles*, Dylan wrote that his uncles fought in World War II along with the Russians and that the Soviet threat seemed "not quite real."[54]

"With God on Our Side" culminates with a theological question about whether Judas Iscariot had God on his side when he betrayed Jesus. Some have interpreted this line as commentary on free will and others see it as Dylan questioning God's existence. Theology professor and Dylan author Stephen Webb has argued that this line means Dylan expresses humanity's incapability of understanding God's will. Webb posits that since Judas carried out God's plan, the notorious traitor actually had God on *his* side.[55] Whatever Dylan's intention, the song clearly douses the idea that whatever actions undertaken by the United States are automatically just. Dylan flashed his writing skill by mixing American history, theology, and a contemporary political issue into one song.

Civil Rights

The civil rights movement not only addressed a legal and moral wrong, it challenged the power of "legitimate authorities" around the country. The system of southern segregation was kept in place not just by violent criminals, but by the very persons who were sworn to uphold the law. And because segregation was partially a system of laws, those who ruled over it could argue the legitimacy of their positions and authority. The individuals who fought for civil rights were common people, many of them students, and the movement often lacked definitive leadership. To engage in protest, activists could march in the streets, walk into a diner and sit at a lunch counter, go to a public school, or attempt to register others to vote. As historian Massimo Teodori explains, the civil rights movement saw "no separation between the masses and intellectuals."[56]

Surprisingly, the only song published in *Broadside*'s first five issues that dealt solely with civil rights was Marilyn Eisenberg's "Freedom, Freedom Riders."[57] Despite the initial absence of civil rights songs in *Broadside*, before the end of 1962, they filled its pages. The editor's notes from December 1962 referred to "dozens" of songs "out of the Negro Freedom movement in the South." *Broadside* quoted Robert Shelton's *Sing Out!* article claiming that "freedom songs represent probably the greatest mass topical songwriting rage in this country since the days of the organizing drive of the labor movement in the 1930's."[58] While the songs poured in, both black and white college-age students risked their physical well-being and their lives working for the Congress for Racial Equality (CORE) and SNCC on voter registration drives and Freedom Rides.

Bob Dylan unquestionably supported civil rights and believed in the equality of all people. As a teen in Hibbing and throughout his life, he demonstrated egalitarian views on race. Dylan, as African American singer Victoria Spivey said, "had no color denomination."[59] His unequivocal support of racial equality and civil rights did not assuage his typical uneasiness concerning organizations. While he told Nat Hentoff that SNCC was "the only organization I feel a part of spiritually," he found the NAACP old and attempting to "use" him. The Hentoff interview was one of many that revealed Dylan's suspicion of formal organizations and the intentions of the older generation.[60]

Dylan's songs such as "The Lonesome Death of Hattie Carroll" and "Only a Pawn in Their Game" confronted the ramifications of institutionalized racism in a manner that dug deeper than simply "all people should be equal," and will be discussed in the next chapter. Bob Dylan's early work often addressed civil rights and the injustice experienced by so many citizens in postwar America. Although the denial of civil rights is inherently unjust, not all of Dylan's songs utilized justice as the centerpiece.

In fall of 1962, Dylan wrote "Oxford Town" about James Meredith's attempt to integrate the University of Mississippi. Initially Meredith had been barred, but after Kennedy administration pressure, Mississippi Governor Ross Barnett grudgingly acquiesced to allow Meredith to attend the school. In order to prevent Meredith's entry, segregationists started a riot and two people died in the disturbance. Dylan reports the racism and violence in a very direct manner, simply stating that Meredith went to "Oxford Town" and, for no other reason than the color of his skin, violence erupted. The song makes no attempt to delve into the causes of racism or make a broader statement about hypocrisy and injustice as he did with "Hattie Carroll' and "Only a Pawn." The song displays no real judgment on Dylan's part; he merely lets the facts tell the story and allows them to be shame enough.

Appearing in the same issue of *Broadside* as "Oxford Town," "Paths of Victory" represents another Dylan civil rights contribution. "Paths" did not specifically address a civil rights episode, but that quest can be understood as a future "victory" over racism and segregation. Given the context of its writing and lyrical clues, such as a troubled past but a brighter future, it seems likely that civil rights was the main inspiration.[61] In late 1962, civil rights became popular subject matter for *Broadside*, evidenced by five songs that dealt directly with the James Meredith/University of Mississippi situation. They appeared in the issue preceding the publication of "Oxford Town" and "Paths of Victory." The five songs were "Talkin' Ole Miss" by Gene Greenblath; "The Ballad of Oxford, Mississippi" by Phil Ochs; "The State of Mississippi" by Richard E. Peck; an ode to Mississippi's governor, "Ross Barnett" by Carl Stein; and Bruce Jackson's "Ballad of James Meredith."[62] By this time, the New Left levied many social critiques, but the civil rights movement had become their primary cause.

Dylan's best-known songs from this era were considered political on some level. Many of his lesser known titles also contained civil rights themes. Two songs, "Long Ago, Far Away" and "Ain't Gonna Grieve," were not released on Dylan's early albums and he never played them live, according to his official website. They finally appeared on *Bootleg Series 9: The Witmark Demos 1962–1964*, which was released in 2010. "Ain't Gonna Grieve" attempts to strike an optimistic note, calling on "brothers" and "sisters" to join in and asserting that people are "all one color." Dylan intends "Long Ago, Far Away" to be ironic, if not overly obvious. It provides a litany of evils such as slavery, war, poverty, murder—and claims that these things happened in the past but not anymore. The stanza that opens the song references someone who spoke of "peace and brotherhood" and as a result was crucified.[63] Other folk writers, such as Matt McGinn in "He'd Have Been in Trouble Too," employed Jesus as a counterexample to the political situation in the United States. The comparison was tragically apt as civil rights activists continued to be martyred over the next few years.[64]

"Playboys and Playgirls" ties together nearly every early-Dylan New Left theme imaginable. In the song Dylan calls out numerous offending parties such as "fallout shelter sellers," Jim Crow, lynch mobs, those who speak insanely of war, "red baiters and race haters," "money makers" and prison walls. Pete Seeger, who performed the song with Dylan at the 1963 Newport Folk Festival, claimed that a million people would eventually be singing it, but Dylan never officially released it and it remains an obscurity.[65]

Bob Dylan's second album, *The Freewheelin' Bob Dylan*, contains two classic anthems: "A Hard Rain's A-Gonna Fall" and "Blowin' in the Wind." In April 1962, Dylan debuted "Blowin' in the Wind" at Gerde's Folk City and stated it was not a protest song, and added that he did not write protest material.[66] Dylan also told *Sing Out!* that songwriters had an obligation to address social issues.[67] Whether he meant this, or he thought it a professionally expedient answer to satisfy his audience, is unknown. His announcement prior to "Blowin' in the Wind" came at a time when he had been writing topical or political songs for about two months. It is unlikely that his reputation as a protest singer could have been solidified in anyone's mind yet. It appears that he began trying to shed expectations even before they could be fully formulated. Regardless of Dylan's intent, his reputation grew rapidly. In May 1962, "Blowin' in the Wind" appeared in *Broadside*. In the same issue, Pete Seeger wrote that some considered Dylan "to be the nearest composer we have had to Woody Guthrie in recent years."[68]

Some of Dylan's compatriots were slightly less than impressed with "Blowin' in the Wind," but it resonated with folk audiences and radio listeners via Peter, Paul and Mary's version, which reached #2 in August 1963 and became the fastest selling single in the history of Warner Brothers Records.[69] The song came out at a perfect historical moment. The optimism of the early 1960s still resonated, youth-led political movements had begun, and there was little competition on the airwaves from similar material. The lyrics asked "how long" cannon balls would fly, people could exist before they were free, and when a man would be recognized as a man. It became a New Left anthem for its peace and rights message, but its lack of specifics allowed it to become a timeless classic, and future activists for numerous movements adopted the song. Ironically, people looked to Dylan for answers even though "Blowin' in the Wind" is mainly comprised of a series of questions. That the answer can be found "in the wind" is not entirely helpful to those seeking guidance.[70]

Despite his reputation as a prophet and conscience of his generation, Dylan offered very few concrete answers and did not claim to possess them. The song's success was owed in part to subject matter whose meaning was not narrowly defined. Like most of his best work, "Blowin' in the Wind" left listeners with room to navigate. Dylan provided the outlines and fans filled in the spaces. In the mid-1970s, when asked whether he wrote his early songs for commercial reasons, he responded, "I wrote them because that's what I was in the middle of." He admitted being caught up in the song's potency: "I felt 'Blowin' in the Wind.' When Joan and I sing it, it's like an old folk song to me. It never occurs to me that I'm the person who wrote it."[71]

Upon scrutiny and the passage of time, works often lose the potency that initially captivated audiences. Songs saddled with the historical significance of "Blowin' in the Wind" have to be appreciated in the context of their day, not just measured by their lyrical or musical deftness. Because the song has been the soundtrack to so many 1960s images, it is hard to envision it coming from any other time. Ian Bell, in his compelling *Once Upon a Time: The Lives of Bob Dylan*, states that "Blowin' in the Wind" was an anthem of the 1960s and would have had a slim chance of success in any other era.[72] Perhaps Bell thought that the song belonged to a simpler time and would not have been as well received later, but he is not explicit in his analysis.

After the 1960s, Americans became more cynical and maybe the song's poignancy would have been lost on a less optimistic public. If that is true, the irony is that Dylan's influence had a part in changing the expectations of listeners and the content of popular music. In 1971, John Lennon's "Imagine" reached #3 on the Billboard charts. It asked listeners to imagine a utopia without greed, violence, or religion. Lennon's message is no less naive than Dylan's in "Blowin' in the Wind." Paul McCartney and Stevie Wonder's "Ebony and Ivory" and Three Dog Night's "Black & White" both topped the charts (1982 and 1972, respectively). The use of piano keys as well as ink and paper as metaphors calling for racial harmony are exceedingly trite compared to Dylan's song. In this context, "Blowin' in the Wind" probably could have achieved success in just about any other time. If nothing else, it proved that for decades after 1962, "message" songs had the ability to sell in large amounts and reach a wide audience. The appeal of such songs and Dylan's writing skill are why he had such a hard time shaking his reputation as the "Voice of a Generation."

Generational Differences

In August 1963, Dylan wrote "When the Ship Comes In" in response to being denied a hotel room because of his appearance.[73] The piece has two direct religious references aimed at the powerful toppled by underdogs: Pharaoh's Army and Goliath. More than religious, it is a song of generational lines being drawn. Though one would never know the inspiration from the song's lyrics, Dylan clearly felt more connection to the growing youth movement than his public statements indicated. The concept of long-haired youth and bewildered parents is overdone, but there is no question that appearances themselves were becoming political statements. As the 1960s unfolded, the style of one's hair and clothes were reliable indicators of an individual's mindset in terms of civil rights, the war in Vietnam, and cultural attitudes.

By the end of 1963, the songs Dylan wrote, sang, and recorded earned him the reputation as the most significant performer of the folk movement. Though his own versions did not achieve chart success, he clearly was an artist on the rise. With notoriety came the added pressure of expectations on Dylan. A recurring theme in his public life has been his refusal, or perhaps lack of desire, to conform to the standards that the public sets for him. In late 1963, Bob Dylan's discomfort with the public perception—that he was a political performer and spokesperson of his generation—reached a symbolic peak. Three weeks after the assassination of President John F. Kennedy, Dylan received the Tom Paine Award at the Emergency Civil Liberties Committee's Bill of Rights dinner. An uncomfortable and intoxicated Dylan insulted the crowd and stated that he saw in Lee Harvey Oswald something of himself.[74]

During his rambling acceptance speech, Dylan spoke at length about generational differences and the pride he felt in being young. He stated that it was not "an old people's world" and that when individuals lose their hair, "*they* should go out." Dylan expressed his discomfort with those in power who made rules for him, and he essentially dismissed the whole purpose for the night by calling politics "trivial."[75] Dylan left the stage to a stunned and hostile crowd. After the controversy, Dylan stated that he did not like the makeup of the audience who "had nothing to do with my kind of politics." The liberal establishment crowd was too bourgeoisie, conventional, and old. The speech illustrated Dylan's lack of connection to the mainstream liberal movement and also the generational rift that existed.

After the debacle, he wrote a semiapology claiming that he was not a "speaker nor any politician."[76] Though this cannot be considered the main reason why Dylan began to shift away from folk music, it likely contributed to him turning from his association with political songs and activism. Allen Ginsberg claimed that the ECLC gave Dylan the award, "but he had declared his independence of politics because he didn't want to be a political puppet or feel obligated to take a stand all the time. He was above and beyond politics."[77]

In December 1963, shortly after the ECLC debacle, Dylan visited an SDS National Council meeting, which accused spy Alger Hiss also attended. During a break, Dylan indicated that he might be willing to participate with the Economic Research Action Project (ERAP), an organization that sought to unite working-class northern communities along socioeconomic rather than purely racial lines. Dylan warned the organizers to be careful due to the fallout from the singer's ECLC speech. He also told them that he would perform some benefits, but never returned their calls.[78] During this time, Dylan seemed to be somewhat interested in political engagement. In February 1964, Dylan and his friends, who embarked on a cross-country car trip, stopped by a miner's strike in Harlan County, Kentucky, to lend support to the workers. They dropped off clothes, perhaps considered planning a benefit, and departed.[79] Later, Phil Ochs sarcastically dismissed those who sought "Folk Points" by going to Harlan or Mississippi, both of which Dylan did.[80]

In January 1964, in between the ECLC episode and his visit to Kentucky, Columbia released *The Times They Are A-Changin'*, Dylan's most overtly political album. If Dylan had grown weary of the folk/protest designation, this album did not reflect it. The title track, to listeners still dazed from the Kennedy assassination, must have seemed prophetic. Dylan's timing proved fortuitous: "The Times They Are A-Changin'" coincided perfectly with political events that occurred in 1964, such as the Freedom Summer, the Berkeley Free Speech Movement, and the presidential election between Barry Goldwater and Lyndon Johnson.

In the song, Dylan threw down the generational gauntlet, warning parents and elected officials to "heed the call" and either assist or get out of the way.[81] Joan Baez noted that "nothing could have spoken better for our generation than 'The Times They Are A-Changin'.'"[82] As with "Blowin' in the Wind," lyrically, "The Times" could be applied during any point in history. If the song had been released in 1974, and fans had grown accustomed to hearing it accompanying images of Nixon's resignation and ongoing violence in Southeast Asia, it would also seem remarkably of *that* time. It is an excellent song, but the mythos of the 1960s has institutionalized it. Record buyers, however, did not immediately catch on. *The Times They Are A-Changin'* proved Dylan's most successful album to date, two spots higher than *Freewheelin'* but reaching only #20 overall. If Dylan was the "Voice of his Generation," at this time his peers chose to not buy his albums and singles in large quantities. This is not to suggest that his cultural and musical importance is diminished, but rather that his core audience made up a smaller number of devoted listeners than often assumed. However, he successfully tapped into a sentiment, especially among the young, that the country was on the verge of a historical precipice. Dylan, whether he wanted it or not, achieved the status of New Left prophet. He reached this apex, but it was with one foot out the door.

Stepping Out

In the period between *The Times They Are A-Changin'* and Dylan's next album, *Another Side of Bob Dylan*, a momentous musical event took place. In February 1964, the Beatles arrived in America and made an immediate impact on Dylan and the country. Their success is often cited as a primary reason why Dylan decided to abandon topical songs and go electric. However, he hinted at his movement away from the folk scene prior to that. In the summer of 1963, he wrote "For Dave Glover," which appeared in the program for the Newport Folk Festival and in *Broadside*. In it, he detailed his inability to sing old folk songs and proclaimed the need to sing his own. "Dave Glover" presented something of a "standing on the shoulders of giants" moment as Dylan acknowledged that the old songs inspired him to create his current work. The stream of consciousness piece served as part declaration, part social critique. It mentioned civil rights and "a seventy year ol' senator who wants t[o] bomb Cuba." "For Dave Glover" also echoed the New Left critique of modern society with lines about robbing the Constitution, censoring the mind, pushbutton food, super highways, and the incongruence of white collars, white hoods, "and the white man's suntan lotion."[83]

Within the Greenwich folk movement there existed an uneasy relationship between commercial success and a performer's authenticity. They considered "selling out" or "going commercial"—essentially any mass appeal—as apostasy on the part of the artist. The pressure exerted on performers to remain true to the cause meant that diversion carried ramifications, political and otherwise. Liam Clancy says that Dylan's success made many in the folk crowd jealous, and they turned it into a question of morality.[84] Folk performer and Dylan compatriot Happy Traum says that once an artist enters music-making professionally, "you strive for commercial success because that's the way you eat." He dismisses stories of artists who pass up monetary reward as "myth."[85] Dylan became more successful than anyone at the time could have imagined. How uneasy he felt about this is hard to ascertain. He told *Life*, "My records are selling and I'm making money," but added, "It makes me think I'm not doing right."[86] Certainly Dylan sought financial reward, but he did not always take the most obvious career path and certainly made decisions that were not necessarily commercially motivated.

In the early 1960s, when Dylan came to New York, a lucrative folk scene did not exist according to one of the deans of the folk crowd, Dave Van Ronk.[87] Echo Helstrom, Dylan's high school girlfriend, met with him in Minneapolis after the release of his first album and claims that Dylan told her folk music would be the avenue by which he would achieve success.[88] According to Joan Baez, Dylan said that he only wrote the protest songs, which he dismissed as "shit," because "news" sold well. He added that he "never was into that stuff."[89] Baez refused to believe it, replying that his songs were too earnest to be a ruse.[90] Some have seized upon this as proof that Dylan had no connection to any of the sentiments he expressed in the songs of this period. Joan Baez accurately recognized Dylan's belief in human equality. He also said that people were "betrayed by our silence" when we do not speak out against injustice.[91] Although he sought commercial success, he also sought artistic fulfillment and possessed a need to keep developing.

In 1964, Dylan had frequent opportunities to capitalize on current events to further his reputation as a political singer-songwriter. Joan Baez performed at a Free Speech sit-in in Berkeley, but Dylan did not. Mickey Schwerner, James Chaney, and Andrew Goodman were kidnapped and murdered in Philadelphia, Mississippi, but another "Only a Pawn in Their Game" or "Oxford Town" did not come forth. Many fans expected that Dylan would write a new batch of protest songs for these events. Perhaps he figured that he had already said what he needed to about these subjects and feared being typecast. Those close to the singer were privy to his views on topical songwriting. He told Phil Ochs that politics was "bullshit" and said to another friend that he "stopped thinking in terms of society." He proclaimed that his refusal to be a part of social issues stemmed from the fact that he was outside of society. Internalizing the effects of the Kennedy assassination, Dylan believed that anybody who attempted or spoke out for real change would be killed, including himself.[92] He certainly had the ability to write songs about the aforementioned issues and could have financially capitalized on them. This is why his exit from playing purely that type of music should be understood primarily as an artistic move rather than one driven solely by profit.

In a one-day session in June 1964, Dylan recorded *Another Side of Bob Dylan* and Columbia released the album in August. *Another Side* represented a move away from specific or topical songs. They now reflected a more personal approach, the lyrics less concrete or even absent of political messages. Over the years, some music critics have credited this album with inventing the singer-songwriter genre. With *Another Side*, Dylan certainly seemed to be distancing himself from standard folk music and direct political statements. The pressure of being the "Voice of a Generation" weighed on him. Tom Wilson, who produced four Dylan albums plus "Like a Rolling Stone," said that the performer was "not a singer of protest so much as he's a singer of *concern* about people." Wilson also added that Dylan did not have to write "about Medgar Evers all the time to be effective."[93] The album dropped a number of clues about the new direction Dylan headed.

New Left activists and folk fans, who were sometimes one and the same, believed in the moral rectitude of their political causes. In addition, they viewed the music as a means to bring about necessary social and cultural change. This led to a sentiment that the stakes were high and the battle lines clearly drawn. A major intellectual player on the Greenwich folk scene, Izzy Young describes the folk crowd as "very black and white," and that they demanded to know "which side are you on?" Young believes that both he and Dylan drew the folk crowd's ire for not definitively picking a side: "They had all decided he was on their side—oh boy! He's one of us!" Young recalls that Dylan started writing songs that were not "about some dying coal miner, and now—oh, no! He's not one of us! He's a traitor, and he's a hypocrite, and he's good for nothing."[94]

Dylan found the lack of options far too limiting for his artistic development. He said, "I was doing that four years ago. Now there's a lot of people writing songs on protest subjects." He added that of the protest singers he heard, they had an "emptiness which is like a song written 'Let's hold hands and everything will be grand.' I see no more to it than that. Just because someone mentions the word 'bomb,' I'm not going to go 'Aalee!' and start clapping." He also believed that the views of the audience contributed to the limitations of that style. "Sure, you can make all sorts of protest songs and put them on a Folkways record. But who hears them?" Dylan pointed out the insular nature of folk records by observing that those who "do hear them are going to be agreeing with you anyway. You aren't going to get somebody to hear it who doesn't dig it." He understood the relative narrowness and self-selection of pop culture consumers. "People don't listen to things they don't dig." If you can find a cat that can actually say 'Okay, I'm a changed man because I heard this one thing—or I just saw this one thing.'"[95]

Several of the songs on *Another Side* hinted at a renunciation of his "protest singer" persona. "It Ain't Me Babe" could be a message to a woman, or perhaps to the folk crowd whose expectations he seeks to get out from under. In "My Back Pages," he warns against viewing life in terms of "black and white." He also claims that he had been an older, more serious folkie who now was a younger, more playful performer. Two albums earlier, he sang in "Bob Dylan's Dream" that it was easy "to tell black from white."[96] Now, Dylan wished to be free from any definitions as obvious as a protest singer or political writer. He had referred to his early period work as his "finger pointing" songs. In the humorous "I Shall Be Free No. 10," Dylan sings that it isn't any use "talking to me" because it is the same thing "as talking to you."[97] He apparently wanted to tamp down expectations, and it seemed an admission that he did not have answers and fans should cease to assume that he did. Additionally, it can be understood as an attempt to democratize by claiming that he and fans existed on the same level and that he was not privy to any arcane knowledge.

Another Side of Bob Dylan peaked at #43 on the album sales chart. It represented a decline of 23 spots from *The Times They Are A Changin'* and the lowest since his debut.[98] Obviously, fans preferred the original side of Bob Dylan. Some members of the folk establishment criticized Dylan's departure on *Another Side*, while others saw it as Dylan pushing forward as he claimed in "For Dave Glover." In January 1964, he wrote a letter to *Broadside* that tackled the issues he was having with being famous and asked out loud if he was a messiah—"hell, no I'm not" came his answer.[99] In *Sing Out!*, Irwin Silber complained about the direction Dylan's songs were headed, calling them "inner directed."[100] Silber, among others, wanted Dylan to remain a writer of topical songs and poster boy for the folk scene. Since *Another Side of Bob Dylan* tanked, relatively speaking, and if sales were Dylan's primary concern, then it seems plausible that he would have retreated to the formula of *Times They Are A-Changin'*—a format already proven successful. Instead, Dylan doubled down and remade rock and roll.

The general atmosphere of the mid-1960s promoted artistic experimentation and musical innovation. Over an 18-month period, Bob Dylan released three albums of music made mostly with electric instruments. When the first of the trilogy, *Bringing it All Back Home*, was released, the Beatles' most recent LP, *The Beatles for Sale*, consisted of only eight originals. It contained typical boy/girl relationship lyrics, including a Dylan-influenced "I'm a Loser." The Rolling Stones and Kinks, playing mostly blues covers, had a nominal amount of original songs in their repertoire, and the Who had yet to release an LP. The Beach Boys and Motown made ear-pleasing pop but did not stray far from their successful formulas or experiment lyrically. The youth, in tune with the change to a more sophisticated sound, stood ready to coalesce around a cultural and spiritual revolution. Dylan's quantum artistic leap in 1965 inspired the Beatles to reach further on their album from the same year, *Rubber Soul*. The group added the sitar, new production values, and put greater thought into their lyrics.

So much has been made of Dylan's decision to employ electric instruments that very little new light can be shed upon the event and its ramifications. Disagreement about what happened at the Newport Folk Festival, even by those who were there, obscures any absolute truth. Clearly some of the folk crowd at Newport, or other venues such as Forest Hills, saw Dylan as a sellout and booed him. To many folk fans, acoustic music represented authenticity, while electric instruments meant commercialism. As far as purists were concerned, the Beatles' records were simply for teeny-boppers. In reality, Dylan's adaptation of electric instruments was less of a sellout than the numerous schlocky cover versions of "Blowin' in the Wind," of which dozens existed.

The ever-restless Dylan wanted to expand his parameters. "I get very bored with my old songs," he said, drawing a line of demarcation after a three-year career. "I can't sing 'With God on My Side' for 15 years." Dylan defended his decision by stating, "If anyone has imagination, he'll know what I'm doing. If they can't understand my songs they're missing something."[101]

Whether Dylan foresaw singing those songs anymore or not, numerous imitators tried to cash in on his style. The most obvious was the rough-voiced, Dylan knock-off, Barry McGuire. In August 1965, his version of "Eve of Destruction" reached #1 on the *Billboard* Top 40, a feat Dylan never accomplished. Phil Ochs thought McGuire's song, written by P. F. Sloan, "imitative and weak" and compared it unfavorably to "The Lonesome Death of Hattie Carroll."[102] Research into popular music demonstrates that a sizable number of young listeners, despite the song's lack of irony or subtlety, misconstrued or did not comprehend the message of "Eve of Destruction."[103] Apparently, most radio listeners and record buyers gave little serious thought to Dylan's work, but rather followed popular trends. Those perhaps a little older or more politically involved had different expectations of Dylan and continued to believe that popular music had transformative powers. Willing or capable artists cashed in on that sentiment and the naiveté of audiences. Considering that an imitation Dylan sold well with "Eve of Destruction," the authentic version should figure to do even better. However, Dylan understood the risk of being reduced to a caricature and released nothing remotely similar to "Eve of Destruction" for years.

Typically the word "political" refers to an active pursuit of an office, the exertion of power, or grappling with an issue. However, rejection or disengagement with the process has political ramifications as well.[104] Much like the Beats, Dylan's conduct and art were political, though not linked to any movement. This is the type of anarchy that best describes his political approach in the mid-1960s. He did not have to scream "Down with the state!" to convey a message of disaffection with the mainstream political process or society. At this point, nearly every one of Dylan's actions and utterances carried influence. He did not need to be overtly political in order to have a political impact. Many listeners assuming the significance of Dylan's lyrics developed their own intellectual response. In this way, Dylan became an exemplar of anarchistic thought and deed.

Those who thought Dylan's new sound was a repudiation of an earlier self or a compromise of his values were wrong. Even though his new songs proved extremely successful, there was no reason to expect that they would. *Another Side of Bob Dylan* was a commercial disappointment compared to *The Times They Are A-Changin'*. A greater leap would, in theory, take him that much further from his original audience. The idea that there was a guaranteed new set of fans necessarily waiting for him is a fallacy. The music Dylan turned out in 1965 was not obviously commercial. There were no Beatlesque harmonies, no cloying love songs, nor any danceable tunes. In his medium, he has been compared to artists such as James Joyce, Pablo Picasso, or Frank Lloyd Wright. As Dylan himself said in the documentary *No Direction Home*, nothing else sounded similar to "Like a Rolling Stone."[105] This is not to say that the music was atonal experimentation; his blues-infused rock was not completely dissimilar from the Rolling Stones or Animals. But the idea of releasing those words combined with that sound, to the listening public, proved a radical artistic move. It reflected experimentations in theater and art as well as the flourishing of the Counterculture. Dylan was by no means the first artist to push boundaries, but now young people, influenced by Dylan's songs and Beat poetry among other things, began to challenge the status quo. Some members of the New Left and folk crowd fell away from Dylan, but as his new songs helped to encourage a burgeoning Counterculture, they pointed the way to the absurdist politics of the Yippies and others.

Increasingly, rock musicians needed to "say something" in order to be taken seriously by their peers, music critics, and certain fans. Lyrics needed to be, or at least appear to be, substantive. In rock and roll's evolution, Bob Dylan set the pace. In May 1966, he released his third installment of mid-1960s masterpieces, the double album *Blonde on Blonde*. His contemporaries, influenced by his previous records, started to play catch up. The Beatles took another leap after *Rubber Soul* and released *Revolver*; the Beach Boys offered *Pet Sounds*. It is hard to imagine either group would have recorded "mature" albums of this nature without Dylan expanding the parameters of rock and roll. By 1967, this change became partially evident when sales of LPs, a format that contained enough room for a proper statement, outsold the 45 RPM format.

Rejection of Mainstream Society

Though not the exclusive domain of the New Left, criticism of a society deemed hollow, artificial, and stifling proved popular in the 1960s. A *New York Times Magazine* article described Dylan's attitude as "rude defiance of all authority and scorn for the Establishment, which he put down with unrelenting and unforgiving bitterness."[106] This quote represented a mainstream media attempt to explain Dylan and his influence. Dylan, obviously fed up with trying to explain himself, told the press, "All my songs are protest songs. You name something, I'll protest about it."[107] There seemed to be a need in society to identify a Pied Piper figure who led the youth astray. Dylan, because of his high profile and songwriting skill, became that symbol. As documented earlier, the feeling of unease among college students and other young people started before Bob Dylan made any allusions to it.

In the songs from his early career, Dylan addressed injustice and inequality. In the next period, he wrote songs that seemed to speak out against the shallowness of society. Dylan said that people now knew "the bullshit of everything," and that it was "a circus world."[108] He became a more mature rock and roll version of Holden Caulfield as he railed against the phonies and artifices of the culture. Dylan's criticism became more abstract, less about concrete issues such as racism and more akin to the Beats and the dissatisfaction of New Left radicals. Joan Baez summed up the difference between Dylan and herself, though they both criticized society, by claiming Dylan's approach suggested that nothing could be done, "so screw it. And I say just the opposite." She feared his message had become "Let's all go home and smoke pot, because there's nothing else to do."[109]

"Subterranean Homesick Blues" kicked off *Bringing It All Back Home* and provided all the evidence needed that Dylan's songwriting had changed. Listeners, looking for meaning, found bits and pieces of countercultural statements jumping out. Dylan sang that after spending "twenty years" in school, the fate that awaited youth was placement on a "day shift." Academic endeavor, often maligned by the New Left, seemed even more pointless from that vantage point. The desirability of attempting to please others and become successful was called into question. Dylan's ongoing suspicion of those in power came through resoundingly with some of his most famous lines.

He informed listeners that they did not "need a weatherman" to gauge which way the wind blew. Inspired by the line, an SDS splinter group in the late 1960s named itself the Weatherman and later was commonly known as the Weather Underground or the Weathermen. In case listeners missed the hint the first time around, later in the song Dylan directly advised them to not "follow leaders."[110] On one level, it existed as a reflection of the New Left's suspicion toward those in power. On another, it appeared to be a thinly veiled attempt to escape from his designation as "Voice of a Generation." Ironically, at a time when questioning authority and leaders became more common, Bob Dylan could not shed the leadership labels he wished to avoid.

The crowning achievement of Dylan's antithetical approach was "It's Alright, Ma (I'm Only Bleeding)." In fall of 1964, Dylan began performing the song in concert. It played out as a seven-minute manifesto against the artificial and commercial nature of society. Some understand the phrase in the first stanza that there is "no sense in trying" as a nihilistic sentiment along the lines of Joan Baez's comment that Dylan forsook any attempts to change society. However, one stanza later, he advocates for continuous growth with the line that if a person is not "being born," they are "busy dying."[111] The notion of change, rebirth, and transformation is a constant thread in Dylan's career.

Dylan attacks tacky commercialism with a line about "flesh colored Christs" and observes that nothing seems "sacred." He notes that advertising exists to deceive the populace into thinking that they are something they are not. As a result, people become lost in consumerist fantasy. Simultaneously, real life takes place around them, but they are not attuned to it. Dylan paints a bleak picture of a society built on "fake morals," where money "swears" rather than talks. In this landscape, the masters make rules for the wise and foolish. In the age of the imperial presidency, Dylan knocks the office down a notch by declaring that even the president must "stand naked." This antihierarchical statement is the equivalent of saying that the chief executive puts his pants on one leg at a time.[112] The ideas Dylan expressed dovetailed with concepts being voiced all over America by young people. New Left leaders such as Carl Oglesby were far more politically aware than Bob Dylan. Oglesby's speech, often titled "Trapped in a System," attacked Lyndon Johnson's Vietnam policy and indicted corporate liberalism. Oglesby's argument separated the sides by age rather than by the usual liberal/conservative dichotomy. He described capitalism, politics, education, and other institutions morphing into a "system" that indoctrinated youth and resisted reform.[113]

"It's Alright, Ma" was written a year before "Trapped in a System," and the message of both conveyed the sense of people being stuck. Dylan employs "rat race" in a pejorative manner similar to his use of "day shift" in "Subterranean Homesick Blues." The rat race means a virtual enslavement of workers that keeps them focused on material things and engaged in a consumerist competition with their neighbors—keeping up, in other words, with Mrs. and Mr. Jones. Thus, these people hate their jobs and find themselves trapped. As a result, they "despise" those who are free from such constraints and wish to keep them buried "in the hole." It is a pit of debt, despair, and self-loathing. This is the vision of society that first the Beats then the Hippies, among other Counterculture types, spoke out against. Though he shared a general worldview with many in the student movement, Dylan consistently remained outside any easy political definition because he doubted the effectiveness of activism and was not aligned with any particular program. Regardless, many people at the time assumed that they understood Dylan and that his politics aligned with theirs.

What Others Thought

Dylan's reputation as a poet and political philosopher grew, and his significance began to be debated by journalists, academics, and cranks. Robert Shelton complimented Dylan's ability to create songs that allowed for listeners to interpret for themselves. Shelton called "Desolation Row" "another of Mr. Dylan's musical Rohrshachs [sic] capable of widely varied interpretation."[114] Because the songs were ambiguous, fans ascribed more precise meaning and metaphorical significance than Dylan intended. There were critiques of society to be sure, but the political content became stylistic. Dylan's transformation did not destroy the old format of popular music as is often suggested. Saccharine ballads continued to shoot up the charts. Rather, it opened the door to possibilities and made Dylan even more popular because listeners assumed his message to be political. In a self-perpetuating way, it made him more important. If politics is the art of the possible, then this was in fact political music.

Fans and critics heaped praise on Dylan, and professors debated Dylan's poetic and literary worth. Not all of them were convinced that he was the "Poet of His Generation." In a 1965 *New York Times Magazine* article, a critic stated that Dylan was not "a writer of any consequence—he's simply a pop-culture figure." He allowed that Dylan's imagination was interesting, "but his ideas and his techniques are dated and banal" and rooted in the Depression Era. He concluded by stating "like most pop-culture heroes, Dylan will soon be forgotten—he'll quickly become last year's vogue writer." In contrast a pro-Dylan critic said that he is "taking poetry away from the academicians...and giving it back to the masses." If Dylan read the article, he probably appreciated being described as a poetic populist. Pulitzer Prize-winning poet Louis Simpson scoffed that the term "poet" was thrown around too loosely and that he was not shocked: "American college students consider him their favorite poet—they don't know anything about poetry."[115]

Whether praise or criticism, Dylan commentators generally accorded him undue significance outside of the rock medium. A New York record executive credited Dylan with altering songwriting—a valid claim. He asserted that before Dylan, "all of the hit songs were lachrymose teen-age laments about unhappy high school love affairs." However, because of Dylan's influence, "the hits are about things like war, foreign policy and poverty." He credited Dylan's early songs such as "Masters of War" and "Blowin' in the Wind" with spawning "imitators [who] are now making it big with folk-rock songs like 'Eve of Destruction,' 'Home of the Brave,' and 'We Gotta Get Out of This Place.'"[116]

Dylan significantly impacted rock lyrics but statements such as these overestimate his influence on the Top 40. A cursory examination of the *Billboard* Charts from the time when the *New York Times Magazine* article was published shows Top-10 hits for adult contemporary trumpeter Herb Alpert, vocal groups such as the Four Seasons and the Shangri-Las, and crooner Dean Martin. Though the Byrds' "Turn! Turn! Turn!" reached #1 that week, no songs that were discernibly about poverty or foreign policy cracked the Top 40 (unless one stretches the intent of "England Swings" by Roger Miller beyond belief).[117] Two studies, one from T. Horton and the other from James Carey, found that boy/girl themes declined from 1955 to 1965, rock's first decade. Horton noted that 83 percent of lyrics in 1955 contained romantic themes, while Carey discovered it had slipped to 65 percent by 1966.[118] Bob Dylan's songwriting was probably the single most important reason why. While the number of love songs decreased, they were not necessarily replaced with solely political work. For example, songs such as "Yellow Submarine" and "Get Off of My Cloud" were neither love nor political songs. Dylan demonstrated that political songs could be profitable and expanded the subject matter of rock and roll to include the nonlinear, absurd, and outright surreal.

The record executive quoted in the *New York Times Magazine* proceeded to oversimplify the causation of young people's political involvement. He asserted that Dylan's music held "a great deal" of the "responsibility for the surprising interest the younger generation has today in serious questions like civil rights and Vietnam." Further, he believed that Dylan probably possessed "more direct influence on what's going on with young people in America today—protest marches, picketing, and so forth—than almost any other one person in the country."[119] Dylan certainly had *some* effect on changing attitudes, if for no other reason than people thought he did. The tendency throughout the years has been to overstate the amount of real political influence the singer exerted.

When a cultural phenomenon such as Dylan hits, people seek an explanation of its cause and impact. During the 1960s, journalists grappled for answers about both social changes and Dylan's popularity. Those attempts grew into mythologizing the singer and what he stood for. Years later, historian John Morton Blum would claim that Dylan "infused his lyrics with political as well as cultural radicalism." This statement is essentially true, but the next one is not: "His 'Highway 61' and 'Desolation Row' carried obvious anti-war and anti-American connotations."[120] This is a perfect example of the Dylan-as-totem type of thinking. Since there were antiwar and anti-American beliefs among the young and Dylan wrote "political songs," then his work must have contained these themes. Anti-American sentiment is not evident in "Highway 61" or "Desolation Row," and obvious antiwar themes do not exist either.

A more comical assessment of Dylan's influence appeared in *Rolling Stone*. In 1967, Los Angeles advertising executive Ken Granger, connected with an organization called Truth About Civil Turmoil, wrote a script, and created a filmstrip entitled "The Hippies." It put forward the theory that Dylan was an unknown songwriter until communist sympathizer John Hammond signed him to Columbia. Granger cited a comment made by Clive Davis, a Columbia/CBS Record executive, who referred to Dylan as "the leading cultural force among young people of today." Granger claimed that "The Times They Are A-Changin'" "made questioning American standards the 'in' thing to do." Granger's comments seem laughable, but they demonstrate the significance people attributed to Bob Dylan and the power of his music to shape the youth.[121]

The aforementioned examples reflect a popular version of the 1960s, one in which countercultural youth battled racism, challenged the military-industrial complex, and pointed the direction to a better world. In this 1960s, Bob Dylan's protest songs provided the soundtrack and helped fuel the conflagration that roared through America. The impact of this on the popular understanding of Bob Dylan has been twofold. First, it has been taken for granted that Dylan's politics aligned with left-wing activism. The reality is that Dylan's public persona and the politics of the New Left ran on parallel tracks for a time. Since that label and all others proved too limiting, he diverged. Second, Dylan has been credited with an outsized influence on political attitudes and events. Although Dylan significantly reshaped rock and roll, the impact that popular music and any specific musician had in affecting real change is debatable. At a 1965 press conference, Dylan unequivocally denied the political importance of his music: "I'm not a preacher. Songs can't save the world, I know that."[122]

A third misconception, but one that does not directly pertain to Bob Dylan, overestimates the number of young people committed to leftist political ideals. Most young people of the 1960s never seriously challenged the status quo or social conventions. Many of those who did only participated to a small degree and ended up living typical or mainstream lives. Some, however, completely turned away from the dominant culture of their parents' generation. This "tiny minority of the youth," whom history professor Theodore Roszak dubbed the "Counterculture," created their own lifestyle. Its defining features were more than long hair or experimentation with drugs and sex, because those things enticed many mainstream youth as well. The true Counterculture members turned their back on most of the economic, religious, and political norms found in the dominant culture.[123]

The New Left attitude Dylan most embodied at this point was the advocacy of individual freedom unconstrained by a bankrupt society. "Ballad of a Thin Man" constitutes this perfectly. The ominous piano, the constant badgering of "Mr. Jones," and the surreal imagery makes it a Counterculture classic. The hallucinatory nightmare describes "one-eyed midgets," people shouting bizarre requests, and a beleaguered Mr. Jones who knows "something's happening" but is unaware of "what it is."[124] Whether Dylan had an individual or a group of people in mind for Mr. Jones is not definitively known. The obvious interpretation is that the song lambasts the philistines of society and draws a clearly defined line between those who get it and those who do not. Dylan informed a journalist of that idea when he bitingly commented, "People that listen to me don't read your paper."[125] Dylan truly did speak for a sizable number of people who, like him, were outsiders but had now become the in-crowd.

Counterculture and Radicalism

In February 1965, President Johnson ordered Operation Rolling Thunder, an escalation of bombing and then, in March, a full-scale invasion of Vietnam. As the civil rights movement began to splinter, the New Left coalesced around the antiwar movement and became radicalized. Young people were no longer content to hold hands and sing "We Shall Overcome." US cities exploded in race riots and antiwar activists took to the streets. Looking back, Dylan comments that he has no fondness for a time he refers to as "cruel."[126] As the decade wore on, many young people became more radical in the pursuit of their ideals. Bob Dylan, the Vietnam War, and civic unrest are all closely associated with the 1960s. However, Dylan had very little to say about these things while they happened. The *Bringing It All Back Home* liner notes (1965) are one of only three direct written references Dylan made to Vietnam in his lyrics or writings and the only one while the conflict took place. Even then, the line was hardly an antiwar statement. In the typical Dylan stream of consciousness style that he used for most of his nonlyric writings, it merely referred to someone blaming him for the "riots over in Vietnam."[127]

Beat poetry and novels influenced Dylan's literary sense. Dylan held Jack Kerouac in high regard and had a personal friendship with Allen Ginsberg. In the early 1960s, the Bohemian/Beat lifestyle existed apart from the politically active New Leftists. While the Beats rejected many of the trappings of polite society, the New Left members who engaged in political causes tended to look and act relatively mainstream. In the early and mid-1960s, the Bohemian origins of the Counterculture movement grew slowly until it expanded rapidly after 1967.[128] Dylan took the foundation that the Beat Generation provided and built upon it. Whether Dylan's lyrics described dwarves of "gray flannel" or fires being shot "full of holes," nothing of the sort had been put down on vinyl before. The growing Counterculture imbibed Dylan's influence as well as that of other artists and intellectuals. Groups such as the Living Theater and Andy Warhol's Factory, among many others, pushed the boundaries of their creative mediums. Dylan did not give rise to all of this, but it coexisted in a mutual reinforcement of kindred spirits.

The Counterculture Hippies and the more serious-minded political activists who led many of the student organizations often did not get along with one another.[129] In 1967, Emmett Grogan and Peter Berg of the Diggers—a communal, anarchist political group—disrupted an SDS meeting. The less flamboyant SDS members were not amused by the Diggers' absurdist behavior. The Diggers, Yippies, and Merry Pranksters represented groups who affirmed the personal approach to politics, but the Counterculture was not generally a political movement in the classic sense of the word.[130] Of course, in some cases the cultural and political movements overlapped, but too frequently the media lumped all long-haired young people into the same category. The Hippies offered "a concept, an act of rejection, a militant vanguard, a hope for the future." According to one underground newspaper, they "openly refused to be used anymore to be manipulated, coerced, and destroyed as human beings."[131] In the early 1960s, SDS had sought serious political change via participatory action and at the same time they called attention to cultural issues as well. The Counterculture frequently affected politics on a personal level and often "dropped out." Toward the end of the 1960s, some activists who were disillusioned and beat down by defeat turned participatory politics into violent action.[132]

Culturally, the changes in style and fashion were akin to an LP being played at 45 RPM speed. On a superficial level, between 1964 and 1969, radically different outward appearances developed in students from the same college campus. The length of hair and style of dress typically belayed their general political outlook. In 1968, 750,000 college students identified with the New Left, but many more adopted some aspect, be it hairstyle, sexual activity, or drug experimentation, of the Counterculture.[133] Another estimate is that America had two million Hippies, but most of them were not on college campuses.[134] Dylan underwent some of the transformation as well. The album covers, spanned by less than three years, for *The Times They Are A-Changin'* and *Blonde on Blonde* reflected the transformation from a Steinbeck-like folkie to a wild-haired hipster. Though the consummate outsider, Dylan did not exist completely disconnected from the cultural upheaval that took place around him.

One of the great ironies of Dylan's career is that as an artist he has been inexorably tied to the 1960s, but he virtually disappeared at its height. The year 1967's so-called Summer of Love, the traumatic year of 1968, and the continuation of the war all passed with Dylan essentially detached. After he backed off from public demands following his motorcycle accident in 1966, Dylan released only two more albums during the 1960s: *John Wesley Harding* and *Nashville Skyline*. He also wrote and recorded numerous songs, most of which became *The Basement Tapes*, with the Band in Woodstock, New York. All of it was almost directly opposite of what one would expect. Rather than ornate and psychedelic, the songs were stripped down and countrified. For some Counterculture types, this represented a betrayal of sorts on Dylan's part. As the political intensity magnified, many expected Dylan to provide commentary against the war or the political violence that seemed to tear the country apart. Dylan saw futility in the attempt to remake a corrupt society via the political process or revolution. During this period, visitors to his home noted that he read the Bible and suggested that they do so as well. Dylan's semireclusive life for the next seven years saw him change his music style, focus on his family, and make few public appearances.

Dylan often remained out of step with the 1960s Counterculture. Though his hair grew longer and his clothes changed, Dylan did not merely follow the trends and fads of the time. He never donned beads, a psychedelic caftan, or dashiki nor did he ever associate with LSD guru Timothy Leary. There was no possibility that Dylan would have suggested that his audience "tune in, turn on, and drop out." He told Nat Hentoff that he "wouldn't advise anybody to use drugs," although opium and marijuana were "not drugs; they just bend your mind a little." He added that *"everybody's* mind should be bent once in a while."[135] Even though the much-ballyhooed culmination of the Hippie ideal occurred virtually around the corner from him, he did not play the 1969 Woodstock Festival. He later said that it did not excite him and that he "didn't want to be a part of that thing."[136] The "Summer of Love" of the Hippies and Bob Dylan the "Voice of a Generation" both exist, in large part, as media constructs. They are simple and prepackaged and applicable when needed. Dylan may have hinted at "All You Need Is Love" with "Tell Me That It Isn't True," a country-sounding tune proclaiming love to be "all there is" and that it made "the world go round." But instead of wearing a brightly colored *Sgt. Pepper* suit or *Magical Mystery Tour* costume, the man on the *Nashville Skyline* album cover looked like a country bumpkin.

While Dylan retreated to his home and family, the New Left experienced major fissures. The much-more-radical Weathermen took over SDS. Additional splits emerged with the formation of groups such as the Revolutionary Youth Movement, Worker Student Alliance, and Revolutionary Youth Movement II. SDS had been the focal point of the New Left, and when it disintegrated, the notion of a unified movement did as well.[137] The earnest New Leftists of the early 1960s still existed, but "Counterculture" could be applied to any number of political or lifestyle choices. The politics of the Counterculture have been described as "the politics of anarchism—of decentralization, rural romanticism, and libertarianism."[138] Using this definition, Dylan's political outlook mirrored the Counterculture, but he never expressed a desire for activism or leadership. During the late 1960s, he also had the luxury of being able to retreat to a rural setting.

Dylan's actual connection to "The Movement" remained minimal though many tried to draw him in, much in the same way the folk crowd had wanted to preserve him. The *Berkeley Barb*, an underground newspaper, attributed the line about not trusting anyone over 35 to "Dr. Dylan." In fact it was CORE and Berkeley Free Speech participant Jack Weinberg who coined the phrase, and originally the age he gave was 30.[139] The *Barb* got it wrong, but actual Dylan phrases were borrowed by the radical movement. In addition to the Weatherman reference, demonstrators at the 1968 Chicago convention chanted "the whole world is watching," paraphrasing Dylan's line from "When the Ship Comes In."

In the 1970s, Dylan unequivocally stated that the so-called Hippie dream had little to do with him: "The flower generation—is that what it was? I wasn't into that at all. I just thought it was a lot of kids out and around wearing flowers in their hair takin' a lot of acid. I mean what can you think about that?"[140] In the 1980s, Dylan had not strayed from that sentiment. Over a decade later, he told *USA Today*, "From '66 on, I was trying to raise a family and that was contrary to the whole epidemic of the '60s." He added that many "people were running away from home and trying to get away from their parents. That was never intentional on my part, trying to run away from *anything*." Dylan has consistently maintained his disconnect from the 1960s stereotype and has kept a tight connection to his children: "My family was more important to me than any kind of generational '60s thing. Still is. To find some meaning in the '60s for me is real far-fetched."[141]

Dylan's 1975 interview with *People* reiterated his lack of political involvement but revealed some of his sympathies: "I'm not an activist. I am not politically inclined. I'm for people, people who are suffering. I don't have any pull in the government." He echoed that 30 years later in the *No Direction Home* documentary when he stated that being on the side of people who are suffering is not political. The *People* article noted that Dylan did not like the accusation that he shied away from the antiwar and other protest movements that "his music catalyzed."[142] With Dylan, it is hard to tell what annoyed him more—the accusation that he distanced himself from the antiwar crowd or the assumption that his music was responsible for the protest movement.

At no time during the 1960s did Dylan make a public statement opposing the Vietnam War or release a song that directly opposed it. A 1990 *Rolling Stone* review of Dylan's West Point concert opened with the line

"Bob Dylan, it has been said was the person most responsible for ending the Vietnam War." The source for that claim is not cited and where the author originally heard that sentiment is a mystery. From a historical standpoint, the statement itself is preposterous. Using no known fact ever written about the American conflict in Vietnam, it distorted Dylan's political significance, the actual reasons the war concluded, and the historical truth about Dylan's stance concerning Vietnam.[143] Considering what Dylan said—or did not say—about the war while it took place, the comment becomes even more bewildering.

The war polarized America in the late 1960s and very little room existed for not being clearly on one side or the other of the issue. In an interview with John Cohen and Happy Traum in *Sing Out!*, Dylan took his typical long-view approach. In interviews, before and since, he has refused to get overly concerned about current events. When Cohen addressed the recent assassinations of Robert Kennedy and Martin Luther King Jr., Dylan reminded him that "the specific name or deed isn't any different than that which has happened previous to this." He added that "progress" brought about monetary change but very little substantive improvement. Toward the end of the interview, Traum asked Dylan about an artist's responsibility to speak out against the war. Dylan, thinking specifically of a painter friend, responded that he knew "very good artists who are for the war." Dylan tried to explain that he appreciated the artist's paintings and did not feel a need to engage in a debate concerning Vietnam. Traum persisted, telling Dylan that he could not see how he and the painter, who was for the war, could "share the same basic values." Dylan responded that he knew the man for a long time, he respected him, and they were friends. He concluded in his ever-oppositional manner by asking Traum how he knew that "I'm not, as you say, for the war?"[144]

This did not represent Dylan tacitly approving or disapproving of the conflict, but rather his annoyance with the questioning and Traum's implication that views on Vietnam should define friendship, admiration, or respect. Dylan's views on the Vietnam War essentially amounted to an approach where he did not bother getting worked up about a given war, since they had existed for millennia and would continue to exist. In his mind, a song or a speech would not bring about political change. However, this disengagement frustrated many on the Left who thought Dylan belonged to them and that he should march lockstep with their beliefs.

As the 1960s wound down, the New Left movement began to disintegrate for numerous reasons. The violence at the 1968 Democratic convention helped to elect Richard Nixon as president and create an impression of a violent and anarchic Left. This partially diminished support for leftist ideas, and as it dropped, support for conservatives increased among incoming college freshmen in the fall of 1970.[145] The movement's inherent suspicion of leaders and basic aversion to dictates made moving in the same direction nearly impossible. Fatigue and disillusionment set in as the New Left continued to incrementally lose ground and suffered a crushing blow in Nixon's 1972 landslide reelection.

The 1970s

The early 1970s proved largely to be a continuation of the difficulties of the late 1960s. The war in Vietnam ground on and the country remained deeply divided. As the 1970s continued, Americans contended with a new set of problems. The economic downturn affected many young people just out of college, especially those who had children to support. American society experienced political, social, and cultural fragmentation. Social and political movements such as civil rights and antiwar protests existed, but the scope broadened to include women's rights, gay rights, the environmental movement, and others. Musically, the singer-songwriter milieu, heavily influenced by Bob Dylan, explored both the artist's inner world and societal issues. Fashion conscious glam rock, ponderous progressive rock, the aggressive sounds of hard rock, beat-heavy funk, and mellifluous soft soul competed for the record buyer's dollar. Dylan still commanded a central position in the rock pantheon, but the competition widened as a new generation sought music of its own and grounding in a world that seemed adrift.

Searching for answers, some joined religious or spiritual groups in an attempt to find what Christopher Lasch deemed "psychic self-improvement."[146] The quest for physical betterment flourished, as did commitment to lifestyles that included health food and jogging. The search for answers did not always provoke improvement, as many struggled with drugs or alcohol and the divorce rate skyrocketed. Throughout the decade, fans still looked to Dylan for direction out of the morass. Some expected that he would return as some sort of Prodigal Son. Public appearances, interviews, and songs were scoured for clues that indicated he had not abandoned politics. Critics too got into the act as they hailed nearly every one of his 1970s albums as some type of return to form. *Rolling Stone* proclaimed Dylan "back" with 1970's *New Morning*.[147] The idea persisted into the 1990s that the folk/protest Dylan was the "old" and authentic Dylan, and that he would return Messiah-like to deliver a message of political salvation.

College campuses exploded in the spring of 1970 following Richard Nixon's announcement that he expanded the war into Cambodia. Ohio's Kent State University witnessed the most infamous episode of campus unrest when National Guardsmen shot and killed four students and wounded nine others. The event served as inspiration for Crosby, Stills, Nash, and Young's Top-20 hit song "Ohio." Edwin Starr's forceful "War" topped the charts in July 1970.[148] Dylan did not contribute to the antiwar catalog, though it almost certainly would have proved profitable for him to have written such a song.

In the summer of 1970, Dylan received an honorary degree from Princeton. He wrote about the event in the song "Day of the Locusts." *Rolling Stone* chronicled the ceremony, stressing Dylan's reluctance to attend and his discomfort with the event when he did. Most of the class that day wore white armbands with peace symbols on them, and Dylan chose to don one as well. This is the only documented, overt gesture Dylan made on behalf of the antiwar effort. Since Dylan seldom did things just because someone wanted him to, it is a safe conclusion that he genuinely agreed with the sentiment. Ben Salzman, an aide to Dylan, suggested that he had agreed to accept the award "as a gesture to the student movement and as to what has been happening on campuses across the country."[149]

Dylan's first major public appearance of the 1970s was the Concert for Bangladesh, a benefit organized by George Harrison. Dylan had to be coaxed by Harrison to perform, but when he did, it prompted many to believe that Dylan had returned to reclaim his rightful place as the "King of Protest." An enthused record executive at the concert exclaimed, "He's coming back to protest."[150] Many thought this would begin a renaissance of Dylan activism, but Jonathan Cott in *Rolling Stone* tempered people's expectations and warned them to not assume Dylan's return to protest music.[151] In the mid-1970s, Dylan played a handful of other benefit concerts including Students Need Athletic and Cultural Kicks (SNACK) in San Francisco and a benefit for Chile's CIA-overthrown socialist government at Phil Ochs's behest.[152] In addition, he got closely involved with Rubin "Hurricane" Carter's cause, which will be discussed in chapter 3.

The sense that the old Dylan had reappeared, "singing those songs that had so much power in the days of protest and radicalism," excited his fans.[153] In reality, Dylan never made himself a visible radical in the same way that John Lennon did. The former Beatle wore his politics for the world to see. Lennon released "Power to the People," "Give Peace a Chance," and "Happy Xmas (War Is Over)," as well as appearing publicly with Jerry Rubin, Abbie Hoffman, and other "Movement" figures in the early 1970s. In contrast, Dylan may or may not have met with Black Panthers Huey Newton and David Hilliard. He was typically elusive when questioned, and if they did meet, nothing came of it. Cautious as ever, Dylan advised, "In this day and age one can't put one's faith in organizations and groups just like that."[154]

Many observers of the music scene assumed that Dylan's 1971 single "George Jackson"—also discussed in chapter 3—marked a return to protest music. Borrowing a line from Joan Baez's "To Bobby," *New York Times Magazine* journalist and Dylan biographer Anthony Scaduto wrote an article entitled "Won't You Listen to the Lambs, Bob Dylan?" Scaduto theorized that "George Jackson" was Dylan's response to the challenge issued by Joan Baez, critics, and radicals to take up the banner of political music once again. "George Jackson," according to Scaduto, "could have been written by the young Bob Dylan who wrote 'Blowin' in the Wind' in 1962." The profile assumed that this meant that Dylan had "returned to so-called message songs."

In the past, many fans believed that Dylan had abandoned them, or "The Cause," and had turned on the singer. Scaduto alleged that critics "charged him with caring more about the steady growth of his investment portfolio than the problems of the world; of being a 'capitalistic pig' to use the shrill rhetoric of the radical movement."[155] Scaduto noted that Dylan demonstrated concern about how the public perceived him. The singer asked, "You can quote radicals who are up on me, right?" The journalist responded "that the article would address radicals who were down on him." Dylan pressed, "You are not gonna paint me on only one side, of the radical thing, are you?"[156] As always, Dylan maintained that the "Voice of His Generation" role was nothing that he had signed up for. He told the magazine, "I said 'not to follow leaders, to watch parking meters.' I wasn't going to fall for that, for being any kind of leader." He continued that "the media made up that crap—that Dylan, the Rolling Stones, the Beatles were leaders. We didn't know anything about it, and what's more didn't want any part of it...Nobody should look to anybody else for their answers."[157]

The singer's late 1960s retreat to the countryside still rankled "those who depended on him and believed he was a prophet," and they could not comprehend that the man who wrote "Visions of Johanna" then wrote "Country Pie."[158] By the early 1970s, some members of the Counterculture had begun a "back to the land" movement of their own, including rural communes. Though it may not have been a conscious emulation, once again young leftists followed Dylan's lead.

Counterculture disillusionment with Bob Dylan was only part of the overall trend in a country whose citizens lost faith in government and authority in general. In the early 1960s, the Kennedy administration's "Best and Brightest" projected an image that the government was being run by the most competent men in the country. By the 1970s, that faith had vanished amid public disclosures of the Pentagon Papers and Watergate Scandal, both providing proof of official misdeeds by those in power. In 1975, 70 percent of Americans thought that the government lied frequently. Coupled with an economic crisis, energy crisis, and loss in Vietnam, pessimism hung over the country and it spiraled downward in a "Crisis of Competence." By mid-decade most Americans believed the president to be "just another flawed individual in a society with many failings."[159] The president now did "stand naked," and most leaders did not seem worth following in the first place.

Dylan Reemerges

If Dylan had been the committed left winger that many made him out to be, it seems likely that he would have had much to say about Watergate and Richard Nixon. During his tour with the Band, in 1974, the line from "It's Alright, Ma" about the president's nakedness drew the biggest cheer.[160] Dylan wrote the lyric when Lyndon Johnson lived in the White House, but the political implications transcended party alliances and individual office holders. Dylan opened the Rolling Thunder Tour in Massachusetts by wearing a Nixon mask throughout the first song.[161] He addressed the crowd by observing that Massachusetts was the only state that did not vote for Nixon in the 1972 election and added, "We didn't vote for him either."[162] Rolling Thunder witnessed Dylan more loquacious than normal; however, partisan political statements onstage were highly unusual for him.

Critic Ralph Gleason, a longtime Dylan advocate, offered his observation about the connection between Nixon and Dylan. Gleason noted the contrast between Nixon's retreat "further into the womb of his Florida and Camp David hideouts" and the public return of "that other great American recluse, Bob Dylan." Gleason somehow believed that the two things were related. He concluded that "Dylan's songs and the pressures he generated had more to do with creating a society in which it was possible for Nixon to thoroughly fuck up and be caught at it and threatened with impeachment, than politicos are likely to believe." It is difficult to imagine how Dylan's music could be related to Nixon's actions, but to a small degree, perhaps Dylan's songs that called authority into question contributed to the response. Gleason alluded to Dylan's influence "because he changed the way we thought and through that, the way others thought. Now is the time, of course, for Dylan to re-emerge." Gleason believed that Dylan's audience had grown into maturity and, as a result, they would understand his music in a new way. He offered up an almost messianic role for the singer: "Things happen at the right time, at least some times, and I am sure this is one of them."[163] Apparently, in Gleason's mind, as Nixon slunk away from the morass of Watergate, Dylan emerged to deliver his saving message.

The return of the politically directed Bob Dylan never came, other than ephemerally. Yet the Dylan mythos continued to grow, and when he decided to embark on his first tour in eight years, anticipation soared. Expectations of the tour were immense, and it proved highly profitable. *Rolling Stone* added to the hyperbole, stating, "Most music lovers would agree that America owes a great deal to Bob Dylan. And now Bob Dylan apparently is ready to collect."[164] One month later, when asked by *Rolling Stone* what kind of feeling he got singing his "protest and message" songs for the first time in years, Dylan rather uncharacteristically did not dodge the question or bristle at the classification. He simply answered, "It's just reinforcing those images in my head that were there, that don't die, that will be there tomorrow." His answer found him in a rare charitable mood concerning audience expectations as he stated, "In doing so for myself, hopefully also for those people who also had those images." Dylan called the 1960s a "new time" in which people became united in their political thinking. He continued, "There's still a message. But the same electric spark that went off back then could still go off again—the spark that led to nothing." Looking both forward and back, he added, "Our kids will probably protest too. Protest is an old thing. Sometimes protest is deeper, or different—the Haymarket Riot, the Russian Revolution, the Civil War—that's protest."[165] This marked one of the few times up to that point that Dylan had acknowledged that some of his music could be classified as protest music. But he pointed out that 1960s activism did not accomplish much and seemed small in comparison to other periods.

Newsweek's January 14, 1974, cover proclaimed "Dylan's Back!" The article interviewed several Chicago concertgoers about their thoughts and expectations for Dylan. One concert attendee reiterated the return theme, hoped that Dylan would provide a message or a sign, and thought that it was the "start of a new era." A painter from Phoenix enthused, "I'm looking for something new again. He's a leader, a pacesetter."[166] As ever, Dylan downplayed expectations and confirmed his desire to be free of them, maintaining "I'm not looking to be that new messiah." He also rejected the notion that he was an idol: "They aren't people, they're objects. But I'm no object."[167]

In the mid-1970s, the United States continued its rightward political turn. In 1976, both *Time* and *Newsweek* published proclamations that it was the "Year of the Evangelical." For many disillusioned by the failure of political movements to affect real change, religion provided an opportunity at self-fulfillment.[168] Between 25 and 33 percent of Americans said they were born-again Christians.[169] Jimmy Carter's election represented a triumph of a not-so-liberal Democrat over a somewhat conservative Republican. The Ford and Carter presidencies each claimed a certain conservative appeal, be it economic or religious. Born again and fiscally conservative, Jimmy Carter was a far cry from the liberalism of Lyndon Johnson or the urbane chic of John Kennedy. Running as an outsider to politics as usual, Carter wore denim and quoted Dylan lyrics. Dylan laughed when he heard that Jimmy Carter had been mentioning his songs on the campaign trail and commented, "People have told me there was a man running for President and quoting me. I don't know if that's good or bad. But he's just another guy running for President."[170] Two years earlier, Jimmy Carter, while chief executive of Georgia, met with Dylan at the governor's mansion.[171] Dylan's 1976 comments about Carter did not give the indication that Carter had impressed Dylan all that much. In 1978, Dylan spoke more warmly about Carter to *Rolling Stone*.

Prior to his campaign for president, Carter mentioned his admiration for Christian theologian Reinhold Niebuhr and Dylan in a Georgia Law Day speech. Carter credited Niebuhr with informing his sense of justice. He then claimed that "the other source of my understanding about what's right and wrong in this society is a friend of mine, a poet named Bob Dylan." Carter said that "Like a Rolling Stone," "The Times They Are A-Changin,'" and the "Ballad of Hattie Carroll" helped him "appreciate the dynamism of change in modern society." Interestingly, the title that Carter quoted is the name of a song that Don West wrote about Hattie Carroll, not Bob Dylan's, which is, "The Lonesome Death of Hattie Carroll." Two years later in Madison, Wisconsin, Carter again referred to Dylan as a friend.[172] How familiar Carter actually was with Dylan's music and Dylan himself is debatable, but in his 1978 *Playboy* interview, Dylan reciprocated and called the president a friend who had his heart "in the right place."[173]

Beginning in the mid-1970s, disco—which began as a subculture scene—grew into a mainstream phenomenon. By the end of the decade, disco songs represented the single most identifiable style on the Top 40 charts. Many of Dylan's musical contemporaries such as the Rolling Stones, Paul McCartney, and Rod Stewart flirted with a disco sound on some of their albums and singles. Dylan, never one to merely follow trends or what was fashionable, did not. To some disco represented a vapid, decadent lifestyle and a threat to rock's authenticity. In 1967 and 1968, as psychedelic music became the rage, Dylan released country-sounding albums. In the late 1970s, Dylan veered away from the crowd once again. As economic and foreign policy woes beset America, many sought escape in a musical style that celebrated hedonism and deemphasized political messages. Dylan eschewed the fad, embraced Jesus, and became an Evangelical Christian.

The cultural turmoil unleashed in the 1960s fostered the religious revitalization of the 1970s. Some people gravitated toward New Age spirituality while others sought renewal within familiar faiths. Americans who felt threatened by the challenges to traditional roles, moral standards, and lifestyles often sought reassurance in a religious belief that preached the inerrancy of the Bible. For many Americans in the mid-1970s, the tumult of the previous decade had made the world appear irredeemable. For these believers, an apocalyptic cleansing and return by Jesus Christ seemed the only viable solution to the current corruption. Since they expected an imminent end of the world, it meant that political solutions were unnecessary. Combining elements of the Counterculture and fundamentalist Christian belief, the Jesus People movement spread among the disaffected. With his personal life a mess, Dylan—who had previously turned to the Bible as a source of inspiration—embraced a new theology and joined the Jesus People in 1978–79. (Details will be examined in chapters 5 and 6.)

In the mid-1960s, Dylan released three electric rock albums; in the late 1970s–early 1980s, he released what is commonly referred to as his religious trilogy. The first two, *Slow Train Coming* and *Saved*, were entirely comprised of religious material while *Shot of Love* consisted of both religious and secular music. Religious themes made frequent appearances on subsequent albums as well. This period surprised most fans and disappointed many as well. When put into the context of Dylan's overall worldview, his conversion may not necessarily seem obvious, but on some levels it made sense. Throughout his songwriting and interviews, Dylan had expressed disdain and dismay at a world he perceived to be superficial and corrupt. Though others sought answers from him, he offered none. Now he believed that he had finally found a solution, but many fans ignored his message.

One of the ironies of Dylan's new religiosity is that whether intended or not, his past contributions had influenced countercultural challenges that spurred the religious reaction. Paul Williams wrote brilliantly on Dylan's conversion. Approaching the subject from essentially an agnostic perspective, he noted that Dylan's Christian songs "turned around our preconceptions as to who is 'us' and who is 'them.'" Williams observed that a connection between Dylan's religious songs and ones like "Positively 4th Street" existed. The difference was that with his gospel music, Dylan pointed the finger at those who were not born again.[174] Regardless of the specific theme, the moralistic culture that informed his worldview influenced Dylan to call attention to the shortcomings of society.

To many, the type of Christianity Dylan embraced represented intolerance and reactionary thought. Williams wrote that when he heard the news, he had hoped Dylan had become something akin to a Catholic Worker activist. That type of personalist approach would have focused on issues of poverty, human rights, and perhaps environmentalism, rather than apocalyptic eschatology.[175] Dylan's conversion distanced him from many on the Left while the type of Christianity he embraced removed him even further from the mainstream. Once again, Dylan emerged as an outsider.

Not all of the critical reaction to Dylan was negative. Jann Wenner reviewed *Slow Train Coming* in *Rolling Stone*. He opined that the album eventually could be considered Dylan's greatest of all time. Wenner trotted out the "Dylan as Generational Spokesman" notion and theorized that the singer "was tied up in the social and political themes of the last ten years." The suggestion was that Dylan's inconsistent output reflected the confusion American society felt in the 1970s. He also reiterated the popular "Dylan's back" theme. According to Wenner, "Bob Dylan has, at long last, come back into our lives and times, and it is with the most commercial LP he's ever released." The production and musicianship make it one of the best sounding albums in his catalog. The public agreed as *Slow Train Coming* rose to #3 on the charts.[176] Wenner chose to view the album as messages about love, patriotism, and sometimes religion. He claimed that the song "Slow Train" was the type of "state of the union" song "that Bob Dylan has put on every record he's ever done." Heaping on praise, Wenner called it Dylan's "most mature and profound song about America." The review used the phrase "religious symbolism" and downplayed the Evangelical aspect of the lyrics. Even though he enjoyed *Slow Train Coming*, Wenner seemed unable to completely accept that Bob Dylan was committed fully to the belief that Jesus Christ was the Messiah and that the End Times loomed.[177]

The 1980s

Ronald Reagan symbolized the completion of the conservative path America started to take during the 1970s. Germany and Great Britain also moved to the right with Helmut Schmidt and Margaret Thatcher coming to power. Yuppies replaced Hippies as the iconic cultural stereotype. Counterculture heroes like Bob Dylan and (Black Panther) Eldridge Cleaver became born-again Christians, and (Yippie) Jerry Rubin worked on Wall Street. Tragically, a deranged fan gunned down John Lennon outside his home. As the late Beatle sang at the start of the 1970s, the dream was over. Style over substance proliferated within US popular culture. Television programs such as *Lifestyles of the Rich and Famous* and primetime soap operas like *Dallas*, *Dynasty*, and *Falcon Crest* showcased ostentatious displays of wealth or the machinations of the rich, powerful, and manipulative. For a songwriter who criticized the phoniness of society, the 1980s provided an easy target—when Dylan chose to engage it. An undercurrent of 1960s activism existed and some middle-aged Baby Boomers sought to relive their youth. Many liberals and radicals openly opposed Reagan's policies and people marched to increase AIDS awareness, as did demonstrators on both sides of the abortion issue. However, many of the ex-New Leftists, who had begun their lives enjoying material comfort, returned to lives of affluence.

The advent of MTV changed the shape of the music industry and marginalized many acts from the 1960s and 1970s. Not as photogenic as they were a decade or two before, many aging musicians found minimal success in the increasingly image-conscious industry. Dylan's forays into video provided few instances that would likely attract a younger fan base. Slick and stylized, MTV threatened to make elder statesmen artists like Bob Dylan irrelevant. Unfortunately for him, Dylan's 1980s musical output did not help combat that trend. His songwriting often remained strong but the songs themselves were mired in the ill-fitting sheen of 1980s production values. Overall, the decade proved erratic for Dylan. He remained a legend but was seemingly disconnected from what had made him great in the first place. Ultimately, Dylan launched a career-resurgence virtually unrivaled in show business, and by 2015 his cultural relevance had outlasted MTV's.

Opposition to the Vietnam War was a cornerstone of the New Left and Counterculture. To further evidence Dylan's distance from these movements, his most direct songwriting about the topic did not occur until the late 1970–mid-1980s. During this period as well, the United States began to confront the legacy of its involvement in Vietnam. The Vietnam Veterans' Memorial was constructed in Washington, DC, while academics, journalists, and the media attempted to assess and reconcile the war's meaning. Hollywood flooded the market with movies such as *Apocalypse Now* and the exaggerated patriotism of *Rambo II*. In the late 1970s, movies such as *Coming Home* and *The Deer Hunter* had portrayed the difficulty veterans experienced and the effects of the war on American society. The songs where Dylan referenced Vietnam dealt entirely with the soldiers' experience rather than peace themes. In 1978, Dylan addressed the topic with a line in one of his most obscure songs, the unreleased "Legionnaire's Disease." The impact was negligible, since very few people ever heard the line about an uncle who fought in the war and then fought another one "all by himself."[178]

In 1985, Dylan released "Clean-Cut Kid," which appeared on *Empire Burlesque* and more fully examined the theme. Not explicitly defined as a song about a Vietnam veteran, the storyline provides obvious clues with mention of napalm and the spilling of blood. The song traces the rise and fall of a Ron Kovic *Born on the 4th of July* figure: the Clean-Cut Kid. The Kid lived out an all-American youth, playing baseball, joining Boy Scouts, and marching in the band. Dylan's distaste for corporate consumer culture shines through as he informs listeners that the Kid was "well fed," feasting on Burger King, Wonder Bread, and Coca-Cola. America's 1980s economic situation caught Dylan's attention when he adds that the Kid's parents lived in a house that "they don't own" and the Kid himself went in debt when he "bought the American dream."[179]

As the song unfolds, it references a ubiquitous "they" who manipulated the young man in a variety of ways. "They" made him a killer, gave him drugs, and forced him to return to the "rat race" without providing the necessary means to adjust. Employing a faceless, nameless "they" harkened back to the New Left's utilization of Establishment or System to label the elite who make the rules and pull the levers of society.[180] Songs Dylan has written such as "Clean Cut Kid," "Masters of War," and "It's Alright, Ma" demonstrate a belief that manipulation, coercion, and dishonesty rule the world, and he frequently seeks to distance himself from that. He asked rhetorically in a 1984 Westwood One Radio interview, "Do you have to be part of the machine...so what if you're not part of the machine?"[181] In Martin Keller's interview with Dylan in 1983, he expressed a healthy distrust of the media. He claimed that most people's attitudes "are determined by the newspaper they read this morning."[182]

Dylan had long since left Hibbing, but he would have been well aware, coming from the Iron Range, that young, working-class men saw military service as their patriotic duty when called upon. Whether or not Dylan's upbringing influenced his attitudes toward the war, "the Iron Range was deeply resistant to the peace movement during the Vietnam War...When there was a rally, the local newspapers did not cover it."[183] Neither speaking out for or against the actual war, Dylan recognized the inimical effects it had on soldiers and their families. A constant throughout his songwriting and public statements, he feared the manipulation brought on by putting faith in organizations, leaders, or ideologies.

During the early and mid-1980s, Top 40 hits containing political or social commentary were uncommon. Bucking the trend, Bruce Springsteen's 1984 release *Born in the USA* became one of the decade's biggest selling albums. Incredibly, seven cuts from the album broke into the Top 10. Comparatively, Dylan has logged 12 Top 40 hits in his entire career. In typical Springsteen fashion, several of the songs addressed economic difficulties or another social ill, including the plight of Vietnam veterans. In a sense, Springsteen wrote the type of protest songs many expected of Dylan since the 1960s. Though its intent was social critique, many listeners mistook the message of "Born in the USA" as a fist-pumping patriotic anthem. During the heyday of Reagan-inspired nationalism, ironic or satirical statements about America were lost on much of the public.

Many young people during the 1960s thought that the messages of peace, love, and equality would change the world. In the increasingly monetized 1980s, cash played the transformative role. The rock benefit may have reached its peak visibility during the decade, but Dylan seemed to have mixed opinions on their efficacy. In 1986, he said that there could "never be too many benefits" and maintained that "someone has got to say something."[184] He remarked at Live Aid that some of the money should be used to help American farmers, which inspired Willie Nelson to create Farm Aid. Dylan spoke less than enthusiastically about people's intentions concerning charity: "While it's really great that people are supporting USA for Africa or Farm Aid, what are they really doing to alleviate poverty?" He called it "guilt money": "Some guy halfway around the world is starving so, OK, put ten bucks in the barrel, then you can feel you don't have to have a guilty conscience about it." Dylan admitted that it did some good, but it would not wipe out social ills and people could not save themselves.[185] Even if he doubted the impact that benefit concerts could have, Dylan took part in many. In 1982, he participated in an antinuke show with Joan Baez. He also performed on 1985's "We are the World" and antiapartheid "Sun City" benefit singles. He played an Amnesty International show in 1986 and Neil Young's Bridge School charity in 1988.[186] Even the fictional Dylan character, Jack Fate, was released from prison to play a benefit concert in *Masked and Anonymous*.

A generation of artists that in some ways could be considered Dylan's progeny began to flourish at the end of a decade known for big-haired heavy metal bands, drum machine-backed pop groups, and new wave synthesizers. Tracy Chapman and Suzanne Vega broke into the Top 10 playing what amounted to acoustic protest music with their hits "Fast Car" and "Luka," respectively. College radio stalwarts R.E.M. took a page from Dylan's mid-1960s repertoire and produced songs with lyrics oblique and often indecipherable. Despite sonic murkiness, R.E.M. mastered Dylan's ability to convey the impression that their songs held unlocked, deeper meanings. In 1989, Dylan himself released what most observers considered his strongest album of the decade, *Oh Mercy*, containing "Political World" and "Everything Is Broken."

The 1990s

In 1992, the country elected Bill Clinton, the first Baby Boomer president. At that time, Bob Dylan's public career had stretched 30 years. Clinton's political triangulation and corporate-friendly economic policies marked a further shift toward the elite Center in the Democratic Party. Dylan started appearing in history textbooks, and his reputation as a 1960s icon was firmly solidified in conventional wisdom. However, Dylan watchers still grappled with reconciling the historical figure with the man who performed and recorded in the present.

The same *Rolling Stone* article that credited him with ending the Vietnam War reviewed his West Point concert. The author observed that in the mid-1960s, "It would have been heresy to predict that he would sing at the United States Military Academy—to an enthusiastic sellout crowd, no less." Acknowledging that both the world and Dylan had changed since then, the author allowed that "maybe it made perfect sense for him to play at West Point and to reveal another side of Bob Dylan after all these years." He suggested that the paradox found "in Bob Dylan's singing at West Point seemed totally lost on him." Dylan often welcomes incongruence and was likely aware but unconcerned about any irony. The article noted that when he performed "Masters of War," the song was "met with a cool response from the cadets down front." Considering Dylan consistently played contentious electric concerts in the mid-1960s and gospel shows in the late 1970s, the "cool response" assuredly would not have bothered Dylan in the least.[187]

As the 1980s ended, Dylan seemed to have found his stride. He made critically acclaimed records as a member of the Traveling Wilburys and as a solo artist on *Oh Mercy*. It seemed to observers that he had recaptured some of his old magic. However, *Under the Red Sky*, his follow-up to the acclaimed *Oh Mercy*, proved somewhat of a disappointment. Dylan continued his now-familiar method of scattering social commentary in bits and pieces among his songs. In "TV Talkin' Song," he derided television's corrosive influence. Some songs like "Unbelievable" contained minor critiques against greed, such as a line about the land of "milk and honey" turning into one of "money." Others, such as "Wiggle Wiggle" and "2 × 2" seemed to have no real lyrical direction.

Within a few years, Dylan and his music began to appear in television advertisements and the accusations of "sellout" that began when he plugged in his electric guitar, returned. This time, critics had more apparent evidence at their ready. As Baby Boomers aged, Madison Avenue geared its focus toward retirement accounts, luxury cars, and other accoutrements of success. Often, for added Boomer appeal, 1960s music accompanied the commercials. Dylan had always spoken warily of the commodification of music. In the 1980s, he lambasted "soulless and commercial" music used to "push some product down your throat." He also expressed skepticism toward corporate sponsorship of tours.[188]

However, in the mid-1990s, he began to license his songs for advertisements. Coopers and Lybrand, an accounting firm, first used "The

Times They Are A-Changin.'" Whether it represented a sellout as some critics maintained, it further showed that by the twenty-first century, nearly everything was for sale. This certainly ran counter to the attitudes he expressed early in his career when he mocked materialism, greed, and misplacement of values in songs such as "Talkin' World War III Blues," "Talkin' Bear Mountain Picnic Massacre Blues," and "It's Alright, Ma," to name only a few. If nothing else it reflected the dichotomous nature within Bob Dylan. He has never denied himself the luxury of having money but has also understood the oppressive power it wields and, in line with his Minnesota heritage, has not been ostentatious with his personal wealth. In *Masked and Anonymous*, Val Kilmer's character points out that people borrow money to buy things that depreciate in value while they own them. In a 1960s interview, Dylan objected to someone owning a Cadillac when someone else was in the gutter.[189] Four decades later, he appeared in television commercials for Cadillac. The commercialization of music and commodification of culture is a worthy debate. Obviously, Dylan has not been unswerving in his rejection of them when his actions are compared to his words.

In the 2000s, Dylan and/or his music appeared in commercials for Victoria's Secret, Chobani, and Pepsi. During the 2014 Super Bowl, in addition to "I Want You" being used to sell yogurt, Dylan appeared in a Chrysler advertisement with his song "Things Have Changed" playing in the background. The ad writers did a credible job, capturing Dylan's phrasing as he narrated lines such as "One thing you can't import from anywhere else: American pride," and "Is there anything more American than America?" Not solely a directive to "buy American," he advised viewers to "let Germany brew your beer" and "let Asia assemble your phone."[190] Dylan received a significant amount of negative reaction from those who called him a sellout (it was hardly his first commercial) and a promoter of Asian sweatshops (a stretch). The United Autoworkers Union was not among those complaining. It was at least a partial rejection of globalization.

Bob Dylan has suffered, probably more than any other artist, from unrealistic expectations. The version of Dylan from his early and mid-twenties has been frequently held up against every other thing he has done. No one takes Pete Townshend and Roger Daltrey to task for getting old or seriously expects Mick Jagger to be a "Street Fighting Man" in his seventies. But Dylan's political songs have been so strongly associated with his image that many people are unwilling to let go of his image as a Counterculture hero. In the *No Direction Home* documentary, Joan Baez explains that people still ask her if Dylan is going to show up at a protest march or sit-in that she is attending—a notion she laughs at.

For an individual who by all accounts is not interested in electoral politics, sees society as irreparable, and possesses skepticism toward authority, the accolades Dylan has received are remarkable. Bill Clinton awarded him a Kennedy Center honor, George W. Bush named him an honorary Texan, and Barack Obama awarded him the Presidential Medal of Freedom. Continuing the practice of attributing political accomplishments to the singer, Dylan biographer Daniel Mark Epstein claims that Dylan helped put Obama in the White House.[191]

Throughout the years, Dylan evolved as an artist, though many wanted what was not possible. Those who expected him to return to a lost era did not grapple with the question of how long Dylan could write the same type of song before people stopped listening. Had he remained the darling of the New Left by writing topical songs, he would have been relegated to a hopelessly dated niche market.[192] In the 1980s, he told ABC's *20/20* that he wrote protest songs, but that "real protest songs" were written in the 1930s and 1940s. He stated that he maintained "a strain of that type of thing...it's just more broad now."[193]

The political landscape of the United States has changed more than Bob Dylan. When asked in the 1990s if current events such as the Oklahoma City bombing had an effect on his songwriting, he replied, "Chaos is everywhere: lawlessness, disorganization, misrule. I don't know if it impacts my songwriting like it used to."[194] Although he claimed not to be inspired by current events, Dylan—well into his fifth decade of music making at the time of the interview—was still being sought out for commentary on them.

CHAPTER 3

Freedom and Justice

During the years following World War II, the notion of freedom in America manifested itself in a myriad of new ways. There were Freedom Schools, a Freedom Summer, Free Speech Movement, free love, free markets, and Young Americans for Freedom. To some, particularly those on the Left, freedom was a legal concept being denied to minority groups who sought equality within an oppressive society. It also existed as an abstract ideal pursued by those who felt shackled spiritually or intellectually. Norm Fruchter, a civil rights and New Left activist, commented that "an individual is free only when he can effectively control, and carry out, all the decisions affecting the way he lives his life."[1] In June 1963, Students for a Democratic Society (SDS) approved the essay "America and New Era," which stated bluntly that their "hope is human freedom."[2]

To others, freedom could not be realized *within* society. Student activist Raymond Mungro, in *The Road to Liberation*, explained that he possessed everything society required for success: education, whiteness, financial stability, and earning potential. However, Mungro claimed that he was "everything but free"—"And it is freedom alone that I cherish and that I must achieve."[3] The sense that mass society proved confining gave rise to greater individual expression and what historian Grace Elizabeth Hale deems the "romance of the outsider."[4] Rebels, outlaws, and activists possessed, or at least strove for, levels of freedom unavailable within the mainstream.

In the 1950s, the Beats championed freedom of expression and the celebration of what they deemed an authentic lifestyle. Versions of Beat ideas, though somewhat altered, moved from the bohemian fringe into the mainstream. The New Right movement of the 1950s and 1960s also used the language of freedom to further their cause. Conservatives believed in the necessity of protecting economic freedom from government overreach. Freedom of expression, freedom of action, freedom from oppression, and freedom from government intrusion—all entered public discussion. To activists of the 1960s, regardless of their political stripe, the quest for freedom meant overcoming powers deemed illegitimate, corrupt, or misguided.

The concept of personal development flourished on college campuses and among popular culture figures. Part of this intellectual climate was the rejection of expectations, either real or imagined, that society foisted on the young. Boxing great Muhammad Ali exclaimed, "I don't have to be what you want me to be. I'm free to be what I want."[5] Young people sought to engage and change a society they viewed as belonging to them.

In the early 1960s, Bob Dylan effectively tapped into the zeitgeist's desire for freedom, and his songs both reflected and advanced it. His politics do not fit into any specific paradigm, much less the standard American party labels. Instead, what he expressed was closer to a notion of personalism that encompassed traditions not present on the usual Left-Right spectrum. The overarching themes of freedom, justice, and equality were not the exclusive claim of any political tradition.

In the 1960s, many activists came to the conclusion that political change alone could not solve America's ills and that nothing less than a cultural upheaval was necessary to challenge the dominant institutions and power structures of the country.[6] According to James Farrell's book *Spirit of the Sixties*, the concept of freedom had "incredible resonance in American culture and activists used it liberally."[7] Although this value is by no means strictly American, it exists at the heart of the country's political heritage. Dylan cherished the idea of freedom and his background reinforced the importance of the concept. Over a span of a career from the early 1960s into the twenty-first century, Dylan has called into question all power structures, be they political, legal, economic, or social.

During his early years as a songwriter, Dylan addressed these issues in a generally direct, straightforward manner. In topical songs about specific events such as the murder of Medgar Evers in "Only a Pawn in Their Game" or, in a more general sense, "Blowin' in the Wind," Dylan voiced discontent with a society tilted in favor of the privileged and which shunted aside those who were not. Robert Shelton, a journalist for the *New York Times* and an early Dylan advocate, wrote, "Despite the singer's age, he is very deeply concerned with the world around him. He cares about war, poverty, injustice, and discrimination."[8] In the liner notes to *Biograph*, a 1985 career retrospective, Dylan echoed Shelton's assessment. He addressed his own songs in the context of his reputation as a protest singer, explaining that it was "not protest for protest sake but always in the struggle for peoples' freedom, individual or otherwise," adding, "I hate oppression, especially on children."[9]

In the mid-1960s, Dylan's lyrics became more opaque and less literal. If the songs were no longer topical, his lyrics exemplified a search for personal freedom by circumventing standard definitions and expectations. Thus, the expression of freedom in Bob Dylan's art became less overtly political on a societal level but more individual and existential. This transformation did not make his work any less significant. In fact, many listeners found it far more revolutionary than his previous style. As some of his ardent folk music fans questioned Dylan's commitment to politics, he refused to surrender the freedom to write the type of song that he wanted, at the time he chose to write it. Either intuitively or expressly, he understood that to be labeled or categorized resulted in objectification, or becoming a thing. To be pigeon-holed, or to be exactly what others wanted him to be, was tantamount to losing freedom.

Dylan's desire to avoid the constructs others sought for him mirrored Existentialist philosopher Karl Jaspers, who wrote, "What makes freedom possible for me is that I myself do not become an object."[10] Dylan's contemporaries in the student movement voiced a similar concern, with one of the "dominant conceptions of man in the twentieth century" being "that he is a thing to be manipulated."[11] Resisting that development, Dylan—a notoriously tough interviewee—told *Disc Weekly* in 1965, "You're using me. I'm an object to you."[12] Instead, he sought to define himself through his work, as he claimed to *Newsweek*: "I am my words."[13] Four years later, Dylan told the same magazine that he believed that his self and his songs were separate, but hoped that his song was "everybody's song."[14]

Dylan's application of the concepts of freedom and justice evolved, but they continued to find a place in his body of work. He advocated individual free will, equal treatment by the law, and a life outside public expectations. By the late 1970s, Dylan found freedom in obedience to Jesus Christ. To many, this was a direct contrast to his earlier self. In actuality, it marked another door opened by Dylan. The doctrine of his particular Christian belief stressed freeing oneself from enslavement to sin and became another manifestation of freedom in his life. With the arrival of the 1980s, Dylan continued, though with less overt religious zeal, to criticize a society he saw as corrupt and confining. Even in songs that did not deal directly with the concept of freedom, Dylan made numerous references to slavery, servitude, and abuse of power. Regardless of the context, freedom seemed to never be far from Bob Dylan's mind. His songs of justice do not address vengeful retribution but rather a universal notion of equality and morality, including but not limited to legal, social, individual, and economic.

Consistently in interviews and other public forums, Dylan has resisted and recoiled from attempts by others to define who or what he is. Dylan has rejected labels, whether as protest singer, spokesman for his generation, or adherent of a certain religious tradition, because these things place limitations on him. Dylan has been able to remake himself numerous times because he has been unwilling to allow "society's pliers" to bend him.[15] Pete Seeger, in a letter to his father, speculated, "Maybe Bob Dylan will be like Picasso, surprising us every few years with a new period."[16] The Picasso analogy has been a favorite for numerous Dylan biographers and commentators. Regardless of whether the analogy is apt, it is not hyperbolic to compare Picasso's contribution to painting and Dylan's transformation of popular music's boundaries. Dylan's acute awareness of the concepts of freedom and justice and his ability to address them through song catapulted him to stardom and created expectations that he somehow had the answers to questions that have plagued humankind for millennia.

The progression of Bob Dylan—from Woody Guthrie impersonator to star on the rise in Greenwich Village to rock and roll trailblazer—is well documented in the many biographies about him. Early in his career, he stood out among a crowded field of folk performers. Dylan's political songs, even from his earliest attempts, revealed a young man who not only recognized and called attention to injustice, but also tried to explain the deeper sociological manifestations of it. He typically presented a view more nuanced than simply "injustice is wrong." Dylan's songs did not merely lament the existence of racism or war, ideas that would have been obvious to almost his entire audience. Instead, he produced insights less immediately apparent but which resonated with audiences and fellow musicians.

Beyond any artist of the twentieth century, Bob Dylan compiled a catalog of songs that inspired, confounded, entertained, and redefined the medium in which he worked. Dylan's first four albums, released between 1962 and 1964, are considered his "folk/protest" output. His debut, *Bob Dylan*, contained only two original songs, sold poorly upon its release, and had minimal impact. The other three albums are considered classics of the era and genre. In addition, Dylan wrote dozens of songs during this period that did not appear on the aforementioned albums. This brief but fertile phase contained Dylan's most easily identifiable examples of songs directly dealing with freedom and justice. His growth as a songwriter in this short span was as rapid as it was remarkable.

Legal Justice

In February 1962, Dylan played a Congress of Racial Equality (CORE) benefit. Around that same time, he began to write and sing political material.[17]

A burgeoning romance with Suze Rotolo, an intellectually and politically active young woman, inspired Dylan to write songs that have often been deemed "protest songs." According to Dylan, he would ask Rotolo to verify the accuracy of his material and he claimed that Suze was "into this equality freedom thing long before I was."[18]

When he arrived in Greenwich Village, many on the folk circuit considered Dylan a political neophyte lacking astuteness, an idea confirmed by fellow musician Dave Van Ronk in the documentary *No Direction Home*. At the start of 1962, there was no reason to expect that the young man would become the most revered contemporary songwriter within 18 months. "The Death of Emmett Till" was one of the earliest examples of Dylan's engagement in politically themed material. The somewhat clumsy lyrics only hint at the greatness the young songwriter would soon achieve. Not exactly straight from the front page, Dylan wrote the song nearly seven years after the murder, which took place when both Till and Dylan were 14 years old.[19]

Hinting at a technique that he frequently employed going forward, Dylan did not focus merely on the evilness of the act and of those who committed the crime, but also admonished a society that failed to provide justice for Emmett Till. The song addressed the torture and murder of Till and proclaimed the brutality too horrible to repeat. Dylan spent roughly half the song calling attention to the absence of justice after Till's murder. The two men, Roy Bryant and J. W. Milam, despite overwhelming evidence, were acquitted of the heinous crime, and Dylan placed some of the responsibility for racism on American society. He asked sympathetic listeners to remind others that the Ku Klux Klan continued to keep hatred alive. The young songwriter ended the piece on a hopeful if not clichéd note. He implored listeners to give everything they could to make America a better place. "The Death of Emmett Till" will not rank among Dylan's greatest works, but compared to other topical songs of the time, it proved a solid effort. However, in short order, Bob Dylan began to stand out among the artists in the Greenwich Village scene.

The following year, he explored the concepts of race and social injustice with greater results on *The Times They Are A-Changin'*. Two songs, "The Lonesome Death of Hattie Carroll" and "Only a Pawn in Their Game," provided powerful examples. "Only a Pawn" recounts the murder of NAACP worker Medgar Evers by white supremacist Byron De La Beckwith. Rather than an outright condemnation of a racist murderer, Dylan subtly confronts the historical relationship of power, class, and race in the South. In the second stanza, he explores the idea that racism is institutionalized by the political elite and provides a buffer between African Americans and well-off whites. He expresses this attitude in lyrics that accuse southern politicians of manipulating poor whites. In Dylan's view, the elite convinces poverty-stricken whites that since they possess more than blacks, they should be satisfied with their lot. To Dylan, the man who "fired the gun" and killed Evers is not to blame, but rather guilt falls on those who wield political and economic power in the South.[20] In this scenario, De La Beckwith is the pawn, indoctrinated and misguided through the educational system and inflammatory speeches of politicians.

Dylan's populist sympathies are evident in "Pawn." Three times in the song he employs the phrase "poor white" and the word "poverty" once. Reasons stemming from economic inequality and manipulation of the lower class, more than condemnation of racists or racism, are the defining features of the song. The implication in "Pawn" is that the material conditions of most whites and blacks in the South could have made them natural allies, if not for artificially constructed racism. This is not to suggest that Dylan consciously employed a Marxist analysis of southern politics, though he was exposed to some of the ideas by Dave Van Ronk, among others.[21] Rather, in his desire for a just society, Dylan developed a nuanced understanding of power relationships. In his work and interviews, he continually viewed elites with suspicion. The poor and powerless, if not championed, are at least framed in a sympathetic light.

Although historians may debate the validity of his interpretation of southern history, it was an impressive feat that a 22-year-old could capably weave into a song. For a young songwriter, the easy route would have been to condemn De La Beckwith, or Bryant and Milam, and focus lyrics on the immorality of racism and racial violence. Instead, even men as vile as racist murderers became more than one-dimensional. "Only A Pawn in Their Game" became a staple of Dylan's early live repertoire. In July 1963, only weeks after Evers's assassination on June 12, he performed it at a Greenwood, Mississippi, voter registration drive and again in August for the historic March on Washington—an event attended by Medgar Evers's brother Charles, who recalls hearing the song, perhaps for the first time that day.[22] The March on Washington witnessed Martin Luther King's famous "I Have a Dream Speech." Organized by civil rights, labor union, and religious groups, it was a coalition event—North and South; black and white; Christian, Jewish, and Muslim—and featured ample music, including gospel singer Mahalia Jackson.[23]

"Only a Pawn in Their Game" resonated with Charles Evers and the song remains a poignant memory for him. In a recent interview, Evers recalls, "My dear friend Aaron Henry, who died a couple years ago, always would sing it. And that's how it really got deep into me because Aaron and I were so close and he and Medgar were so close." Henry was the state president of Mississippi's NAACP chapter and Medgar Evers was field secretary. When

Medgar Evers was murdered, Charles took his place. Asked what he thought of "Only a Pawn," when he first heard it in the 1960s, Evers responds, "If a white man can do that for us...Back at that time, you know, very few white people were helpful to us. When I heard the song it just knocked me off my feet." Evers agrees with Dylan's assessment that blame went beyond Medgar's murderer to a system of institutionalized racism that pitted poor whites against blacks, especially in the Deep South: "That's true. It went on in the South and throughout the country. Jackie Robinson and I were very personal friends and Jackie couldn't stay in a single hotel in Chicago, New York, St. Louis, and no place else." Charles Evers adds that while "Mississippi was a little more violent," he experienced "bigotry and hatred all over": "You know, after my brother was killed, I went to Chicago and we couldn't go nowhere near Cicero. Gosh, so much bigotry and hatred over there the Negro didn't have a chance to go to Cicero in the North." Asked if he wanted to add anything about Dylan or his involvement in the 1960s, Evers concludes, "Not really. I think Dylan's work speaks for itself. And he wrote the song for Medgar."[24]

On *The Times They Are A-Changin'*, Dylan exposed the flawed American judicial system again in "The Lonesome Death of Hattie Carroll." It relays a recent event, with a few liberties taken by Dylan, of an African American woman who was struck by William Zantzinger, a wealthy tobacco plantation owner. Hattie Carroll is never identified as black, though she was, and the song implicitly conveys this fact. A drunken Zantzinger hit Carroll, who had been serving drinks for a Baltimore high society function, with his cane, and eight hours later she died.[25] Whether the blow directly caused her death or not, Dylan unquestionably guides the listener to that conclusion. The racial overtones are obvious but the tragedy of an innocent woman's death and the fact that she left behind 11 children are not the song's centerpiece. Instead, as Dylan unfolds the story, he warns at the end of each stanza that it is not yet time to cry for Hattie Carroll. As with "Emmett Till," the lyrics of "Hattie Carroll" focus on the shortcomings of the court system as Zantzinger received a six-month sentence for his deed. The song culminates with the statement that race and class create different systems of justice in America.

Finally, upon revealing this ultimate injustice, Dylan suggests that listeners weep for the result—not merely an innocent woman's death and her motherless children, but the absence of legal equality. In both songs, Dylan took a tragedy and used it to illustrate something larger about the failings of American society and its legal proceedings. In 1963, none of this would have been news to African Americans but many white Americans had been able to ignore the disparity in the country's system of justice.

The manner in which Dylan handled the events in "Pawn" and "Hattie Carroll" provided two variations of how his music confronted race, class, and the justice system. Both William Zantzinger and Byron De La Beckwith were racist whites and responsible for the death of African American civil rights activists. In "Hattie Carroll," Zantzinger's racism is not a focal point of the song. In fact, the subject is not explicitly broached. Dylan references some of Zantzinger's boorish behavior that night and a *Time* magazine account of the episode mentioned Zantzinger's use of racial slurs toward the African American staff.

Byron De La Beckwith intentionally murdered Medgar Evers in response to the latter's activism. Carroll participated in the Civil Rights Movement but Zantzinger did not kill her *because* she was an activist. Zantzinger knew that he could strike and unintentionally kill Carroll and face minimal consequences *because* she was poor and black and he was rich and white. Though De La Beckwith was arrested shortly after the killing, Dylan kept him nameless in "Pawn." Perhaps Dylan found him not worth acknowledging. Zantzinger is named and demonized for his actions, but Dylan even went so far as to claim that De La Beckwith was not to blame. A quick glance at the facts and one would guess that De La Beckwith would have received a greater degree of Dylan's scorn. Ultimately, there was one main difference between the two men. Zantzinger was wealthy, connected, and entitled; De La Beckwith was poor, ignorant, and manipulated. Dylan resented Zantzinger's abuse of power and his exploitation of privilege. Apparently, in Dylan's eyes, Zantzinger's behavior was inexcusable and the judge's ruling reprehensible. De La Beckwith, on the other hand, was both a victim and a perpetrator.

In the early 1960s, regardless of how much or how little he identified himself with it, Dylan belonged to a community of folk singers and topical songwriters. Phil Ochs, a fellow folk singer and admirer of Dylan's talent, wrote a piece for *Broadside* entitled "The Art of Bob Dylan's 'Hattie Carroll.'" Ochs reported overhearing, after a concert, "a well known commercial folk singer criticizing" Dylan's work as "another one of those black and white songs." A different artist called it "too preachy." Ochs understood the "many pitfalls that Dylan might have fallen into while treating such a delicate and difficult subject." He continued, "It would have been easy to describe the event and ask, 'Wasn't that a terrible shame, don't let her die in vain,' and put the usual sarcastic 'land of the free' line at the end."[26] Ochs's assessment of the song and its strengths proved accurate, and ultimately Dylan's writing abilities created the notoriety that allowed and necessitated his movement away from the folk music scene.

Though an artist of considerable reputation, in 1963, Dylan had not yet realized the magnitude of his fame. Many other writers' songs were published in *Broadside* and, as expected, themes such as civil rights, workers' rights, and antiwar were commonly employed. Oftentimes numerous songs appeared on a specific subject matter. When multiple songwriters presented similarly themed topical work, in almost every case Dylan's contribution became the definitive version. For example, in late March 1963, *Broadside* published a song by Don West called "Ballad of Hattie Carroll." Since her death occurred in February 1963, and Dylan's version was not recorded until October and contains the result of the trial, West's "Hattie Carroll" could not have been influenced by Dylan's. What the West song lacked was the deeper societal criticism present in Dylan's version. West's version of the story alludes to class distinctions but does not explore much beyond the mere tragedy of Carroll's death and the circumstances surrounding it.[27] Phil Ochs also penned a song dealing with the murder of Medgar Evers. Titled "The Ballad of Medgar Evers," it appeared in *Broadside* in July 1963, also shortly after the murder.[28] Two issues later, *Broadside* published Tom Paxton's "Death of Medgar Evers."[29] In both examples, the tragedy is addressed and deplored, and Evers lionized. This is not to say that any of these songs are poor; it is just that they lack the depth and nuance of Dylan's.

Not only are "Till" and "Carroll" indictments of American courts and the lack of justice for African Americans, they can also be understood in the context of the growing cultural gap between many of those in Dylan's age group and the generation in power. The institutions of justice allegedly with "no top and no bottom" proved their racial, class, and gender biases, at least to Dylan and many other young people.[30] In the 1960s, a growing awareness emerged, whether acutely or vaguely, among younger people that American society was not as free and just as they had been taught. Carl Oglesby summed up this disillusionment when he wrote, "Blame those who mouthed my liberal values and broke my American heart."[31] At the time, the vast majority of Americans still had faith in the System but this would soon be lost. Dylan became a herald for the growing lack of confidence Americans had for their political and legal institutions.

Dylan did not limit his critique of the imbalanced scales of justice to the plight of African Americans. In "Percy's Song" and "Seven Curses," Dylan again indicts corrupt or callous judges. In these songs, both fictional, the courts do not carry out the expected type of justice. Neither song appeared on a Dylan album from the era but popped up decades later on *Biograph* and *Bootleg Series 1–3*, respectively. In "Percy's Song," a driver kills four passengers in an automobile accident. For the negligent motorist, the judge imposes a 99-year sentence, an excessively harsh punishment according to Dylan, who serves as the song's narrator. Since the driver is a friend, Dylan decides to confront the judge, who is inflexible, arbitrary, and angry at being challenged. Perhaps realizing that his decision has a weak foundation, the judge offers no rationale and forces Dylan from his chambers. Though the driver is technically guilty of vehicular manslaughter and the negligent death of four other people, the judge is the recipient of the song's antipathy.

Though fictional, "Seven Curses" suggests Dylan's views on authority figures and socioeconomic class. The song features a character named Riley who steals a horse, is caught, and is sentenced to death by hanging. Declining a payment of gold or silver, the judge offers the man's freedom in exchange for a sexual encounter with Riley's daughter. Despite her father's pleas to not do so, she acquiesces. However, the judge does not intervene on her father's behalf and the following day he is hung. Though not as clear-cut examples of injustice as "Till" and "Carroll," these two songs implicitly reflect an emerging generational rift and growing distrust of the power establishment by Dylan and others of his age group. Dylan, the young artist, wrote the songs for an audience of primarily young listeners. The judge character in both songs can be assumed to be an older man. "Seven Curses" also suggests an element of class disparity and the notion that those who lack connections and privilege cannot receive justice. We see once again a criminal, in this case a horse thief, cast as the sympathetic character; the supposedly respectable figure, the judge, is not. In "Percy's Song" and "Seven Curses," the crimes committed by the powerless figures are noted but not elaborated upon and certainly not condemned.

The songs discussed thus far demonstrate an artist who deemed abuses of power and acts of injustice a greater moral violation than breaking a law. As noted in an earlier chapter, Dylan's background suggests that he believed in a universal source for ideas of justice and freedom. Many of his songs contained the message that human judges, laws, or politicians may be the source of power in society, but they are not necessarily legitimate authorities. These Dylan songs illustrated the many discrepancies in America, and students who belonged to organizations such as SDS noticed as well. Todd Gitlin, an SDS leader, wrote, "In a supposedly fluid America, it is class that apportions a man's share of justice, health, culture, education, ordinary respect—as any visit to a jail, an emergency room, a theatre, a college or a municipal bureau will illustrate."[32]

Dylan never caused much trouble as a young man, but prison and outlaws played recurring roles in his work. Throughout his life, Dylan has identified with rebels and outsiders, whether James Dean as a teenager or Lenny Bruce as a 40-year-old man. Joan Baez describes her relationship to Dylan as one of "fellow outlaw."[33] Romanticizing outlaws has been a common theme within the American musical and folk traditions that influenced him. In the 1980s and 1990s, Dylan covered songs such as "Pretty Boy Floyd," "Black Jack Davey," and "Stack a Lee." Though these characters are rogues at best and violent criminals at worst, they are frequently portrayed admirably. In some of Dylan's early work, he presented prisoners in a sympathetic light. He often described them as victims of a society that failed them. This is not to say that Dylan excused the criminal act but he instead emphasized the humanity of the criminal.

This thinking was what brought the wrath of the Emergency Civil Liberties Committee down upon Dylan, following his Tom Paine Award acceptance speech, when he stated that he saw some of Lee Harvey Oswald in himself. Though he did not express it explicitly as "hate the sin, love the sinner," at the very least it suggested empathy with the sinner's plight. Dylan has rarely condemned criminals but rather attempted to understand the individual circumstances that created them. It is a tactic used in "Folsom Prison Blues" by Johnny Cash, a man for whom Dylan had great mutual admiration, and by singers of outlaw songs in the folk tradition.

Dylan employed compassion for a criminal in writing "The Ballad of Donald White," one of his lesser-known songs of the era. Most likely inspired by a documentary he saw on television called *A Volcano Named White*, Dylan told the story of a 24-year-old drifter unable to adjust to society, who found existence more comfortable inside a jail than out.[34] Due to overcrowding, Donald White was set free against his wishes, and he eventually committed a murder and was subsequently executed. Dylan casts White as a sympathetic character and indicts the society that both creates and fails to care for him. Throughout his career, Dylan has empathized with violent criminals, even when their plight may not have been caused by an injustice but rather their own actions. Dylan asked, "When are some people gonna wake up and see that sometimes people aren't really their enemies, but their victims?"[35] This rhetorical question echoes the last line in "Donald White."

Officially unreleased until it appeared on *The Bootleg Series Volumes 1–3*, "Walls of Red Wing" further demonstrated Dylan's exploration of prison and its inhabitants. Situated along US Highway 61 in Minnesota, Red Wing is the site of the state's juvenile reformatory. Because he fabricated the details of his youth, some believed that "Red Wing" was autobiographical, but Dylan spent no more time incarcerated in Red Wing than Johnny Cash did locked up in Folsom Prison. Whether he actually ever saw the facility at Red Wing depends upon the route he took out of the Twin Cities to Madison, Wisconsin, and New York City after high school. He may have passed by the detention center, but one of Dylan's friends from Duluth, Jim Beron, spent time in Red Wing for truancy, and that might have inspired the song.[36]

The lyrics of "Walls of Red Wing" induce sympathy for the youth sentenced to the facility. Dylan's portrayal of the structure as an imposing Bastille-like dungeon assumes a fair amount of poetic license. The actual Red Wing facility is far less foreboding, at least physically, than Dylan describes. However, for many of the young men who entered it, the psychological intimidation could very well have made it feel threatening. At the end of "Walls of Red Wing," Dylan sings that some of the boys would be incarcerated in St. Cloud. Observing that some juveniles eventually would become inmates at the state penitentiary implies that Red Wing will be unsuccessful in reforming them. From the sentiment of "Donald White," Dylan clearly did not possess much faith in the redemptive capabilities of the prison system. For good measure, in "Walls of Red Wing" he surmises that some inmates will end up becoming lawyers. Based upon Dylan's portrayal of judges, this does not suggest that they necessarily would be on the right side of the law by becoming lawyers. "Walls of Red Wing" was not a major statement on the failure of the American penal system, but Dylan focused on the plight of the individual caught in an unjust society rather than falling back on typical 1950s and 1960s juvenile delinquency/teenage rebel clichés.

Economic Justice

The Progressive and New Deal eras saw Americans begin to address the issue of poverty in new ways. By the mid-1960s, Lyndon Johnson was waging a "War on Poverty" that he hoped would alleviate the condition. Though he never addressed Johnson's Great Society, Dylan's sympathies obviously resided with the poor. Bob Dylan's youth in northern Minnesota's political climate exposed him to ideas and provided experiences that created sympathy for the economically dispossessed. Folk legend Woody Guthrie was one of his heroes and influenced the young Dylan's artistic development. As a Great Depression era troubadour, naturally Guthrie's oeuvre contained songs that addressed the economic struggles of the average American. Woody's son, Arlo Guthrie, says that his father stood for the "little guy" and for an outsider's point of view.[37]

Dylan championed underdogs and outsiders and excused or downplayed their actions if they broke the law. At the same time, he vilified judges, police, and the privileged, especially when their actions negatively affected the underclass. Three Guthriesque songs, "Man on the Street," "Only a Hobo," and "He Was a Friend of Mine," remained unreleased until *The*

Bootleg Series Vols. 1–3 in 1991. The first two Dylan wrote. The third he adapted and recorded for his eponymous first album, but it did not make the final cut. The three songs follow a similar track: an indigent man dies on the street. In "Man on the Street," a police officer jabs the dead man, "who never done wrong," with his billy club. The officer guards a society that alternately fears, loathes, and disregards the impoverished transient. Dylan's distaste for authorities who abuse their power became evident in the recorded version when he replaced the phrase "billy club" with "bully club."[38] As the title suggests, "Only a Hobo" comments on society's lack of regard for the destitute and the fact that nobody cares when "one more is gone."[39]

Dylan wrote "The Ballad of Hollis Brown" about a South Dakota farmer driven to murder his family and commit suicide due to overwhelming hard luck and misery. One of the bleakest offerings in Dylan's catalog, the song appeared on *The Times They Are A-Changin'*. The pounding rhythm and desperate lyrics create a sense of foreboding and doom, or as *New York Times* journalist Robert Shelton writes, "an almost physically discomforting intensity."[40] Thus, when Dylan reaches the last line that after the seven deaths, seven more people are born, it leaves listeners to contemplate the futility of Brown's hardscrabble life. However, the birth of seven new people also opens the door for an optimistic interpretation—if one so chooses. When the song appeared in *Broadside*, it bore the title "The Rise and Fall of Hollis Brown: A True Story," and that is also how he introduced it for the *Witmark Demos*, now found on *Bootleg Series Vol. 9*. Though not technically a true story, it may be "inspired by true events."[41] Despite Brown being defined as a child murderer, the song does not condemn him for these actions. If anything, Dylan guides listeners to understand Brown as truly pitiful and the deaths by his hand as mercy killings.

Dylan explored a different avenue of social justice in "Who Killed Davey Moore?" He wrote "Davey Moore" as a commentary on the exploitative nature and physical toll of boxing, as well as American society's love of violent spectacle. Essentially pulled from the front pages in March 1963, Dylan wrote the song about a boxer who died in the ring. The song appeared in *Broadside* and on CD for the *Bootleg Series 1–3*.[42] If Dylan found boxing barbaric in 1963, it was not a sentiment he retained. Boxers show up in "I Shall Be Free No. 10" and "Hurricane" and, later in life, Dylan sparred as a means of physical fitness. At the beginning of each stanza, Dylan poses the question "Who Killed Davey Moore?" In attempting to answer the question, the song implicates such culprits as Moore's manager, Moore's opponent, a sportswriter, and a gambler. As he works systematically through the song, each character, when the question is posed to him, denies culpability.

Once again, Dylan sought a broader social explanation for an individual's predicament and allowed for two possible interpretations. The first is that society collectively, for entertainment, money, or other exploitative reasons, was to blame and Moore was a victim. The second possibility is that Dylan used the episode as a lesson in personal free-will and demonstrated that Moore ultimately was responsible for his own actions, and attempting to lay blame elsewhere amounted to a cop-out.[43] Considering the other songs we have seen from Dylan in this time period, the former explanation is probably closer to his intent.

In the song's live version, a line about boxing not being allowed in Cuba would elicit a loud, favorable response from the audience. It should be noted that Cuba's boxing ban extended only to professional boxing, as amateur boxing flourished and the country's teams did very well in the Olympics and other international events. Music critic Ralph Gleason writing about Dylan noted that "if we were a truly moral people, there would be no professional boxing." Gleason also called Dylan "a genius, a singing conscience and moral referee as well as a preacher."[44] Once again, a topical Dylan song had company in *Broadside*, this time from Phil Ochs's "Davey Moore," a song that decried the boxer's death but did not go beyond labeling those involved in the boxing profession as "vultures."[45]

By the end of 1963, Dylan's social justice songs had earned him the crown of "Voice," "Conscience," and "Poet" of his generation and the expectations that went with such a lofty title. An examination of his work up to this point reveals a very talented songwriter, but the limitations of topical material became the impetus for Dylan to break out of the mold others cast for him. The irony was that by writing songs concerned with freedom for others, he had lost much of his own, at least artistically speaking. Dylan biographers make a point of describing his refusal to meet expectations or his propensity for taking new and unexpected directions. Dylan existed within but not as a part of the culture, society, and institutions that surrounded him. Whether in his hometown of Hibbing or the folk scene, Dylan saw the need to formulate an exit strategy and implement it.

Resisting Definition

Dylan underwent a lyrical metamorphosis on his fourth album, *Another Side of Bob Dylan*, when he moved away from specific issues and songs about people such as "Hattie Carroll" and "Donald White." The new songs were more lyrically grand but less accessible. Previously, he had dabbled in this type of indirect writing on songs such as "A Hard Rain's A-Gonna Fall," and now it became his primary means of expression, at least for the next few years. For example, the song "Chimes of Freedom" contains the word "freedom" in the title but makes no specific claims as to where, when, or how it is being either exercised or denied. This is not to say that the indirectness makes the song any less potent; in fact, the wordplay and imagery place it alongside Dylan's epic masterpieces. This style will be Dylan's hallmark and influence countless artists.

In "Chimes," he issues a series of incongruent images and characters such as an "underdog soldier" and a "mistitled prostitute." Dylan brings another outlaw figure into the song, in this case a "misdemeanor" one. He also reiterates, albeit in a slightly different manner than his earlier work, the notions of social justice and the inmate as victim. "Chimes of Freedom" references the "unharmful, gentle" individual who happened to be "misplaced" in a jail cell. Beyond use of the term "underdog," "Chimes of Freedom" clearly suggests a song for the downtrodden. The chimes toll for the "luckless," "abandoned," "foresaked," "outcast," and "mistreated," among others.[46] What this results in is a song that conveys freedom in a general sense but cannot be specifically pinned down.

The type of music Bob Dylan was making suggested an artist replacing the confinement of serious political songwriting with the new personal type of freedom advocated by so many others of this time. Dylan, whether intentionally or unwittingly, became an icon for this burgeoning sense of freedom. When the public bought into "Dylan the Protest Singer" and began to demand a prescribed image, he understood the artistic limitations that accompanied these expectations. Dylan recalled being introduced at the Newport Folk Festival by Ronnie Gilbert of the Weavers. She told the crowd that Dylan appeared from out of a need to deliver messages that required expressing. She culminated by announcing, "I don't have to tell you. You know him, he's yours." The notion of ownership chafed Dylan at the time, and 40 years after the fact it still sat uneasily with him. He wrote about the event in *Chronicles Volume One*: "What a crazy thing to say! Screw that. As far as I knew, I didn't belong to anybody then or now." He continued, "But the big bugs in the press kept promoting me as the mouthpiece, spokesman, or even conscience of a generation. That was funny."[47] He told Paul Robbins in 1965, "I'm not going to tell them I'm the Great Cause Fighter or the Great Lover or the Great Boy Genius or whatever. Because I'm not, man. Why mislead them?" He said that these labels were "just Madison Avenue selling me, but it's not really selling me, 'cause I was hip to it before I got there."[48]

Many in the folk music scene were not amused by the direction he went. When he sang about "mutiny," in "Chimes of Freedom," Dylan may have thought that charge would be leveled against him. There is no question that he had grown weary of the expectations to write purely political songs and chose a new artistic vision. Dylan cut his ties to the folk movement with "My Back Pages." The paradoxical refrain that he had been older then but was younger now declares his independence from an earlier persona. He sings of a "self-ordained" professor who speaks of liberty being "just equality in school." This may be understood as a critique of the mainstream liberal notion that integration was the end goal for the Civil Rights Movement. While the legal gains were important, it amounted to only a partial victory if unofficial segregation remained. For northern whites who considered themselves pro-civil rights but never left the comfort of their own social class, southern desegregation proved an easy position to take. Historian C. Vann Woodward called this northern-liberal-led vision of civil rights "neo-paternalism" and accused its advocates of "unconscious condescension."[49]

Though integration was a necessary component of the Civil Rights Movement, open access was not the same as true liberty. The push for integration ignored the existence of institutional racism's deep roots in America, which remained unaddressed by many whites. Lyndon Johnson's inability to grasp why the cities burned even after he had signed the Civil Rights Act into law reflected the disconnection. Dylan understood the complexity of civil rights issues as evidenced by comments to Paul J. Robbins. Dylan wholly supported the cause but his antithetical worldview informed his understanding of organizations and institutions. He explained that civil rights became "proper" and mainstream: "It's not 'Commie' anymore... But when you get beneath it, like anything, you find there's bullshit tied up in it."[50] Dylan voiced his disgust with the media, its portrayal of civil rights, and how it missed the big picture. "There's people living in utter poverty in New York. And then again, you have this big Right to Vote." He bemoaned the futility of politics, asking, "Who are they going to vote for? Just politicians; same as the white people."[51]

Dylan's comments coincided with the direction that the Civil Rights Movement took in the mid- and late 1960s. As official means of segregation broke down, activists placed more emphasis on ameliorating the effects of institutionalized racism, such as poverty. A growing number of young people believed that the movement no longer served their interests and it began to splinter and radicalize. In 1966, the Student Nonviolent Coordinating Committee (SNCC) voted to remove white members, and Stokely Carmichael expressed the need for "Black Power." No longer were the majority of African Americans—the young in particular who demanded their rights—content to serenely endure violence or gratefully accept white northern "help."

On a lighter note, Dylan addressed politics and fame, among other topics, with "I Shall Be Free No. 10," an updated version of "I Shall Be Free" from *Freewheelin' Bob Dylan*. The opening stanza indicates that Dylan no longer feels the need to speak for anybody— assuming that he ever did. He asserts that he is the same as everyone else and that it is "no use" to talk with him because it would be the same as talking to anyone else. He gets a sarcastic dig in at Cold War fears by proclaiming that it would be "pretty scary" if the Russians beat the United States to heaven. The next stanza contains lines about Barry Goldwater marrying Dylan's daughter, which he says he would not allow for all of Cuba's farms.[52] None of these amounted to blistering political statements when compared to his earlier work. However, subversive lyrics resonated with listeners.

Anarchy and Personal Freedom

Depending on one's point of view, Dylan's next move may have been his most overtly political act. He changed himself from an acoustic folk performer, saddled with being the conscience of his generation, into a cryptic rock and roll hipster. Dylan's lyrics continued their transformation into more obscure and elliptical styles, and they are the musical equivalent of the 1964 bus ride Ken Kesey and the Merry Pranksters embarked upon. This manifestation of freedom became that of self-expression and a desire to go—as the Pranksters' bus read—"Furthur," artistically and personally. Dylan, who spoke out for justice and equality for others, now desired freedom of his own. A decade later, still fighting the expectations of others, he told *TV Guide*, "Greed and lust I can understand, but I can't understand the values of definition and confinement. Definition destroys."[53]

Between January and August 1965, when he recorded *Bringing It All Back Home* and released his second masterpiece, *Highway 61 Revisited,* Dylan led a musical revolution that contained political, cultural, and social overtones. The following year, Dylan presented *Blonde on Blonde,* the third installment of his electric rock output. With these albums, Dylan raised the bar for all other popular music artists of the period. The songs Dylan recorded in 1965 and 1966 were some of his greatest and most popular. Neither discernibly about a single subject nor linear in their progression, his music captivated the imaginations of listeners. If Dylan intended them to be about something specific, only he knew what—and he wisely chose to not explain himself. His work became impressionistic, open to the listener's interpretation. The perplexing and vivid imagery constituted its strength and much of his songs' appeal. He liberated himself from the confines of the folk scene and his fellow artists from narrow subject matter. Dylan's music proved to be participatory as it allowed the listener to engage in the process of creating meaning for his songs.

Songs such as "Queen Jane Approximately," "It's All Over Now, Baby Blue," and "4th Time Around" were not just "about" freedom—they evoked it. The young man from Hibbing now wrote expressionistic songs that fans and critics mined for deeper meaning. Dylan moved from a critique of injustice and a lack of freedom on a societal and institutional level, to a glorification of freedom and individual expression. Perhaps Dylan decided, or always knew, that an attempt to change society on a broad scale was not feasible, and instead he chose to concentrate on an inner world. Or perhaps it was never his intention, as he said in 1974, to "remake the world" or lead a "battle charge."[54] Most likely he simply grew tired of the scene, the style, and the limitations. If this is the case, Dylan could not have presented a better example for artistic freedom. As he would sing on "Just Like Tom Thumb's Blues," neither fortune nor fame were what they claimed.

There was no single moment in which Bob Dylan declared independence from the folk music scene. In retrospect, Dylan dropped clues throughout 1964. The lyrics on *Another Side* suggested an artist on the move, an individual escaping someone else's expectations. The live versions of songs not yet released on LP, such as "It's Alright, Ma (I'm Only Bleeding)" and "Gates of Eden," undisputedly captured an artistic revolution. By the time of the ballyhooed July 1965 performance at the Newport Folk Festival, the transformation had become total. At that concert he played "Maggie's Farm," a song infused with a populist sentiment that had appeared on *Bringing It All Back Home* in March of that year.

The degree to which his songs should be explicated is the listener's prerogative. In 1965, it truly was Dylan alone who wrote songs of this nature, and most other popular music of the time was devoid of any possibility for this type of analysis. "Maggie's Farm" is a prime example of Dylan's new conceptualized personal freedom. In its entirety, the song explores power relationships between Dylan the singer and Maggie and her family. The song begins with Dylan's declaration that he refuses to labor "on Maggie's farm" any longer. He complains of having a head filled with ideas that drive him insane. If that is metaphorical and represents his new musical direction, then Maggie and her family are the folk crowd and deny him the freedom to do it. They tell him to "sing" as he slaves, and her father and brother abuse Dylan by extinguishing cigars in his face and fining him. This occurs while the National Guard stands watch by the door, condoning the injustice and protecting the perpetrators. Maggie and her family threaten Dylan's personal liberty, as do the critics and fans who think they own him and want the singer "to be just like them."[55]

Familiar themes of power and freedom can be found in "It's Alright, Ma (I'm Only Bleeding)," but they are hallucinatory compared to his earlier work. The song is a tour de force of social grievance, disillusionment, and despair, and a treasure trove of lines for Dylanologists. The central issues are no longer the injustices of corrupt judges but people trapped and who "must obey" an authority for which they have no respect. They hate their jobs and their futures and therefore "speak jealously" of people who are free—people who do not succumb to the trappings of a hollow society. Dylan understands that liberty frightens people who do not want to accept the responsibility of being free. Activists, members of the Counterculture, or simply "longhairs" learned this lesson when their quests for freedom were met with hostility. Dylan reminds listeners that "the masters" create rules for the wise "and the fools."[56]

Later in 1965, Dylan upped the creative ante with *Highway 61 Revisited*. Although his songs from this era have been analyzed repeatedly, formulating a coherent thematic perspective from them is difficult. His admiration for Beat self-expression provided the most obvious cultural touchstone. Dylan, via his lyrical approach, proved to be an exemplar of this type of freedom. Some labeled the music Dylan pumped out during this period as anarchic. He may have advocated an anarchistic type of freedom, one without rules or at least without coercion, but not of violent confrontation. The media concocted numerous taglines in an attempt to capture Dylan's essence, a practice he disdained. In *Chronicles* and his *60 Minutes* interview, he facetiously referred to himself as the "Archbishop of Anarchy," but he gave no indication that he ever actually bought into that myth.

During 1965, Dylan became an undisputed international superstar and experienced mainstream success with "Like a Rolling Stone" reaching #2 on the *Billboard* charts. In Dylan's ultimate single, he warns "Miss Lonely" who "had it made," "dressed so fine," and attended "the finest schools," that the roles would be reversed. He had already explored variations of tables-being-turned in songs such as "The Times They Are A-Changin'" and would again in "Like a Rolling Stone's" musical and thematic partner, "Positively 4th Street." Dylan held in contempt those who sneered at or blatantly disregarded individuals on the outside looking in, even though the same could have been said about him.[57]

Though not explicitly a political subject, "Tombstone Blues" references "city fathers," "the chamber of commerce," "the commander-in-chief," and "king of the Philistines," along with "slaves," "prison," and shoeless factory workers.[58] In Dylan's earlier style, he met those who abused power head on, whether the "Masters of War" or William Zantzinger. Now he became subversive, turning the game on its head and making authorities look ridiculous. As he warned in "Ballad of a Thin Man," something was happening, but the Mr. Jones he addressed did not know what it was. Dylan's intuitive moves suggested a creative artist, sensitive to the culture around him, somewhat influenced by pharmaceuticals, who desired to test the boundaries of his medium. In doing so, he inspired others to question and explore aspects of their own lives.

His live shows became contentious as members of the crowd booed the music played with electric instruments. The following year, he recorded a double album, *Blonde on Blonde*. The album contained familiar settings and archetypes, but they now received a psychedelic treatment. In "Visions of Johanna," Dylan replaces the courtrooms discussed earlier, such as the one that featured William Zantzinger, with a hallucinatory setting where "infinity" becomes the defendant. In "Most Likely You Go Your Way (and I'll Go Mine)" the judge character, previously a symbol of corrupted power, now simply "holds a grudge."[59] Dylan's catalog contains numerous references to trials, courts, slaves, and servants. The song does not have to be "about" those subjects to mean that freedom was on Dylan's mind. Because of his reputation as a political songwriter, fans and critics scrutinized every word he uttered.

In the mid-1960s, Dylan's contemporaries in the music world followed his lead and asserted notions of personal freedom as well. Though he did not write songs that overtly proclaimed an individual freedom to do exactly as one wished, Dylan influenced this type of thinking. Within the realm of popular music, he served as the pacesetter. Prominent artists such as the Beatles, the Rolling Stones, and Jimi Hendrix moved toward songs of that nature. For example, the Beatles' song "The Word" appeared on *Rubber Soul*, an album that the group recorded partially in an attempt to keep up with Dylan's level of innovation on *Bringing It All Back Home* and *Highway 61 Revisited*. The song urges listeners to "say the word," which turns out to be "love." By doing so, they will "be free" and also, as lead vocalist John Lennon sings, be like him. The song, however, is not really a statement about freedom, political or philosophical, and Lennon and McCartney probably use "free" to rhyme with "me."[60]

In Jimi Hendrix's "Stone Free" and The Rolling Stones' "I'm Free," both artists advocate freedom of action. Essentially, they express a message stating that they are free to do whatever they want, whenever they want. It was not a call to anarchy but rather a proclamation aimed at a youth culture that desired greater latitude in lifestyle choices wrapped up in a vague notion of freedom. Some teenagers naturally envisioned a life wholly free to do and be whatever they wished. If nothing else, these songs illustrated a chasm between wealthy rock stars and their listeners.

Dylan's expression of freedom was open-ended because he advocated few things in particular, but he served as an exemplar of a deeper existential type of freedom. He sings in "Gates of Eden" about men whose freedom is total and who can do anything they want except die.⁶¹ With contractual pressures aplenty, Dylan could not do exactly as he wanted. Fans perceived an image to the contrary, which, combined with the cultural atmosphere, created a powerful archetype. During the 1960s, ideas of independence and nonconformity flourished among the young. The Kinks sang that they were unlike everyone else, and their Mr. Joneses were a "Well Respected Man" and a "Dedicated Follower of Fashion." Kris Kristofferson, who worked as a janitor in the Nashville studio where Dylan recorded *Blonde on Blonde*, addressed freedom in a hit for Janis Joplin: "Me and Bobby McGee." The song's two lovers possess nothing and live free because they have nothing to lose.⁶²

Dylan opened up rock and roll to virtually limitless subject matter and provided the format's greatest lyrical contributions. On multiple occasions, all four Beatles acknowledged their admiration of Dylan and his influence on them. In 1967, the Velvet Underground released songs about heroin, sadomasochism, and transvestites. That same year, the Doors explored the Oedipal Complex in their song "The End." Both groups contained lyricists who owed a debt to Dylan's writing. Though Dylan's songs very rarely broached these gritty types of topics, he more than any other artist opened the door for expanding topical parameters. His entire catalog—rather than an individual song such as "Jet Pilot," a one-minute throwaway with a surprise ending that reveals the "woman" in the song is really a man—encouraged the Velvet Underground to push the boundaries of rock and roll subject matter. In 1970, the Kinks hit the Top 10 with "Lola," a song that provides clues less than subtle concerning cross-dressing and homosexuality. Six years earlier, an achievement of that order would have been unimaginable. Dylan begot the transformation that other performers took in ever-evolving directions.

Although it is easy to overestimate music's role in society's cultural shifts during the 1960s, it should be acknowledged as a contributing factor. Songs such as "Mr. Tambourine Man" and "Rainy Day Women #12 and 35" may or may not be about drugs. Ultimately, what any of his songs were about is actually less important than what people *thought* they were about, or the manner in which he inspired other artists. Dylan and the music he wrote embodied a trait that a successful politician also possesses: the ability to have another's perceptions projected onto him.

The irony for Dylan is that the concept of freedom flowed through his songs and the culture (either expressed or implied), yet the expectations of being Bob Dylan threatened to make him a virtual prisoner of his fame. It is likely that he used a 1966 motorcycle accident—the severity of which is disputed—to escape a punishing concert schedule. "The pressures were unbelievable," Dylan recalled. "They were just something you could never understand because they did such weird things to my head."[63] Dylan rested and recuperated in upstate New York and transformed himself yet again. Dylan's period as rock and roll wild-haired hipster was, as U2's Bono said two decades later, "a brief flash of lightning," striking with as much force and vanishing as quickly.[64]

Dylan's late 1967 album, *John Wesley Harding*, proved transformational. In 1964, he had stepped away from his image as a Dust Bowl balladeer and protest icon. He now shed his rock and roll persona and entered a rural family man period. The manner in which he expressed himself lyrically did not indicate a radical departure but rather a continuation of his artistic exploration. Sonically, however, the album reflected a stripped-down, slightly country feel. If playing electric music betrayed his folk fans, his next period confused those who expected a continuation of Dylan the rock and roll oracle.

His outlaw fascination continued with the title song on the album *John Wesley Harding*. Dylanologists can endlessly puzzle over his intention when he named the album after John Wesley Hardin, a late-nineteenth-century gunslinger and brutal murderer. The other riddle is why Dylan added a "g" to the last name. Whether he simply thought it sounded better or did it accidently is unknown, but what is apparent is that Dylan turned his character into a hero. Contrary to the song, there is no evidence that the real John Wesley Hardin was friendly to poor people, and he certainly harmed a few men, probably of varying degrees of honesty.

The idea of someone being persecuted by the powers that be flows through *John Wesley Harding*. Dylan's Harding was accused of a crime, but the charges "could not be proved."[65] Dylan reversed his early form of songwriting from primarily nonfictional subjects to fictional ones, but continued to employ freedom, justice, and populist themes. In the song "Drifter's Escape," the main character returns to a setting familiar in Dylan's earlier work, the courtroom, but on this album it was unlike those portrayed in "Hattie Carroll" or "Seven Curses." The Drifter on trial does not know what crime he committed, though his moniker suggests someone potentially dangerous, or at least an individual on the fringes of society. As per Dylan's usual portrayal, he intends that listeners find the Drifter a sympathetic character. The Drifter never receives habeas corpus yet is convicted and hauled off to jail.

On *Harding*'s "As I Went out One Morning" Dylan referenced Tom Paine, the firebrand of the American Revolution. Paine, more than anyone of his time, presaged the democratic ideals of the country. The author of

Common Sense advocated democracy, women's rights, and the end of slavery. He fell out of favor as the revolution became more conservative and ended his life as an outsider. Thomas Paine also happened to be the namesake of the Emergency Civil Liberties Committee award Dylan received in late 1963. Dylan may have scoffed at the suggestion that any these things were interconnected, but since he did not bother to explain himself, listeners drew their own conclusions.

Characters who represent different sides of power, freedom, and law—a thief, a prince, and a servant—appear in "All Along the Watchtower." *John Wesley Harding* also contained songs about a "Lonesome Hobo," a "Poor Immigrant," and a semioppressive "Dear Landlord." "Wanted Man," Dylan's collaboration with Johnny Cash, written around this time, did not appear on the album and represented another version of a favored theme, the outlaw song. The material Dylan wrote at this time returned frequently to the constructs he employed throughout his career.

It may be a stretch to assert that a randomly placed word or phrase represented a great advocacy for personal freedom or the plight of the poor. Dylan already wrote those songs in the early 1960s, and it seems unlikely that he would abandon the ideas developed during his formative years. Most likely, he simply explored new ways of expressing them. As an artist, Dylan understood that he could only write a particular type of song so often before it became redundant and the audience lost interest. He also needed to seek varying styles and sounds, lest he "just get bored." Instead of an entire song devoted to the injustice done to Hattie Carroll, he now advocated personal existential freedom suggesting that we should not live by another "man's code."[66]

Because the Bob Dylan myth and reputation already existed, people pored over the songs. Jean Strouse reviewed *John Wesley Harding* for *Commonweal* in an article entitled "Bob Dylan's Gentle Anarchy." In Strouse's analysis, the album conveyed the "anarchy of everyone doing his own thing, assuming that freedom can exist only outside the laws and layers of society. The outsiders—outlaw, hobo, immigrant, joker, thief, girl in chains, drifter, saint—form an existential community simply in reaction to 'them.'"[67] Strouse's language was reminiscent of the classic Dylan line about the necessity of being honest if one chose to "live outside the law."[68]

Freedom of Contentment

John Wesley Harding dabbled in a country music sound and *Nashville Skyline* fully exemplified the country persona that Dylan projected in the late 1960s. Absent are any statement songs much beyond the joys of being with "the one you love."[69] What came through at this time was a picture of a man liberated from the pressures of constant touring and eager to debunk the myth that his utterances contained world-changing power. In 2004's *Chronicles Volume One*, he says as much and writes about his wife and children who he "loved more than anything else in the world." In addition, he demystified his reputation by stating that he was not a "preacher performing miracles."[70] Dylan's folk songs advocated a universal freedom for all, and his electric songs displayed a personal freedom of expression. Now Dylan experienced for himself the freedom of living the life he wanted. In 1969, *The Hartford Times* explained that the Beatles and Dylan "abandoned the leadership quest in pop. [Dylan] brought together the momentous unison of folk and rock, and now he seems to be happy just being himself."[71] After a punishing tour schedule, constant demands, and ensuing hype, nothing could have been more freeing than a period of domestic bliss.

The pastoral gentleness of Dylan's music on the *New Morning* album reflected his contentment. With paeans to family life such as "Time Passes Slowly" and "If Not for You," it exuded a warmness that makes it a dark horse favorite among many fans. The word "free" makes an appearance on "If Dogs Run Free," and with female jazz scatting it is one of the more unusual sonic arrangements in Dylan's catalog. He sings that by doing your thing, you can "be king."[72] And in the youth parlance of the late 1960s and early 1970s, the phrase "Just do your own thing" suggested the possibilities of creating their own culture—the Counterculture.[73] It is hard to tell whether the line is meant to mirror the Hippie sentiment or gently mock it. Throughout the song, Dylan repeats "If Dogs Run Free" and asks "Why not me?" and "Why not we?"[74]

As the 1960s turned into the 1970s, ideas of personal freedom, individuality, and the need for self-expression proliferated. Once understood as a novelty, they now found their way into mainstream culture. A variety of recordings captured these sentiments. "Free to Be…You and Me" and "Everybody is a Star" by artists as diverse as Marlo Thomas & Friends and Sly & the Family Stone, respectively, placed on the charts. Television shows aimed at children such as *Sesame Street* and animated movies like *The Point* reflected it as well. *Harold and Maude* featured Cat Stevens's ode to self-expression, "If You Want to Sing Out," and continued the promotion of the sense that society prevents its members from experiencing authentic lives.

Many Americans believed that their corrupt institutions could not provide justice and audiences thrilled to vigilante movies. In *Dirty Harry*, a cop tired of a weak and ineffectual court system took matters into his own hands and appealed to those who craved law and order. *Billy Jack*, named for the film's main character, was a Vietnam veteran who protected the students and faculty of the countercultural Freedom School by forcefully battling racism, discrimination, and violence. Films that portrayed outlaws-as-heroes such as *Bonnie and Clyde*, *The Sting*, and *The Godfather* helped to define the era of filmmaking. Despite having contributed to the rise of these sentiments, many believed that Dylan no longer promoted them. More than any other artist, Dylan had to combat unrealistic expectations created for him by the public. The belief among critics and the record-buying public that he would return like some sort of Prodigal Son or Messiah to sing "protest music" reflected a lack of understanding concerning both Bob Dylan and human nature.

During the 1970s, Dylan wrote a few topical songs that harkened back to his protest days. In terms of quality, they constituted a mixed bag. In 1971, he released the single "George Jackson." For those who believed that Dylan's main function as a songwriter was to write politically charged protest songs, it served as an indication that he had mounted a comeback. The song used themes of injustice and the misunderstood, jailed criminal that Dylan had employed in songs almost a decade earlier. Similar to Donald White, George Jackson had a long rap sheet and at the time of his death was incarcerated at San Quentin. Jackson wrote a book entitled *Soledad Brother* that described the deplorable California prison system and his experiences in it. While imprisoned, Jackson became a leader among inmates within San Quentin and was later killed by guards during an alleged escape.[75]

George Jackson epitomized the type of figure Dylan frequently heralded: an inmate whose talents of expression won others to his cause. However, Dylan's lyrics seemed disingenuous to many listeners. He sang that he "really loved" Jackson but the two never met. In addition, the image of Dylan waking up with tears in his eyes was hard to believe as were lines about San Quentin prison guards fearing Jackson's "love" and "power."[76] As Dylan frequently does in songs of this nature, he indicts society. He theorizes that the world is a prison and some inhabitants are "inmates" and others "guards." The song hit the airwaves and barely made a dent. It topped out at #33 on the *Billboard* Top 40, which may, in part, have been due to the fact that some AM stations refused to play it either because of its "philosophy" or that it used the word *shit*.[77] It may also have suffered because it is not among his best and listeners found the sentiment unconvincing.

Dylan may well have been moved by Jackson's story, but few listeners connected. In a 1971 *New York Times Magazine* article on Dylan, Anthony Scaduto interviewed a young singer who stated that he had been "radicalized by the Bob Dylan of the mid-1960s." The musician claimed, "I just don't believe he means those words. I don't believe he loves George Jackson, or relates to any of it anymore." The singer interviewed raised questions about Dylan's motives, claiming that the song smacked "of calculation, of Dylan being afraid he's losing his audience." As so many Dylan followers did, he drew contrasts with Dylan's earlier work: "People believed it when he sang about Emmett Till and Hattie Carroll and all the others who were destroyed by the system. I believed it back then. I don't believe it about 'George Jackson.'"[78] The poor showing for the single cannot be attributed to the record-buying public being uninterested in politically themed music at the time. In the early 1970s, songs that contained overt messages such as "Power to the People," "Ball of Confusion," "Peace Train," and "What's Going On," to name a few, either entered or stalled just outside the Top 10. Coincidentally, Dylan's next tale of injustice, "Hurricane," about jailed boxer Rubin Carter, also reached #33.[79]

Whether Dylan believed strongly in the quality of "George Jackson" is hard to gauge. He cut two different versions of it but never played it live. A variety of interpretations emerged to explain Dylan's reasoning behind the song. Some understood "George Jackson" as an intentional sabotage to get people off his back, while others saw it as a well-intentioned but poorly executed attempt to address subjects dear to him, and finally there were those who viewed it as a cynical but failed attempt to sell records. Scaduto weighed in: "It is clear he has been afraid that if he speaks out again in protest he will once more be burdened with that prophet's cloak that weighed so heavily on him."[80] It is possible that the song was a ploy to recapture the glory of a former self. More likely, Dylan saw George Jackson as a victim of society and felt compelled to comment on his death. What is certain is that the song was written and released quickly and had a half-baked quality. Infamous Dylan watcher A. J. Weberman dug through Dylan's garbage for clues into the singer's life. Weberman believed that what he called the Dylan Liberation Front (DLF) needed to free Dylan psychologically and convince him to return to protest writing. Weberman offered "George Jackson" as evidence that the DLF caused Dylan to alter his ways and become politically engaged once again.[81]

In the mid-1970s, Dylan's personal life underwent upheaval with a protracted divorce from his wife, Sara. *Blood on the Tracks* and *Desire* partially chronicle this personal turmoil. Critics and fans rank *Blood on the Tracks* not only among Dylan's very best, but also among the greatest albums of all time. The singer's pain on the album is evident and Dylan, caught up in his personal troubles, makes very little social commentary. He followed a 1970s musical trend, albeit one he pioneered the previous decade, by releasing an introspective, singer-songwriter type of album. "Tangled Up in Blue" perhaps a shrouded autobiographical commentary on the 1960s, contains references to someone who dealt in slaves and a street where "revolution" was "in the air."[82]

Desire, the follow-up album to *Blood on the Tracks*, contained "Hurricane." Cowritten with director Jacques Levy, it became one of Dylan's most famous political/justice songs. Dylan, in a deviation from his typical approach, spoke directly, often, and openly about the need to get boxer Rubin "Hurricane" Carter released from prison. Carter, not nearly as peaceful as Dylan and Levy portrayed, had a violent and checkered history before his arrest. Police in Paterson, New Jersey, stopped the outspoken Carter and charged him with a triple murder. In the subsequent trial, inconsistencies and dubious testimony against Carter led to his conviction. This raised questions regarding the fairness of the proceedings and caused many to think that he was a victim of gross injustice. Whatever the reality of the case, after Carter mailed Dylan a copy of his book *The Sixteenth Round*, the singer became convinced that the courts had railroaded Carter.[83] Dylan went to the prison that housed Carter and the two men developed a mutual admiration—so much so that Carter referred to Dylan as a "brother."[84] Joan Baez saw Dylan's involvement in the cause as a confirmation that he still concerned himself with the suffering of others. She commented that she did not expect Dylan to "champion my causes" and that he was "not an activist." However, she continued that this did "not mean he doesn't care about people. If that were so, he wouldn't have written 'Hurricane.'"[85]

Once again, a story of injustice moved Dylan to write a song and, in this case, become a very public advocate for its subject. Dylan ignored or fictionalized aspects of Carter but believed that the boxer was a victim of a corrupt and racist system. He also points out that the privileged, or the "criminals" who commit their acts wearing suits, are allowed to go free.[86] Dylan addressed this notion of white collar criminals again in the 1980s on "Sweetheart Like You" with the line that those who "steal a little" are put in jail and those who "steal a lot" are made kings.[87] "Hurricane" was a "protest song with the gritty urgency and outrage that had once enflamed a whole American generation," according to an article in *People*.[88] Beyond the fact that Dylan sang about a specific protest issue once again, the themes of justice, privilege, and race connected "Hurricane" to "The Lonesome Death of Hattie Carroll" and "Only a Pawn in Their Game." Dylan's support of the underdog and distrust of those in power never wavered.

"Joey," one of Dylan's more peculiar subject choices, was a number written about mob boss Joey Gallo. Gallo was the only protagonist who was both nonfictional and non-African American to be featured in a Dylan justice/trial song. Though a cynical move to build his own power, Gallo reached out to African American gangs and maintained friendly relations with fellow prisoners who were black.[89] Dylan sang that in prison Joey's best friends were black because they understood what it meant to live in a society that placed "a shackle" on them. After his release, Gallo's charm attracted people, and he possessed a certain chic among his high society friends. Perhaps Dylan empathized with the idea of Gallo the outsider as early in the song Dylan sings that Joey was on the "outside" of any "side there was."[90] Although some of the people depicted in Dylan's songs were unfairly persecuted—Rubin Carter, for example—that claim is difficult to make about Joey Gallo.

Hardly a misunderstood outsider, the mobster conducted a war between organized crime families, participated in the rape of a prison inmate, poisoned another, and beat his wife, among a variety of misdeeds. He was a brutal, mentally unstable, and violent man, not unlike the actual John Wesley Hardin. As he did in "Donald White" and "George Jackson," Dylan expressed sympathy for a criminal who he believed society had treated unjustly. Some Dylan chroniclers have written the song off as a spoof. In a review for *Creem* entitled "Bob Dylan's Dalliance with Mafia Chic," rock critic Lester Bangs eviscerated "Joey," picking apart the many misrepresentations within it. Typically unfazed by criticism, in 1991, Dylan called the song "great" and in 1987 started playing it live.[91]

In 1975, Dylan kicked off one of his most famous concert tours. He conceived of the Rolling Thunder Revue as a contrast to modern rock shows that had become spectacles replete with pyrotechnics, lasers, and other gimmicks. Striking a note for traditional America, Dylan and his entourage stopped by Plymouth, Massachusetts, before embarking on the tour. Having only toured once since 1966, a Dylan show was a special event and audiences came out to see and hear the artist at work. On *Bootleg Series 5*, which consists of songs culled from the tour, an audience member can be heard calling for Dylan to play a protest song. Dylan, with a response that borders on contemptuous, growls "Here's one for ya" and launches into "Oh, Sister," a song whose categorization as "protest" is not obvious in the least.[92] For a decade, Dylan dealt with people who could not accept that he had changed his sound and style. He was succinct when he spoke about fans and critics who wanted him to reconcile with an earlier image they had created for him. Always seeking freedom from that expectation, Dylan spat, "Those people were stupid. They want to see you in the same suit. Upheaval distorts their lives."[93]

Joan Baez said that on the Rolling Thunder tour, Dylan would "say ridiculous things to the audience, which would try to decipher his words as if they had just sprung from the holy tablets up on the mountain." Dylan's reputation as mystic oracle kept audiences enthralled, but Baez was less impressed. She wrote, "Bob's songs seemed to update the concepts of justice and injustice. And if the songs were not about justice, he made you think they were, because of his image, his rejection of the status quo, set against the mounting turbulence in the country."[94] While partially using the tour to help Rubin Carter's cause, he also performed a Woody Guthrie song, "Deportee (Plane Wreck at Los Gatos)," a handful of times with Joan Baez in May 1976. The song is an ode to Mexican migrant laborers who died in an airplane crash after being deported to Mexico. "Deportee" fits the classic Dylan pattern: sympathy for the dispossessed and calling attention to the callous treatment they often receive from society. At this point, Dylan himself sought escape from an unraveling personal life and the road offered him a certain freedom.

Spiritual Freedom

After the Rolling Thunder Revue ended, Dylan's marriage officially did as well. His next release, *Street Legal*, proved to be another transitional album. Though very few rock fans could have anticipated Dylan's next move, in retrospect *Street Legal* demonstrated the work of an artist with major concerns on his mind. The record invoked religion, apocalyptic imagery, and a corrupt society. Lyrically, it remained typically obscure but contained some of Dylan's most intriguing work. "Señor (Tales of Yankee Power)" did not directly address a single topic. Reading the title, one may have expected a blistering commentary on the US government's Latin American policy, but none existed. Instead, the song unfolds with a tale that is vaguely menacing and filled with confusion. Toward the end of the song, Dylan suggests that he and Señor should "overturn these tables."[95] This imagery immediately conjures Jesus upsetting the tables of the Temple moneychangers. The episode was Jesus's most direct attack on institutionalized power and a reaction to a practice that he found profane. For the next several years, Dylan wrote songs and gave interviews in which he called attention to what he saw as an increasingly corrupt society.

In "Changing of the Guards," Dylan uses lyrics to explicitly disavow the need for organizations. His contempt for those in power remains in "No Time to Think" and its line about "fools making laws." Dylan then lists a series of -isms: "socialism," "patriotism," "materialism," as well as "liberty," "equality," and "tyranny." Untrustworthy judges, who had made so many appearances in Dylan songs, now on *Street Legal* "will haunt you." The album seemed to be the work of an artist experiencing the creeping malaise of the late 1970s. In a post-Vietnam, post-Watergate, present-Energy-Crisis America, Dylan was tapped out, frazzled, and looking for answers.[96]

When Bob Dylan converted to Christianity, most people reacted with shock. The born-again, evangelical variety that he chose turned off many who saw it as reactionary. Paul Williams, in *Dylan—What Happened?*, asked, "Has this poet/hero of stalwart individualism joined forces with the enemies of personal and religious freedom?"[97] In the late 1960s and early 1970s, the Jesus People movement emerged as some Hippies "rebelled against not just the lifestyle but also the liberal religion of middle-class America and took up conservative forms of Christianity."[98] Dylan joined the outside-the-mainstream Jesus People in the late 1970s.

At first glance, Dylan seemed to have repudiated everything that he had espoused since the 1960s. However, within Christianity, there exist several themes that Dylan found appealing. First, the New Testament promotes social justice and advocates for the poor. Second, Dylan always appreciated an outsider, and in the secular world of rock music an embrace of religion made him just that. Third, Christian doctrine preaches a concept of freedom, realized by breaking the chains of sin.

Usually assumed to be opposites, obedience and freedom coexist within the concept of submission to God's authority as a means of freedom. Jesus told his disciples, "You will know the truth, and the truth will make you free." The apostle Paul wrote that those who have been "set free from sin" have "become slaves of righteousness." Similar thought can be found throughout Paul's letters (e.g., "For freedom Christ has set us free" and "Where the spirit of the Lord is, there is freedom").[99] The concept of freedom as obedience to God can be found in the Puritan heritage and a secular version of this exists within the social contracts of John Locke and Jean Jacques Rousseau. Dylan's personal turmoil certainly led him to seek answers, and what he found kept him traveling along the path he had always trod.

The albums that comprised Dylan's gospel period—*Slow Train Coming*, *Saved*, and *Shot of Love*—were not as radical of a departure as they seemed at first glance. Dylan dealt with his newly adopted Christian notion of freedom on *Slow Train Coming*'s first song, "Gotta Serve Somebody." The message rings through that whether a "doctor," "thief," or "businessman," everyone must "serve somebody" and the choice is quite simple: Satan or God. Dylan ticks off a litany of social ills in "When You Gonna Wake Up," including wrongly accused "innocents in jail," "lawbreakers making rules," and "gangsters in power."[100] On *Saved*, Dylan most directly employs the metaphor of sin as a form of slavery in "What Can I Do for You?" He expresses his gratefulness to Jesus, who released him "out of bondage."[101]

Dylan rejected organizational hierarchy at virtually every turn and the type of Christianity that attracted him lacked that feature and existed well outside the American religious mainstream. As Dylan forged a new belief system, he carefully differentiated between religion and Jesus. In a radio interview, Dylan said that religion was "repressive" and "another form of bondage," but Jesus did not preach religion. Dylan rejected prescriptive rituals as a false path to the kingdom of "a Master Creator," of "a Supreme Being in the Universe."[102] Into the 1990s, Dylan continued to express the idea that it is "God who gives you the freedom."[103] In 1995, he commented that *Slow Train Coming*'s "Precious Angel" "probably emancipated me from other kinds of illusions."[104] Dylan came across like most recent converts, excited by his newfound faith and wanting to share the freedom he found in Jesus with everyone else—whether they wished to receive the message or not. Throughout his career, Dylan had called attention to social problems and abuse of power, and for the first time he offered what he thought were legitimate solutions to these issues. But few of those who had hung on his words back then were listening now.

Within his Christian perspective, his distrust of organizations and authority figures never wavered. Fifteen years after Dylan first warned listeners about following leaders, he advised against putting stock in groups such as the Moral Majority. Rather than forfeiting personal freedom to an earthly leader, Dylan urged people to "Get in touch with Christ yourself. He will lead you. Any preacher who is a real preacher will tell you that: 'Don't follow me, follow Christ.'"[105] A few years later, he stated that being a part of modern society was akin to "turning a deaf ear to all that can save you, while pursuing a wall, a strange mirage. Seeking freedom where freedom isn't, and both your feet are caught in a trap, and you're bleeding to death but you can't feel it 'cause you're high on the drugs of illusion." He then went on to list a number of atrocities committed in the name of religion. Dylan added succinctly, "Today's religion is tomorrow's bondage."[106]

The 1980s and Beyond

Critics often depict the 1980s as Dylan's creative nadir. However, there existed some strong songwriting and a continuation of common themes. As Dylan progressed into middle age, working in an industry geared toward those decades younger, the weight of his words carried less social resonance. Within American culture, the idea of freedom increasingly became commercialized. The notions of personal freedom advocated in the 1960s became expressed as freedom of product choice for consumers. Starting in the 1980s and continuing, Dylan's songs and interviews confronted materialism in society. In later years, Dylan would also use his songs and person in a variety of commercial advertisements. For the time being, however, Dylan remained outside of societal trends.

Infidels—a suggestive title—was an enigmatic album and contained multiple instances where Dylan forayed into what could be called political writing. Though the production values epitomized some of the worst of the 1980s, the songwriting is intriguing. "Jokerman" opens the album and finds Dylan as inscrutable as ever.[107] The song plays out like a video collage of apocalyptic images: a demagogue manipulating crowds, "false-hearted judges," a rich man in the "fiery furnace," and civil unrest. Those looking for clues that Dylan had abandoned Christian doctrine pointed to his mention of Deuteronomy and Leviticus, two of the law-themed books of the Torah. Rather than discarding one set of beliefs for another, Dylan continued to employ all of his influences. Biblical themes of all sorts, instead of needing to be excavated, were openly exposed on *Infidels*.[108]

In "Jokerman," freedom is right "around the corner," but since truth is far away, things don't look hopeful.[109] Dylan's message seems to be that without truth—living in accordance with God's expectations—one cannot have freedom. He asserted a similar line of thinking on "Lord Protect My Child," an outtake from *Infidels* that appeared on the *Bootleg Series 1–3*. He sings of reconciliation between humans and God, and claims that men will continue to live in chains until that day. Dylan's religious views underwent great scrutiny at this time, and outside observers reported that he had forsaken Christianity and embraced Judaism. It is likely that he integrated aspects of both traditions and carried his personal relationship with God forward in a manner only fully understood by Dylan himself. (The next chapter will consider the question in detail.)

Of all of the songs in which Dylan addresses justice, "I and I" is one of the few instances where he broaches the idea of it being punitive. It contains a perplexing line about a "stranger" teaching Dylan to see, in the "beautiful face" of justice, the ancient maxim "an eye for an eye and a tooth for a tooth."[110] What he means by this has been interpreted in many ways. Larry Yudelson believes it to be a "Jewish justification of his Christian phase" but does not elaborate beyond that.[111] Seth Rogovoy argues in his excellent *Bob Dylan: Prophet, Mystic, Poet* that the line signals Dylan's rejection of Christianity and the stranger was perhaps a rabbi he associated with in the early 1980s.[112] Some have understood it in a dispensational context—in other words, a difference in God's Jewish and Christian message. Dylan's late 1970s and early 1980s Christianity certainly contained a healthy dose of eschatological End-Times thinking prevalent among dispensationalists.[113] If nothing else, it demonstrates the complexity of Dylan's work and the difficulty in staking a claim to his meaning.

In 1988, Dylan embarked on what is now called the Never Ending Tour, a term he dislikes because the label attempts to set parameters on him. The following year, he released what is often considered the highlight of his 1980s output, *Oh Mercy*. It kicks off with "Political World." Considering the 1960s nostalgia of the period, it was a potentially loaded choice. Dylan speeds through a series of social ills and images such as wisdom being locked in jail.[114] The song signaled, to many critics and fans, that once again the "old" Dylan was back. However, the notion of a true Dylan who existed in the early and mid-1960s, and then was lost, and now is found again is patently wrong. Bob Dylan the songwriter and musician underwent many superficial changes, and he experimented with different ways of expressing similar themes.

On 1992's *Good As I Been to You*, Dylan chose to record "Black Jack Davey," an outlaw song that reaches back not only musically to an earlier Dylan period, but thematically as well. "Arthur McBride," from the same album, is the tale of two cousins taking a stroll on Christmas morning. The narrator and McBride encounter a three-person military contingent and are encouraged by the sergeant to enlist. He extols the virtues of a fine uniform and the good meals provided by the military. Arthur McBride notes that while the offers of money and adventure are "charming," they come with the risk of being sent to war at any time. He refers to his cousin and himself as "single and free" and observes that the sergeant possesses neither his clothes nor control over his life. Incensed, the sergeant threatens the pair, who in return beat the soldiers bloody and continue with their walk. If the song's sentiment appealed to Dylan, it is likely due to its freedom and antiauthority elements rather than a simple antimilitary sentiment.[115]

When, once again, many began to write off Dylan, he reemerged in 1997 with *Time Out of Mind* and a series of strong albums that continued through 2012's *Tempest*. In "Mississippi," from 2001's *Love and Theft*, Dylan sings about being trapped or "boxed in," a fear that has spurred him to evolve throughout his career.[116] Dylan's unwillingness to be defined and his need for an exit strategy came through in a 1970s conversation with Anthony Scaduto: "Me, I gotta keep a place for me."[117] Early in Dylan's cowritten movie *Masked and Anonymous*, Jack Fate, the character played by Dylan, languishes in an underground cell. His release having been secured by unscrupulous concert promoter Uncle Sweetheart, Fate comments to his now-former jailer on the way out, "I ain't felt free in a long time." The jailer responds, "Keepin' people from being free is big business."[118]

In the 1980s, Dylan began to frequently express dissatisfaction with consumerism, artifice, and a rootless modern American culture set adrift. In 2009, he told *Rolling Stone* that he found it "unnerving" that so many teenagers were constantly plugged into various forms of media. He stated that it robbed them of their "self identity," but ultimately they were free to do what they wanted. Dylan immediately added, "As if that's got anything to do with freedom. The cost of liberty is high, and young people should understand that before they start spending their life with all those gadgets."[119]

In 2012, President Barack Obama awarded Dylan the Presidential Medal of Freedom, presumably based on his 1960s output, but his advocacy of freedom and justice has gone far beyond just that period. As an artist, Dylan has advocated freedom and justice, sought the ability to express himself in meaningful ways, and wished to be liberated from labels applied by others. Whatever the manifestation, Dylan's notion of freedom transcends categories and continually shapes his outlook.

CHAPTER 4

Conversion and Culture

The relationship between Christ and Caesar, between the Church and the World, has been the subject of thought, debate, and sometimes bloodshed for thousands of years. Each side claims to hold a trump card of allegiance, whether natural or supernatural. Conflicting loyalties can cause problems for a society. Collaboration can produce a sacralism that combines two types of potent power: secular and religious. While seeming to promoting harmony, this can also cause problems in the long run (and in the short run for those falling outside of the governmental/ecclesiastical mainstream).

Competition between the eternal and temporal has inevitable political implications. God is said to be at the center of Christianity, but the religion operates in an earthly context of time and space, including specific nation-states with rulers, laws, and customs. Context cannot be ignored and it often overshadows the spiritual.

In seeking to understand how these pieces fit or do not fit together, we will make use of Niebuhr's classic book *Christ and Culture*. Shining a spotlight on one of five models of how the two relate will set the stage for understanding Bob Dylan's politics since 1979. The Christ Against Culture theological position leads to the ideology of Christian anarchism.

The Conversion of Dylan

It is important to consider the authenticity of Bob Dylan's Christian conversion and ongoing faith in Christ. If chapter 6 of this book is going to describe Dylan as an example of Christian anarchism since 1978, we have to show two things: that he remains a Christian and that he is an anarchist. His anarchism—before and after 1978—is easily established, but a brief flirtation with Christianity in 1979–81 does not a Christian anarchist make…at least not when speaking of Dylan in the present tense. So it is important to verify his continued Christianity.

As he later recalled, Bob Dylan had always known that "there was a God or a creator of the universe and a creator of the mountains and the sea and all that sort of thing," but had not been "conscious of Jesus and what that had to do with the supreme creator." He "had always read the Bible" but had "only looked at it as literature."[1] Raised in a Jewish family, he primarily grew up reading the Hebrew Scriptures (i.e., the Tanakh or Miqra—Torah, Prophets, Writings—or what Christians call the Old Testament). Still, he was acquainted with the New Testament as a culturally literate young man, even if he viewed it in literary terms only.

As an artist and a moralistic social critic, Dylan included a multitude of biblical quotations and allusions in his songs during his pre-1979 period. The most famous examples are "Blowin' in the Wind," "A Hard Rain's A-Gonna Fall," "The Times They Are A-Changin'," "I Shall Be Released," "All Along the Watchtower" and other songs on *John Wesley Harding*, and "Forever Young." When Dylan began his own publishing company, in 1971, he named it Ram's Horn Music. The ram's horn or shofar has been a musical instrument used by the Jewish religion since ancient times.

Although Dylan indulged in some of the decadent behaviors of the typical rock star in the 1960s and 1970s, he had a reputation among music fans for being more virtuous than average. This may have been because he was well-mannered and cherubic-looking when he began his career, had a moralistic persona during his protest song days, and/or had a tendency as a private person to keep his extramusical activities out of the spotlight. During an interview with Dylan for *Rolling Stone*, in 1978, Jonathan Cott said, "When I was waiting to pick up my ticket for your Portland [Oregon] concert last night, I happened to ask the woman behind the desk where all these kids were coming from. And she said: 'For Bobby Dylan, from heaven—for Black Sabbath, who knows?'" Neither Cott nor Dylan—nor the ticket woman—knew that Dylan was on the eve of a religious awakening that he would credit to heaven.

The details of Dylan's conversion—a silver cross being thrown on stage at a concert in San Diego, a personal encounter with Jesus in a motel room in Tucson, the influence of his girlfriend Mary Alice Artes, and his talk with ministers from a Los Angeles church—can be found in various biographies.[2] In describing his conversion to Karen Hughes, in May 1980, Dylan said, "Jesus put his hand on me. It was a physical thing. I felt it. I felt it all over me. I felt my whole body tremble. The glory of the Lord knocked me down and picked me up."³ The interview does not say whether this occurred in the motel, in connection with the ministers, or at some other time in late 1978–early 1979.

The intense personal aspect of Dylan's touch by Jesus reminds us of the Christian mystical experience of brilliant scientist-mathematician Blaise Pascal in 1654. After he died, a piece of paper written by Pascal, describing the spiritual experience, was found sewn into the lining of his doublet (jacket). Dylan's personal encounter with Christ and subsequent reading of the Bible led to dramatic changes in his thought, lifestyle, music, and career. This was not an arid intellectual or abstract theological exercise for Dylan. As he told Hughes, "Christianity is not Christ and Christ is not Christianity." Being a Christian means that "you're talking about making Christ the Lord and the Master of your life, the King of your life."[4]

As a new Christian, Dylan was zealous. He did not embrace a feel-good, namby-pamby, Kumbaya sort of Christianity. It was biblical, no-other-way, fire-and-brimstone, end-of-the-world, all-consuming, 100-proof Christianity. This produced shock and dismay among many of Dylan's fans and associates.[5] On the other hand, evangelical Christians were excited about the famous new addition to the fold. After seeing Dylan perform in Santa Monica, in November 1979, veteran pop star and born-again believer Pat Boone told the press, "It's one of the gutsiest things I've seen in my life. I wanted to shout, 'Hey listen—for a generation he asked the questions, and now he's giving you the answers. Why don't you just listen?'"[6]

Earlier in November, Dylan did something unprecedented. He spent the first two weeks of his new concert tour in the same venue—the Fox Warfield Theater in San Francisco—singing brand new songs. They were from his successful, recently released album titled *Slow Train Coming*, and for his second Christian album, *Saved*, which would be recorded in early 1980. He refused to sing any of his famous, preconversion songs.

Despite negative local newspaper reviews from opening night and some hostility from old fans expecting to hear the old songs, the stay in San Francisco was generally positive for Dylan. There was a problem, though, that foreshadowed his increasingly strained relations with the evangelical Christian world. Because it played an important role in Dylan's estrangement from the institutional church and helps to explain why he has resorted to a lonely, individualistic type of Christianity for the past 30 years, it is worth recounting at length. Dylan's personal assistant at the time, Dave Kelly, remembers:

> We had tried to get all the churches in the area to pick a night—fourteen nights—give it to each different church, different denomination, to come

out and bring their youth groups... To talk to the people as they left and invite them to church because he knew that he couldn't follow up with them. If he's preaching the gospel and he's getting them in this state where they're ready, he wanted—he thought—but... He didn't understand how political the church was. And he did hate it when he found out what it was like. It did great damage to him, I think, spiritually. But none of the churches would participate. It was my job to call them. None of them would participate unless they were the only ones... So we ended up with no single church coming out to support what he was doing... Can you imagine how damaging that was to a new convert? He's taking death threats every day of the week. And he's out there fighting... They're out in the back and they won't even help... So, he just got it: the church was political as well. And he wasn't interested in that.[7]

The story is sad and sheds new light on the vehemence with which Dylan would later express his opinion of politics. In 1984, Dylan expressed the opinion that politics is a tool of Satan and that it kills rather than bringing anything to life. In all likelihood, he was not only thinking about the secular world of elections and government, which he had long despised, but the institutional church as well. Something that was designed to be beautiful and pure—the Bride of Christ—had become corrupt and disgusting—a Whore. Emulating the world, the pseudochurch is more Babylon than Bride. Revelation, one of Dylan's favorite books of the Bible, describes the Great Harlot—compromised through conceit, manipulation, greed, politicization, and fornication with the kings of the earth—as being "drunk with the blood of the saints and the blood of the martyrs of Jesus." This may be one reason, among many, that politics kills. What happened in San Francisco was one small example that he experienced personally. Politics killed an opportunity to minister to those who heard Dylan sing and preach the gospel.[8]

Dylan and Judaism

In the two-year period between the release of *Shot of Love* (1981) and *Infidels* (1983), two contradictory rumors suggested that Dylan's "Christian phase" was over. He had either lost interest in religion and returned to his worldly lifestyle of drinking and carousing, or he had embraced Orthodox Judaism as an alternative to Christianity.[9] No doubt Dylan's personal life was not above criticism from a moral perspective—as is true for all of us—but that says little about his faith commitment or his status in relation to the grace of God. As for a return to his Jewish roots, this perception was sparked by events such as attending the bar mitzvahs of his sons and studying with some rabbis in Brooklyn. But this proved nothing. Dylan did not reject his Jewishness when he knelt before Yeshua, whom he saw as the Jewish Messiah.[10] From a spiritual point of view, Dylan did not see Christianity as a rejection or replacement of his Jewishness. He saw it as a completion or fulfillment. From the perspective of traditional Judaism, this is a patronizing or insulting thing to say, but it is, nonetheless, the perspective of Jesus and the first-century Jews who followed him. This is the teaching of the New Testament, which was composed almost entirely by Jewish writers.

Dylan's gospel album *Saved* featured Jeremiah 31:31 on the inner sleeve: "Behold, the days come, saith the Lord, that I will make a new covenant with the house of Israel, and with the house of Judah." It is significant that he chose a Bible passage that bridges the gap between the Old Covenant and the New Covenant, between Judaism and Christianity. A fellow Jewish convert to Christianity, Hollywood composer Al Kasha, played a role in Dylan's conversion, after meeting him at the Vineyard Church. Many of the songs for *Slow Train Coming* were written at Kasha's home.[11] During his first year in fellowship with Christians in Los Angeles, Dylan became friends with Keith Green, another Jewish convert to Christianity (see chapter 6). Ethnically and culturally, Dylan remained Jewish after becoming a Christian. It was part of who he was and it would stay with him. Yet that is not the same as being an adherent of the religion of Judaism.

In March 1982, Dylan was in California for the bar mitzvah of one of his sons, perhaps Samuel. In June 1983, *New York* magazine reported that Dylan was studying with the Lubavitch (Chabad) sect of Orthodox Jews in Brooklyn. This was in the midst of his work on the *Infidels* album. In September 1983, Dylan was in Jerusalem for the bar mitzvah of his son Jesse. In August 1986, Dylan recorded "Thank God," a song popularized by Hank Williams, at a concert sound check, backed by Tom Petty and the Heartbreakers. The video clip was shown the following month on the Lubavitchers' Chabad antidrug telethon. Dylan added a clip at the end appealing for money and praising Chabad for its work against the powerful and profitable illegal drug trade.[12]

These four events sparked rumors that Dylan had abandoned Christianity and embraced Orthodox Judaism. Rabbis affiliated with the Lubavitch (Chabad) sect encouraged that perception. The reality was not so simple and not so suggestive of Dylan abandoning Christ. Regardless of his own religious views, it was natural for a father to attend his sons' bar mitzvahs. Dylan's children were being raised in Judaism, under the guidance of their mother Sara and their grandmother (Dylan's mother) Beatrice "Beatty" (Stone) Zimmerman Rutman. In June 1984, Mick Brown spoke with Dylan in Madrid. Recalling the previous September, Brown wrote, "He was in

Jerusalem last Autumn for his son Jesse's bar mitzvah—'his grandmother's idea,' he smiles. Israel interests him from 'a biblical point of view,' but he had never felt that atavistic Jewish sense of homecoming."[13]

The photograph of Dylan in Israel, by ex-wife Sara, on the inner sleeve of *Infidels*, was taken at the time of the bar mitzvah. Dylan is kneeling on the Mount of Olives above Jerusalem. This has not only Jewish but also Christian significance as the place from which Jesus Christ ascended into heaven after spending 40 days with his disciples (post-Resurrection). It is also the prophesied place to which Christ will someday return.[14]

In his July 1983 interview with Martin Keller, Bob Dylan was asked about his recent search for his "so-called Jewish roots" (Keller's words). In an amazing reply, Dylan described an array of Old Testament figures: Joseph, Moses, Jacob, Gideon, Deborah, Esther, Reuben, Samson, King David, King Saul, Elijah, Isaiah, and Jeremiah. He also mentioned John the Baptist from the New Testament. He concluded, "We're talking about Jewish roots...Yeah these are my roots, I suppose. Am I looking for them? Well, I don't know. I ain't looking for them in synagogues with six pointed Egyptian stars shining down from every window, I can tell you that much."[15] This was a telling comment. He specifically rejected the idea that his reconnection with his Jewish heritage had anything to do with Jewish synagogues. Instead, it was based on the Hebrew Scriptures (Old Testament) but also on the New Testament (written almost entirely by Jews).

Dylan's reference to "six pointed Egyptian stars" is a disparaging reference to the Star of David (sometimes called the Shield of David). It is the symbol of modern Zionism and the modern state of Israel, but there is no evidence that it was ever used by King David. Its widespread use for Jewish identity began in the Middle Ages. Also known as a hexagram, it is sometimes linked to paganism and the occult.[16] Some sources identify it as the Seal of Solomon favored by Jewish Kabbalists and partly trace its association with Jews back to pagan Egypt, perhaps through Solomon's marriage to the daughter of Pharaoh.[17]

A few months later, Dylan was interviewed by Robert Hilburn. Hilburn wrote, "Dylan has reportedly spent much time recently at Chabad Lubavitch, a hard-line Hasidic Jewish center in Brooklyn." When asked about erroneous news reports that he had recorded an album of Hasidic music for a reputed label called Mitzvah Records, Dylan treated it as a joke: "You can say I'm planning to make 20 records for them. Say I'm going to make all my records from now on for them."[18]

It may be significant that Dylan chose to sing a gospel song for his contribution to the Chabad Telethon in 1986. The last verse of the song, which refers to Jesus as "the Master" and quotes his prayer to the Father while on the cross, may have been edited out before broadcast but was more likely omitted by Dylan because it would not have been appropriate for a telethon sponsored by an Orthodox Jewish group. In the first verse, which Dylan did sing, he referred to a "straight (strait) and narrow" road, which is language derived from the King James Version of words Jesus spoke to his disciples.[19]

In August 1988, Dylan's stepdaughter Maria married Peter Himmelman, a devout religious Jew. That same year, Dylan appeared for a second time on a Chabad Telethon. This time, he appeared live and played the harmonica while son-in-law Himmelman sang "Hava Nagila." Dylan wore a yarmulke.[20] In 1990, Dylan provided a blurb praising a book on sexual modesty for an Orthodox Jewish rabbi based in St. Paul.[21] Bob Dylan's occasional participation in events for Hasidic/Orthodox Judaism does not indicate a rejection of Christianity. It seems to be tied to family and to a shared moral outlook. Becoming a Christian does not mean a rejection of one's Jewish heritage since Christ himself and all of his original disciples were Jews. It is possible that Dylan also hopes to maintain a bridge to pious Jewish traditionalists—as opposed to Jewish atheists—in the hope that he may influence some to consider the messianic claims of Jesus.

In a recent interview, Dave Kelly, who was Dylan's personal assistant in 1979–80, gave his assessment of Dylan's involvement with "the hierarchy of Judaism within America, which comes out of Flatbush." He recalled, "I saw when the rabbis first were sent to him—the Lubavitch out in New York, Rabbi Schneerson and his people, who were the cutting edge people in America, among the Orthodox Jews...And he [Dylan] was very much against them at the time. But I saw them then force him—through his mother, I think—force him to have to study with them. But he wasn't interested in that at all." When asked what he thought about the mid-1980s rumors that Dylan had moved away from Christ, that he had returned to his worldly ways or embraced Orthodox Judaism, Kelly replied,

> The media and the industry wanted to believe that. What I saw clearly was the pressure for him, at the very least, to study with the [Lubavitch/Chabad] rabbis. He'd never done that. And he didn't realize what an insult it was to their Jewish community. He didn't see that. He didn't see why that would be the case. He didn't see how iconic he was. It would be like Barbra Streisand becoming a Christian...And I think that hurt him. He didn't mean to hurt them. And then there was the pressure. If you don't study with them and give them a chance.

According to Kelly, the executives for Dylan's label were predominantly Jewish. Although most were secular Jews, Kelly believes that they responded to pressure from the nation's Orthodox Jewish establishment. Dylan did not like the political power of the rabbis and had no interest in looking for a different Messiah after finding Jesus, but his record label responded to rabbinic pressure, at one point threatening to not release the next Dylan album. Kelly says, "And next thing I know, I hear that he's studying with rabbis. So I know that was compromise. He's not stupid, right?...He couldn't do a thing. Not releasing a record was just not an option for him."

"If Dogs Run Free" is an upbeat Dylan song, but Kelly uses a canine metaphor that is less pleasant: "I don't think he'd ever pulled their [Columbia Records] chain enough to know that there was a limit to it. He'd got to the end of the yard like the dog on a chain and he was pushing against it. 'Oh oh, this is actually a chain. I could just run around the yard and think I'm free.' So that's what had happened."[22] With record execs being tired of the Christian persona, they were hoping that Dylan would move on to a less-controversial, more socially acceptable phase. Kelly continues, "They [the Orthodox hierarchy in New York City] came first to the label people...And they said, 'We gotta pull *your* chain now. You've got too much responsibility to the Jewish community...We let you do whatever you want to do...We don't really care. But [you can't let Dylan do this].'"

Of course, Kelly is not suggesting that there was a Jewish conspiracy to keep Dylan in the fold. Aside from one particular group—leaders of the Lubavitch sect of Hasidic Jews—there was no organized effort. There was nothing malevolent about it. The reaction of the group was natural enough. The desire to keep a famous cultural figure from rejecting traditions that you are dedicated to preserving is a normal response.[23] Living in a free country afforded them an opportunity to talk with Dylan. The confluence of religious, economic, and family pressure may have been uncomfortable for him but it was not so surprising and he rolled with it—even if it gave rise to inaccurate rumors.

From Kelly's perspective, Dylan finally agreed to meet with the Lubavitch rabbis for at least three possible reasons: encouragement from his mother, he felt bad that his public conversion had upset or embarrassed fellow Jews, and pressure from above by the economic powers at Columbia. So Dylan made an effort to give the "very learned men" (in Kelly's words) a chance to explain their religion. Referring to the request that he listen to the Orthodox rabbis, he told Kelly, "I can do that."[24]

Dave Kelly stopped working for Bob Dylan in 1980, after his first gospel tour ended. News that Dylan was studying with the Brooklyn rabbis did not surface until 1983. Kelly writes, "Yes, the record label seemed to be putting pressure on him during the time I was with him, to at least spend some time with the rabbis studying. The argument presented seems to have been that it was only fair to give them as much time to present their views as Bob had given to the Vineyard pastors." He adds, "I can only assume the pressure continued until he finally agreed, a few years later. However, the studying may also have been happening privately long before the public became aware that it was happening." In the end, the experience must not have been all negative because Dylan continued his association with the Jewish rabbis in the coming years despite his continued Christianity.[25]

In 1984, Dylan told *Rolling Stone* that the Old Testament and New Testament were "equally valid" to him. He also said, "I believe in the Book of Revelation," and went on to refer to the coming Antichrist. Twenty-eight years later, he repeated the line about Revelation word-for-word to a different interviewer for the same magazine.[26] The Revelation of Jesus Christ to his disciple John is a New Testament book. During the 1984 interview, Dylan said that he could find common ground with both Christians and Orthodox Jews. He agreed that yes, he would suggest to the latter that they should look into Christianity if he were asked, but that mainly he was focused on making music.[27] Dylan was clearly uncomfortable talking about the specifics of his religion at this point in time, but his answers, terse though they may be, are still revealing.

In an interesting 1985 interview with *Spin*, Dylan asserted, "Whether you want to believe Jesus Christ is the Messiah is irrelevant, but whether you're aware of the messianic complex, that's all that's important." Even though he seemingly brushes off the importance of belief in Jesus Christ, his use of that phrase—name plus title—is important. Christ means Messiah (Greek and Hebrew words, respectively, for "Anointed One"). No Orthodox Jew would call Jesus of Nazareth "Jesus Christ" because it would be calling him the Messiah. Dylan continued, "This world is scheduled to go for 7,000 years. Six thousand years of this, where man has his way, and 1,000 years when God has His way. Just like a week. Six days work, one day rest. The last thousand years is called the Messianic Age. Messiah will rule. He is, was, and will be about God, doing God's business."[28] While there are parallels to the Old Testament, this is straight out of the New Testament. Revelation chapter 20 identifies the time period, and this is known as the "Millennium" (1,000 years).

Describing the Great Tribulation that precedes the Millennium, Dylan mentioned the "mark of the beast" from Revelation (chapter 13) and said,

> People don't know how to feel holy... They don't know what God wants of them. They'll want to know what the Messiah wants... People are going to be running to find out about God, and who are they going to run to? They're gonna run to the Jews 'cause the Jews wrote the book,

and you know what? The Jews ain't gonna know. They're too busy in the fur business and in the pawnshops and in sending their kids to some atheist school. People who believe in the coming of the Messiah live their lives right now as if he was here... The scriptures back me up. I didn't ask to know this stuff. It just came to me at different times from experiences throughout my life. Other than that, I'm just a rock 'n' roller, folk poet, gospel-blues-protest guitar player.[29]

During his 1986 world tour, Dylan introduced the song "In the Garden," from the album *Saved*, by saying, "I want to sing you a song about my hero." This was not the act of an Orthodox Jew since the song is all about Jesus Christ as Lord and Savior. Dylan sang both the black spiritual "Go Down, Moses" and his own "In the Garden"—upholding both the Old and New Testaments—when he performed in Tel Aviv, Israel, in September 1987. Two days later, he closed his concert in Jerusalem with "Gotta Serve Somebody" and "Slow Train."[30]

Dylan the Christian: A Passing Phase?

Like a submarine, Dylan's faith has been mostly submerged since 1981. This does not mean that it has disappeared. Dylan's concert set lists (including his choice of cover songs), his cagey-yet-illuminating interview remarks, and his use of biblical language, including New Testament words, in his songs all attest to his continued Christianity.[31] In addition to evidence cited earlier, in connection with the Judaism rumors, there are many things that can be mentioned from 1983 through 2015.

Within a year or two of his conversion, Dylan was estranged from the evangelical wing of institutional Christianity. The self-serving, short-sighted, and spiritually tone deaf reaction of San Francisco churches when he sought to involve them in his music ministry was a harbinger of things to come. His personal assistant at the time, Dave Kelly, recalls the believers who should have rallied around Dylan and helped him as a new convert:

> They didn't see him changing the way they thought he should change...He never really was embraced by the church. What they're judging is outward social activities and how he should act and how he should talk...He doesn't have a pastor that nurtured him. The pastor [Kenn Gulliksen] who brought him to the Lord...[was preoccupied with personal issues] almost immediately after he brought Bob into the church...And that was pretty devastating to him.[32]

In July 1983, Dylan was interviewed by Martin Keller of *City Pages*, a Minneapolis publication, and the interview was widely syndicated. He was getting ready to release *Infidels*. Keller told Dylan, in connection with the line in "Man of Peace" about Satan, "People hearing that may take it to mean that you're still involved with Christianity." Dylan responded, "So what if they say that?" He told Keller that *Shot of Love* was his favorite album, going on to say, "To those who care now where Bob Dylan is at, they should listen to *Shot of Love* off the *Shot of Love* album. It's my most perfect song. It defines where I am at spiritually, musically, romantically and whatever else. It shows where my sympathies lie. No need to wonder if I'm this or that. I'm not hiding anything. It's all there in that one song." In 1984, he told MTV that *Shot of Love* remained his favorite album.[33] The song "Shot of Love" includes a clear reference to following Jesus, specifically the cost of discipleship.[34] Meanwhile, the new album, *Infidels*, was full of biblical imagery, including references to both Christ and Antichrist.

When asked, in October 1983, if he still considered himself to be born again, Dylan said, "I don't think it is relevant right now. First of all 'born again' is a hype term. It's a media term that throws people into a corner and leaves them there. Whether people realize it or not, all these political and religious labels are irrelevant. That was all part of my experience. It had to happen. When I get involved in something, I get totally involved." When asked if he regretted anything from the *Slow Train Coming* period, he responded, "I don't particularly regret telling people how to get their souls saved. I don't particularly regret any of that. Whoever was supposed to pick it up, picked it up. But maybe the time for me to say that has come and gone. Now it's time for me to do something else... Jesus himself only preached for three years." When asked if he planned to do some of his *Slow Train Coming* songs on future tours, he said, "Yeah. I'll probably do a few of those. I get letters from people who say they were touched by those [gospel] shows. I don't disavow any of that."[35]

Not wanting the media to throw him into a corner, he distanced himself even more from the "born-again" label in 1984. When Kurt Loder of *Rolling Stone* asked if his three 1979–81 albums were not "inspired by some sort of born-again religious experience," Dylan answered, "I would never call it that. I've never said I'm born again. That's just a media term. I don't think I've ever been an agnostic. I've always thought there's a superior power, that this is not the real world and that there's a world to come." Dylan was dodging the label by 1983–84 for good reason, but his statement was clearly inaccurate. Jesus used the born-again phrase with Nicodemus. In an interview with Karen Hughes in May 1980, Dylan had said, "Being born again is a hard thing... Conversion takes time because you have to learn to crawl before you can walk... You're re-born but like a baby." In an interview with Robert Hilburn in November 1980, Dylan had said, "I truly had a born-again experience, if you want to call it that. It's an over-used expression, but it's something that people can relate to. It happened in 1978."[36] Already by the time of this Hilburn interview, Dylan had grown a bit leery of the "born-again" designation. His concern grew as he saw how it was used to dismiss his music and thought.

Interview magazine later published some outtakes from Scott Cohen's *Spin* interview of September 1985. In response to the prompt "One Last Favor I'd Like to Ask," Dylan said, "Resist not evil, but overcome evil with good." When asked to identify "Several Things Still Blowin' in the Wind," Dylan's second answer was "the wages of sin." His responses were quotations from three New Testament verses—one by Jesus and two by Paul. The verse containing Paul's warning about sin makes reference to "Christ Jesus our Lord."[37]

In an interview with Denise Worrell, in 1985, Dylan commented, "I don't think each person has his own individual truth. How could you have your own personal truth? Who would give it to you?" He was quite revealing when asked about his religion:

> I don't want to talk about what I've become or became because that sets people off into role playing... So, whatever it is that I am manifests itself through what I do, what I say, not by what title I want to put on myself, or other people may want to put on me. That's why I've stayed away from all that stuff all the time. I mean, I know you can call somebody something like "born again" and then you can dismiss that. As long as you can deal with it on a level of, like, a cartoon, you can dismiss it.

In an interview with *Newsweek*, in 1997, Dylan recalled a momentous event during his European tour with Tom Petty and the Heartbreakers from a decade earlier. On October 5, 1987, in Locarno, Switzerland, he had an epiphany. (His memoir calls it a "metamorphosis.") Contemplating retirement from music and having a crisis of direction, that night Dylan gained new energy and new purpose. A line came to him: "It's almost like I heard it as a voice. It wasn't like it was even me thinking it. *I'm determined to stand, whether God will deliver me or not.* All of a sudden, everything just exploded."[38] Dylan's line is paralleled in Daniel 3:10–18. Dylan has been steeped in the apocalyptic portions of the Bible since his conversion in 1978–79. Daniel ranks right beside Revelation as a primary source of End-Times information. A Dylan thought or Divine message echoing the book of Daniel, with its emphasis on defying the evils of Babylon while living in its midst, makes perfect sense.[39]

Honored for Lifetime Achievement at the Grammy Awards, in February 1991, Dylan gave an unusual acceptance speech. He quoted his father as saying, "Son... you know it's possible to become so defiled in this world that your own mother and father will abandon you. And if that happens, God will always believe in your own ability to mend your own ways."[40]

In a March 1991 interview with Eliot Mintz, Dylan spoke against the desire for a *legacy* because the word is linked to *legend*, which in turn is linked to *legion*. For Dylan, that is a problem because Legion is a name for the Devil, referring to a New Testament encounter between Jesus and a demon-possessed man. He said, "If you try to attain some type of righteousness in this world you don't want to leave a legacy." He linked legacy with pride, which leads to downfall. Discussing "Every Grain of Sand," from *Shot of Love*, Dylan reiterated Jesus's comment that the hairs on our head are numbered and his belief in a God of purpose.[41] A dozen years after performing the contemporary Christian song "Rise Again" in concert, Dylan recorded it in the studio in June 1992, with a Chicago choir.[42] It is a song about the crucifixion and resurrection of Jesus.

In his October 1997 interview with *Newsweek*, Dylan said, "Here's the thing with me and the religious thing. This is the flat-out truth: I find the religiosity and philosophy in the music. I don't find it anywhere else. Songs like 'Let Me Rest on a Peaceful Mountain' or 'I Saw the Light'—that's my religion. I don't adhere to rabbis, preachers, evangelists, all of that. I've learned more from the songs... The songs are my lexicon. I believe the songs."[43] Despite the claim of being truthful, this is not the whole truth. Clearly, Dylan also finds important things in the Bible. But the statement reflects his anarchistic, individualistic approach to life, his distrust of human authority—partly coming from a long-held philosophy and partly coming from rejection by the institutional church in 1979–80. The first song Dylan mentions was by the Stanley Brothers and is a song of family and home more than of faith. The second song, by Hank Williams, is a gospel song that specifically identifies Jesus as the Savior.

In December 1997, Dylan was a recipient of the Kennedy Center Honors Lifetime Achievement Award. He chose three songs to be performed for the televised concert event: "The Times They Are A-Changin'" (performed by Bruce Springsteen), "Don't Think Twice, It's All Right" (David Ball), and "Gotta Serve Somebody" (Shirley Caesar). It is significant that Dylan chose his hit Christian song as the only example of his post-early-1960s work. Dylan was clearly pleased with Caesar's performance.[44]

From 1999 through 2002, Dylan repeatedly sang covers of southern gospel songs in concert, including "This World Can't Stand Long" (almost 40 times) and "I Am the Man, Thomas" (almost 60 times). The first, popularized by Roy Acuff, is an apocalyptic song. The second, by Ralph Stanley, is about the resurrected Jesus showing his nail-scarred hands to his doubting disciple. In his Oscar-winning song "Things Have Changed" (2000), Dylan mentions the Bible's apocalyptic warning about the world. Over 20 years after its last live appearance, Dylan began singing "Saving Grace" again in 2003 and has sung it 16 times since.

Modern Times was released in 2006. It was full of biblical imagery.[45] *Together through Life* was released in 2009. In comparison to *Modern Times*, there was much less spiritual content. Dylan worked with former Grateful Dead lyricist Robert Hunter on the songs. The only song that had clear biblical references was the only song Dylan wrote by himself: "This Dream of You." It had three New Testament allusions.[46]

Later in 2009, Dylan surprised people by releasing a Christmas album that combined his ragged voice with smooth arrangements and female backup singers reminiscent of the 1950s. People wondered if *Christmas in the Heart* was a joke or satire. It was sincere. Dylan included secular songs celebrating season, snow, and Santa, but also religious songs devoted to the birth of Jesus. In November 2009, Dylan gave an interview promoting the Christmas CD that was published by the North American Street Newspaper Association. The interviewer, Bill Flanagan, told Dylan that he sounded like a true believer on "O Little Town of Bethlehem." Dylan replied, "Well, I am a true believer." When asked if he had a favorite Christmas album, he replied, "Maybe the Louvin Brothers. I like all the religious Christmas albums. The ones in Latin. The songs I sang as a kid." Flanagan noted, "A lot of people like the secular ones," which prompted Dylan's response, "Religion isn't meant for everybody."[47]

Dylan's *Tempest* album, released in 2012, was not what he had originally intended. He told Mikal Gilmore, "I wanted to make something more religious. I just didn't have enough. Intentionally, specifically religious songs is what I wanted to do." He added that it takes considerably more concentration to successfully record ten songs on the same religious theme than it does to assemble something like *Tempest*.[48] Apparently, Dylan was planning a sequel to *Saved* or *Shot of Love*. Even as recorded, *Tempest* was an outgrowth of Christian religion.[49]

When we consider Dylan's recorded output during the past 30 years, the only other main component, besides Christian spirituality, is the love songs that he has included on his albums since *Freewheelin'*. There is a bit of overt sociopolitical content, which will be noted elsewhere, but not much.

There are no lyrics of rabbinic Judaism or political Zionism. There are no suggestions that Dylan is interested in atheism or astrology, Buddhism or Hinduism. The Christian influence stands out.

A full-length interview of Dylan by Mikal Gilmore was published later in 2012. He told *Rolling Stone*, "No kind of life is fulfilling if your soul hasn't been redeemed." Asked about specious accusations of plagiarism in recent years, Dylan was defiant: "These are the same people that tried to pin the name Judas on me. Judas, the most hated name in human history!... Yeah, and for what? For playing an electric guitar? As if that is in some kind of way equitable to betraying our Lord and delivering him up to be crucified. All those evil motherfuckers can rot in hell."[50] Over 30 years after his conversion, Dylan's words during this interview make his spiritual allegiance crystal clear. Even if we had no other evidence concerning the status of Dylan's faith today, these three words—"betraying our Lord"—would be enough.[51]

As Dylan himself explained in his 1983 interview with Robert Hilburn, while he does not regret "telling people how to get their souls saved," the time for expressing that in such stark terms "has come and gone." He noted that even Jesus's preaching ministry only lasted three years. Dave Kelly observes that while many evangelical Christians in the 1980s thought that Dylan "should be an evangelist his entire life," this was not his calling. It was "a momentary thing" coming from "the zeal of a new convert." Kelly explains: "He's done it as good as anybody could ever do it. No need to continue to do it... He's an artist. And he stopped for a moment being a pure artist and went into what any new convert would do... he went into an evangelistic kind of outreach: 'Let me tell you, you gotta listen to the Lord.' Preaching salvation. But he's a prophet. He doesn't see himself as a preacher at all."[52]

Because Dylan was largely abandoned by fellow evangelicals in the early 1980s, Kelly thinks that he may have "stunted growth in certain areas that Christians would consider vital." Referring to the man who hired him in 1979, as he prepared to go out on the road for the first time as a believer, Kelly says, "But it doesn't change his view of Christ. 'Is Christ the Savior or not?' is what separates a Christian from the non-Christian, really. It's the Savior himself and the need for the atonement. And that's never gonna be gone. 'Cause once you know that's true, you know it's true."

Dylan continues to vocalize his Christian faith through music and interviews. Most evangelical Christians—infatuated with popularity, ambition, power, money, and other worldly values—long ago wrote off Dylan as the big one who got away. They are no longer interested in Dylan because they have a shallow understanding of what it means to be a Christian and he has chosen to stay away from the Contemporary Christian Music and Religious Right subcultures. We may conclude that Bob Dylan is a private, sensitive individual who refuses to cheapen his relationship with the Savior in order to please evangelical Christendom and refuses to end that relationship in order to please the materialistic, self-satisfied, God-rejecting world system. In this age, that leaves him in a kind of no-man's-land—which may be fitting for a man who has a prophetic calling.

Niebuhr's Christ and Culture

H. Richard Niebuhr's book *Christ and Culture* was first published in 1951 but has had lasting influence because he created a model that is time transcendent. Its ongoing relevance can be seen in the thought and music of Bob Dylan beginning with his conversion to Christianity in 1978–79. Niebuhr, a professor of Theology and Christian Ethics at Yale Divinity School, belonged to the neo-orthodox school of Protestant theology. Neo-orthodoxy was developed by Swiss and German theologians, most notably Karl Barth, in the years following World War I. Richard Niebuhr's more famous brother was fellow theologian Reinhold Niebuhr of Union Theological Seminary.

Richard Niebuhr devised a classic framework for analyzing the relationship between Christianity and the world. He identified five responses to the question, "How should the church relate to the surrounding culture?": Christ Against Culture, Christ of Culture, Christ Above Culture, Christ and Culture in Paradox, and Christ the Transformer of Culture.

Niebuhr also calls the Christ Against Culture position the New Law type and Radical Christianity. Referring to those who hold this position, Niebuhr speaks of

> their common acknowledgment of the sole authority of Jesus Christ and the common rejection of the prevailing culture. Whether that culture calls itself Christian or not is of no importance, for to these men it is always pagan and corrupt. Neither is it of first-rate significance whether such Christians think in apocalyptic or in mystical terms. As apocalyptics they will prophesy the early passing of the old society and the coming into history of a new divine order. As mystics they will experience and announce the reality of an eternal order hidden by the specious temporal and cultural scene.[53]

For each of the five Christian cultural positions, Niebuhr identifies several examples from church history. For Christ Against Culture, he identifies the apostle John (specifically, the letter of I John); Tertullian (third-century theologian, known as the Father of Western Christian Thought for his extensive writings in Latin); Anabaptists (Mennonites, Amish, and other groups with roots in the sixteenth-century radical wing of the Protestant Reformation); Society of Friends (George Fox, John Woolman, and other Quakers during the first century or two of their existence); Leo Tolstoy (Russian novelist and social philosopher); and Søren Kierkegaard (Danish philosopher and Lutheran). Two decades after Niebuhr was writing, the Jesus People Movement in the United States would exemplify the same tendencies. The ideology of Christian Anarchism is associated with this position (see chapter 5). Bob Dylan is an example of someone who, for the most part, identifies with Christ Against Culture.

The Christ of Culture position, also known as the Natural Law type and Accomodationism, does not see any conflict between Christ and culture (or at least the dominant culture to which such Christians belong). Seeing harmony between the church and the world, human nature is seen as basically good, sin is underplayed, and reason is exalted. It is the opposite of Christ Against Culture. In the American context, this cultural assimilation of Christians includes both upper-class capitalists—with the Rockefeller family at the center of theological modernism ("liberalism") in the twentieth century—but also less-affluent fundamentalists and evangelicals.[54]

The Christ Above Culture position, also known as Synthesis, sees unity between Christ and culture but also sees the two as distinct. It is cooperation without merger, like two horses harnessed together pulling in the same direction while each maintaining its identity. The difference between the two is maintained and Christ, as revealed in Scripture and church tradition, is given priority in a way that is not to be found with the Christ of Culture position. Room is found for theology *and* philosophy, supernature *and* nature, revelation *and* reason. The world (as distinct from the church) is viewed more positively than by the Christ Against Culture and Christ and Culture in Paradox positions, but less positively than by the Christ of Culture position.

The Christ and Culture in Paradox position, also known as the Oscillatory type or Dualism, argues in favor of a both-and approach. There is considerable polarity and tension between the church and the world, but the latter is not as fully rejected as with the Christ Against Culture position. At the same time, an emphasis on the Fall, human sin, and divine grace is more common with this position than with Christ of Culture and Christ Above Culture. All of human life is tainted by sin but this does not mean that the mundane aspects of human life are scorned or shunned. Culture is fallen but is still part of God's providential plan and Christians have roles to play in culture. Dualists embrace the ethic of being "in the world but not of the world."

The Christ the Transformer of Culture position, also known as the Conversionist type, agrees with the Against and Paradox positions about the prevalence of sin in culture but also believes that God's sovereign rule extends to culture and Christians are therefore called to be involved. This involvement consists of transforming those parts of culture in need of change and bringing them into conformity with God's will, thereby building the Kingdom of God on earth. This position has a more positive view of culture than Against and Paradox partly because it stresses the goodness of God's creation—beginning the scriptural narrative not with redemption but with creation.[55] Human culture has great potential for good because what the Fall perverted can be restored through conversion. This is conversion not only of individuals but also of structures and practices.

If we think of Niebuhr's positions on a linear spectrum running from hostility toward culture on the left side to embrace of culture on the right side, the positions would be in this order: Christ Against Culture, Christ and Culture in Paradox, Christ Above Culture, and Christ of Culture. Christ the Transformer of Culture transcends the spectrum because it contains elements of the other four positions. As with Christ of Culture, there are Christians of opposing political points of view that share the Transformationist position. The content of the transformation may be quite different even as the theological justification for seeking such transformation is similar.

Dylan and Culture

The life and writing of Bob Dylan exemplify a type of Christian engagement with popular culture that is mostly antithetical. Dylan influenced pop culture and made a name for himself, in the early 1960s, as a talented and perceptive creator of protest songs. As he moved from overt, sociopolitical "finger-pointing" material to introspective, psychedelic "folk-rock" material, he retained his adversarial stance vis-à-vis the dominant trends and institutions of society. His conversion to Christianity in 1978 did not symbolize a renunciation of his countercultural stance. Rather, it was a clarifying, broadening, and deepening of his position.

During the past three decades, Dylan's Christian perspective has been woven like a thread through his songs (both recorded originals and performed covers). His theology is based on three sources: the ancient Jewish prophetic tradition, the Jesus Movement tradition coming out of the early 1970s, and the Christian tradition in folk-country-and-blues music. The example of Dylan reminds us that engagement with popular culture does not have to mean endorsement or emulation. It also reminds us that a transformative approach to culture does not have to mean involvement in electoral politics or government. Dylan remains apolitical, which is, in itself, both an engagement with and a rejection of our culture. Dylan's emphasis on what Kuyper called *antithesis* is not the whole story, for a Christian world and life view, but it is part of the story.

If Bob Dylan were an isolated example of an artistic, intelligent Christian who has dabbled in theology, his perspective would be of limited value for the wider community of Christians. But we can place Dylan in a wider context of a distinct and important tendency within Christianity. Thinking of Niebuhr's five types of Christian response to culture, Dylan is clearly in the Christ Against Culture camp. He "uncompromisingly affirms the sole authority of Christ over the Christian and resolutely rejects culture's claims to loyalty." One of Dylan's favorite books of the Bible is Revelation, which is "radical in its rejection of 'the world.'"[56]

Dylan's conversion to Christianity in 1978 occurred in the context of the southern California-based Jesus People Movement of the late 1960s and early 1970s. The so-called Jesus Freaks and their allies sought a restoration of the purity and simplicity of the first-century church. This included an emphasis on contemporary social ethics but also an eschatological yearning for the Second Coming. The apocalyptic aspect of the movement was seen in the popularity of musician Larry Norman's song "I Wish We'd All Been Ready" and writer Hal Lindsey's best-selling book *The Late Great Planet Earth*. After his conversion, Dylan went through a period of intense Scripture study under the teaching of ministers connected with Vineyard Christian Fellowship, a loose-knit denomination that began as a Bible study in the Hollywood living room of Norman. The Bible teaching included an emphasis on Revelation, the Olivet Discourse of Christ (Matthew 24–25), and the Old Testament prophetic books, as understood by dispensational premillennial theology. This was the kind of Bible prophecy popularized by Lindsey in the 1970s. (See chapters 5 and 6 for details.)

While Niebuhr mitigates the anticulture nature of Revelation because it was written in the context of Roman persecution, the Jesus People and Dylan did not see the book as dated or fulfilled. One of the unique aspects of Dylan's concert tour in 1979–80 is that he spent considerable time between songs giving Bible-based insights and advice to his audiences. Many longtime fans were confused and angry. Coupled with Dylan's refusal to sing any of his old, pre-Christian songs, some fans heckled, others walked out. It began hurting ticket sales as word of the new, religious Dylan began spreading in the media. In 1979, Dylan told a radio interviewer, "People say, 'Bob don't do that stuff.' It may be costing me a lot of fans. Maybe I'll have to start singing on street corners. Still I'll give all praise and glory to God." On the stage in San Francisco, he remarked, "Hmm. Pretty rude bunch tonight...You know about the spirit of the Anti-Christ? Does anyone here know about that? Ah, the spirit of the Anti-Christ is loose right now...If you want rock'n roll, you go down and rock'n roll. You can go and see Kiss and you can rock'n roll all the way down to the pit!"[57]

As a new Christian, on tour in 1979–80, Dylan made use of his famous 1960s persona to promote the gospel. In Omaha, he said, "Years ago they...said I was a prophet. I used to say, 'No I'm not a prophet.' They say, 'Yes you are, you're a prophet.' I said, 'No it's not me.' They used to say, 'You sure are a prophet.'...Now I come out and say Jesus Christ is the answer. They say, 'Bob Dylan's no prophet.' They just can't handle it." When a fan in San Francisco shouted the Dylan lyric about getting stoned, from "Rainy Day Women #12 & 35," while he was speaking about Scripture, he used the interruption to segue into introducing the next song: "Hangin' on to a Solid Rock Made Before the Foundation of the World." At a concert in Hartford, he recalled singing songs during a 1965 appearance in the city: "One was a song called *Desolation Row*. Huh? You're clapping now, you weren't clapping then...They didn't understand what I was singing about. I don't think I did either [laughs]...So it must have taken a while for *Desolation Row, Maggie's Farm, Subterranean Homesick Blues* and all that stuff to catch on, because it wasn't accepted very well at the time."[58]

Many of Dylan's mini-sermons focused on the End Times. In San Francisco, he said, "There's gonna be a war called the Battle of Armageddon which is like something you never even dreamed about. And Christ will set up His kingdom and He'll rule it from Jerusalem. I know, far out as that may seem this is what the Bible says." In Albuquerque, he said, "I told you 'The Times They Are A-Changing' and they did. I said the answer was 'Blowin in the Wind' and it was. I'm telling you now that Jesus is coming back, and He is!—And there is no other way of salvation...Jesus is coming back to set up his Kingdom in Jerusalem for a thousand years."[59] Dylan's belief in a future, literal, earthly reign of Jesus Christ was in the tradition of Tertullian (AD 160–225), father of Latin theology and fellow proponent of Christ Against Culture.[60]

Church Out of World

Other major themes of the Christ Against Culture type are also present in Bob Dylan's work. For example, he recognizes the biblical and oppositional distinction between the Church and the World. This distinction is foundational to the Christ Against Culture position and is well-represented in the New Testament. The word "church" comes from *ekklesia* (*ecclesia*) in Greek, meaning assembly of the called-out ones.[61] The Church is called out of the World, as Christ himself declared.[62] (Of course, this is a spiritual separation, not a physical one.) Even earlier in

God's covenant relations with humankind, we see the same principle at work with ancient Israel. The word "holy" means "set apart." The same root gives us the words "sanctify" and "saint." Jesus prayed, "Thy kingdom come, thy will be done, on earth as it is in heaven," and told Pilate, "My kingdom is not of this world."[63]

Niebuhr is correct in pointing out the prominence of the anti-*kosmos* imperative in the writings of John—namely, Revelation and the epistles. I John is particularly emphatic, declaring, "Love not the world, neither the things that are in the world. If any man love the world, the love of the Father is not in him."[64] The Church is set in opposition to the World (as an organized system dominated by fallen, ungodly values) partly because Satan is described as the prince of this world during the present age.[65] Because of these contrasting loyalties, Christ set forth alternate ethics for an alternate society—not for some perfected future but for the fallen present, which is precisely why the commands are so difficult yet important.[66]

In addition to references in his songs, Bob Dylan made clear reference to these Christ Against Culture verities when he preached on stage in 1979–80. He told one audience, "The Bible says, 'Friendship with the world is the enemy of God.' In other words, a friend of the world is the enemy of God. I know that sounds really strange, but sometimes the truth is hard to take. But the truth will set you free." He told another crowd, "You know Satan's called the god of this world, that's true, and it's such a wonderful feeling when you get delivered from that."[67]

Of the five cultural positions defined by Niebuhr, Christ the Transformer of Culture is one of those that most encourages engagement with politics. It does so because government offers the attractive possibility of wholesale social transformation through law-making and law-enforcing. This seems to be the opposite of the apolitical Christ Against Culture position that places no faith in worldly institutions to regenerate or sanctify. Yet the two do not have to necessarily clash. They can complement. Active cultural engagement does not have to mean general cultural affirmation. Culture would not be in need of transformation if it were not seriously flawed. Abraham Kuyper, Dutch theologian and statesman from a century ago, recognized this and called it "antithesis," which means contrast or opposition...in other words, "against."[68]

During a London radio interview in 1981, Dylan expressed the hope that his music, over the years, had been "a healing kind of music" because there was too much "sick music" in the world: "It's made by sick people, and it's played to sick people to further a whole world of sickness." In "Things Have Changed" (2000), Dylan declared that all of the world's truth is nothing more than "one big lie."[69]

Spiritual Maturity and Artistic Nuance

In trying to engage culture during his early days as a Christian, Dylan sometimes sounded superficial and seemed ham-fisted. He was often criticized for sounding like a second-rate Moral Majority scold during his *Slow Train Coming* period. Even some of his sympathetic fans cringed at some of his lines.[70] The reference to Arabs in "Slow Train" sounded jingoistic and bigoted. Mentioning adulterers and pornography in "When You Gonna Wake Up" seemed to be a silly sounding of false alarms...although the next line was better (gangsters/power, lawbreakers/rules).[71] One critic attributed such clunker lines to "sloppy writing" and Dylan's desire to "make a conscious connection for the public between the early 'protest-singer' Dylan (still his best-known image) and the present-day born-again Dylan."[72] While this is probably true, spiritual immaturity was probably also a factor.

In 1979, Dylan linked his gospel rap in concert one night to the brand-new Iranian hostage crisis, referring to the Shah of Iran having "plundered the country, murdered a lot of people, escaped." He went on: "Now here's what Jesus would have done. Jesus would have gone back. See, that's what Jesus did."[73] He had a point, but such a simplistic approach whereby every current event is merely grist for the evangelistic mill is not the best example of Christian engagement with culture.

Six years later, Dylan exhibited considerably more spiritual depth when he discussed American culture and the ways of the world. He told an interviewer, "I've never been able to understand the seriousness of it all, the seriousness of pride. People talk, act, live as if they're never going to die. And what do they leave behind? Nothing. Nothing but a mask." He condemned the commercialization of the world in a way that went beyond Accept-Jesus-as-your-Savior-or-you'll-be-in-big-trouble:

> Everything's a business. Love, truth, beauty...Spirituality is not a business, so it's going to go against the grain of people who are trying to exploit other people...A lot of crooked people give a lot of money to charity. That all means nothing. If there's evil behind good, it doesn't make the good good. No matter how many hospitals they're building. It's all bullshit. It's called vanity of vanities. That's what the world is run on. That's how the machine turns, so if you go against that in any way, you're an outlaw.[74]

Dylan's comments about songs on his *Biograph* box set compilation (1985) also indicate a level of Christian maturity and thought that was, understandably, lacking in the 1979–80 period. In his interviews with Cameron

Crowe, printed in the booklet and on the inner sleeves, Dylan said some amazing things that are well worth reading. Commenting on "Every Grain of Sand"—one of his most beautiful, hymn-like postconversion songs—he provided all kinds of nuggets of wisdom. Dylan had not changed his commitment to revealed truth or his allegiance to Christ as king, but he had a richer vocabulary and was able to engage a wider area of culture than in earlier years. The *Biograph* booklet contained perceptive Dylan commentary on the commercialization of rock music, even if he himself would eventually succumb to the temptation (e.g., his absurd commercial for Victoria's Secret in 2004). He also contrasted more organic, genuinely talented music with popular culture.[75] Throughout his interviews, he was both very interested in the world and deeply spiritual in a way that critiqued that world. The prose of Dylan that accompanies *Biograph* is as profound and provocative as anything he wrote in the 1960s.

Since the early 1980s, Dylan has retained his faith in Christ while moving toward a more mature engagement with culture. While he is a clear example of the Christ Against Culture position, this is not to say that Dylan's stance in relation to culture and non-Christians is one of utter negativity or complete rejection. Being in oppositional mode to the world, as an organized system, does not mean opposition to every aspect of life in the world. It means rejection of the dominant spirit and direction of the world—specifically, rejection of the "'arrangement' under which Satan has organized the world of unbelieving mankind upon his cosmic principles of force, greed, selfishness, ambition, and pleasure."[76]

In 2014, after referring to his forthcoming album of Sinatra covers as containing "songs of great virtue," Bob Dylan told an interviewer, "People's lives today are filled with vice and the trappings of it. Ambition, greed and selfishness all have to do with vice...We don't see the people that vice destroys. We just see the glamour of it—everywhere we look, from billboard signs to movies, to newspapers, to magazines. We see the destruction of human life."[77]

Yet God is not absent even in such a spiritually benighted milieu. In a recent interview, Dylan remarked, "I see God's hand in everything. Every person, place and thing, every situation." This is what Abraham Kuyper called "common grace." Of course, Dylan is no Pollyanna or Pangloss. He also recognizes the existence of sin, falsehood, and evil. "Roll On John" (2012) is an example of Dylan's appreciation for art, justice, and truth flowing through humanity regardless of individual spiritual allegiance. Bob Dylan is a Christian; John Lennon was not. Yet Dylan can pay tribute to Lennon because he appreciates his positive contribution of shining a light in a dark world. With his keen sense of justice and great artistic ability, Dylan himself was a conduit of common grace in his pre-Christian years of the 1960s and 1970s.[78]

An emphasis on personal conversion rather than cultural conversion has political implications. It encourages Christian anarchism. At the same time, personal conversions produce ripple effects and there are incremental social changes that come from such individual changes. But they do not produce a wholesale transformation of culture—certainly not in a spiritual, saving sense and certainly not through government. In May 1980, Dylan told a crowd in Toledo, "Jesus is for everybody. He came to save the world, not to judge the world. Education's not gonna save you. Law's not gonna save you. Medicine's not gonna save you. Don't wait too long... Salvation begins right now, today."[79]

CHAPTER 5

Christian Anarchism

The pairing of the words *Christian* and *Anarchism* may seem an unlikely, if not impossible, marriage of ideas. Is not Christianity the defender of order and tradition? Do not God and Country fit together as appropriately as Mom and Apple Pie? What could anarchism, with its bombs and chaos, have to do with steeples and stained-glass windows?

Christian anarchism is a relatively rare ideology, in terms of number of adherents, but it is an important ideology. Christian anarchism was the political philosophy underlying much of the abolitionist movement in nineteenth-century America. It played an important role in the early days of Protestant fundamentalism. It contributed mightily to efforts on behalf of civil rights and peace during the 1960s. It encompasses various shades of theological orthodoxy. Its twentieth-century adherents ranged from one of the world's premiere novelists (Tolstoy) to one of the world's greatest songwriters (Dylan). In fact, it is the ideology most exemplified by Bob Dylan since 1979.

Dylan as Christian anarchist sounds like an exotic, maybe unbelievable, concept, but that is because Christian anarchism is rarely considered or examined. Dylan's Christian conversion was revolutionary. It affected every area of his life, including his politics. For half of his life, Dylan has been a Christian. He was converted at the age of 37. As discussed earlier, we should not think of him only as the left-wing protest singer of his youth. Even when young, he was more than that. Certainly he was more than that by the 1980s.

Anarchism

To the average person, the word "anarchy" is apt to mean chaos and violence. The word "anarchist" is likely to conjure up images of the bomb throwers and assassins of the 1890s or punk rockers and juvenile delinquents. When used in its political, nonpejorative sense, anarchy refers to the absence of political authority (i.e., no government). Using this definition, it follows that anarchists are persons who advocate the elimination of government.

Anarchism is actually a broader concept than dictionary definitions would indicate. Many persons who think of themselves as anarchists or who are sympathetic toward anarchism would not go so far as to publicly advocate the immediate abolition of all governments. As with most movements, there are gradualists as well as nongradualists when it comes to anarchism. Many anarchists realize that their utopian vision of a withered-away state is unlikely to occur in the foreseeable future. This being the case, they are content to minimize state power within the current sociopolitical context. Efforts to minimize state power may include electoral politics even though the state and its elections are rejected in theory. People who embrace or are sympathetic toward anarchism often support political decentralization. If taken to a logical conclusion, decentralization would lead to individuals governing themselves (i.e., anarchy).

Some persons would not claim the title "anarchist," but nonetheless have such a strong suspicion of human authority that they come close to anarchism. Some anarchists call themselves "libertarians" because the word "anarchist" has too much of a stigma attached to it. Others call themselves "libertarians" because they believe in a minimal state—a state far smaller and less powerful than the state taken for granted by mainstream politics—while not going so far as anarchy. In this chapter, total anarchists, quasi-anarchists, and radical libertarians will be lumped together. Broadly defined, "anarchism" includes those who favor the maximization of freedom, peace, and/or justice by eliminating, greatly minimizing, or ignoring the state.

Some anarchists are motivated primarily by a love of freedom, others by a love of peace, and still others by a love of justice. Most are motivated by a mixture of the three. Some anarchists are motivated primarily by their love of God. Some believe in violent methods, while others reject the use of violence. Some attempt to dismantle the state; others attempt to ignore it.

Diminution of state authority can be brought about in a number of ways. Most socialistic anarchists and individualistic anarchists directly attack the state, spending much time and effort attempting to eliminate it or at least severely curb its power. A frontal assault is not the only way to undercut the power and influence of human government. There are other ways that are equally, if not more, effective. Christian anarchists tend to use less obvious, less direct ways. Some are intentional, while others are unintentional byproducts of religious thought, feeling, and behavior.

Changing the world through personal example and personal dealings with others casts doubt on the efficacy of politics and the state. Awareness of the self-serving, morally corrupted nature of humanity leads to a healthy distrust of humans, including political leaders. With the republican form of government, the state is delegitimated by widespread disinterest in the political process, by the commonly held perception that most politicians are dishonest and corrupt, and by low voter turnout. Direct communion with God and direct accountability to God serve to undercut human authority (both ecclesiastical and political). The creation of a community separate from the rest of the population provides an alternative to the community controlled by the state (the separation does not need to be physical; it can be spiritual and intellectual).

"Marching to the beat of a different drummer" can be subversive when one publicly challenges fundamental assumptions of one's government.[1] As socialistic anarchist Noam Chomsky points out, this is far more threatening to the state than merely disagreeing with specific policy decisions since most people choose from a narrow range of "acceptable"—as defined by the elite/state—policy options. Knowing that we will not have lasting peace until Christ returns to earth encourages skepticism toward actions taken by political parties and governments in the name of "peace."

General Bases of Christian Anarchism

Christianity is commonly seen as a preserver of tradition, as a bulwark of social order and patriotism. A superficial understanding of history lends credence to this perception. A superficial interpretation of the New Testament also supports this perception. The apostle Paul's words to the Christians in Rome seem to settle the question of the relationship between believers and the state: it is to be a relationship of respect and obedience.[2]

As explained in chapter 4, one of the positions identified by H. Richard Niebuhr in his book *Christ and Culture*, concerning the relationship between Christianity and the world, is Christ Against Culture. Christian anarchism emanates from the Christ Against Culture position because human government is a component of human culture. Christ Against Culture has never been the predominant position in the Roman Catholic Church, the Eastern Orthodox Church, or the largest Protestant denominations, but this position is a stream of thought and action that has produced hostility, skepticism, and indifference toward the state during the past 2,000 years. Historical examples of Christian anarchism include Tertullian and the Montanists, Donatus and the Donatists, Francis of Assisi and the Franciscans, Conrad Grebel and the Swiss Brethren, Menno

Simons and the Mennonites, and George Fox and the Quakers. The Jesus People are a more recent example.

The words of Romans 13 notwithstanding, Christian anarchists in the past and present have drawn on other passages of Scripture to explain their attitudes toward the state. These passages provide the bases of Christian anarchism. There are nine general bases of Christian anarchism, each of which will be briefly considered. In addition to the general bases shared by most Christian anarchists, there are five specific bases: mystical, ecclesiological, eschatological, ethical, and countercultural.

The first general argument for anarchism concerns the sovereignty of God.[3] In "Gonna Change My Way of Thinking," Bob Dylan says that God's authority is the only true authority. He refers to the power of God being manifested through the second coming of Christ in "When He Returns." Christ's power is also mentioned in "Ain't No Man Righteous, No Not One" and "In the Garden."

The second general argument for anarchism deals with human free will.[4] Linked to his belief in liberty and perhaps drawing upon the Hebrew scriptures, Bob Dylan has always had an interest in free will. In "Highway 61 Revisited," God tells Abraham that he can do what he wants in response to the command to sacrifice his son but that there will be consequences for disobedience. A premise of "Gotta Serve Somebody" is the existence of our ability to freely choose to do this or that, to serve the Devil or the Lord. He makes the point in "Ain't No Man Righteous, No Not One" that God can set us free only after we choose to surrender to Him. In "Are You Ready?," he says that the path toward either Heaven or Hell is a decision that each of us makes. The opening verse of "License to Kill" warns about the dire consequences of poor choices coming from man's free will in connection with technology.

The third general argument for anarchism is based on original intent.[5] Bob Dylan notes that kings do not exist within the "Gates of Eden" while those outside of Eden are condemned to be owned by a succession of kings. In "Man Gave Names to All the Animals," he recognizes a type of human government or stewardship in relation to animals within Eden. Human government is unnecessary where God reigns supreme, therefore police do not exist in the "City of Gold."

The fourth general argument for anarchism is based on the universality of the Fall of humanity.[6] Bob Dylan's post-1978 songs are full of references to the universality of the Fall. *Philos* (brotherly love) is an ideal but according to "Slow Train" it is difficult to find it being practiced. In "When You Gonna Wake Up," bad systems of thought range from Marx to Kissinger, and we have a topsy-turvy world in which criminals wield power and rule breakers make laws. The titles of the songs "Ain't No Man Righteous, No Not One" and "Everything is Broken" speak for themselves. Introduction of original sin and satanic power through Adam's transgression is mentioned in "Pressing On." "Trouble" is all about the fallenness of the world. Fallen human nature is mentioned in "You Changed My Life." In "Union Sundown," we are told that violence rules the world. The dominance of corruption, greed, and power is noted in "Blind Willie McTell." The world is described as having been raped and debased, and men are described as being in chains, in "Lord Protect My Child."

The fifth general argument for anarchism concerns the nature of the New Covenant.[7] Bob Dylan's recognition that God primarily deals with individuals rather than with nation-states during the present age stretches back to the early 1960s. In "I'd Hate to Be You on That Dreadful Day," he talks about God's judgment upon the wicked after they die. Judgment of a specific type of wickedness is dealt with in "Masters of War." The accounting for deeds we do on earth that will occur after we die is mentioned in "Ain't No Man Righteous, No Not One" and "Are You Ready?"

The sixth general argument for anarchism deals with freedom from the Law. Bob Dylan has always had a rebellious, antinomian side to him. It comes out in songs that praise rebels and criminals. But this was never simple nihilism, even in the 1960s. He was making an unstated distinction between legitimate authority and illegitimate authority. As a cynic—or a realist—he believes that most human authority is illegitimate in its foundation or perverted in its practice. For example, in "No Time to Think," the foolish make laws because they enjoy hurting and imprisoning others. From a young age, Dylan has believed in moral authority and had a sense of justice (e.g., "Masters of War").

Dylan's conversion to Christianity gave a deeper spiritual dimension to his antinomianism. When gangsters are wielding power in "When You Gonna Wake Up," Dylan is condemning illegitimate authority, not authority per se. In "Gonna Change My Way of Thinking," he acknowledges the existence of good rules, including the Golden Rule, but also praises those who are guided by God ("walk in the Spirit," "led by the Spirit," as the apostle Paul puts it). Paul points to a link between our own freedom and love being given to others. He also says that if we follow the desires of the flesh (our fallen nature), we will be in bondage to sin and not able to do what we most want. But if we follow the Spirit we will not be under the Law and will be free to do the things that we most want (and which please God).[8] A parallel to the Golden Rule is found within this passage (Gal. 5:14).

According to "Trouble in Mind," Satan tries to tempt us into being a law unto ourselves. Dylan speaks negatively about criminals in the context of a "Political World." Similarly, law-breaking citizens are the evil norm in "Death is Not the End," and laws and rules being broken and bent are disparaged in "Everything is Broken." In these instances, he is referring to legitimate, God-given authority that is being ignored by the wicked. Such rejection of divine-sanctioned authority will find its culmination in the Antichrist during the Last Days. In II Thessalonians 2, the "man of lawlessness" or "man of sin" is described as a front man of Satan who claims to be God and will eventually be overthrown and destroyed when Christ returns. The law that is being broken and defied by the Antichrist is the Law of God—not the Mosaic Law but rather the eternal, universal Government of God.[9]

The concepts of law and authority are assumed to be diametrically opposed to the concepts of liberty and anarchy, but this is not necessarily true. In the proper, godly context, law and authority *free* human beings. In the improper, satanic context, lawlessness and rebellion *enslave* human beings. It is a matter of legitimacy and spirituality. Sometimes it is right to obey; sometimes it is right to revolt. Sometimes absolute monarchy is best; sometimes anarchy is best. God is able to use each of these things, depending upon who is being obeyed, who is being revolted against, who wields all of the power, and who is sanctioning the freedom.

The seventh general argument for anarchism is based on divine impartiality.[10] Bob Dylan songs speak of this basis. From the beginning of his career, Dylan's belief in equality was implicit in his music, as he notes in "My Back Pages"—a song that expresses regret for being glib, not for being egalitarian. One example is "It's Alright, Ma (I'm Only Bleeding)," which uses nakedness in connection with the President to show that no one is above human vulnerability and the rules of life. In addition to free will, another premise of "Gotta Serve Somebody" is the existence of divine impartiality—all, regardless of occupation or status, are free to choose the Devil or the Lord. The mighty have been brought low in the "City of Gold." The comedian "Lenny Bruce" exposed the misdeeds of those in high positions. In "Angelina," the high and mighty are going to be overthrown (perhaps in Jerusalem or Argentina). The people who appear to be beautiful in "Foot of Pride" are like whitewashed tombs—bearing the whorish mark of Babylon the Great and full of evil.[11]

At a concert in May 1980, drawing on the book of James and alluding to socioeconomic class, Dylan talked about how we often treat people differently because of how they dress: "We treat some persons one way, just because somebody else doesn't have as much, we treat them another way. But we've already judged that person whether we know it or not." The inner sleeve of *Shot of Love* includes a spiritually egalitarian passage from the

Gospels, in which Jesus prays, "I thank thee, O Father, Lord of heaven and earth, because thou hast hidden these things from the wise and prudent, and hast revealed them unto babes."[12]

The eighth general argument for anarchism concerns the distinction between what belongs to government and what belongs to God.[13] With emotion and eloquence, Bob Dylan spoke of how he owed his entire life to God in the songs recorded during his overtly Christian period. Examples include "I Believe in You," "Saved," "What Can I Do For You?," "Property of Jesus," "Every Grain of Sand," and "You Changed My Life."

The ninth general argument for anarchism deals with misplaced loyalty.[14] Going as far back as "With God On Our Side," Bob Dylan has been aware of potential dangers in uniting God and Country (especially in the service of war).[15] In "Ain't No Man Righteous, No Not One," he warns that salvation is not obtained through devotion to any national flag. He quotes Dr. Johnson's famous line about patriotism being the last refuge of scoundrels in "Sweetheart Like You." "Clean-Cut Kid" shows how the government—and parents—systematically use the American Dream to lead young men to destruction through "service to country" (war). The second verse of "License to Kill" may be referring to the same thing. His version of the Irish folk song "Arthur McBride" shows how streetwise young people can see through military recruiting propaganda by imperial governments. The bridge of "Trust Yourself" observes that the world, including the United States, is a land teeming with those who steal and destroy. It is a fallen land dominated by ungodly men. There is no American Exceptionalism foreign policy to be found in Dylan's theology/ideology.

In a 1986 interview, Dylan said, "I'm not particularly into this *American* thing, this Bruce Springsteen-John Cougar-'America first' thing. I feel just as strongly about the American principles as those guys do, but I personally feel that what's important is more eternal things. This American pride thing, that don't mean nothing to me. I'm more locked into what's real forever." When asked if Springsteen and Mellencamp weren't promoting certain principles that have made the country great rather than promoting jingoistic American pride, Dylan responded, "Yeah? What are those principles? Are they Biblical principles? The only principles you can find are the principles in the Bible. Proverbs has got them all."[16]

In addition to drawing upon the nine general bases of Christian anarchism, Dylan has partly based his spiritually inspired anarchism on three specific ways of viewing the world and living his life: eschatological, ethical, and countercultural. Because these three specific bases are not widely known or understood outside of certain circles within the evangelical Christian

Eschatological Basis

Bob Dylan has partly had an eschatological basis for his anarchism since 1979. Eschatology is a basis of Christian anarchism because it stresses forthcoming divine intervention in human history in order to bring about peace and justice on earth, thus encouraging people to shift their hopes from earthly politics and human government to heavenly realities and divine government. The doctrine of the second coming of Christ tends to deflate pretensions of human self-sufficiency and progress. For this examination of Christian anarchism, the word "eschatological" is more appropriate than "chiliastic," "millenarian," or "apocalyptic." Chiliastic and millenarian refer specifically to the 1,000-year reign of Christ on earth (i.e., the Millennium). *Chilioi* is Greek for "a thousand"; *mille* is Latin for "a thousand." Apocalyptic implies a battle between good and evil at the end of the age (i.e., the Great Tribulation and the Battle of Armageddon). *Apokalupsis* is Greek for "reveal" (revelation). Eschatological is a broader term that encompasses all of the events surrounding the second coming of Jesus Christ. It is a theological term referring to the study of "the last things" or "the end times." It is derived from the Greek word *eschatos*, meaning "last."

The eschatological basis has one component (millenarianism) and one implication (separatism) of special relevance to anarchism. Millenarianism refers to the millennial reign of Christ on earth. Separatism refers to separation of the church from the world. The eschatology of some Christian anarchists is characterized by millenarianism and separatism, while that of others is characterized by separatism alone. Dylan has both.

The doctrine of the Millennium teaches that the Kingdom of God will come in power and glory. Jesus's reign will be visible, tangible. Peace and plenty will exist on earth during his reign. Edenic conditions will be restored. God's promises to Israel will be fulfilled when the Davidic throne is reinstituted. The Messiah (Christ) will rule not only Israel but all nations. Although the specific length of time comes from the New Testament book of Revelation, the concept of Jesus Christ ruling on earth for 1,000 years is drawn mostly from the Old Testament. Significant portions of Isaiah, Ezekiel, and Zechariah speak of the Millennium. References to it are also found in Jeremiah, Hosea, Joel, Amos, Obadiah, Micah, Zephaniah, and Haggai.[17]

Those who possess an eschatological basis for their anarchism view the world as a conglomeration of unregenerate human beings plus the culture of that conglomeration. It is a system organized on fallen, even satanic, principles. They believe the system is covertly ruled by evil spirits.[18] They see Christianity as revolutionary. Rather than attempting to reform the world system, they believe that it must be overthrown. While the system cannot be changed, individuals can be changed through regeneration (spiritual rebirth).

During the months following his conversion, Dylan was reportedly influenced by his reading of *The Late Great Planet Earth* by Hal Lindsey, a dispensational premillennialist and Vineyard Fellowship minister. Bible passages speaking of the End Times are especially important to Dylan. This may be related to the fact that dispensationalism teaches that the End Times hold promise not only for the Church but also for Israel. (Dylan is a messianic Jew.) During the 1979–80 period, he introduced some of his songs in concert with apocalyptic words. He told one crowd, "Christ will return to set up His Kingdom in Jerusalem."[19] Dylan's eschatological songs include "Slow Train" (1979), "When He Returns" (1979), "Ye Shall Be Changed" (1979), "Are You Ready?" (1980), "The Groom's Still Waiting at the Altar" (1981), "Caribbean Wind" (1981), "Jokerman" (1983), "Man of Peace" (1983), "Ring Them Bells" (1989), "Cat's in the Well" (1990), and "Things Have Changed" (2000). Dylan accepts the New Testament teaching that the Devil "rules the world."[20]

Ethical Basis

Bob Dylan has partly had an ethical basis for his anarchism. This was true before his conversion to Christianity and has remained true since 1979. Ethics are a basis of Christian anarchism because of their emphasis on personal application of New Testament principles and exhortations, thus encouraging delegitimization of the state, which operates on the basis of opposing principles and propagates opposing exhortations. Ethics are not confined to a personal context; they also exist in a social context. Some Christian anarchists who have an ethical basis for their anarchism are theologically unorthodox humanitarians. In the cases of Tolstoy and Schweitzer, ethics were the only basis for their anarchism. One does not, however, have to be theologically unorthodox in order to possess an ethical basis. The Bible is full of ethical precepts. Theological orthodoxy can be combined with literal interpretation and conscientious application of these precepts.

The Old Testament includes many passages stressing the need for justice, honesty, and compassion, but it also includes some sub-Christian principles and practices. The New Testament is usually the source for Christian anarchists who have an ethical basis. The Sermon on the Mount is a repudiation of the principles of this world, including the principles of human government. People who are poor, hungry, and sad are pronounced "blessed." Disciples are told to turn the other cheek when struck and to love their enemies. During his years of ministry, Jesus stressed the changing of one's heart and behavior rather than the embracing of a creed or the joining of a religious organization.[21]

The ethical basis for Christian anarchism can serve to balance the separatism that is implicit in the eschatological basis. From the biblical perspective of holiness and sanctification, the separation of those who seek to be faithful to God is usually a spiritual and attitudinal separation, not a physical separation. To use a Christian cliché, believers are to be "in the world but not of the world."[22] An easier way of life, however, is to physically withdraw from the wickedness of the world, going the route of Pharisees, exclusive Christian communities, homogeneity of friends, and so on. This unbiblical type of separatism—with tendencies toward self-righteousness, self-centeredness, hyperpietism, hyperindividualism, lack of empathy, dualistic antiphysicality, gospel reductionism, and kingdom underappreciation—can be counteracted by an emphasis on biblical ethics. This separatism/ethics balance is what we see among some Christian anarchists. Dylan is one such person.

On the other hand, an overemphasis on ethics and a neglect of the eschatological can produce an unbalanced, unbiblical type of Christian humanism. The Religious Society of Friends (Quakers) is an example of an originally Christian, anarchistic group that has, for the most part, discarded its eschatological emphasis and attendant separatism. Drawing upon Schweitzer's *Quest of the Historical Jesus*, Quaker scholar Douglas Gwyn notes that George Fox and the early Friends were attempting to recover an emphasis that had been largely lost after the fourth century. Early-twentieth-century Quaker theologian Rufus Jones emphasized the mystic and ethical elements of Quakerism to the exclusion of all else. Gwyn comments,

> It would be unfair to ascribe to Rufus Jones all the excesses of his followers or to ignore his many important contributions, such as his helping to found the American Friends Service Committee. But his interpretation of Fox and early Quakerism not only missed the early Quaker vision, it imposed upon Quakerism a liberal philosophical agenda, carrying Quakers along with a cultural tide that has proven ultimately unfruitful. Liberal Quakerism partakes of an early twentieth-century optimistic humanism that seems woefully inadequate to the problems of this historic age.

Reformed philosopher James K. A. Smith has provided a more recent analysis of Christian worldliness, especially within the context of neo-Calvinism. Smith sums up his point in this way: "*Shalom* is not biblical language for progressivist social amelioration. *Shalom* is a Christ-haunted call to long for kingdom come."[23] Dylan would agree with Smith's argument and he has been able to avoid the worldliness that comes from a lopsided religion of ethics by maintaining an understanding of Christianity that is both ethical and eschatological.

What is the relationship between Christian anarchism and social justice? A majority of Christian anarchists during the past century or so have had a left-liberal tint in terms of economics and politics. The exceptions have not written forcefully or extensively on the subject of social justice, but they, too, have attempted to be faithful to biblical injunctions concerning fairness and equality. The Bible is full of exhortations of concern for the poor, the hungry, the weak, and the oppressed.[24] Many of the prophets of the Old Testament stressed the need for social justice. Jesus Christ warned that a person cannot serve both God and mammon, that it is easier for a camel to go through the eye of a needle than for a rich person to enter the kingdom of God, that people should not lay up treasures on earth and build bigger barns, that the rich man who ignored the suffering of the poor man Lazarus would not be allowed to go to Abraham's bosom, and that merchants and money changers should not turn a house of prayer into a den of thieves.

Theologically unorthodox Christian anarchists have always placed great stress on social justice. This is not surprising since their Christianity is mostly ethical in nature. A distinction can be made between those theologically orthodox Christian anarchists who stress social justice and those who stress individual conversion. Partly in reaction to the Social Gospel emphasis of the modernists, fundamentalists such as A. C. Gaebelein have stressed personal salvation by Christ's atoning death on the cross. Social implications of Christianity have been largely ignored. Most dispensationalists, pietists, mystics, and restorationists have little apparent interest in such matters. In contrast, orthodox Christians in the Anabaptist, Wesleyan, Catholic Worker, and Jesus Movement traditions are often interested in the social implications of Christianity.

Of course, individual conversion and social justice are not mutually exclusive. Many Christian anarchists embrace both. It should also be noted that addressing social justice on a mass level through grand pronouncements is not the only way of expressing social concern. It is possible to express social concern on a daily, one-on-one basis. This is especially important to keep in mind when considering the views of Christian anarchists. It is a serious mistake to define concern for social justice in terms of political activism, welfare spending by the state, and/or violent revolution (approaches favored by the National and World Councils of Churches and other distinctly unanarchistic groups). There are other equally valid ways of addressing social injustice (e.g., anonymous acts of personal charity, providing help to family members, assisting individuals through the local church). These ways are associated with the philosophy of personalism. Christian anarchist examples of personalism include Peter Maurin, Dorothy Day, Albert Schweitzer, and Bob Dylan.

Dylan depoliticized his career in 1964 but his left-liberalism has never gone away. Prior to his conversion to Christianity, his commitment to justice and equality was revealed in songs such as "Chimes of Freedom" (1964), "George Jackson" (1971), and "Hurricane" (1975). As a Christian, Dylan's songs have mostly focused on spiritual matters and human relationships but some contain references to social justice. "Gotta Serve Somebody" (1979) is built on the principle of spiritual egalitarianism. Dylan criticizes the greed and exploitation of big business' project of globalization in "Union Sundown" (1983). He extols Mahatma Gandhi, Martin Luther King, and Jesus Christ in his version of Kris Kristofferson's "They Killed Him" (1986).[25]

In 1986, Dylan said, "To me, America means the Indians. They were here and this is their country, and *all* the white men are just trespassing. We've devastated the natural resources of this country, for no particular reason except to make money and buy houses and send our kids to college and shit like that... What we did to the Indians is disgraceful. I think America, to get right, has got to start there first." A quarter of a century later, in 2012, he spoke of another deep wound in American history and culture: "This country is just too fucked up about color. It's a distraction. People at each other's throats just because they are of a different color. It's the height of insanity, and it will hold any nation back—or any neighborhood back... It's doubtful that America's ever going to get rid of that stigmatization. It's a country founded on the backs of slaves." Dylan took a nuanced view of the Civil War: "If slavery had been given up in a more peaceful way, America would be far ahead today. Whoever invented the idea [of the southern Confederacy as the] 'lost cause'... [It was] No such thing, though there are people who still believe it."[26]

When asked, in 1986, if he was disturbed by preachers "who claim that to be a good Christian one must also be a political conservative," Dylan was skeptical that Christianity can be equated with conservatism. He noted, "Jesus said that it's harder for a rich man to enter the kingdom of heaven than it is for a camel to enter the eye of a needle." Following in the footsteps of the Restorationist wing of the Charismatic Movement, as exemplified by

Chuck Smith of Calvary Chapel and the ministers of Vineyard Fellowship, Dylan disliked the Prosperity wing. At a concert in May 1980, Dylan spent a little time discussing this. Quoting some who say, "If you accept Jesus, everything's gonna be fine," Dylan commented, "That's not necessarily true." He referred to preachers of the "Prosperity Doctrine" who go around saying, "Well, it's your right to have anything you want." While acknowledging that God will meet our needs, he told the crowd that the gospel message must be balanced and implied that such Prosperity preachers would not be going to heaven. In an outtake from Scott Cohen's *Spin* interview in September 1985, Dylan was asked to identify three pet peeves. His first answer was: "Preachers who preach the 'Wealth and Prosperity' doctrine." In the 1986 interview mentioned earlier, he told *Rolling Stone*, "I've heard a lot of preachers say how God wants everybody to be wealthy and healthy. Well, it doesn't say that in the Bible. You can twist anybody's words, but that's only for fools and people who follow fools." He finished with a warning against being "entangled in the snares of this world."[27]

Dylan's interest in social justice can also be seen in his willingness to participate in various music benefits during the 1980s (e.g., USA for Africa recording session, Live Aid concert, Farm Aid concert). In some ways echoing his "Chimes of Freedom" (1964), Dylan's song "Ring Them Bells" (1989) shows concern for the poor, the lost, the blind, the deaf, and the innocent. In his 2003 version of "Gonna Change My Way of Thinking," recorded with Mavis Staples for a CD celebrating his gospel period (1979–80), Dylan comes up with almost entirely new lyrics, including a cynical reference to how, in our present age, the golden rule means that those with the gold rule. Dylan's "Workingman's Blues #2" (2006) begins with a lament for the proletariat's declining economic power and the low-wage effects of globalization.[28] "Ain't Talkin'" (2006), on the same album, speaks of being crushed by power and wealth.

Most Christian anarchists during the past century or so have been pacifists or quasi-pacifists when it comes to conflict and war. Among such Christians, there has been a preference for peace even in the face of patriotic jingoism. This is not surprising since war is a project of government—big, expensive, violent, invasive, restricting, propagandizing government—and anarchists are skeptical of government. Also, Christian anarchists tend to interpret the Bible literally and literal interpretation of the New Testament tends to yield a mandate of nonviolence for Christians. The Old Testament includes cases of divinely sanctioned warfare but also includes signs of a peace ethic: human violence cited as a cause of the Great Flood, the sixth commandment ("Thou shalt not kill"), King David not allowed to build the Temple because he shed too much blood and waged too many wars, and the promise of peace on earth during Christ's millennial reign. Christ's Sermon on the Mount is pacifistic in nature ("Blessed are the peacemakers"; "Love your enemies"), with his saying about turning the other cheek being an aspiration associated with Christian nonviolence.[29]

Theologically unorthodox Christians often contend that the simple, radical message of Jesus was twisted by Paul and other early church leaders. In terms of pacifism, Paul's message coincided with Jesus's message. The book of Revelation prophesies a world government headed by the Antichrist during the last days. The Antichrist will come to power amid promises of world peace but his actions will lead to the Battle of Armageddon.[30] This eschatological scenario partly explains why some Christians oppose political centralization on a global scale and are suspicious of international peace initiatives by politicians.

As we shall see in chapter 7, Dylan combines an emphasis on Bible prophecy, mostly acquired in 1979, with foreign policy emphases that echo the traditions of his home state (Minnesota) and home region (Upper Midwest). Emphases of American patriotism, nationalism over internationalism, peace over war, hostility toward the military-industrial complex, and suspicion that wealthy Northeastern interests drive US foreign policy can be found in Dylan's songs and comments throughout the 1960s and 1970s. The Christian apocalyptic perspective was added—without logical difficulty—by the 1980s. There is continuity between "Masters of War" and "Man of Peace." The first is about open enemies of peace (1963); the second is about a false friend of peace (1983).[31]

Countercultural Basis

Bob Dylan has partly had a countercultural basis for his anarchism. While he had never been an intentional leader of the American Counterculture of the late 1960s and early 1970s, he had been one of its heroes. When he became a Christian in late 1978, it is perhaps not surprising that he did so through the instrumentality of the Christian subculture of the southern California counterculture. Subculture member and 1979–80 Dylan associate Dave Kelly describes these believers as "the classic California hippie Christians."[32]

The Christian counterculture is a basis of Christian anarchism because it stresses the inner life over the outer life, the existence of an alternative society, forthcoming divine intervention in human history, personal application of New Testament principles and exhortations, and the value of some of the ideas of the New Left and the secular Counterculture. These emphases encourage freedom from human authority within the church, a shift of attention from the state to the church, a shift of hopes from earthly politics and human government to heavenly realities and divine government, delegitimization of the state, and consideration of points made by secular radicals and revolutionaries. The Christian counterculture is epitomized by the Jesus People Movement. The Jesus Movement began in 1967, exploded in 1969, and dissipated in 1973. Its members were known as "Street Christians," "Jesus Freaks," or "Jesus People." The movement began on the West Coast of the United States and was centered in California, but soon spread across the country and eventually to western Europe.

The countercultural basis is an amalgamation of the two previously discussed bases plus an infusion of 1960s social radicalism. Given this mixture of anarchistic influences, it is not surprising that "the Jesus People are casebook examples of the Christ-against-culture approach."[33] Since organized Christianity in America is closely tied to American culture, members of the Jesus Movement were largely indifferent or hostile toward the institutional church. The Jesus People played "a distinct kind of counter-cultural role" within the church. They were "critical of the older leadership" of the church, and they "accepted many elements of the youth culture, including individualistic apparel, the bearded, long-haired look of conventional portraits of Jesus, new forms of poster art, and a penchant for guitars and rock music."[34]

The Jesus Movement did not emphasize Roman Catholic mysticism but did focus on something that had some of the same inward, deeper-life elements: Protestant charismaticism. *Charisma* is Greek for "gift." Charismatics believe in the existence and use of all of the spiritual gifts of the New Testament, including speaking in tongues. Historically, charismatics can be traced to the Pentecostal Movement, which arose at the beginning of the twentieth century. Pentecostals, in turn, can be traced to the Holiness Movement of the late nineteenth century. The Holiness Movement emphasized sanctification as a second work of grace and opposition to social evils.

The Jesus Movement has been labeled by one church historian as "largely neo-Pentecostal." Glenn Kittler's book on the Jesus People equates the Jesus Movement with the Charismatic Movement.[35] The charismatic element was an important part of the Jesus Movement but Kittler seems to exaggerate its importance. While many, if not most, Jesus People spoke in tongues and possessed unusual spiritual gifts, some did not. Also, there were other elements of the movement that were of equal importance. And it is a mistake to try to compress the Charismatic Movement into the Jesus Movement. Neopentecostalism began spreading throughout mainline churches in the early 1960s, while the Jesus People arose in the late 1960s. Most Catholic, Episcopal, Lutheran, and Methodist charismatics did not consider themselves to be Jesus People. Most of these charismatics were older, lacked an eschatological emphasis, possessed mainstream social views, and were not hostile toward the institutional church. Kittler's view of the Jesus Movement may have been colored by his close friendship with John Sherrill, a charismatic and author of *They Speak With Other Tongues*.[36]

Despite having *glossolalia* (speaking in tongues) in common, members of organized pentecostalism were not entirely comfortable with the Jesus Movement and the reverse was also true.[37] In comparison with classical pentecostals, charismatic Jesus People tended to be less dogmatic about tongues as the evidence of Holy Spirit baptism. Speaking in tongues was an important part of the Jesus Movement, but it was "by no means the focal point of Jesus People theology."[38]

David Wilkerson, an Assemblies of God minister, was the most important link between pentecostalism and the Jesus Movement. Wilkerson first achieved national prominence ministering to gang members and drug addicts in New York City. He played a key role in starting the Charismatic Movement through the inclusion of words about the baptism of the Holy Spirit in his autobiographical *The Cross and the Switchblade*. This best-selling book was written with the assistance of the aforementioned John Sherrill. In the early 1970s, some viewed Wilkerson as "the one person probably most responsible for the great surge of the Jesus People movement." Linda Meissner, pioneer of the Jesus Movement in the Pacific Northwest, worked at Wilkerson's Teen Challenge Center in Brooklyn in the early 1960s. In the early 1970s, Wilkerson wrote the *Jesus Person Maturity Manual*. By 1980, Wilkerson was associated with Last Days Ministries, which was founded by Keith Green, a singer/songwriter who was a latter-day manifestation of the Jesus Movement.[39]

Jesus People were countercultural in how they interpreted and applied ecclesiology, eschatology, and ethics (e/e/e). The Jesus Movement emphasized *ecclesiology*. Members viewed the church as an alternative society and rejected sacralism, sacerdotalism, and denominationalism. Most were either critical of or hostile toward the institutional church. Members of the movement believed that the institutional church in the United States was no alternative to American society. For many Jesus People, "the established churches have lost significant contact with the Jesus of the New Testament...The church is viewed as just another social organization with a facade of piety whose main task is the caring and feeding of drowsy, apathetic members who are nothing more than copies of their non-church-going, establishment-oriented neighbors." In contrast, the Christian World Liberation Front proclaimed, "He [God] will unite Berkeley Christians with others throughout the world to demonstrate His alternative to the present world system in all of its manifold manifestations." In this and several other respects, Jesus People were restorationists. They saw themselves "as the church of the Book of Acts reincarnate, not as Christians standing in a line of thinkers and workers of the generations between the time of Pentecost and today."[40]

In contrast to organized Christianity, the Jesus Movement was characterized by simplicity of doctrine and worship. Many Jesus People met for worship in homes. If they had formal worship leaders, there was usually a plurality instead of one person dominating everything. Turns were often taken in giving messages of instruction. They sang simple choruses, many of which consisted of Scripture set to music. Much time was devoted to group prayer. In the early 1970s, David Wilkerson wrote,

> *This new church doesn't revolve around buildings.* It's made up of Jesus people who have cleaned up and invited the Lord to make their bodies His temple! The members of this new church worship anywhere: in homes, on the beach, in school, out in the country, anywhere two or three of them get together. They prefer $50 guitars to $50,000 organs. They prefer sitting on the floor or folding chairs rather than on expensive padded pews. They prefer going to meetings in clean, informal clothes rather than the latest fashion.[41]

Jesus People were theologically irenic, but their willingness to embrace other Christians did not mean that they favored the ecumenical approach of the National Council of Churches and the World Council of Churches. Many considered the NCC/WCC approach to be bureaucratic, apostate, and too closely tied to political and economic elites. An account at the time reported, "Pederson said he believed that the ecumenical trend in the Christian world would ultimately be brought to fulfillment from the grass roots, by the Jesus People, and not as a result of any theological or authoritarian compromises at the top." Many Jesus People identified "the institutional church, particularly in its ecumenical manifestations," with the false church of Revelation (i.e., the Great Whore of Babylon).[42]

In addition to an emphasis on a return to biblical norms through literal interpretation of the New Testament, the Jesus Movement's emphasis on ecclesiology can partly be traced to Chinese restorationist church leader Watchman Nee, who was "one of the most widely read theologians" among Jesus People.[43] Nee's writings, including *The Normal Christian Church Life* (aka *Rethinking the Work* and *Concerning Our Missions*), were quite influential in the movement.[44] Nee was influenced by the Plymouth Brethren but went beyond their approach. In the United States, one ecclesiological legacy of the Jesus People was the home church/fellowship movement associated with figures such as Gene Edwards and Charles Schmitt. The Calvary Chapel and Vineyard Fellowship denominations were more institutionalized examples of this legacy. Calvary and Vineyard are loose-knit denominations that call themselves associations of local churches. Chuck Smith was primary founder of the former; Kenn Gulliksen and John Wimber were primary founders of the latter. Gulliksen was a protégé of Smith.[45]

The Jesus Movement emphasized *eschatology*. One of the phrases frequently used by Jesus People was *maranatha* (Greek for "Come, Lord!").[46] This view of Bible prophecy came into the movement through pentecostal and neoevangelical sources as well as through Watchman Nee books. The pre-, mid-, and post-tribulationist varieties of premillennialism were found among Jesus People. Chuck Smith, pastor of Calvary Chapel, was a leading figure of the Jesus Movement and a leading teacher of eschatology for decades.[47] Love Song, a country-rock band popular among the Jesus People in the early 1970s, was a manifestation of Calvary Chapel. One of the group's notable songs was "The Cossack Song," based on a premillennial dispensational interpretation of Ezekiel 38 and 39. It was first released in 1974—five years before the Iran hostage crisis began (November 1979) and the Russian invasion of Afghanistan (December 1979), two events that brought fresh attention to Bible prophecy and helped spark Bob Dylan's apocalyptic raps in concert (1979–80).[48]

The Late Great Planet Earth by Hal Lindsey was first published in 1970 and was one of the decade's top-selling books (more than ten million copies were in print by 1978). The book had "a widespread appeal among the Jesus People."[49] Lindsey was a graduate of Dallas Theological Seminary, a dispensationalist school.[50] After resigning as a Campus Crusade for Christ staff member during the 1969–70 period, Lindsey cofounded J.C. Light and Power House in Los Angeles. By this time, Lindsey had "given up trying to sell organized religion to the younger generation."[51] Instead, he focused on teaching the Bible to Jesus People. By the late 1970s, Hal Lindsey was a pastor with Vineyard Christian Fellowship.

Singer-songwriter Larry Norman, who was under contract in the late 1960s and early 1970s with Capitol Records and MGM Records, was the "poet laureate" of the Jesus Movement.[52] Norman's career—especially during its 1969–76 zenith—was marked by a number of well-crafted eschatological songs. Examples include "Ha Ha World," "Peace, Pollution, Revolution," "U.F.O.," "The Sun Began to Rain," "Six Sixty Six," and "Hymn to the Last Generation." The most influential example is "I Wish We'd All Been Ready," with imagery borrowed from Matthew 24, in which Jesus tells his disciples about the sign of his second coming and the close of the age. Studio versions of "I Wish We'd All Been Ready" were recorded by Norman in

1969, 1972, and 1975.[53] Cover versions of the haunting song were used in the apocalyptic films *A Thief in the Night* (1972) and *Left Behind* (2014 remake with Nicolas Cage).[54] The best-selling series of Christian books that sparked the latter movie borrowed their "Left Behind" title from the chorus of "I Wish We'd All Been Ready." (Norman borrowed the word "left" from Matthew 24.)

The Jesus Movement emphasized *ethics*. Jesus People were characterized by literal interpretation and application of the New Testament. Following the words and examples of Jesus and his original disciples, they tried to simplify their lives. They tended to reject the materialism and consumerism of American culture. They attempted to live out the Sermon on the Mount, including the Beatitudes and the Golden Rule. Jesus People did not believe that good works would save them, but they believed that good works were important. The Christianity of the Jesus People was not merely ethical but it did include an important ethical dimension.

In addition to possessing the *e/e/e* Christian emphases examined earlier, the Jesus Movement was leavened by the New Left and secular Counterculture. The anarchistic nature of the eschatological and ethical bases of Christian anarchism has been examined in detail. The New Left and secular Counterculture were also anarchistic in nature. The New Left's intellectual roots were largely in the anarchistic writings of thinkers such as Henry David Thoreau, Dwight Macdonald, and C. Wright Mills.[55] While members of the Counterculture tended to be less prestigiously educated and less politically doctrinaire in comparison to members of the New Left, they shared the philosophy of anarchism. Writings produced by members of both movements in the late 1960s were clearly anarchistic.[56] Like most members of Students for a Democratic Society (New Left), members of the Counterculture had a "profound distrust of leadership and structure" and tried to create "participatory communities based on decentralized, small-scale technology and an ethic of loving mutuality."[57]

In the early 1970s, scholar Michael Lerner linked the anarchism of the Counterculture with the anarchism of Bakunin, Thoreau, and Tolstoy.[58] In the early 1990s, journalist E. J. Dionne pointed out similarities between the New Left and the Counterculture:

> To say that an individualistic, apolitical counterculture was at odds with a communitarian and political New Left is to oversimplify the complex relationship that existed between the two. Insofar as the New Leftists were launching a cultural and moral rebellion cast as a political revolt, they had much in common with their comrades in the counterculture who were battling for new "lifestyles"...The counterculture paralleled

the left in asserting the value of gentleness over competition, "peace" over "war," living by a code of authenticity today over making "opportunistic" calculations aimed at tomorrow... The convergence of the counterculture and the New Left launched one of the most subversive slogans of the era: "The personal is the political." This slogan demanded a kind of moral accountability that is rare to those involved in politics. It declared that individuals should live their private lives in ways that accorded entirely with their publicly stated principles. A gentle and egalitarian politics demanded gentle and egalitarian behavior in private. Ultimately, this helped create the women's movement.[59]

Socially speaking, this is the milieu out of which the Jesus Movement also arose. The personalism of the secular Counterculture had similarities with the personalism of Jesus, thus facilitating the transition of many Jesus People from the secular Counterculture to the religious Counterculture. An observer at the time pithily described the politics of both secular and religious counterculturalists: "One finds in the counter-culture that distinctly anarchist combination of apolitical disdain (and often ignorance of) the normal political processes combined with a passionate sense of the political responsibility of the individual."[60]

Jesus People tended to be "long-haired, hippie-looking, and alienated from the established churches." Theologically, they were fundamentalists; sociologically, they were not.[61] Many Jesus People had a background of illegal drug use. In the vernacular of the movement, young people who had been "getting high" on marijuana started "getting high" on God. Some who had been "blowing their minds" by taking LSD began "blowing their minds" by reading the Bible. "Speed freaks" became "Jesus freaks." "Flower children" became "children of God." "Street people" began looking forward to "streets paved with gold." The "Age of Aquarius" was traded for the "End of the Age." Like hippies of the late 1960s and early 1970s, Jesus People were attracted to communal living. They had the further example of some of the early Christians, who "had all things in common" and distributed "to each as any had need." Communes were "sprinkled throughout" the Jesus Movement. The secular Counterculture rejected the materialism and consumerism of mainstream, bourgeois society. The religious Counterculture also tended to reject these social traits.[62]

The anarchistic nature of the Jesus Movement is clear from comments by and about Jesus People in the early 1970s. The Christian World Liberation Front (CWLF) "was usually on the same side with the [New Left] radicals in terms of criticizing the Establishment, but the big difference was in the approach to the solutions. The Front said: 'You can't change the System by destroying it. You've got to change people.'" Duane Pederson, publisher of the *Hollywood Free Paper*, took the same approach to sociopolitical problems: "There is only one real solution to our messed up and confused society...The only one that will be lasting and permanent...is to change people...Then, with changed people, we can have a completely changed society."[63] When Chuck Smith of Calvary Chapel was asked, "Is it your idea, then, to send Jesus People out across the country and have them become part of the society where they settle down?" Smith answered,

> I hope not. I think society stinks. Our prayer is that the Jesus People will *convert* the communities where they settle down...We don't have a pollution problem by accident. We don't have a drug problem just because of the pressures of peer groups. We don't have wars just because there is no other way to settle disputes. We don't have corruption in government just because there are weaknesses in our form of democracy. People—society—have brought these problems upon us because people are greedy and materialistic and deceitful and un-loving.[64]

Larry Norman was dismissive of politicians and encouraging of change through personal transformation in his composition "A Song Won't Stop the World" (1969).[65] In the folk protest song "The Great American Novel" (1972), he was even more critical of pretentious-and-false politicians and suggested that perhaps we should all stop voting. "Right Here in America" (1970–71) expressed his view that the church, not the state, is the instrument for saving individuals and bettering society. In the same song, Norman argued that if young Americans stopped marching for peace and started marching for Jesus, then peace would take care of itself. In "Peace, Pollution, Revolution," Norman referred to attendance at peace marches in Washington (1965–70), the Democratic National Convention in Chicago (1968), and the Toronto Rock and Roll Revival (1969) but then concluded that such activities were a waste of time and recommended watching prophetic events in the Middle East instead. Norman's song "The Outlaw" (1972) dealt with the question, "Who was Jesus Christ?" Was he an outlaw? A poet? A sorcerer? A politician? He rejected the politicization of Christ, instead viewing him in spiritual terms. During a 1980 concert in Omaha, he sang, "Sometimes I think biblical Christianity doesn't have much to do with American Christianity."[66]

The skepticism of Larry Norman and other Jesus People in regard to mainstream American society and acculturated Christianity, including bland assumptions about patriotism, were drawn partly from sources such as Watchman Nee and Francis Schaeffer.[67] One ecclesiastical critic of the Jesus Movement "declared that the saddest thing he had to say about the whole thing was that the newly enfranchised kids probably wouldn't vote in the 1972 Presidential election because they cared so little about their country and the world."[68] The prevalence of countercultural attitudes in the Jesus Movement can be seen in opinions expressed by movement members in response to interview questions in 1971–72. Their answers were recorded for posterity in the book *The Jesus People Speak Out!*. The countercultural responses found in the book are representative of the anarchism, egalitarianism, and pacifism of many, if not most, Jesus People.[69]

In his song lyrics since 1979, Bob Dylan has shown that he is in sympathy with the nine general bases of Christian anarchism: sovereignty of God, human free will, original intent, universality of the Fall, nature of the New Covenant, freedom from the Law, divine impartiality, distinction between what belongs to government and what belongs to God, and misplaced loyalty. In addition to the general bases shared by most Christian anarchists, there are three specific bases that are relevant to Dylan: eschatological, ethical, and countercultural. His identification with these bases can be seen through his songs, concert raps, and interviews. Dylan's Christian conversion and discipleship occurred largely within the context of a Christian anarchist movement: the Jesus People. The Jesus Movement was primarily countercultural and eschatological, with an ethical component as well.

CHAPTER 6

Dylan and the Jesus People

It may be interesting to see how the Jesus Movement exemplified Christian anarchism in the 1960s and 1970s but the examination does not mean much for us if we cannot link Bob Dylan to the Jesus Movement. Information about the political thought and practice of the Jesus People is important in a book about the politics of Dylan only to the extent that we can clearly identify Dylan as a Jesus Person. In fact, we can show that Dylan was a latter-day Jesus Person who joined Christianity five or six years after the heyday of the Jesus Movement (1967–73). The movement had dissipated by 1979 but its impact continued and part of its impact was the conversion and discipleship of Bob Dylan.[1]

Dylan's born-again experience began in a solitary context during a concert tour with a silver cross on a stage and a direct encounter with Jesus in a motel room. More importantly, it continued through a Jesus People–created church located in southern California, the epicenter of the Jesus Movement. Establishing the link between Dylan and the Jesus Movement requires historical recounting in some detail, which is what we are about to do. Dylan's personal life, newfound spirituality, biblical emphases, ecclesiastical preferences, and musical interests were interrelated in 1979–84. They combined in a way that reinforced his long-held anarchism yet increased its width and depth through the New Testament. This story has never before been told in detail.

Having been associated with the anarchism of the New Left and the Counterculture during the 1960s, Bob Dylan's conversion to Christianity in the late 1970s reinforced, deepened, and extended his anarchism. One factor in this development is that Dylan's conversion was brought about through Vineyard Christian Fellowship, a church with which Larry Norman was affiliated and which emanated from the Jesus Movement. The Vineyard movement was partly born in Norman's living room in Hollywood. The Bible study that began there grew into Vineyard's first local church, founded in Hollywood by Kenn Gulliksen in 1974. Gulliksen was instrumental in Dylan's conversion and became known as "Bob Dylan's pastor."[2] In the 1980s, Dylan and Norman were acquaintances and admirers of one another's work.[3]

Don Williams was the youth pastor of Hollywood Presbyterian Church in the late 1960s and early 1970s.[4] He founded the Salt Company Coffeehouse and Virgil House Christian Communal. Larry Norman was affiliated with the Presbyterian church and "tried out some of his first rock-gospel compositions" at the coffeehouse.[5] Williams eventually provided important spiritual support for Dylan. Dylan thanked Williams on the inner sleeve of his *Shot of Love* album (1981). In 1985, Williams came out with a book about Dylan's faith. He asserted that the singer was still a Christian despite rumor and speculation to the contrary.[6]

Seeds of salvation were planted in Dylan's life by musician friends who were Christians, including new convert Roger McGuinn of the Byrds and members of the Alpha Band who had toured with Dylan during the Rolling Thunder Revue tour of 1975–76 (T-Bone Burnett, Steven Soles, and David Mansfield; the latter two also toured with Dylan in 1978).[7] Ultimately, it was a fan throwing a silver cross on stage at a San Diego concert, a personal encounter with Jesus in a motel room in Tucson, the influence of his Christian girlfriend Mary Alice Artes (a member of the Vineyard Fellowship congregation in Tarzana), and conversation with Vineyard Fellowship ministers from the West LA congregation that led to Dylan's born-again experience.[8]

Bob Dylan was not involved with Jesus People during the 1967–73 period. By the time Dylan became a Christian in 1978, the Jesus Movement was no longer intact. Nonetheless, his early affiliation with Vineyard Fellowship and other manifestations of the movement indicate that Dylan could be considered a Jesus Person. While Dylan's songs contain no mention of speaking in tongues, they are full of references to the End Times.[9] Hal Lindsey was an associate pastor of the Vineyard Church in the late 1970s. Dylan was influenced by Lindsey's views through his Bible training at Vineyard.[10]

Beginning in 1979 and continuing through the early 1980s, Dylan's politics were intertwined with one of the most important legacies of the Jesus Movement: Contemporary Christian Music (CCM). Based in Southern California (LA area), it was originally known as Jesus Music, with the harder-edged type called Jesus Rock. What mostly began, in the early 1970s, in Calvary Chapel churches and other informal, grassroots examples of spiritual revival, morphed into a religious music industry that imitated the secular music industry. The imitation took the form of profit motive, slick production, marketing hype, self-congratulatory demeanor, emphasis on radio airplay, music charts, award shows, and so on. The center of focus, at least at its corporate level, shifted from the LA area to Nashville (Gospel Music Association, Dove Awards) and Waco (Word Records). The music became more trite, bland, sociopolitically conservative, and centralized in its distribution.[11]

By the late 1970s, CCM was big business. Its commercialization took a toll on its spirituality. Early fathers of CCM such as Larry Norman, John Fischer, and Chuck Girard largely avoided the worldly excesses of the burgeoning industry and, in some ways, acted as a conscience or reminder to newer artists. CCM stars who were affiliated with Calvary Chapel, Vineyard Fellowship, and other countercultural remnants of the Jesus Movement tended to take a less worldly approach to their music. Politically, they were affiliated with what we are calling Christian anarchism. It was to this camp that Dylan gravitated in early 1979.

Dylan and Keith Green

In March 1980, Bob Dylan played harmonica for a song recorded by Keith Green, founder of Last Days Ministries. Backup singers on the track were Charity, Linda, and Howard McCrary—siblings of Regina McCrary, who sang backup on tour with Dylan and on his albums *Slow Train Coming*, *Saved*, and *Shot of Love*.[12] Like Norman, Green was one of the most popular and influential contemporary Christian music artists coming out of the Jesus Movement. Like Dylan, Green was a messianic Jew (i.e., an ethnic Jew who converted to Christianity). Randy Stonehill—best friend of Larry Norman—was a major influence in Green's conversion to Christ in the mid-1970s.[13] Green was part of Vineyard Fellowship before moving his Last Days community to Texas. Dylan met Green through Vineyard in 1979. At one point, Dylan shared the brand new lyrics for *Slow Train Coming* with Green and asked his opinion. On the back cover of the album containing Dylan's harmonica-playing, Green thanked Dylan for "surrendering to Jesus" and allowing him to "share in that joy." Green also thanked Gulliksen for "spiritual counsel and support." While in the recording studio, Dylan told Green that his first album, *For Him Who Has Ears to Hear*, was one of his all-time favorite albums.[14]

As a result of his association with Green, in 1980, Dylan listened to the new LP of the CCM group 2nd Chapter of Acts and loved it. It was a concept album based on C. S. Lewis's *The Lion, the Witch, and the Wardrobe*

(*Chronicles of Narnia*, 1950). Dylan asked the group to open for him on his upcoming Fall 1980 tour, but they declined after praying about it. In thinking about the upcoming tour, Dylan's list of possible songs included the 2nd Chapter of Acts gospel-chart hit "Mansion Builder." (He did not end up performing it, though.)[15] The vocalists of the 2nd Chapter of Acts were the three Ward siblings (Annie Herring, Nelly Greisen, and Matthew Ward). They recorded in the studio for the first time in 1970 when singing backup on Larry Norman's vocal re-recording of "Sweet Sweet Song of Salvation" (a song first released the previous year by Capitol Records).[16] Pat Boone was able to get the Ward siblings under contract with MGM Records, which led to two singles (1972–73). (This was the same period during which Boone's friend Larry Norman was recording for MGM.) Folk singer Barry McGuire—most famous for "Green, Green" (1963) with the New Christy Minstrels and his solo hit "Eve of Destruction" (1965)—became a Christian through the Jesus Movement in the early 1970s. Annie Herring's husband produced McGuire's first Christian album and the Ward trio sang backup.[17] Keith Green's first album, the one so appreciated by Dylan, included the CCM classic "The Easter Song" by Annie Herring.

On July 29, 1982, the Associated Press wire announced, "A CHRISTIAN MUSIC SINGER WAS AMONG 12 PEOPLE KILLED IN A PLANE CRASH IN EASTERN TEXAS LAST NIGHT." The full AP story was short because Keith Green was not a widely known national figure outside of the youthful evangelical subculture, but his death merited a little attention. The first verse of Dylan's "Blind Willie McTell," recorded in May 1983, includes a reference to East Texas being a place where martyrs had fallen. Green cannot be described as a martyr in the sense of dying from persecution but with his prophetic fire he might have been viewed as a casualty of spiritual warfare. The plane crash that took his life could be described as the plane having fallen from the sky. Was Green a martyr in Dylan's eyes? During his last year on earth, Green was moving away from his prophetic, apocalyptic emphasis toward a more mainstream emphasis on overseas missions and opposition to abortion. Dylan, however, may have remembered the zealous young man who was viewed by some evangelicals as a modern-day Jeremiah within the church. "I Pledge My Head to Heaven," the Green song on which Dylan played harmonica, was all about a man who was willing to pay any cost to be faithful to God. It was the song of a would-be martyr. On the other hand, Dylan's reference to East Texas in "Blind Willie McTell" may have nothing to do with Keith Green.

CCM singer-songwriter Dallas Holm, a native of Minnesota, joined David Wilkerson's ministry in 1970. He had been the music leader of Wilkerson's evangelistic crusades for a decade by the time Dylan began singing Holm's song "Rise Again." "Rise Again" debuted during Dylan's return to the Fox Warfield Theater in San Francisco in November 1980. He performed the song nearly a dozen times during his late 1980 western US tour. He sang the song in concert one more time in June 1981. Dylan recorded "Rise Again" in June 1992.[18]

The extent to which Dylan was integrated into the Los Angeles CCM subculture can be seen by looking at *Billboard*'s Inspirational LPs chart for the third week of September in 1980. Debby Boone's *With My Song* was #10 (containing her cover of Dylan's "What Can I Do for You?"), Keith Green's *No Compromise* was #13 and *For Him Who Has Ears to Hear* was #25 (a Dylan favorite), Dylan's *Saved* was #14 and *Slow Train Coming* was #36, Dallas Holm's *Live* was #15 and *His Last Days* was #39 (both containing "Rise Again"), 2nd Chapter of Acts' *Roar of Love* was #18 and *Mansion Builder* was #19 (both Dylan favorites), and Randy Stonehill's *The Sky is Falling* was #21 (produced by Larry Norman).[19]

Dylan and Dave Kelly

Dylan had a personal connection to another Christian rock musician in 1980: Dave Kelly of the band Ark. Founding members of Ark were Kelly and Derek Jeffery, both originally from Scotland. In 1969, in England, the two won a national Battle of the Bands contest sponsored by Apple Records. The prize was a recording contract with Apple. Unfortunately for Kelly and Jeffery, the Beatles were breaking up at this time and Apple was unable to follow through with its promise of a released recording. The two did, however, hang out socially with the Beatles a bit and learned some of the ropes of the music industry through their association with Apple. The band signed with Warner Bros. UK and were the opening act for some of the big British bands in the early 1970s.

In 1976, Kelly moved to Los Angeles and was soon converted to Christ by watching a televangelist. He then converted Jeffery, who had joined him in the United States. The two new Christians became involved with the LA music world (including Stevie Wonder and Tommy Bolin), joined a Vineyard Fellowship church, became friends with Keith Green, and formed the band Ark. Premier blues guitarist Peter Green, founder of Fleetwood Mac, wanted to be Ark's lead guitarist, but when that did not work out, the band turned to Al Perkins, who was a fixture of the West Coast music world, especially of country-rock. Perkins led Richie Furay to the Lord when Perkins was a guitarist with the Souther Hillman Furay Band, a country-rock supergroup formed in 1973 and under contract with Asylum Records. Furay was formerly with Buffalo Springfield and Poco.[20] Perkins had formerly been a guitarist for Stephen Stills's band Manassas and a session player for a variety of bands, including the Rolling Stones and the Eagles. Al Perkins brought a couple Californians on board as fellow band members and in addition to playing lead guitar he produced Ark's first—and last—album: *The Angels Come* (1979).[21] The LP had a retro sound, with Beatleish music and Christian lyrics.

RCA Records had offered to sign Ark but only if they kept overt Christian language out of the lyrics (e.g., saying that Jesus is "the only way"). Lead singer and lyricist Kelly, and his bandmates, were unwilling to compromise on the lyrics, and so they signed with a Christian label instead. Even finding a Christian company willing to release their album was not easy for Ark. Christian record companies did not know what to do with their music because it was not viewed as marketable. It was too rocky to be played on Christian radio and in Christian churches.

As printed on the album cover, the band's name and record's title—*Ark The Angels Come*—were borrowed from John Lennon's quip that was added to the beginning of the McCartney song "Let It Be," on Phil Spector's version of the album (1970).[22] Evangelical critics praised the Ark album as excellent (deservedly so). It won the Album of the Year Award for 1979 from *Campus Life* magazine. Nonetheless, *The Angels Come* was ignored by Christian radio and Spirit Records went out of business shortly after its release. It wasn't long before the band broke up.

Following the demise of Ark, Dave Kelly was asked to join Badfinger—a Beatleish band that began its recording career with Apple—but he declined. Instead, Kelly worked for a time as a tech consultant for Pink Floyd's upcoming The Wall tour.[23] Through a mutual friend at Vineyard, Kelly was asked to meet Bob Dylan at his rehearsal studio in the fall of 1979. The Ark album was on Dylan's turntable. Kelly was shocked when Dylan asked him to become his personal assistant. Dylan told Kelly, "I need somebody that's a Christian, and understands the music business, and can talk on my behalf to the [road] crew and the band, anybody that's around. I'm not comfortable right now...I'd just like somebody there to buffer me." After Kelly became his personal assistant, Dylan began rehearsing for his 1979–80 all-Christian-music tour in support of *Slow Train Coming* and wrote new songs that would debut during the tour and eventually be released on *Saved*. Kelly's recollections of this period would later be quoted by Clinton Heylin in his book *Bob Dylan Behind the Shades*.[24]

Although Kelly had taken on a new role as a confidant of Bob Dylan, he did not completely abandon his own musical career. When Dylan found out that a British Christian label wanted Kelly to record a solo album, he convinced Kelly to move ahead with the project and he gave Kelly his touring band and backup singers for the recording. At first, Kelly told his boss, "That's just silly, I'm not going to leave working with Bob Dylan to make a solo album. I'm not that ambitious"; but Dylan said, "No, you have to. You have to do it."[25] Dylan drummer Jim Keltner, who played drums on the album, was a veteran of George Harrison and John Lennon solo LPs. Keltner acted as band leader and recruited Kinks/Rolling Stones studio pianist Nicky Hopkins for the recording. A couple of the songs were recorded in England at ELO's studio, using that band's string players and arranger. Dylan had offered to play harmonica but Kelly did not want to take advantage of his kindness.[26]

Just before beginning a tour to promote his new album, Kelly's pregnant wife suddenly died of meningitis on Christmas morning 1980 and his baby died a week later. The tour was cancelled. His career as a singer-songwriter was put on hold at that point, but he continued to work behind the scenes in the music industry. He moved on from his association with Dylan but has fond memories of the rock superstar who was his brother-in-Christ.

Dylan and Larry Norman

Looking at the links between Bob Dylan and Larry Norman is useful because Norman was the preeminent musician of the Jesus Movement. To put it another way, Norman was the nation's top example of Christian anarchism in the music world for a decade (1969–79). Dylan assumed this role after his conversion to Christ. The Christian anarchism of Dylan during the 1979–84 period is obvious based on the evidence of his lyrics and interviews, but this ideological view did not arise spontaneously. There was an historical and theological context.

There were other possible political paths Dylan might have taken if his newfound faith had been a different sort of Christianity. When he first listened to *Slow Train Coming*, music critic Paul Williams had "hoped and imagined" that Dylan was into "a Catholic Worker kind of activist Christianity" that focused on peace and justice (rather than sin and salvation).[27] Without its original Peter Maurin-Dorothy Day personal faith, theological orthodoxy, and political anarchism, this kind of Catholic Worker activism probably would have led Dylan into a politics that was not distinct from worldly leftists. He might have become a progressive Democrat or maybe a Green Party member. If he had entered into Christianity through a church allied with the Religious Right, Dylan might have become a dogmatic Republican with special emphasis on opposition to abortion and homosexuality, and support for hawkish American exceptionalism and the Israeli government.

Under either of these scenarios, his theology probably would have been intertwined with worldly partisanship.

Or Dylan could have been converted through the wing of the Charismatic Movement that emphasizes the gospel of health-and-wealth. Under the influence of Copelands and Osteens, Dylan might have become a mainstream Republican with special emphasis on economic prosperity and worldly success. As it actually occurred, Dylan's conversion to Christianity through an institutional heir of the Jesus Movement led to his adoption of Christian anarchism. Given his background as a non-Christian-but-moralistic anarchist, it was a natural fit but not inevitable. This is why ties between Dylan and Jesus People such as Norman are worth considering.

Larry Norman had long blond hair, looking the part of a hippie—or, as he later put it, like the long-haired Jesus with whom he grew up in the 1950s. As noted earlier, he was the "poet laureate" of the Jesus Movement, with "Sweet Sweet Song of Salvation" and "I Wish We'd All Been Ready," from his pioneer Christian rock LP *Upon This Rock* (1969), being two of his early classics.[28] In addition to his music, Norman influenced the Jesus People as creator of the One Way sign (index finger pointing to the sky as a way of redirecting applause to God). He was set apart from many of his Jesus Music peers by his artistic sensibilities and sardonic humor. He was also different because he continued to labor in the vineyard of secular music. Upon release of *Only Visiting This Planet* (1972), he was described by *Variety* as "a new folk-rock singer-composer to be reckoned with."[29] By the mid-1970s, he had become a friend of influential Christian writers such as Hal Lindsey, Francis Schaeffer, Malcolm Muggeridge, and Os Guinness. Norman performed at the Old Fashioned Gospel Singin' concert on the lawn of the White House, hosted by President Jimmy Carter, on September 9, 1979. He sang "The Great American Novel"—an egalitarian, civil libertarian, pacifistic, anarchistic song (not the norm of the day).

After signing a contract with Capitol Records in 1966, releasing two albums on that label (one with his band, one solo), Norman moved to MGM Records for his 1972 and 1973 albums. *In Another Land* (IAL), the third album in what had become a trilogy, was released by Norman's own company, Solid Rock Records, in 1976. The album was exquisitely produced and engineered. Norman was the producer; Andy Johns was the engineer. Johns was a prominent British recording engineer and record producer who had engineered albums for Led Zeppelin and the Rolling Stones, among others, earlier in the decade. His brother Glyn Johns was also a famous engineer and producer, having worked on the Beatles' *Let It Be* (pre-Spector), as well as with the Rolling Stones, the Who, and the Eagles. (In 1984, Glyn Johns would produce Dylan's *Real Live* album.)

Norman had signed with ABC Records in 1974 to distribute Solid Rock releases in secular stores but ABC subsequently bought Word Records, a Christian label, and chose to use their Word subsidiary as the distributor. That meant that *In Another Land* was mostly sold through Christian bookstores. This limited Norman's outreach to the unsaved but increased his profile among evangelical Christians in the late 1970s. It was a bestseller in the Christian context. The album's most famous songs were "The Rock That Doesn't Roll" and "I Am a Servant." Norman's rerelease in 1978 of *Only Visiting This Planet*, stocked in some Christian bookstores, also added to his popularity in the growing CCM market. When the history of Jesus Music (CCM) was published in 1979, it borrowed its title from an OVTP track: *Why Should the Devil Have All the Good Music?*. Pat Boone wrote the prelude; Larry Norman wrote the foreword.[30]

In 1988, *Contemporary Christian Music*—a magazine that exemplified the gospel music industry and which thus had an uneasy relationship with Norman, who was critical of what he saw as the shallow and worldly values of the industry—asked evangelical music critics to identify "The Best Contemporary Christian Albums of All Time." Norman's OVTP was named #1. Dylan's *Slow Train Coming* was #2. Randy Stonehill's *Welcome to Paradise*, produced and released by Norman, was #3.[31] In the 1980s, Norman's recordings influenced Black Francis (Frank Black), singer-songwriter of the Pixies, and the two artists eventually performed together. The Pixies, an alternative rock band that had greater popularity in Europe than at home in America, influenced Nirvana, Radiohead, and Weezer, among other bands.

Larry Norman, theological example of the Jesus Movement and ideological example of its Christian anarchism, had some obvious Dylan connections over the course of his recording career. On Norman's first MGM album (1972), "The Great American Novel," was a protest song reminiscent of Dylan's 1963–64 period. Another song on the album, "Reader's Digest," was patterned after "Subterranean Homesick Blues." On Norman's second MGM album (1973), "Nightmare #71" lyrically resembled the surrealism of Dylan's mid-1960s period. When Norman recorded "Song for a Small Circle of Friends" for *In Another Land* (1976), he included a newly written verse about Dylan, embellished with harmonica. The first track on IAL, "The Rock That Doesn't Roll," quoted the title line from "Like a Rolling Stone." Recorded in 1976–77 and released in 1981, Norman's *Something New Under the Son* was a blues-rock album containing several echoes of Dylan's *Bringing It All Back Home*. The inner sleeve contained photographs replicating the pictures on the front and back covers of Dylan's LP, with Norman replacing Dylan. The song "Larry Norman's 97th

Nightmare" was patterned after "Bob Dylan's 115th Dream," complete with false start and laughter.[32] Either when he performed at the White House in September 1979, or later that month, Norman gave President Carter inscribed copies of his own OVTP album and Dylan's just-released *Slow Train Coming*.[33]

After he became acquainted with Dylan, to some degree, during the 1979–80 period, Norman planned an album of Dylan songs called *Before and After*, designed to be a tribute to Dylan from 1962 to 1982. Side One would feature preconversion songs; Side Two postconversion songs. One track, "Just Like a Woman," was released by Norman in 1981.[34] *Before and After* was never released but a second track, "Positively 4th Street," was finally issued in 2003. Presumably, Norman's studio recording of "When He Returns," released in 1998, was also intended for *Before and After*. The 1998 CD also included Norman's song "Oh Little Sister," patterned after Dylan's "Oh Sister."

Pat Boone was "a very close friend" of Larry Norman by the early 1970s.[35] In the late 1970s, one of the first reports about Dylan's shocking conversion to Christianity was the rumor that he had been baptized in Boone's swimming pool. The story was incorrect, but Boone, like Norman and now Dylan, was a prominent member of the evangelical Christian community in Los Angeles. His daughter, Debby Boone, who had a mega-hit with "You Light Up My Life" in 1977, included a cover of Dylan's new song "What Can I Do For You?" on her 1980 album. It was released prior to Dylan's version on *Saved*.[36]

In 1979, Bob Dylan was fully converted to Christ through Vineyard Christian Fellowship and was biblically educated for four months through its school of discipleship. Vineyard Fellowship began in 1974 as a Bible study in Larry Norman's living room on Wednesdays. In 1976, after noting that "we've had a lot of Jewish people become Christians at our Bible studies and church meetings," Norman described the roots of Vineyard:

> A lot of artistic people would meet at our house for meetings...Bible studies. And after a while there were so many of us, we had to meet somewhere else, and then somewhere else. Now it's so huge that we have several ministers and a school in the mornings...different classes from 8:00 to 12:00 for people who really want to study the Bible. We've got really great teachers. It's called The Vineyard and our pastor is Ken Gulliksen. It's a real home. It's so nice to have a tight family of artists.[37]

This 1976 description was part of the interview that accompanied Norman's *In Another Land* album. Three years later, Dylan would receive ministry, baptism, and discipleship through Vineyard. In the late 1990s, Norman recalled,

> When I met Ken Gulliksen he was a student of Chuck Smith's. He said he wanted to reach out to people in music. I had already begun a Bible study for actors and musicians so I said he could lead the weekly studies because I was on tour so often. We both agreed to call our meeting The Vineyard. I supplied all of the artists and their friends from my own phone book. I paid for all of the food and drinks. I even gave Ken money to help support Joanie and him. We held it in my living room from 1974 to 1977 when I had to go on my world tour. By then we had so many people that we had to divide the kids into several different houses and meet on Sundays at the Leo Carillo Beach because it was free (no rent) and we had over 200 kids attending by then.[38]

An interesting possibility is that the Dylan-Norman musical relationship may have gone both ways. Dylan was an obvious musical influence, over the years, on Norman. It is possible that Norman influenced Dylan in 1979. Norman's song "Without Love You Are Nothing" was first released on vinyl on *Bootleg* in 1972. Later that year, it was more widely released by MGM on the album *Only Visiting This Planet*. In the United States, it was a DJ single (45) under the name "Without Love." In the United Kingdom, it was released as a single under the name "Righteous Rocker, Holy Roller." A short new version of the song, under the name "Righteous Rocker #3," was included on the album *In Another Land* (1976). Allen Flemming, a friend of Larry Norman and a person familiar with his archives, comments, "With Dylan the influence of Larry is an obvious one. Play *Righteous Rocker* and then play *Gotta Serve Somebody*. But again, like with U2, Dylan never mentions Larry in any way that can be substantiated."[39]

Could Dylan's song "Gotta Serve Somebody," a hit single and opening track on Dylan's first Christian album (1979), have been inspired by Norman's song "Without Love You Are Nothing" (aka "Righteous Rocker")? Musically, Norman's song is more hard-rock than blues-rock but there are lyrical similarities. Norman begins with the words "You could be." Dylan begins with the words "You may be." The verses of both songs are a listing of an array of occupations and life circumstances. The choruses of both songs begin with the word "But." Norman's song repeats the key two-word phrase from the title four times. Dylan's song repeats the key two-word phrase from the title three times. The last line of the last verse of the Norman song contrasts shaking hands with the Devil with giving one's life to God (Devil or God). The chorus of the Dylan song contrasts serving the Devil with serving the Lord (Devil or Lord).

Is it plausible that Dylan was inspired by Norman? Given the context of Vineyard Fellowship and the involvement by Dylan in the LA Christian music scene, the answer is "Yes." It might seem implausible that Dylan, a living legend, would hang out with, and be influenced by, culturally insignificant musical inferiors (relatively speaking). And yet he did and was. As a new believer, Dylan was humble enough that he was willing to learn from spiritual elders—even if they were physically younger and musically less-gifted than himself. Norman was more talented and musically accomplished than most of his CCM peers but obviously he was not on the same level as Dylan.

Allen Flemming comments, "I think it is nearly impossible that Dylan was not influenced by Larry. Not only is the evidence there in the songs but think about it like this: Imagine anyone meeting Dylan right after Dylan's conversion in late 70's. Dylan, the greatest songwriter of the century. What music are you going to recommend he listen to in order to build his faith? Larry Norman, maybe Bruce Cockburn and Johnny Cash, but above all Larry."[40]

Flemming also draws an interesting link to early Dylan: "Norman was our crazy, lyrical, rebel poet who knew the Name of the Answer blowin' in the wind Bob Dylan sings about. Larry thought he was writing 'Why Don't You Look Into Jesus' to Janis Joplin but I think he was writing it just as much to give a Name to the answer in Dylan's song *'Blowin' in the Wind.'* The same answer in the wind given in John 3:8 by Jesus. Jesus!" This passage in the gospel of John contains the conversation between Jesus and Nicodemus about being born again. Dylan called attention to it in his song "In the Garden."[41] Telling the seeking Pharisee that he should not marvel about the need to be born again, Jesus added, "The wind blows where it wills, and you hear the sound of it, but you do not know whence it comes or whither it goes; so it is with every one who is born of the Spirit." The Greek word *pneuma* can be translated spirit, wind, or breath. It appears at the beginning and end of John 3:8, usually translated "wind" in the first instance and "Spirit" in the second.

The odds that Dylan listened to *Only Visiting This Planet* in early 1979 are quite high. If he was listening to albums by Keith Green, 2nd Chapter of Acts, Dallas Holm, and Ark—and we know that he was—he probably had Larry Norman on his turntable at least once. As a new Christian, Dylan was looking for musical role models. Norman may have been an acquaintance through church. Since Dylan borrowed ideas from New York folk-music scene friends in the early 1960s, would do the same from Humphrey Bogart movies in the mid-1980s, and from an obscure Japanese writer (Saga), a largely forgotten Civil War poet (Timrod), and a long-dead Roman poet (Ovid) in the 2000s, he could easily have been inspired by the father of Christian rock music as he prepared to make his own Christian rock album.[42]

Of course, this has nothing to do with plagiarism. Great artists take existing material and build on it—enhancing and reinterpreting. Dylan has operated in this way from the very beginning. It is possible, perhaps likely, that Dylan heard one of Norman's records, liked the song, and wrote his own song in the wake of that listening. Although first released in 1972, the MGM album containing "Without Love You Are Nothing" was rereleased in 1978. So it was circulating at the time Dylan was writing the songs for *Slow Train Coming*.

There are additional clues that suggest Dylan heard and was influenced by *Only Visiting This Planet* (OVTP). There are similarities between Norman's "The Great American Novel" and Dylan's "Slow Train." Both tracks are state-of-the-union ("protest") songs examining contemporary American culture in the light of Christian spirituality. Both draw upon the last line of the Star-Spangled Banner. Both have grain/starve juxtapositions. Both refer to human laws being irrelevant. Both mention brotherhood as a stated ideal that is contradicted by reality.[43] A recurring Norman theme in both "Great American Novel" and another song on OVTP, "Reader's Digest"—the pastiche of "Subterranean Homesick Blues"—is criticism of the US government's expensive obsession with travel to the moon. Dylan does not address this subject in "Slow Train," but he does in two *Infidels* songs four years later: "License to Kill" and "Union Sundown." He also complained about the space preoccupation in spoken comments during the 1980s.[44] As noted earlier, such similarities could be purely coincidental. Whether any Dylan song was influenced by any Norman song, the more important point is that Dylan the new Christian came out of the countercultural Jesus Movement that included Norman and the ideology of Christian anarchism.

Dave Kelly, who appeared earlier in this chapter as leader of the Christian rock band Ark and personal assistant to Dylan in 1979–80, cannot imagine any Larry Norman influence on Bob Dylan. When asked about a possible connection between Norman and Dylan, Kelly dismisses the idea out of hand: "No, I don't think Larry had any effect on Dylan. People have asked me that before. See, Larry—how can I say this kindly?...When I met Larry, it was like meeting Pink Floyd for the first time, particularly Syd Barrett the singer. It was as if he was one of the wounded warriors. It's like he wasn't all there. You could talk to him and then he would just drift off. Say strange things."[45] Comparing the talent of Norman unfavorably with that of Keith Green, a friend of Dylan, Kelly says, "From a musical perspective, I think Bob, and others, saw him as a sort of amateur. He was famous because he was an amateur with long hair in the Jesus Movement that wrote songs... [Larry] could never be taken serious in the pop world, in the mainstream world. He wasn't talented enough to do that." Kelly makes the point that standards are "much, much lower" in the Christian music world.[46]

As Dylan's aide and friend during the crucial *Slow Train Coming/Saved* period, as a fellow Christian affiliated with Vineyard during this time, and as a rock musician, Kelly's thoughts carry weight. However, it is possible that his disappointing meeting with Norman the man has colored his impression of Norman the musician. It may be that Kelly has not listened to Norman's classic albums recently. To say that Norman was amateurish and lacked the talent to succeed beyond the Christian music world does not comport with the facts. Listening to the five major albums recorded by Norman from 1969 to 1977—from *Upon This Rock* to *Something New Under the Son*—shows that he had talent. The fact that he never rose to the same heights after this peak period does not negate the point. One of the albums that was self-produced and not released on a secular label—*In Another Land* (recorded 1975)—may be the best of the five. It has polished production and first-rate lyrics, melodies, and musicianship.

In his assessment of Norman, Kelly mentions his persona as a long-haired Jesus Movement figure but seems to forget Norman's career in the secular music world. A third-rate talent would not have been kept under contract by Capitol Records for a solo album after his stint with People. His time with the band included a Top-20 single with Norman as colead vocalist. Nor would a third-rate talent have been signed by MGM Records after he left Capitol. *Only Visiting This Planet* received positive reviews from (secular) music trade publications.

His track record in the late 1960s–early 1970s proves that Norman's talent exceeded the relatively low standards of the Christian music industry. Also, an amateurish musician would not have been given entrée into George Martin's recording studio or been able to later attract Andy Johns as sound engineer. And surely the Library of Congress must have some vetting process by which they decide which nominated music albums are chosen for the prestigious National Recording Registry in a given year.

Of course, even if Norman was more talented than Kelly is giving him credit for being, this does not prove any Norman-to-Dylan influence. Kelly apparently never heard Dylan mention Norman during the 1979–80 period, but this does not mean Dylan could not have heard *Only Visiting This Planet* in early 1979 (when he was writing the *Slow Train Coming* songs and before Kelly came on board).

In an interview with a British Christian magazine, in 1984, Norman told an interviewer, "Well people used to tease me and say Oh, you're a Christian Bob Dylan and then when Dylan became a Christian in my Bible study they'd say to him Oh you're a secular Larry Norman." When asked, "Do you know Dylan?," Norman replied, "Not really well." Asked what he thought about Dylan's latest album, *Infidels*, he was enthusiastic. Norman praised *Slow Train Coming* even more, calling it "the finest gospel album ever written," and added, "I'll never write one as good as that. He'll never write one as good as that—nobody will... That album is like a prayer, it's a beautiful prayer."[47]

Within the commercialized evangelical Christian subculture, Larry Norman was often accused of being egotistical and of creating a self-aggrandizing career mythology, including name-dropping. It is interesting that Norman did not take any credit for inspiring Dylan's *Slow Train Coming*. There was either no inspiration from *Only Visiting This Planet*, there was inspiration but Norman did not recognize it, or he recognized it but did not mention it because he was being humble. In 1988, Larry Norman commented on Dylan's relationship with the evangelical world: "It really hurt me to hear people yelling at Dylan's concerts when he sang two old songs in the middle of his Christian songs. I don't think he should be criticized for singing his old songs. I think they say a lot about his thoughts and, really, the feelings and thoughts of this generation." Norman saw Dylan as someone who continued to serve God even though he had distanced himself from institutional Christianity: "I thought Dylan was doing a wonderful job of balancing his presentation at concerts... I'm sorry that he became wounded by us [Christians] because he finally decided if we wouldn't accept his fellowship then he wouldn't offer it. I think he's rightly more concerned about his relationship with God than he is concerned about his relationship with us."[48]

Norman's brother, Charles "Charly" Norman, was part of the LA rock scene by the late 1980s and was Larry's latter-day lead guitarist. Writing in 1988, Larry Norman shed more light on his connection to Dylan: "At Christmas Charly bumped into Bob Dylan and they talked a little about my music. Bob told Charly he was a fan and wanted to know if I had anything new coming out, because, you know, I hadn't done any new albums since he became a Christian." Charles Norman elaborated on the encounter in an interview for this book. Returning to California from Sweden, he saw Dylan on an airport bench outside at LAX. When Dylan asked about his guitar case, Charles said he was a musician who toured with his brother Larry Norman. Bob Dylan "did like a double-take and said, 'Yeah, Larry Norman. That's your brother? Wow. Cool. I love his music, man. What's he doing?'"

After some small talk, Dylan said, "Tell your brother I said Hello again. Man, I love what you guys are doing." Charles was elated by the conversation but Larry showed no great emotion when he told him about it.[49]

Despite abundant talent, contracts with secular record companies, and influence within the evangelical Christian world, Larry Norman never resided in the stratosphere of popular music in terms of cultural fame, musical influence, and commercial success. To put it another way, he was not in the same league as Bob Dylan and his friends/peers/colleagues the Beatles, Johnny Cash, and U2. Nonetheless, Norman had peripheral connections to these superstars. For about a year, the Beatles and Larry Norman (as a member of the band People) were label mates on Capitol Records (1967–68). During his 1968 visit to the United States to announce creation of Apple Records, at a Capitol function, Paul McCartney told Norman that he liked People's hit single "I Love You," but John Lennon was always Norman's favorite Beatle.[50]

In June 1972, Norman appeared with Johnny Cash, among others, at the Explo '72 festival in Dallas, sponsored by Campus Crusade for Christ. The two singer-songwriters were featured on Side One of the soundtrack album.[51] When Cash died in 2003, Norman wrote a remembrance for *Christian Musician Magazine*.[52]

According to Norman, U2 was influenced by his Christian rock records when they began their career as a rock band that was three-fourths Christian in the late 1970s. (Bono experienced a Christian conversion in 1976, the same year he joined what became U2, and two of his bandmates followed.)[53] Norman had an international career, with overseas record releases and concerts. He appeared at Royal Albert Hall in London in 1972, 1973, 1975, and 1981. Norman was a friend of British pop superstar Cliff Richard, a fellow Christian. In 1978, Richard released a Top-40 LP containing three Norman songs. Norman appeared at the Greenbelt Festival of Christian music, held each August in England, in 1979, 1980, and 1981. During his first two Greenbelts, Norman appeared with his own band. At Greenbelt '81, he made a surprise appearance at the end of a Sheila Walsh song. U2 also made a surprise appearance at Greenbelt in 1981.[54] Referring to U2, Norman's brother Charles says, "They were totally inspired...Of course they would have heard of Larry's music." When U2 was in LA for the *Joshua Tree* tour, in 1987, they had someone who worked for them call Norman because they wanted to meet him after the concert. That fell through but they eventually met, and Bono and Norman kept in touch by e-mail.[55]

Norman's friend Allen Flemming recalls from their conversations that "Larry's initial reaction to U2 was that they did not talk about Jesus openly enough. But with time Larry saw that what they were doing truly was advancing the kingdom." Norman was "very supportive of Bono's efforts" to encourage US and Western European governments to forgive debts of poor countries and to encourage drug companies to donate AIDS medicines to Africa.[56]

When Larry Norman died in 2008, at the age of 60, Bono sent flowers to his family in Oregon.[57] In 2014, the Library of Congress announced that Norman's *Only Visiting This Planet* (1972) and U2's *The Joshua Tree* (1987) were two of the 25 recordings chosen for preservation through its annual National Recording Registry (2013). They were two of only three rock albums that year.[58]

Dylan and Bono (U2)

Like Dylan, Bono of U2 can be described as a latter-day manifestation of the Jesus Movement. Bono (Paul Hewson) is the band's lead singer and songwriter. U2 began in 1976 when its members were in their mid-teens. They were students at Mount Temple Comprehensive School in Dublin. The band went under a couple different names before settling on U2. Of the four lasting members of U2, three were born-again Christians (Bono, The Edge aka David Evans, and Larry Mullen; Adam Clayton was not, at this time).

The Christian band members were having a crisis of spirituality by the time the band was getting ready to record its second album, *October*, in the summer of 1981. Bono, Edge, and Larry were part of a charismatic home-church called Shalom Fellowship. They attended twice-weekly meetings of the evangelical Christian group. They got up at 5 a.m. for devotions (Bible study and prayer).[59] Bono experimented with speaking in tongues.[60] Shalom was an outgrowth of the Jesus Movement. A communal group, it was antimaterialism and prosocial justice. This reminds us that an apolitical, anticultural stance does not necessarily negate concern for the poor and oppressed.[61]

When Shalom leaders expressed concern about the worldliness of rock music, Edge decided to quit the band and Bono followed his lead. Mullen, on the other hand, was unhappy with Shalom. Eventually, U2 decided they could reconcile their faith and their music.[62] All of this spiritual and emotional turmoil helped to produce a great album. With Bono taking the lead in writing and singing, *October* would be U2's most explicitly Christian release. *October* reflected not only the spiritually intense, charismatic-flavored emphases of the Jesus Movement but also its Christian anarchism and emphasis on change through apolitical personalism.[63]

The influence of Watchman Nee, a key theologian and role model for Jesus People, can be seen in the lyrics of *October* and in the spiritual turmoil of the band members during its recording. His classic book *Love Not the World* was especially relevant. In 1989, Bono told *Mother Jones*,

> We [U2 members] were just being pulled in two different directions. A lot of it was based on the idea of the ego. We'd been reading a lot of Watchman Nee, a Chinese Christian mystic. His idea was: "Unless the seed shall die and be crushed into the earth, it cannot bear fruit." [John 12:24–25] Rock 'n' Roll had this idea: "It's *me!*"... Like, "Out of my way, looking out for number one, 'I Can't Get No Satisfaction!'" Watchman Nee's attitude to that would be: "So what? What's so important about you anyway?" (*laughs*) So it was like we were being torn in two... In the end, I realized it was bullshit, that what these people [in Shalom] were getting close to with this idea was denial, rather than willful surrender.[64]

Although U2's album *War* (1983) marked a public turning-away from the cultural isolation of *October*, both albums shared a Christian spirituality and anarchism. *War* addresses sociopolitical issues, but it does so from a Christian anarcho-pacifist point of view.[65]

Exhibiting both a Christianity that transcends conventional Left/Right politics and a pragmatic desire to get things done, in the 1990s, Bono developed a reputation as someone who was willing to work with a wide variety of politicians and businessmen, including right-wing Senator Jesse Helms (R-NC). (His approach drew scorn from left-wing ideologues who detested his lack of "purity.")[66]

Bono and Dylan share similar politics (although Bono places more trust in politicians). Both have been grounded since youth in a populist pulling-for-the-underdog worldview.[67] Both imbibed Jesus Movement-inspired Christian anarchism in the late 1970s–early 1980s. Given these commonalities, it is not surprising that the two men became friends. Bono joined Dylan's social circle in the 1980s. On their *Rattle and Hum* album (1988), U2 covered Dylan's "All Along the Watchtower," performed a song cowritten by Dylan, who provided a backing vocal ("Love Rescue Me"), and had Dylan play organ on one track ("Hawkmoon 269").[68]

Decentralism and Populism

Clearly, Bob Dylan's biblical understanding and spiritual practice were linked to the legacy of the Southern California-based Jesus Movement, particularly in its musical manifestation, in the years following 1978. In 1999, Dylan's former pastor Kenn Gulliksen told an interviewer at the Jesus People Reunion in Anaheim, which had 16,000 participants, that he thought

Dylan remained a Christian believer and that his brothers and sisters in the Lord should be praying for him. Associated with the Calvary Chapel movement before cofounding the Vineyard Fellowship movement, Gulliksen had returned to Calvary Chapel by this time.[69] In his politics, Dylan embraced a type of Christian anarchism partly because he was anarchist-minded before his conversion and partly because he was discipled by the anarchist-minded Christians of Vineyard Fellowship, with their emphasis on personalism, eschatology, and counterculture.

In chapter 5, *anarchism* was broadly defined to include those who favor eliminating, minimizing, or ignoring the state. It could be asked, if abolishing the state is not a realistic goal, what should anarchists do? They can try to minimize and ignore the state. The creation of true democracy would represent a true minimization of the state. It is a relatively small step from the genuine democracy of Thomas Jefferson to the individualistic anarchy of Henry David Thoreau. Noam Chomsky notes, "Jefferson's concept that the best government is the government which governs least or Thoreau's addition to that, that the best government is the one that doesn't govern at all, is one that's often repeated by anarchist thinkers through modern times."[70]

Jefferson was not an advocate of democracy in its purest sense (e.g., as experienced by Athens). Nonetheless, his ideology was amazingly democratic. The truth of this statement can be seen when one considers the aristocratic context in which he lived, including his maternal relatives and national colleagues. Jefferson was clearly a populist rather than an elitist. Dylan can be accurately described as a Jeffersonian in his politics, given his populism, agrarianism, and "isolationism." As noted in chapter 1, Dylan said in 1976 that he would vote for Thomas Jefferson if he were alive because he "knew what was happening." Three years later, referring to inflated egos, outdated laws, and foolish attempts to manipulate the Devil, Dylan suggested that Jefferson would be stunned to see modern America.[71]

Creation of the Port Huron Statement by Students for a Democratic Society in 1962 is often seen as a starting point of the New Left, an anarchistic movement. The statement's call for "participatory democracy" expresses a yearning for genuine democracy. What passes for democracy in the United States is actually, by classical definition, aristocracy. Based upon the research of elite theorists and the testimony of many persons involved in the political process, it could be argued that the United States is a specific type of aristocracy: plutocracy (rule by the wealthy). Since elimination of the US government is probably never going to occur, anarchists who wish to do something other than attempting to ignore the state could try to minimize the state. They can do this by working against aristocracy and plutocracy. They can urge the democratization of society to disperse power from the few to the many. They can advocate political and economic decentralization.

Dylan the Christian Monarchist

Bob Dylan is a premillennialist when it comes to eschatology. Premillennialism is built upon a belief in the literal reign of Jesus Christ on earth. Dylan believes that Jesus will rule as king for 1,000 years when he sets up his throne in Jerusalem, and he sees this as a supremely good thing. Dylan can be described as a monarchist in this way.[72] Dylan is also an anarchist and a populist.

One person ruling over everyone else on the planet is the opposite of decentralization. Unelected, absolute monarchy—even if benevolent—is about as far removed as one can get from democracy and anarchy. How do we account for this apparent discrepancy between Dylan's support for anarchy and democracy in the present and his support for monarchy in the future? A serious Christian knows that allegiance to Jesus Christ takes precedence over everything else, including ideology, but there must be some way to integrate support for these competing forms of government into one intellectual framework.

Ironically, a solution is suggested in the writings of a pagan philosopher. In contrast to the elitism and hostility toward democracy found in the *Republic* of Plato, his later, smaller, and less-well-known work titled *Statesman* sees some value in democracy and contains remarkable parallels to biblical eschatology. After arriving at his first definition of the statesman-king, Plato presents the myth of the age of Kronos (Cronos). Plato is teaching a political philosophy in *Statesman* that is both more realistic and less elitist than the one taught in *Republic*.[73]

The *Statesman* has direct application to the seemingly conflicted ideologies of Dylan and other anarchistic Christians. During the age of Kronos, humans were under divine sovereignty and had no need for human rulers. The peaceful, prosperous, and anarchistic age of Kronos corresponds to life in the Garden of Eden. The time when Kronos will take control of the universe once again, thereby creating a new golden age, corresponds to the Millennium. According to Plato, rule by the statesman-king is the one true form of government because "the best thing of all is not full authority for laws but rather full authority for a man who understands the art of kingship and has wisdom." The statesman-king corresponds to Jesus Christ, who will someday rule earth as a just and wise king. Because statesmen-kings are such rarities, there are six imitative forms of government. Imitative rulers must strictly adhere to cultural norms and laws rather than following their own private agendas if they wish to successfully imitate the statesman-king.

Plato's scenario does not explicitly include sin or Satan but his words have application to a deeper, more biblical understanding of earthly politics. Because Satan is the clandestine ruler of this world during the present age, the human rulers of the various nations are typically under Satan's dominion and operate according to his "cosmic principles of force, greed, selfishness, ambition, and pleasure."[74] This being the case, the human rulers are not governing according to God's laws. Regardless of the form of government found in any given nation, none of the national governments are governing according to God's laws. Taking Plato's ranking of the six imitative constitutions, we can thus eliminate the first three forms of government. Nowhere on earth today is there a monarchy, aristocracy, or democracy governing according to God's laws. This leaves us with democracy (not according to laws), oligarchy, and tyranny. Plato comments,

> The rule of the many is weak in every way; it is not capable of any real good or of any serious evil as compared with the other two. This is because in a democracy sovereignty has been divided out in small portions among a large number of rulers. Therefore, of all three constitutions that are law-abiding, democracy is the worst; but of the three that flout the laws, democracy is the best. Thus if all constitutions are unprincipled the best thing to do is to live in a democracy.[75]

Christians such as Dylan believe that all national rulers in our world flout God's laws and reject the principles of his Kingdom. For this reason, democracy is the best form of government. In a sinful world with politics dominated by Satan, the safest situation is for political power to be as decentralized as possible. Satan being the prince of this world, it is best that government be "weak in every way." Of course, a far more desirable situation can be envisioned: the overthrow of Satan's power and the commencement of rule by Jesus Christ. In such a situation, the value of democratic rule by the people pales in comparison to monarchic rule by the Messiah. As Plato says, "When constitutions are well ordered [according to laws], democracy is the least desirable, and monarchy, the first of the six, is by far the best to live under—unless of course the seventh [i.e., the statesman-king] is possible, for that must always be exalted, like a god among mortals, above all other constitutions."[76] In Dylan's view, Jesus Christ is not only a man capable of being a just and wise king; he is also God and can thus be a statesman-king. He is truly a god among mortals and will rule as such during the Millennium.

In reconciling Dylan's simultaneous belief in divine monarchy and human anarchy/democracy, we could say that the political philosophy of Christians should be that of "All or Nothing." They should look forward to monarchy—specifically, a world government headed by Jesus Christ (the *All* form of government). In the meantime, they should support anarchy because humans are sinful and Satan is the current ruler of the world (the *Nothing* form of government). Although abolition of the state is a noble ideal, it is not realistic, and so Christians should concentrate on other types of anarchism—namely, ignoring the state and minimizing the state. They can attempt to ignore the state by realizing that they are citizens of heaven and by recognizing the church as an alternative society. They can attempt to minimize the state by supporting genuine democracy (the *Little* form of government). In theory, Christians should support "All or Nothing," but in practice they may have to support "Little" until they are given "All." According to Dylan—and the New Testament—on that day, "the kingdom of the world" will become "the kingdom of our Lord and of his Christ."[77]

During his first coming (advent), Jesus was largely an undercover king. But this is not the whole story. As a Jew who read the Bible, including the Hebrew Scriptures (the Old Testament from a Christian perspective), before his 1978–79 conversion, Dylan presumably would have come across the two sides of the Jewish Messiah foretold by the prophets and celebrated by the psalmists. The suffering Messiah *and* the reigning Messiah; Isaiah 53:3–12 *and* Isaiah 2:2–7. In the New Testament, the rabbi Yeshua (Jesus) is described as laying claim to both of the messianic aspects. He is the savior for all peoples sent by God from heaven *and* the heir to the Davidic throne of Israel. His kingdom is other-worldly (heaven) *and* this-worldly (earth).[78]

Dylan's monarchism is theological more than ideological because it focuses on Jesus's second coming. It looks to the future. Still, it is true that Dylan, in his own indirect and idiosyncratic way, has inspired some citizens of the Kingdom to make a difference in the here-and-now. When Jesus prayed, "Thy kingdom come, thy will be done, on earth as it is in heaven," he meant, among other things, God's will for government and society. Christians who think about such things find it amazing that they are able to help fulfill, in some measure, the Lord's Prayer. They do so even as they also pray, "Come, Lord Jesus."[79]

Dylan the Christian Anarchist

Intentionally or not, Bob Dylan was "the New Left's most resonant troubadour," as the biographer of New Left father Dwight Macdonald puts it.[80] Dylan was also the preeminent hero of the less overtly political, more lifestyle oriented Counterculture that developed in the late 1960s. Like the New Left, the Counterculture was anarchistic. The message of Dylan's first all-electric album, *Highway 61 Revisited*, was clear: Protest is not going to change the world; change yourself and you will change the world. It could be argued that Dylan did more as a rock star to revolutionize American society than he did during his days as a folk singer. His songs stimulated self-understanding and change in millions of young people. In his 1946 article "The Root is Man," Macdonald called for the creation of small fraternal groups—organized according to the principles of pacifism and non-coercion—that would challenge the government by draft refusal, evasion, argument, and encouraging attitudes of disrespect, skepticism, and ridicule toward the state and all authority.[81] Twenty years later, Dylan put these attitudes on vinyl and people bought copies at their local record store.

Bob Dylan's electorally apolitical, anarchistic stance, so evident in the 1960s, did not change when he became a Christian in late 1978. Two years after his conversion, Dylan said, "When I walk around some of the towns we go to... I'm totally convinced people need Jesus. Look at the junkies and the winos and the troubled people. It's all a sickness which can be healed in an instant. The powers that be won't let that happen. The powers that be say it has to be healed politically."[82]

In May 1980, during a concert in Providence, Dylan told the crowd that they didn't realize that "the Devil's behind politics." A week earlier, he told a crowd, "They're running for president now. They're gonna save the country... But you can't save nothing unless *you're* saved."[83] During the same concert tour, he repeatedly told his fans, "I've never told you to vote for nobody" but now he needed to tell them that "Jesus is the way of salvation."[84] When asked, in 1983, if there were any political songs on *Infidels*, Dylan said,

> I don't write political songs. Political songs are slogans. I don't even know the definition of politics. At one time it could have been a good thing, but right now it's all part of that so-called corruptible crown. Like you know, the law is a good thing until it's used against the innocent. Politics could be useful if it was used for good purposes. For instance, like feeding the hungry and taking care of the orphans. But it's not. It's like the snake with its tail in its mouth. A merry-go-round of sin. All you hear about are US interests in Latin America. But what are those interests? You can't find out. Show me an honest politician and I'll show you a sanctified whore. You know that old story about the murderer who kills the judge and puts on his robe. But he's still a murderer.[85]

In a 1984 interview, Dylan remarked, "I think politics is an instrument of the Devil. Just that clear. I think politics is what kills; it doesn't bring anything alive." When asked whether it makes any difference who is president, Dylan said he didn't think so. He went on to put things in historical and personal perspective, noting that he had already seen several presidents come and go in his lifetime. He added, "How can you deal with Reagan and get so serious about that, when the man isn't even gonna *be* there when you get your thing together?"[86] Around the same time, on tour in Madrid, Dylan said, "There's a lot of different gods that people are subject[s] of. There's the god of Mammon. Corporations are gods. Governments? No, governments don't have much to do with it anymore, I don't think. Politics is a hoax. The politicians don't have any real power. They feed you all this stuff in the newspapers about what's going on, but that's not what's really going on."[87]

The following year, however, Dylan acknowledged a potentially good side to politics—provided that it is referring to grassroots endeavors of the people rather than dishonest machinations of the politicians. Referring to the New Left and 1960s social movements, he told an interviewer, "Politics have changed. The subject matter has changed. In the '60s there was a lot of people coming out of schools who were taught politics by professors who were political thinkers, and those people spilled over into the streets. What politics I ever learned, I learned in the streets, because it was part of the environment. I don't know where somebody would hear that now." Pointing to identity politics and multiculturalism, he added, "Now everybody wants their own thing. There's no unity."[88]

In 1986, when asked if some of his postconversion songs were signs that he had moved to the political right, Dylan responded, "Well, for me, there is no right and there is no left. There's truth and there's untruth, y'know? There's honesty and there's hypocrisy. Look in the Bible: you don't see nothing about right or left...I hate to keep beating people over the head with the Bible, but that's the only instrument I know, the only thing that stays true."[89] Dylan was asked by the *Los Angeles Times*, in 2001, if he had been interested in the 2000 election between Bush and Gore. He commented, "Did I follow the election? Yeah, I followed to see who would win. But in the larger scheme of things, the government is irrelevant. Everybody, everything can be bought and sold."[90]

On election night in 2008, Dylan was playing a concert in Minneapolis. He presumably knew that Obama had won the election or was likely to win it. Referring to his bass player, Dylan said, "Tony Garnier, wearin' the Obama button. Tony likes to think it's a brand new time right now. An age of light. Me, I was born in 1941—that's the year they bombed Pearl Harbor. Well, I been livin' in a world of darkness ever since. But it looks like things are gonna change now." This was interpreted as an unprecedented political endorsement by Dylan but the language is ambiguous. Was he praising Garnier or gently mocking him? Dylan himself was not wearing an Obama button. Unlike many rock stars, he had not publicly endorsed his candidacy against McCain. Given the embarrassingly disastrous nature of the G. W. Bush years, Dylan may have been relieved that a Bush-clone would not continue that trajectory. But the words used by Dylan were qualified. Garnier "likes to think" and it "looks like" change is on the horizon. In other words, Dylan may have been referring to Garnier's wishful thinking and to the appearance of change when no change is likely on the most important matters. The spiritual language that he used—"age of light" and "world of darkness"—also argue against Dylan suddenly exhibiting a naive faith in a particular politician. Looking at eternal values and being skeptical of political hype and the latest fad, Dylan would most likely have taken the hope hoopla surrounding Obama with a grain of salt.

In 2012, Dylan was interviewed by *Rolling Stone*. In the context of talking about racial prejudice and the curse of slavery, he was asked, "Did you hope or imagine that the election of President Obama would signal a shift, or that it was in fact a sea change?" Dylan answered, "I don't have any opinion on that. You have to change your heart if you want to change." Dylan brushed off the interviewer's suggestion that Obama had sparked widespread hostility because of race, saying that previous presidents had received similar opposition. When asked, "Do you vote?," Dylan replied, "Uh..." When asked, "Should we vote?," Dylan gave a perfunctory answer: "Yeah, why not vote? I respect the voting process. Everybody ought to have the right to vote. We live in a democracy. What do you want me to say? Voting is a good thing." The interviewer then asked again if Dylan himself votes. Dylan smiled and said, "Huh?" He refused to evaluate President Obama's first-term performance in office, saying, "What do I think of him? I like him. But you're asking the wrong person. You know who you should be asking that to? You should be asking his wife what she thinks of him. She's the only one that matters. Look, I only met him a few times. I mean, what do you want me to say? He loves music. He's personable. He dresses good. What the fuck do you want me to say?"[91] All of this was spoken like someone who has no interest in electoral politics.

In an interview with Bill Flanagan to promote *Together Through Life*, in the spring of 2009, Dylan was asked about politics. He gave a typical disparaging assessment: "Politics is entertainment. It's a sport. It's for the well groomed and well heeled. The impeccably dressed. Party animals. Politicians are interchangeable." Flanagan asked him if he doesn't "believe in the democratic process." Dylan replied, "Yeah, but what's that got to do with politics? Politics creates more problems than it solves... The real power is in the hands of small groups of people and I don't think they have titles." Later that year, when asked by Flanagan why he decided to donate the profits from his *Christmas in the Heart* CD to three particular charitable organizations, Dylan said, "Because they get food straight to the people. No military organization, no bureaucracy, no governments to deal with."[92]

Dylan's anarchism is reflected in many of his postconversion songs. In "Gonna Change My Way of Thinking" (1979), he says that God is the only legitimate authority. In "Lenny Bruce" (1981), he praises the controversial comedian of the 1960s. Dylan approvingly notes that Bruce exposed the misdeeds of the high and mighty. This rebellious attitude led to Bruce being labeled as crazy because he did not follow the rules.[93] Dylan's skeptical attitude toward human authority comes out in "Sweetheart Like You" (1983), a song in which he paraphrases Dr. Johnson's observation that patriotism is the last refuge of scoundrels and Augustine's observation that he who steals a little is a pirate (criminal) while he who steals a lot is an emperor (king).[94] "Political World" (1989) is a completely negative song. In a political world, love has no place, wisdom is jailed, mercy is put to death, courage is extinct, and peace is unwelcome. In "Everything is Broken" (1989), he refers to all of the things that are broken in the political world of the present fallen age. The title of Dylan's 1993 album seems to sum up his attitude toward human authority: "World Gone Wrong."[95]

If we try to think of a prominent Christian anarchist in the United States or elsewhere today, no one will come to mind. This is an indication of how standardized and compromised Christianity has become. Ironically, this cookie-cutter, culturally comfortable type of religion is most pervasive among Bible-believing Christians—the very group that should be most antithetical to worldly norms and most open to thinking outside of the box because they claim to take the words of Scripture seriously.

In some ways, this literalism does have countercultural effects. In the Western world, the overall narrative and plain meaning of specific passages of the Bible lead most theologically orthodox Christians to refrain from glorification of homosexuality and to reject same-sex marriage. Yet one senses that the most vocal of the antihomosexuality champions lack the spirit of the Kingdom of God even if they have its letter. This hinders their cause because it is short on nuance and context. Righteousness can thereby be too easily dismissed by others as self-righteousness. One also wonders how much this opposition to homosexuality is rooted in the Bible and the Holy Spirit versus in cultural tradition and self-satisfied insularity.

Most of these advocates of biblical norms and spiritual holiness fail to extend their countercultural approach to areas that are less convenient to their national and political allegiances. Believers in God who can see the inherent problems or harm of homosexuality and abortion rarely see weaknesses or sin with materialism, capitalism, military-centered patriotism, subtle-but-ingrained racism, culturally ordained sexism, commodification of nonhuman living creatures, violence, or war. To question or oppose these things would put American Christians—especially white, affluent, older American Christians—in the personally uncomfortable position of going against their own lifestyle and the political assumptions of their friends and neighbors. It would be inconvenient and embarrassing. So the hard sayings of Jesus and the lyrics of Mary and the warnings of James and the implications of Genesis are ignored. Or simply never noticed. The average American evangelical Christian is too conformed to the world to even realize that he or she needs to be transformed by a renewal of the mind.[96]

This is where someone like Bob Dylan could have a beneficial effect. Granted, he is not known as a Christian anarchist and his influence is negligible among the very brothers and sisters in Christ who are most in need. Still, he stands as an example of someone who uses Bible literalism and Spirit transformation to question some of the basic assumptions of our dominant culture.

A little over a century ago, the world recognized the spiritual radicalism, the Christian anarchism, of Leo Tolstoy. He made a name for himself as a novelist but became a social philosopher. Dylan follows in this tradition of literary-figure-as-cultural-critic. Sadly, though understandably, Dylan's role as an explicitly Christian witness has been muted. Since the 1990s, he has also been too willing to give precious space on his infrequent new studio recordings to second-rate love songs rather than to spiritually informed denunciations of folly and evil. This is regrettable but we should be more grateful for what we have than frustrated by what we don't. Dylan remains standing as a voice of cultural dissent. A personally inconsistent but still-compelling scourge of institutionalized nonsense. An undercover example of Christian anarchism.

CHAPTER 7

Dylanesque Politics in the Real World

"All or Nothing—or Little" may be an interesting abstraction but what relevance does it have for the real world? Successful politicians do not go around calling themselves Christian anarchists. Even Christian politicians are discreet and selective in talking about the lordship of Christ. They do not want to alienate voters and donors. They do not want to acquire the reputation of being a religious nut. Are there examples of politicians who are different from their peers—in the way that Dylan is different from fellow singer-songwriters—when it comes to religion and philosophy, rhetoric and policy? If we cannot identify such examples, talk of Christian anarchism remains pie-in-the-sky. An intellectual abstraction is neither helpful nor historical.

Can Dylan's politics be applied to the real world of power in Washington, DC? While Dylan himself is indifferent or hostile to electoral politics, are there any examples of Dylanesque politicians? Are there examples of Christian anarchists who are sincerely committed to the Kingdom of God and are encouraging decentralized power, liberty, community, democracy, morality, social justice, and peace in the fallen world in which we live? Are there examples of Christians who seem to have an "All or Nothing—or Little" philosophy, who believe not only in worldly separatism but also in social ethics?

Dylanesque Politicians

Interviewed on tour, in Dayton, Ohio, in May 1980, Dylan said, "God will stay with America as long as America stays with God. A lot of people maybe even the President, maybe a lot of senators, you hear them speak and they'll speak of the attributes of God. But none of them are speaking about being a disciple of Christ."[1]

At the time, President Jimmy Carter was one of the nation's most famous born-again Christians. In the wake of Watergate, he emphasized Christian morality and his Southern Baptist roots while running for the White House in 1974–76. He also had a couple of Dylan connections. As governor of Georgia, he had hosted a postconcert party in Atlanta during Dylan's 1974 tour. After winning the Democratic presidential nomination, in 1976, Carter quoted a line from "It's Alright Ma (I'm Only Bleeding)" during his acceptance speech at the national convention in New York City. Despite Carter's highly publicized faith and links to Dylan, the singer was willing to implicitly criticize Carter in 1980. He was making a fair point. Once Carter was elected, for the most part he governed like most other politicians. His public references to God were generic, as is typical of presidents. His pragmatic streak continued as president. (While he touted his honesty during the campaign, he was known for fuzzy positions and for talking out of both sides of his mouth.) He paid lip service to human rights, but his foreign policy was guided by traditional realpolitik concerns of power and profit. Although Carter has been a more principled Christian after leaving the White House, his time in office was not characterized by Kingdom values. For this reason, he is not a good example of a Dylanesque politician. Another recent evangelical president, George W. Bush, also fails in this regard.[2]

Christian anarchism is inherently antiestablishment. If we find politicians in DC possessing aspects of this ideology, they will necessarily be antiestablishment—both politically and economically. Whatever else they were, Presidents Carter and Bush were not antiestablishment. As a candidate, the former allied himself with David Rockefeller of Standard Oil, Chase Manhattan Bank, and the Trilateral Commission. On the national level, the latter was the political creation of the Wall Street wing of the Republican Party that had earlier opened doors for his father and grandfather.

Thinking of the modern era of American politics during the past 55 years (since 1960), there are some federal elected officials who have been populists, who have emphasized the common good, who have tried to make peace rather than war. Senator Paul Wellstone (DFL-MN) and, even more consistently, Senator Russ Feingold (D-WI) come to mind from the 1990s and 2000s. However, they have been adherents of Judaism so they do not fit so well with Christian anarchism. Like Dylan, they have been Jews; unlike Dylan, they have not been converts to Christianity.[3]

Further back in time, we find a pair of Protestant evangelicals in the 1960s and 1970s: Senators Mark Hatfield (R-OR) and Harold Hughes

(D-IA). Hatfield was an evangelical Baptist. Hughes was a born-again Methodist. Both were near-pacifists. They were leading liberals/progressives within their respective parties, but their concern for the sanctity of life and belief in nonviolence extended to unborn babies. Hatfield continued in the Senate through the 1990s.

On January 12, 1991, Hatfield was one of only two Republicans in the Senate to oppose a resolution endorsing President George H. W. Bush's planned war against Iraq. The other GOP member who opposed the Persian Gulf War was Senator Chuck Grassley (R-IA). The Senate vote occurred five days before the bombing of Baghdad began and five weeks before Dylan performed "Masters of War" at the Grammy Awards. Grassley, an evangelical Christian, has been a conservative populist since joining Congress in the 1970s. He is not a pacifist but is skeptical of the military-industrial complex. He is a critic of monopolistic agribusiness even though he is from a farm state. He is a common-sense constitutionalist who has earned a reputation for being a maverick within his own party. He upholds the same principles of government even when Republicans are in the White House. In some ways, Grassley is a throwback to the Robert La Follette and Robert Taft traditions within the party.[4]

Two self-identified heirs of La Follette liberalism were Senators Wayne Morse (R/I/D-OR) and William Proxmire (D-WI). Both supported democratization of politics, emphasized frugal government, and opposed imperial wars. Morse was a leading voice for these principles from the 1940s through the 1960s. Proxmire carried the torch from the 1950s through the 1980s. Morse cast one of two votes in the Senate against the prowar Gulf of Tonkin Resolution in 1964. The only House member to publicly oppose the Resolution was Congressman Eugene Siler (R-KY), a Taft conservative. Morse and Proxmire were not known to be religious men, but Siler, a devout Southern Baptist, exemplified a type of Christian politics that dissented from the norms of the wealth-and-power establishment in the 1950s and 1960s. Earlier, in the 1940s and 1950s, Congressman Howard Buffett (R-NE), another Taft Republican, played a similar role.[5]

More recent Christian politicians who have been critical of Wall Street, centralized power, internationalism, and/or globalization include Congressman John Ashbrook (R-OH), Senator Jesse Helms (R-NC), Congressman Larry McDonald (D-GA), Senator Tom Coburn (R-OK), and Congressman John Kasich (R-OH). They have been evangelical Protestants and conservative populists. Other Christian statesmen who come to mind are Senator Jim DeMint (R-SC) and Congressman Jeff Fortenberry (R-NE).

We can also include Roman Catholics such as House Assistant Majority Leader David Bonior (D-MI), Congresswoman Marcy Kaptur (D-OH),

Congressman Dennis Kucinich (D-OH), and Congresswoman Cynthia McKinney (D-GA). They have been liberal populists. Governor Jerry Brown (D-CA), a Catholic who has been influenced by Buddhism, was a prominent national voice for alternative values from the 1970s through the 1990s, but he has been more conventional and establishment since that time.[6] Older examples include the liberal populists Senator Frank Church (D-ID), a Presbyterian, and Senator James Abourezk (D-SD), a Greek Orthodox. However, Church and Abourezk were not known for their Christian faith. The same can be said for two populist mavericks elected to the US Senate in 2006: Jim Webb (D-VA) and Jon Tester (D-MT).

In his May 1980 interview in Dayton, Dylan talked about being a disciple of Christ. In contrast to the spiritual truths he was sharing, he said, "I wouldn't have much to offer anybody who wants to know about politics or history or art or any of that. I've always been pretty extreme in all them areas anyway." Dylan's comment says something about the ideological nature of Dylanesque politicians. There is a reason that they are often depicted as extremists by the corporate media, who act as gatekeepers of respectability. Dylanesque politicians are usually on the principled Left or principled Right rather than in the pragmatic Center with its mammon and empire. This makes sense because discerning Christians who are acquainted with power often recognize the spirit of Antichrist and Babylon in the Center. The words of Larry Norman apply in this context: "There are extremes in life," and the truth is found "in the extremes" because "the truth is far from the lie."[7] This maxim is not always applicable but it applies here and the perspective resonates with Dylan.

In September 2001, the Senate voted 98–0 and the House voted 420–1 to authorize President George W. Bush to use military force as he saw fit in retaliation for the 9/11 terrorism. As a result, he began the longest war in US history: the Afghanistan War. Citing her Christianity as the main reason for being the lone dissenter, Congresswoman Barbara Lee (D-CA) said, "I take my faith seriously. I'm not going to wave the Bible...But let me tell you: I am a person of deep faith. I think my vote was based in my religion and my faith. Where else do you go to at a time like this?"[8]

Congressman Chris Smith (R-NJ), a Catholic, is prolife and prolabor, supportive of human rights and critical of globalization. Congressman Ron Paul (R-TX), a Protestant, has been a leader of conservative populism and libertarianism from the 1970s through the 2010s. His allies in the House have included Jimmy Duncan (R-TN), Walter Jones (R-VA), Virgil Goode (D/I/R-VA), Justin Amash (R-MI), and Thomas Massie (R-KY). His son, Senator Rand Paul (R-KY), is a better politician than Ron Paul, possessing both the pluses and minuses that accompany that talent. As an antiestablishment leader, Rand Paul's national career began with a bang when his maiden speech on the Senate floor criticized the moral weakness of the many compromises of his famous predecessor Henry Clay. However, once Senator Paul began having his own presidential ambitions, compromising became an increasingly frequent mode of operation for himself.

Barry Goldwater and George McGovern

When thinking of Dylanesque politicians, one possibility is Senator Barry Goldwater (R-AZ). He was the 1964 Republican presidential nominee. As mentioned in chapter 1, in his *Chronicles* memoir, Dylan surprisingly says that Goldwater was his "favorite politician" in the early 1960s.[9] Even when wrong, Goldwater seemed to be above-average in integrity and courage, in the context of national politicians. Since Dylan didn't like phonies, this would have appealed to the young singer. With his libertarian philosophy, Goldwater may have sometimes been in the vicinity of the second half of the "Christian anarchist" label, but he was never known for being Christian. He was a secular statesman who intrigued young Dylan but the mature Dylan, as a Christian, would probably have found Goldwater's worldview to be more deficient.

Another possibility is Senator George McGovern (D-SD), a man with Christian roots who was born and raised in one of the states that borders Dylan's Minnesota. He was the 1972 Democratic presidential nominee. In some ways, McGovern was the most Jeffersonian ("radical") Democrat nominated for president since W. J. Bryan in 1908. Although he was an electoral hero of the New Left and the Counterculture and was widely viewed as ultraliberal in 1972, McGovern had a conservative side to him, as well. Like Bryan and the Populist Party of the 1890s, he was conservative in the sense of wanting to return to earlier American traditions.[10] McGovern is not a perfect fit for the "Christian anarchist" designation, however, because he tended to be a statist who looked to the federal government to solve problems. And while born into a family headed by a Wesleyan Methodist minister, McGovern himself did not hold to the evangelical faith of his father.

Despite being seen as opposites in the 1960s and 1970s, Goldwater on the Right and McGovern on the Left shared a number of important traits. They were both more principled than the average politician. They were both largely Jeffersonian (despite Goldwater's militarism and McGovern's statism). They were both populists who clashed with their party's establishment. They both lost presidential elections in landslides partly because they were abandoned by these establishments. In 1968, Goldwater told his aide Karl Hess, "When the histories are written, I'll bet that the Old Right and the New Left are put down as having a lot in common and that the people in the middle will be the enemy."[11]

Mark Hatfield and Harold Hughes

Of course, in some ways, this is an exercise in absurdity. We can almost imagine a Dylan lyric on the subject from his jokey, surreal-dream 1964–65 period: "Ridin' down the road with Jerry Brown and Jesse Helms / My head it was a-hurtin' / / Thought I saw, pumpin' gas, Liz Taylor and Richard Burton / It was premium."

Many of these politicians have had a Jeffersonian vibe but none have had a Dylanesque vibe. Bob Dylan is a unique individual, and his career as a poet and musician does not easily lend itself to finding close equivalents among the political class. Still, if Dylan has a discernible politics—and we think he does—we must be able to find ideological compatriots who share some of his basic values and tendencies. Specifically, those who try, as Christians, to be loyal to the Kingdom of God even as they live out their daily lives in the portion of the fallen world we call the United States of America. Of the examples mentioned earlier, Mark Hatfield and Harold Hughes probably come closest to the Dylan model, if we can imagine that model being translated from music into statecraft.

In 1970–71, Senator Hughes explored a candidacy for the 1972 Democratic presidential nomination. He decided against running partly because his Christian pacifism would have prevented him from launching nuclear weapons against innocent civilians overseas as commander-in-chief of the armed forces during the Cold War. The overarching factor was his unwillingness to lose his soul through political compromises. And he knew that "man's relationships cannot be changed by political acts and alliances alone, but change must start in his heart." When deciding to retire from the US Senate rather than seek another term, he told the press, in September 1973, "Rightly or wrongly, I believe that I can move more people through a spiritual approach more effectively than I have been able to achieve through the political approach."[12] This is the same viewpoint that Dylan would express in the early 1980s when he remarked that "people need Jesus" but "the powers that be" say that social ills must be "healed politically."[13]

Hatfield was touted as a 1968 presidential possibility by young peace-minded Republicans. Hughes seriously considering running for the presidency four years later. Politically savvy observers assumed that Hatfield and Hughes were too honest and too radical to ever gain the White House. Part of the problem with both men, from a pragmatic, establishment point of view, was that they had a consistent prolife ethic, from abortion to war.

Governor Hatfield became the nation's first prominent Republican to publicly oppose the Vietnam War in 1965. Governor Hughes placed antiwar candidate Eugene McCarthy's name into nomination at the 1968 Democratic National Convention in Chicago. Working with George McGovern, in 1970, Senator Hatfield cosponsored the McGovern-Hatfield amendment that would have ended Vietnam War combat operations and set a deadline for withdrawal of US troops by cutting off funds. The amendment failed because of opposition from President Nixon, most Republicans, and hawkish Democrats. Senator Hughes supported it.

On September 21, 1973, Harold Hughes proved that his mind had not been polluted by the false philosophy of Henry Kissinger (to paraphrase Dylan in "Gonna Change My Way of Thinking").[14] He voted against the confirmation of Kissinger as secretary of state, saying that he had "a chilling, chessboard view of the world" and his philosophy was "inimical to the long range cause of world peace and inconsistent with the moral purpose of our nation."[15] Hughes was on the losing side—Kissinger was easily approved by a vote of 78–7.

Four months after the *Roe v. Wade* decision, in which seven men—including six Republican appointees—struck down all state antiabortion laws, Hughes and Hatfield worked together to introduce a constitutional amendment to protect unborn life.[16] The reader may or may not agree with the abortion views of Hatfield and Hughes, but the point here is that they were politicians trying to consistently apply their Christian principles. In the process of this application, they were countercultural in the sense of going against the tide of both upper-class, elite mores and grassroots progressive attitudes.[17] Right or wrong, this took courage and it is indicative of a Dylanesque flavor to their politics.

After becoming a born-again Christian later in the decade, did Bob Dylan agree with Hughes and Hatfield on abortion? It seems as though criticism of abortion would have fit well within "Slow Train," "Gonna Change My Way of Thinking," or "When You Gonna Wake Up" (1979), but it is not there. In the song "Lenny Bruce" (1981), the hero is complimented for not having decapitated any babies, which could be a reference to abortion. In "Foot of Pride" (1983), Dylan mentions casual, merciless infanticide in the context of Revelation 17:5. The following year, in an interview, Dylan declined to join the antiabortion political crusade, however. Dylan told *Rolling Stone*, "I personally don't think abortion is that important." Asked if abortion is taking a human life, Dylan replied, "Well, if the woman wants to take that upon herself, I figure that's her business. I mean, who's gonna take care of the baby that arrives—these people that are callin' for no abortion?" It was a libertarian, prochoice response but Dylan did not argue against a moral dimension to abortion. Later in the chapter, we will see that he put abortion into a wider context of commercialized contraception that encourages casual sex.[18]

A Christian publisher issued Senator Hatfield's book *Between a Rock and a Hard Place* in 1976. While he was an evangelical Baptist himself, Hatfield's theology had roots in, or at least congruence with, the Anabaptists of sixteenth-century Europe. The Anabaptist movement was the radical wing of the Protestant Reformation and was an example of Christian anarchism.[19] In the United States, its legacy can be seen among the Amish, Mennonites, Hutterites, and (partly) Church of the Brethren. The list of sources in the endnotes of Hatfield's book is replete with Christian anarchists, including Tolstoy, John Howard Yoder, Cecil John Cadoux, Thomas Merton, and E. F. Schumacher (plus non-Christian anarchists Mohandas Gandhi and Erich Fromm).[20]

The radical nature of Hatfield's Christ Against Culture theology—even as he actively engaged culture in the imperial city—can be seen in every chapter. He describes the National Prayer Breakfast, on February 1, 1973, at which he was a speaker. At the Washington Hilton Hotel that morning, he was seated at the head table between Rev. Billy Graham and President Richard Nixon amid 3,000 other people.

Hatfield began his speech by warning his colleagues about "the real danger of misplaced allegiance, if not outright idolatry" through failing to distinguish between "the god of an American civil religion and the God who reveals Himself in the Holy Scriptures and in Jesus Christ." He described the god of civil religion as "a loyal spiritual Advisor to power and prestige, a Defender of only the American nation, the object of a national folk religion devoid of moral content." He cited Jesus's warning in Luke 6:46 about "false petitioners," and said, "We sit here today, as the wealthy and the powerful. But let us not forget that those who follow Christ will more often find themselves not with comfortable majorities, but with miserable minorities." Continuing with his prophetic tone, Hatfield called for repentance. He closed by citing Romans 12:2, saying, "Lives lived under the Lordship of Jesus Christ at this point in our history may well put us at odds with values of our society, abuses of political power, and cultural conformity of our church... We must continually be transformed by Jesus Christ and take His commands seriously... Then we can soothe the wounds of war, and renew the face of the earth and all mankind."

Nixon aides were angry and Graham was annoyed.[21] It was an astounding thing to do, and it is reminiscent of Dylan's unwelcome speech at the Emergency Civil Liberties Committee dinner in December 1963. Unlike

Hatfield, Dylan was young and drunk but the same prophetic speaking-truth-to-power vibe is present in both. For the most part, the messages fell on deaf ears as the respectable crowds bristled at the gauche, offensive, crazy remarks (from their perspectives).[22]

Billy Graham, a friend of Hatfield, wrote a letter of gentle admonishment to him afterward. Graham was more cutting in a private telephone conversation with his friend Nixon. The evangelist always had a regrettable tendency to fawn over presidents. For example, during this conversation, the tape reveals Graham saying that he agrees that Nixon is "the greatest President that we've ever had in the history of America" and "I believe the Lord is with you." Nixon shrugs off the comments made by Hatfield but says that they were in "rather bad taste" and were "out of line." Graham agrees but goes further. He was mortified: "Oh, it was terrible. I sat there so embarrassed, I didn't know what to do." Graham thinks that Hatfield should have thanked "Mr. President" for brokering a ceasefire in Vietnam (after waging war for four years). That would have been Graham's preference, "Instead of getting up [and] talking about the sins and so forth. It really was terrible." When Nixon calls Hatfield "a strange fellow sometimes," Graham agrees, saying, "I don't understand him. He is the big disappointment in political life." Nixon suggests that Hatfield is just pandering to campus radicals. Graham responds, "Yes, but to use a platform like that in your presence at a Presidential prayer breakfast which we leaned over backwards all these years to keep non-political, and to get up and do a thing like that was just inexcusable. And if he has any part in it next year, I don't intend to go." Graham then adds, "And you know the interesting thing about it is that Harold Hughes is getting deep into this [Senate] prayer breakfast thing and he goes to every single meeting. He's on every committee, and pretending to be, you know, a great Christian."[23]

In Chapter 9 of *Between a Rock and a Hard Place*, Senator Hatfield is skeptical of the Just War Theory. Rooted in the theology of Augustine and Aquinas, this theory could be used to limit war-making but far more commonly it has been used to excuse war-making. In application, the emphasis has been on justification not justice, on rationalization not restraint. Hatfield argues, "War is always a terrible evil. It is never good nor glorious. Nothing about a just war makes that war good; it is never more than a necessary evil... The Bible constantly condemns war and equates it with humanity's worst sins. Further, outright militarism always falls under God's judgment, and is never an option for the Christian." He then contrasts what he sees as the perspective of Christ with that of American culture: "A far different attitude pervades society and infects churches. War is frequently glorified.

Righteous in cause, war is seen as virtuous in conduct. History's greatest moments are the wars successfully won...In America we do not mourn over past wars; we extol them...even when the motives were obviously tarnished with imperialism."[24]

Hatfield even raises a cultural issue that is almost never considered by Americans, writing, "Millions of dollars are spent on toy guns and games of violence for our children, who can grow up believing that war is natural and even fun." When Bob Dylan was asked about seemingly endless wars, eight years later, in 1983, he responded, "You know the toy manufacturers that make guns and tanks for small children? They are as much to be held responsible for death and destruction of the planet as any important arms manufacturer. They're just doing it for little people. They're the ones who start the assembly line of death. They light the match. In the end there's a supreme judge they'll have to answer to for this."[25]

Partly grounded in the decentralist Republican tradition of Robert Taft, Hatfield is critical of big government and big business. He writes, "People believe the federal government has grown too big; that it spends too much money to accomplish far too little; that what it does spend it frequently wastes; that it has lost touch with its citizens; that it employs too many presumptuous bureaucrats...To an unsettling degree, they are right." He argues that bureaucracy has led to alienation by average Americans in the face of "the massive size of society's corporate and political apparatus" and "complex centralization of modern institutions."[26]

As a young politician, Hatfield was an early supporter of General Dwight Eisenhower for president and was an Eisenhower delegate at the 1952 national convention when Senator Robert Taft lost his third and final race for the White House. Hatfield had not supported Taft when he had the chance, but in 1970–71 he was calling himself a Taft Republican in order to draw a contrast between his views and the militarism and imperialism of the party's mainstream.[27] Hatfield's appreciation for Taft apparently was sparked by a deepened understanding of power and the world. This coincided with his deepened understanding of Scripture and the Kingdom of God.

By this time, Hatfield admired the work of Murray Rothbard and the libertarian economist/activist reciprocated by endorsing Hatfield for president in 1970. Rothbard distinguished Senator Hatfield from Mayor John Lindsay, a silk-stocking Rockefeller Republican, saying the two were not ideologically similar. Instead, Rothbard identified Hatfield as a classical liberal "devoted to the creed of a strictly limited government: limited at home and abroad." Rothbard went on to observe, "Mark Hatfield sees that the only hope for liberty on the political front is to forge a new coalition, a coalition combining the libertarian ideas of both Left and Right." Rothbard quotes Hatfield as having recently said, "I have not, like Faust, sold my soul to politics," but he does not specifically mention his Christian faith. In Mark Hatfield's case, it was his radical Christianity that allowed him to rise above the falseness of party labels and ideological categories to see the common good and the deeper principles.[28] The same was true for Harold Hughes. And Bob Dylan.

International Relations

The foreign policy of Bob Dylan can be summarized as a trio of negatives: antimilitarism, anti-imperialism, and antiglobalization. Summarizing his views in their oppositional format is fitting because the singer-songwriter has more often spoken as a critic of a morally bankrupt status quo than as an advocate of alternative approaches. More as a prophet denouncing evil than as a visionary suggesting good. But we if we want to put things more positively, we can say that Dylan stands for peace, republic, and local economy (with corresponding skepticism toward war, empire, and global capitalism). More specifically, we can say that emphases of nationalism over internationalism, peace over war, hostility toward the military-industrial complex, and belief that wealthy Northeastern interests drive US foreign policy have been present in Dylan's recordings and interviews since the early 1960s. These tendencies were supplemented by his full embrace of the Jewish/Christian prophetic tradition beginning in 1979.

Tor Egil Førland of the University of Oslo sees a consistent foreign policy message in the songs of Dylan stretching from the early 1960s to the early 1990s: "It contains two central elements. One—aversion to war—leads to protests against its effects on individuals caught in the war machine, and to finger-pointing at munitions makers and defense authorities. The other element consists of a rejection of foreign trade because of its effects on US producers, and leads Dylan to blame Eastern or foreign capitalists." As a "midwestern isolationist" from Minnesota, Dylan could be thought of as a musical latter-day Charles Lindbergh Sr. or Henrik Shipstead.[29]

The word "isolationist" is an insulting epithet first used in the 1930s by imperialists ("internationalists"). It was used to describe nationalists and peace-minded Americans like Shipstead and the younger Lindbergh who resisted entry into a second European war because they had a negative assessment of the first such war 20 years earlier and because they adhered to traditional US foreign policy. Following Washington, Jefferson, and John Quincy Adams, "isolationists" wish to avoid foreign quarrels and entangling alliances. In other words, they wish to isolate the American people only from military and political ties that are likely to draw them into unnecessary wars that have little to do with genuine national defense.[30] "Isolationists" support engagement with the rest of the world when it comes to knowledge and friendship, free travel and free trade.

Dylan wrote some classic antiwar songs during the early part of his career, including "Blowin' in the Wind" (1963), "John Brown" (1963), "Masters of War" (1963), and "With God On Our Side" (1964). Since his Christian conversion, he has written and/or performed other antiwar songs, including "Clean-Cut Kid" (1985), "They Killed Him" (1986), and "Two Soldiers" (1993). In 1980, he told an interviewer, "People don't look at war as a business. They look at it as an emotional thing. When you get right down to it, however, war—unless one people need another people's land—is a business."[31]

Dylan participated in the Peace Sunday concert in 1982. In "Union Sundown" (1983), he said that violence, not democracy, rules the world. In an interview for *Biograph*, in 1985, he mentioned that the Devil rules the world and so Dylan equates violence with evil. Also in connection with *Biograph*, he said, "Did you ever hear that to conquer your enemy, you must repent first, fall down on your knees and beg for mercy? Does West Point teach that? I don't know, I do know that God hates a proud look." He also touched on his familiar theme of the military-industrial complex, mentioning "the armaments manufacturers selling weapons to both sides in a war, inventing bigger and bigger things to take your head off while behind your back, there's a few people laughing and getting rich off your vanity."[32]

Dylan told an interviewer in 1986 that there would be "no moral value" to having US troops intervene in Central America and that he disagreed with the bombing of Libya. In "Political World" (1989), he said that peace is unwelcome in a political world. He pointedly sang "Masters of War" in concert at the US Military Academy at West Point in October 1990 as the US government moved toward war with Iraq. He sang the same song during the Persian Gulf War at the nationally televised February 1991 Grammy Awards ceremony, on the occasion of receiving a Lifetime Achievement Award.[33]

Dylan's liner notes for "Two Soldiers" (1993), a nonoriginal song about the Civil War, mentioned "war dominated by finance (lending money for interest being a nauseating & revolting thing)."[34] Talking about the Civil War, in 2012, Dylan said, "If you want to know what it was about, read the daily newspapers from that time both the North and South. You'll see things that you won't believe... It's nothing like what you read in the history books. It's way more deadly and hateful. There doesn't seem to be anything heroic or honorable about it at all. It was suicidal. Four years of looting and plunder and murder done the American way." At the same time, Dylan did not take the Confederate nostalgia position of simply blaming the horrors of war on Lincoln: "The United States burned and destroyed itself for the sake of slavery. The USA wouldn't give it up... The whole system had to be ripped out with force... A lot of destruction to end slavery. And that's what it really was all about." He correctly identified what was immediately at stake after the election of 1860: "They [Lincoln and the leading northern Republicans] weren't trying to take the slaves away. They just wanted to keep slavery from spreading."[35]

Dylan has denied that "Masters of War" is an antiwar song. When asked by Robert Hilburn of the *Los Angeles Times* to give an example of a song that has been widely misinterpreted, Dylan responded, "Take 'Masters of War.' Every time I sing it, someone writes that it's an antiwar song. But there's no antiwar sentiment in that song. I'm not a pacifist. I don't think I've ever been one. If you look closely at the song, it's about what Eisenhower was saying about the dangers of the military-industrial complex in this country. I believe strongly in everyone's right to defend themselves by every means necessary." Shortly thereafter, in an interview with Mikal Gilmore of *Rolling Stone*, Dylan reiterated the point: "I've said before that song's got nothing to do with being anti-war. It has more to do with the military industrial complex that Eisenhower was talking about."[36] In these comments, Dylan was apparently sincere. But he was overstating his case. He was speaking in the wake of 9/11 and at the time (2001) he probably supported the war in Afghanistan as a just means of eradicating terrorism that had killed thousands of innocents. Dylan is both pacifist-minded *and* patriotic-minded.

Right after making his comments to Hilburn about "Masters of War," Dylan spoke on related subjects that had a patriotic theme. He said, "I think something changed in the country around 1966 or so. You'll have to look at the history books to really sort it out, but there are people who manipulated the Vietnam War. They were traitors to America, whoever they were. It was the beginning of the corporate takeover of America." He later added, "If we're not careful, we'll wake up in a multinational, multiethnic police state—not that America can't reverse itself. Whoever invented America were the greatest minds we've ever seen, and [people] who understand what the Declaration of Independence and the Bill of Rights are all about will come to the forefront sooner or later."[37] This is not a hippie-dippy "peace, love, and granola" viewpoint. This is coming from a more nuanced place of nationalism and populism.

Dylan's criticism of "a multinational, multiethnic police state" foreshadowed the setting of his film *Masked and Anonymous* (2003).[38] As a lifelong advocate and practitioner of ethnic inclusiveness, Dylan was not objecting to a multiethnic society per se. He was objecting to a police state coupled with a globalistic type of multiculturalism imposed from above by transnational corporations lacking loyalty to America and treasonous politicians willing to sell out American traditions for personal wealth and power.

Is this type of patriotism of the Left or of the Right? It is of both. In mixing nationalism with populism, it echoes both the Old Right and the New Left. There is a figure of national stature with comparable views on economic and foreign policy: Ralph Nader. Nader and Dylan are contemporaries, with the former being born in Connecticut to immigrant parents (1934) seven years before Dylan was born in Minnesota to children-of-immigrant parents (1941). Both are of Semitic ethnicity (Nader being Arab, specifically Lebanese; Dylan being Jewish). It is worth examining Nader in some detail to show that Dylan is not an idiosyncratic anomaly. Dylan, like Nader, belongs to an ideological tradition that cuts across simple-minded Left/Right categorization.

Ralph Nader is often caricatured as an ultraliberal, socialist type. He certainly has a progressive side to him but, as with Bob Dylan, conventional wisdom ignores important parts of his life and thought. Nader the crusader for truth and justice has largely derived his worldview from his parents. They owned and operated a restaurant and bakery, and Nader grew up in the small town of Winsted. He was raised by hard-working parents who taught him traditional values that he holds to this day—values like honesty, thrift, fairness, the common good, and a sense of right and wrong.[39] These were the values of small business and Main Street, not big business and Wall Street. Nader is a true believer in concepts like the Constitution, the rule of law, checks and balances, local community, and national sovereignty.

Populists on both the Left and the Right believe that the rise of giant, monopolistic corporations and their influence on government was not a conservative cause. It was a revolutionary rejection of traditional American values—a rejection of competition, free enterprise, and democracy. The values pushed by many Fortune 500 companies often go against the best American traditions. What is conservative about materialism, personal debt, planned obsolescence, and Madison Avenue with its phoniness and artificially created "needs"? In searching for an alternative to big government to check misdeeds by big business, as set forth in his recent book *Unstoppable: The Emerging Left-Right Alliance to Dismantle the Corporate State*, Nader is returning to his youth.[40] He has always had a traditionalistic, small-business, patriotic streak that is compatible not only with Jeffersonian liberalism exemplified by Bryan and La Follette but also with Jeffersonian conservatism exemplified by Taft and Goldwater.

Nader's first publication in a national magazine was "Business Is Deserting America," published in 1960 by *American Mercury*, an Old Right periodical. The article's opening sentence seems to mock foreign aid such as the

Marshall Plan. Nader also refers to the US government's "ingrained gullibility to internationalism." The main point of the article is a condemnation of overseas corporate investment and production.[41] This patriotic emphasis on America First—an emphasis compatible with a humanitarian, nonimperial type of internationalism—has never gone away.

In 1996, Nader wrote an editorial for the conservative *Washington Times* calling on the owners and managers of multinational corporations to say the Pledge of Allegiance at every annual shareholder meeting. He followed this up with letters to the CEOs of the 100 largest US-based corporations. The response? Only one big company said, "Yes, that's a good idea"...and they did not end up doing it. The other 99 were not very interested in pledging allegiance to America. Their loyalties lie elsewhere—perhaps to the Almighty Dollar. Traditionalistic conservatives like Pat Buchanan join Nader in noting the irony: corporations that have been chartered in America and have benefited greatly from government tax breaks, marketing, bailouts, and military protection have little sense of loyalty to the United States of America.[42] It is one downside of globalization. This critique is shared by Bob Dylan.

For sake of clarification, a second example of someone who shares membership in the ideological tradition to which Dylan belongs will be mentioned in passing. Wendell Berry is a contemporary of Dylan and Nader who shares their perspective on economic and foreign policy. He was born in 1934—five months after Nader. Raised in rural Kentucky, Berry has an agrarian emphasis as a farmer and writer. He is a Christian pacifist. Berry is an opponent of plutocracy and globalization. He supports decentralization of political and economic power. Like Dylan and Nader, Berry appeals to both the populist Left and the traditional Right.[43] All three men are bigger than partisan politics.

An examination of four songs written in the early 1960s reveals that Dylan was indeed publicly antiwar during that period of his life. "Blowin' in the Wind" speaks poetically-but-favorably of banning cannonballs. At the time, this language would have evoked thoughts of the Ban the Bomb movement in regard to nuclear weapons. "Let Me Die in My Footsteps" speaks of Dylan's wish that all weapons be thrown into the sea because they are part of a flawed past. "Masters of War" speaks not only of the military-industrial complex but also of the lie that a world war is winnable by anyone. "With God on Our Side" speaks of the irrationality of nuclear war—even when seemingly necessary—and expresses the thought that God will stop the next war if he is truly on our side.[44]

It is true that Dylan is not Leo Tolstoy or A. J. Muste in terms of unswerving commitment to nonviolence at all times and places. He is not a pure pacifist and never has been in that sense of the word. But "pacifist" comes from a French word that goes back to the Latin word *pax*, meaning "peace." Overall, Dylan has been a peace-minded person. So when Dylan says, "I'm not a pacifist," he is right if by "pacifist" he means a no-exceptions antiwar person, but he is wrong if he means someone who usually prefers peace to war. Dylan is not a dogmatic advocate of unilteral disarmament or collective nonviolence, but given his qualifications on war—whether we consider his warning about the plutocratically inspired military-industrial complex or his emphasis on the right of defense (perhaps using the Just War Theory of post-312 Christianity)—over the years Dylan has been far more antiwar than prowar. Most of the time, he has been a de facto pacifist.[45]

One factor in Dylan's tendency to oppose war is his opposition to empire. He believes in national self-defense but understands the distinction between wars of defense and wars of aggression. He does not succumb to the idolatry and folly of American Exceptionalism despite being patriotic. Because he is a patriot who knows history and respects tradition, he prefers a republic at home and abroad instead of an empire with overbearing government domestically and internationally. (Of course, this also fits with his anarchism.) Just as William Jennings Bryan and his allies tried to stop—unsuccessfully—the rise of the US empire in 1898–1900 by appealing to America's origins as a people who cast off distant, imperial rule, Dylan does not see US imperialism as appropriate for a nation of free, self-governing citizens. In addition to using the Declaration of Independence, Bryan used the Bible to oppose imperialism, including a speech based on the story of Naboth's vineyard. Likewise, Dylan's Christianity has reinforced his anti-imperialism. He recognizes that human lust for power will eventually culminate in a global empire of the Antichrist.[46]

Dylan's patriotism is also kept within proper bounds by his sense of fair play (justice) and by his understanding of the relative unimportance of the temporal United States in comparison to the eternal Kingdom of God. At a November 1979 concert, his American patriotism was tempered by his Christian separatism: "Well, let me tell you now: the devil owns this world; he's called the god of this world. Now we're living in America. I like America, just as everybody else does... I love America, I gotta say that... But America will be judged." Referring to the coming End Times, Dylan contrasted faith in the nation with faith in Jesus Christ the "solid rock." This was a very Jesus Movement à la Watchman Nee way of expressing himself. Dylan revealed a similar perspective in a 1986 interview when he said that while he supported "American principles," he considered "eternal things" to be more important.[47]

Dylan's reference in "Slow Train" to Arab oil producers was seen by some as racist and jingoistic. At the time, Noel Paul Stookey—fellow Christian and Paul of Peter, Paul and Mary—wrote that "the political activist has misread the reference to sheiks controlling America's power in 'Slow Train' as a conservative political posture," when "it is, in fact, an accurate portrayal of the larger picture of world greed and man's subsequent dependence upon its luxuries and niceties as though they were life itself."[48] Whether Dylan intended it as a condemnation of greed or globalization or both, it was probably not meant to promote American Exceptionalism or US/Israeli foreign policy.

As mentioned earlier in the chapter, during the 1983 interview in which he called politics "a merry-go-round of sin," Dylan contrasted the potential of US foreign policy ("feeding the hungry and taking care of the orphans") with corporate-driven imperialism: "All you hear about are US interests in Latin America. But what are those interests? You can't find out."[49] Knowing that corporate greed often lurks behind the idealistic platitudes of dishonest politicians, Dylan realizes that what is usually called "national interest" on the global stage is actually the interest of specific individuals belonging to a specific socioeconomic class (mostly working in Manhattan/NYC and DC). In a 1985 interview, Dylan made an analogy between US government-backed Latin American dictators and corrupt politicians during the coming Great Tribulation: "All the Somozas and Batistas will be on their way out, grabbing their stuff and whatever, but you can forget about them. They won't be going anywhere. It's the people who live under tyranny and oppression, the plain, simple people, that count, like the multitude of sheep. They'll see that God is coming." As mentioned earlier, Dylan saw "no moral value" to US military intervention in Central America in 1986.[50]

In his dislike for corporate-driven imperialism, Dylan stands in the tradition of American populism, especially the Midwestern "isolationists." In the 1910s, William Jennings Bryan of Nebraska opposed the dollar diplomacy of the Taft administration and resigned as secretary of state under Wilson when he could not prevent his administration from pushing the US toward entry into World War I. (One decision that upset Bryan was Wilson's approval of Wall Street loans to the British and French governments, thereby undercutting the stated policy of neutrality.)[51]

In the 1920s, Senator Robert La Follette (R-WI) denounced domination of the US State Department by oil companies and investment banks. He pledged, "Your sons shall not be conscripted as a collection agency of private debts... We will end the partnership between our State Department and imperialistic interests, and we will divorce it from Standard Oil and international financiers." Partly inspired by publication of the bestselling book *Merchants of Death*, which exposed the role of the armaments industry in promoting war, in the 1930s, the US Senate created a committee chaired by Senator Gerald Nye (R-ND) to investigate possible corporate influence on the US government in connection with World War I.[52] The Nye Committee placed witnesses under oath, including DuPont executives and banker J.P. Morgan Jr., but its efforts were hindered by Democratic partisans of Wilson and FDR who sat on the committee.[53]

In the mid-1930s, retired Marine Corps Major General Smedley Butler, two-time recipient of the Medal of Honor, was another outspoken critic of corporate-driven militarism. His popular speech "War Is a Racket" was widely distributed when it became a book. All of this foreshadowed criticism of the "military-industrial complex" by President Dwight Eisenhower and the New Left in the early 1960s. This has been a central concern of Dylan's, especially set forth in "Masters of War." *War Is a Racket* even foreshadowed Dylan's song "With God On Our Side." Referring to World War I, Butler wrote, "So vicious was this war propaganda that even God was brought into it. With few exceptions our clergymen joined in the clamor to kill, kill, kill. To kill the Germans. God is on our side."[54]

In a 1935 magazine article, after telling Americans that he had spent 33 years of active duty in the Marine Corps, General Butler wrote, "And during that period I spent most of my time being a high-class muscle man for Big Business, for Wall Street and for the bankers. In short, I was a racketeer for capitalism. I suspected I was just part of a racket all the time. Now I am sure of it." Butler gave specifics, including "I helped in the raping of half a dozen Central American republics for the benefit of Wall Street... I helped purify Nicaragua for the international banking house of Brown Brothers in 1909–12."[55]

There are some recurring themes in US foreign policy since the rise of global empire in the 1890s. One is military intervention in Latin America. Another is the role played by New York–based international investment bankers. When Dylan was questioning supposed "US interests in Latin America," in 1983, he was partly referring to Nicaragua. The Reagan administration was using the CIA-backed Contras in an armed attempt to overthrow the socialist Nicaraguan government because it was hostile to US corporate interests. For years, the US government had supported brutal dictator Anastasio Somoza—mentioned in Dylan's 1985 interview—until he was overthrown by the left-wing Sandinistas. Butler not only referred to US intervention in Nicaragua in 1909–12 but he also mentioned the Wall Street banking firm of Brown Brothers. Under Reagan, Vice President (and ex-CIA Director) George Bush played an important role in imperialist machinations in Nicaragua.⁵⁶ Bush's father, Senator Prescott Bush (R-CT), was a partner of Brown Brothers, Harriman & Co. before going into politics.

Although he was a fellow Republican, Senator Nye publicly criticized President Coolidge for sending Marines into Nicaragua in 1927 to protect investments by Wall Street bankers. He called it "financial imperialism" and said that the government was "helping to crucify a people in Nicaragua merely because Americans have gone there with dollars to invest."⁵⁷ Surprisingly enough, most of the aforementioned critics of war-making were Republicans (La Follette, Nye, Butler, Eisenhower). As mentioned in chapter 1, the leading conservative Republican in the 1940s and 1950s, Senator Robert Taft (R-OH), was an opponent of militarism and imperialism. Unlike his father, President William Howard Taft, Senator Taft was a Midwestern populist. He was not a pacifist but his foreign policy made him more peace-minded than the average Republican or Democratic politician.

Taft supported armed neutrality and national defense as befitting a republic, as opposed to entangling alliances and overseas intervention as befitting an empire. For this reason, he opposed US entry into World War II prior to Pearl Harbor (1938–41) and peacetime conscription through the Selective Service Act (1940). Just as he saw US imperialism behind FDR's push for involvement in the European war, Taft later voted against the United Nations Participation Act (1945), was skeptical of the Bretton Woods Agreements (1945) and the Marshall Plan (1948), voted against the North Atlantic Treaty Organization (1949), and was skeptical of the Cold War because these things seemed to be manifestations of a new American Empire.⁵⁸

In a July 1950 letter, Senator Taft wrote that he had the feeling that the United States was "in real danger of becoming an imperialistic nation," noting, "The line between imperialism and idealism becomes very confused in the minds of those who operate the system." In a 1951 speech, Taft opposed US involvement in French Indo-China, which earned him the distinction of being a proto-opponent of the Vietnam War. One of Dylan's Beat heroes, Jack Kerouac, supported Taft for president in the early 1950s.⁵⁹

A more recent Midwestern "isolationist" who sounds like Dylan in his rejection of corporate-driven imperialism is former Governor Jesse Ventura of Minnesota. On Veterans Day 2014, Ventura, a Navy special operations veteran, said that he could no longer recommend military service: "I hate to say it, but no, I would be a conscientious objector today. I don't believe that the military fights for our freedom. They give them all the ra ra at the stadiums, and they cheer 'em on. But when the veterans come home, we pretty much forget about them. They're old news. They're yesterday's garbage. And it's time to move on to the next war." Referring to active duty military personnel as pawns, Governor Ventura said that "international corporations" are the ones who "truly run our country today." He added, "That's why wars are fought—so the profiteers of war can make money. If we weren't involved in these wars, we would have more freedom."[60]

Economic Globalization

"Isolationists" like Congressman Ron Paul (R-TX) oppose globalization treaties such as NAFTA, GATT, and CAFTA because they argue that these are managed trade for the benefit of large transnational corporations rather than free trade for the common good. True laissez-faire free trade would not require thousands of pages of government-negotiated, government-enforced agreements. Bob Dylan has a similar perspective, with an added eschatological dimension of Babylon and Antichrist.

Despite his American patriotism and Jewish ethnicity, Dylan does not seem interested in assisting or glorifying any particular national government (United States or Israel). At the same time, he opposes the type of internationalism that is promoted by capitalists and imperialists. He sees "traitors to America" behind this endeavor.[61] He also sees this as setting the stage for the Antichrist. He warns that Satan sometimes poses as a "Man of Peace" (1983). Dylan sees evil lurking behind the push for political globalism and economic globalization. In 1984, he warned, "They're gettin' everybody in that frame of mind—like, we're not just the United States anymore, we're *global*...Well, that's what the Book of Revelation is all *about*. And you can just about know that anybody who comes out for peace is *not* for peace...You can't be for peace and be *global*." He then spoke about how transnational corporations are creating one "big *global* country" that is "controlled by the same people."[62]

The unholy alliance between political power, corporate greed, and religious apostasy is described in one of Dylan's favorite books of the Bible (Revelation): "Fallen, fallen is Babylon the great! It has become a dwelling place of demons, a haunt of every foul spirit...for all nations have drunk the wine of her impure passion, and the kings of the earth have committed fornication with her, and the merchants of the earth have grown rich with the wealth of her wantonness."[63]

During the same 1984 interview, Dylan was asked about his new song "Union Sundown," which criticized global capitalism. Kurt Loder asked if the worker in Argentina who was making the Chevrolet car would be "better off" if he weren't making 30¢ per day. Dylan dismissed the paltry wage, saying, "I mean, people survived for 6000 years without having to work for slave wages for a person who comes down and...well, actually, it's just colonization. But see, I saw that firsthand, because where I come from, they *really* got that deal good, with the ore." Dylan was referring to the Iron Range in northeastern Minnesota. He explained how the booming iron ore industry gave way to abandonment as out-of-state mine owners looked for cheaper ways to find ore. He connected his region's history with contemporary global greed and exploitation.[64]

Wayne Cole, a perceptive historian from the Midwest, noted this very thing in his 1962 biography of Gerald Nye. Summarizing the legacy of Nye, a La Follette Republican who represented North Dakota in the Senate from 1925 to 1945, Cole wrote,

> In a sense, the struggle between agrarian isolationists and urban internationalists has been transferred from the United States to the world scene since World War II. The United States, Great Britain, and Western Europe evolved into a huge metropolis with a community of interests in both security and economic matters. This industrial-financial complex has a role in the world economy roughly comparable to the role of the Northeast in the United States. The economically underdeveloped areas of the Near and Middle East, Asia, Africa, and Latin America have a relationship to the North Atlantic metropolis or to the Soviet Union not unlike that of rural North Dakota to the urban Northeast during Nye's senatorial career.[65]

Cole could just as easily have said "not unlike that of rural Minnesota," including the Iron Range. What Dylan calls "colonization" can also be called political and economic imperialism. From the Gilded Age on, there was a domestic version of this, and eventually it became the philosophy that drives globalization.

As mentioned earlier, Dylan's Super Bowl commercial for Chrysler, in February 2014, was at least partly a rejection of globalization. Later that year, referring to American billionaires who are preoccupied with international affairs, Dylan said, "Does it make him happy giving his money away to foreign countries? Is there more contentment in that than in giving it here to the inner cities and creating jobs?... These multibillionaires can create industries right here in America. But no one can tell them what to do. God's got to lead them."[66]

Christian Zionism

Christian Zionism is a mixture of theology and ideology in which evangelical Protestants support the modern nation-state of Israel. More specifically,

Christian Zionists support the Israeli government in its hawkish foreign policy and domineering domestic policy. When Dylan converted in 1978–79, it would have made some sense if he had become a new leader of the Christian Zionist movement. He was Jewish. Even before his conversion, he believed in God and was familiar with the Hebrew Scriptures. He had visited Israel in the early 1970s. He was interested in End Times prophecy and embraced the premillennial dispensational interpretation of Hal Lindsey.

And yet Dylan did not become a Christian Zionist. Why not? Dylan's newfound Christianity was in many ways less-culture-bound than the average American evangelical at the time—partly because it was new and he approached the Bible with the fresh eyes of a convert. Also, he had a more-spiritual, less-politicized understanding of Bible eschatology. Finally, he remained an anarchist in his ideology after his conversion. When it was released in 1983, "Neighborhood Bully" was widely seen as a pro–Israeli government song. This was apparently incorrect. In a 1984 interview, Dylan suggested that the song was referring to Israel during the days of the future Battle of Armageddon rather than to the current Israeli government.[67]

Sexual Politics

Although many of the young Jesus People of the late 1960s shared outward traits such as long hair, beards, and groovy clothes with their secular generational peers, they tended to be more "conservative" (biblical, really) in their sexual attitudes because they were following an ancient book rather than contemporary trends.[68] When he became a Christian, Bob Dylan imbibed some of this skepticism toward free love and its ethic of "If it feels good, do it." By following the scriptural path of the Jesus Movement, Dylan confused and angered many of his admirers among the larger American Counterculture and secular society in general.

As noted earlier, when asked about abortion in 1984, Dylan dismissed its importance. When pressed about abortion being used as a form of birth control, Dylan provided some provocative insights. He called the birth control pill a "hoax." Drawing a responsibility parallel between contraception and prostitution, he decried the double standard that puts the burden on women instead of men. Expressing the suspicion that birth control pills are not safe for women, he connected the dots between scientists creating a drug and drug companies making money off of sexual promiscuity: "Yeah, you can go out and fuck anybody you want now; just take this pill." He summed up by saying, "The problem is not abortion. The problem is the whole concept behind abortion. Abortion is the end result of going out and screwing somebody to begin with. Casual sex."[69]

In the same 1984 interview, Dylan was asked about the recent radical-feminist attempt, inspired by Catharine MacKinnon and Andrea Dworkin, to pass a municipal ordinance in Minneapolis defining pornography not as a criminal violation of obscenity laws but rather as a litigable violation of women's civil rights. Dylan called pornography "pretty deeply embedded" in American society, pointing out that mainstream television is awash in commercialized sexuality.[70]

Dylan's longtime friend Allen Ginsberg, the Beat poet, was openly gay. In January 1980, Ginsberg talked to Dylan backstage after a concert in Denver. Clinton Heylin recounts, "Although Ginsberg talks to him of a God of forgiveness, Dylan retorts, 'Yes, but he also comes to judge.'" At a concert in Hartford, in May 1980, Dylan spent five minutes talking about politicized homosexuality in San Francisco. He drew a parallel to Canaanite cities under God's judgment in the Old Testament: "It's a growing place for homosexuals, and I read they have homosexual politics... Well, I guess the iniquity's not yet full. And I don't wanna be around when it is!"[71]

Dylan was asked about homosexuality in the 1984 interview. He agreed that the Bible says that homosexuality is an abomination but also agreed that his friend Allen Ginsberg, a homosexual, was a good guy. Dylan summed up: "Yeah, well, but that's no reason for *me* to condemn somebody, because they drink or they're corrupt in orthodox ways or they wear their shirt inside out. I mean, that's *their* scene. It certainly doesn't matter to *me*. I've got no ax to grind with any of that." Clearly refusing to play the role of an Anita Bryant or a Jerry Falwell, Dylan distanced himself from the Moral Majority. He took a libertarian stance on the conduct of others without denying that there are biblical and moral problems with homosexuality.[72]

Even though Dylan has not always practiced what he preached during his zealous years (1979–80), at that time he publicly rejected American cultural norms of hedonism and sexual promiscuity. Sounding like a traditionalist condemning the sexual revolution, Dylan told a concert audience in Montreal, "I was talking to a girl the other day who just lives from orgasm to orgasm. I know that's a strange thing, but that's what she's said to do because of these so-called modern times. But she's not satisfied."[73] In 1990, Dylan was featured in a cover blurb for a book by an Orthodox Jewish rabbi in St. Paul that advocated traditional Jewish norms about sexual modesty; it was called *Doesn't Anyone Blush Anymore?*. Dylan wrote, "Anyone who's either married or thinking of getting married would do well to read this book."[74]

When *Slow Train Coming* was released in 1979 and the songs for *Saved* were debuted live, music journalist and longtime Dylan fan Paul Williams asked about the woman mentioned in "Gonna Change My Way of Thinking," "Precious Angel," and "Covenant Woman":

> The question arises—and this would be an invasion of privacy except that the man has proclaimed himself publicly as a servant of God, and thus has specifically raised the issue of his attitudes toward alcohol, fornication etcetera—is she his lover, and if so are they married? And if not, does his literal interpretation of the Bible (for there is much evidence in his new songs that he's a fundamentalist in the sense of living by the written words of Christ) allow for the possibility of unsinful lovemaking between unmarried adults? I would hope that it does, as I regard fundamentalist attitudes towards sex as basically unGodly and would feel a lot more friendly towards a devout Christianity that was more enlightened in this regard. (A secret marriage is the more likely possibility, however.)[75]

Williams, founder of the rock music magazine *Crawdaddy!* (1966), was interested in Buddhist spirituality. Over the decades, he stayed true to the left-wing anarchist vibe of the Counterculture in a way that secular-minded Democrats did not. But Williams shared with typical white Democrats an aversion to traditional Christianity's moral restrictions on human sexual behavior.

In 1984, Dylan said, "It's very popular nowadays to think of yourself as a 'liberal humanist.' That's such a bullshit term. It means *less* than nothing."[76] Dylan seemed to be yearning for a liberalism that was more authentic and more traditional. A liberalism of someone like Harold Hughes and Mark Hatfield, or of their antecedents William Jennings Bryan and Robert La Follette.

In his new rejection of modern sexual mores, Bob Dylan on *Slow Train Coming* struck some longtime admirers as sounding like Jerry Falwell (to their horror). Paul Williams chalked up some of the seemingly jingoistic, self-righteous, moral-condemnation language on the album to "sloppy writing" on Dylan's part. He added, "Nevertheless, if he's going to hang around with fundamentalist Christians, many of whom are ultraconservative simply because they've never been exposed to anything else, he's going to have to be especially responsible about what he says and what views he seems to espouse—in fairness to them, and what he might have to offer them in the way of a broader worldview."[77]

Partly because he was attracted to at least part of the Left, with its emphasis on individuality and common good, Dylan found manifestations of the Religious Right unappealing despite some overlap in viewpoint. In

1980, when asked about political activism by fundamentalist Christians in groups like the Moral Majority, he told an interviewer, "I think people have to be careful about all that... It's real dangerous. You can find anything you want in the Bible. You can twist it around any way you want and a lot of people do that. I just don't think you can legislate morality... The basic thing, I feel, is to get in touch with Christ himself. He will lead you."[78] This statement reflects the Christian anarchism of the countercultural Jesus Movement.

The Establishment Takes Notice of Dylan?

When Dave Kelly was interviewed for this book, he told a bizarre story about an "older gentleman who had the room next to Bob Dylan" in the San Francisco hotel while Dylan performed at the Warfield Theater for two weeks in November 1979.[79] Dylan's management had reserved two floors of rooms in the hotel. Kelly explained that Bill Graham, famous San Francisco concert promoter who was in charge of the tour, would take Dylan and the older gentleman out to a different restaurant each night. Kelly accompanied Dylan. He recalled, "We would get in the limo and Bill Graham would be in it, Bob would be in it, and this old gentleman." At the restaurant, the gentleman would sit between Dylan and Graham.

Kelly continued, "A week and a half in, Bob said something to Bill Graham about this gentleman as if he was the other one's friend... Finally, Bob probably said to Bill Graham, 'So why don't you bring your buddy over tonight we're going to go to this thing.' Something innocent like that. But, anyway, whoever said it first, the other one went, 'He's not my buddy. He's yours.'" This is how they learned that nobody knew who the man was even though he had been next to Dylan in the hotel, with him in the car, and next to him at the restaurants.

Prior to this, the gentleman with an aristocratic bearing had befriended Kelly. He would ask him lots of questions about Dylan: "What his plans were, where he was socially, what kind of activities he's likely to do with the youth in America, his outlook, what his goals were." Focusing on spirituality, Kelly replied by telling the "very English lord type of guy" all about "the End Times stuff" that he and Dylan were into at the time. Given the context of a rock music tour, it was rather surreal but it became even more surreal. A subsequent night, the old gentleman whom nobody knew took Kelly and a friend out to dinner at a fancy restaurant in the Nob Hill neighborhood. Everyone at the $150-a-plate restaurant knew the man by name and he had his own table. Kelly learned that the man was very wealthy with a big mansion on Nob Hill.

After they sat down for dinner, the gentleman told Kelly why he had been hanging out with Dylan. Kelly recalls:

> He says to me, "I work for the Families." And I said, "The Families? Who?" He said, "The Fifty-Five Families." I'm like, "There's Fifty-Five Families? Where?" "*The* Fifty-Five Families." He acted as if I should have known. And he said, "The Fifty-Five Families that basically run America. They own all the companies. They began way back in the Mayflower days. They're still in power." Very matter of factly. "I basically report to them what's going on in my city that might affect the country as a whole. Or politically might change the landscape. Anything that might affect youth and how they react, if they're going to rebel. Anything that affects commerce. I basically just report that. There's nothing"—and he looked at me because he could see I was kind of spooked—"nothing nefarious." [I thought,] "Oh yeah? It's already nefarious because you're reporting to Fifty-Five Families. It don't matter what you're reporting, the part that they even exist is spooky for me." And he says, "Well, they just like to know what's going on. They have people all over the country and San Francisco's my city. I have to let them know."

Most of what Kelly had been telling him was the End Times *à la* Hal Lindsey scenario that Dylan was telling audiences about in song and speech. The old gentleman was fascinated by that. He said, "Look, would you be willing to come with me and tell them what you told me?" He gave Kelly the option of flying, all expenses paid, to either Jupiter Island in Florida or (probably) Aiken in South Carolina.[80] Kelly told me, "You can imagine what I'm thinking at the time. I may never come back. Who am I going to be reporting to? They're going to own me from that point. I mean, what's the deal? ... Needless to say, I declined."

After hearing about the corporate power of the Fifty-Five Families, Kelly was curious about their political perspective. He continues his account: "I said, 'Well, what's their politics?' He said, 'They don't have any. They support both sides. They let the people choose—between their choice A and their choice B.' You know, Pick a card, any card, as long as it's one of mine. It's a very expensive thing. It's not quite an option for somebody else to come on the scene and not support it."

Kelly was unnerved by the seemingly rational, proper-acting man telling him that the Fifty-Five Families control most of the major corporations by hiring front men to serve as CEOs on their behalf and dominate US politics by funding both major political parties. On top of the incredible sociopolitical implications, the Families were interested enough in Dylan to plant someone in his midst to seek information. Kelly: "Can you imagine this older gentleman who has a huge mansion in San Francisco, the entire time that he could, until he was found out, he's got this room next to Bob Dylan, who he has got nothing to do with? I mean, they're not connected in any way. He's an old guy. Talked like an English lord. But he didn't have any choice. He had to do it."

When it was pointed out by this book's coauthor that the Fifty-Five Families sound like an Illuminati conspiracy kind of thing, Kelly responded, "Like that but he kept saying, 'It's nothing scary. It's just a business.' And he tried to take me back earlier and say, 'Look, what's going to happen? You've got these families in the North, you've got these families in the South. They have a disagreement. They fight it out. But they're still there. Nobody's gone. They've always been here." The gentleman drew a parallel to how things were run in old Europe, where it was "all the same people behind" the various national kings and "if there were other problems, they would finance the person that's coming up."

Asked if the man seemed kooky, Kelly replied, "No. Not at all. Very intelligent guy...He wasn't hiding anything from me. He was ready to tell me anything...To him, it was just matter of fact...All he ever did was try to calm my fears." Commenting on representatives of the Families being in major cities of the nation, Kelly said, "Isn't that wild? Just to be aware. And if you're on top of the hill, you want to see people comin' as far away as possible. To deal with it. But, again, he didn't see it as like a military threat or as a secret society thing...I think he just thought it was information gathering for people in power. He didn't see the people in power as corrupt in any way."

If these Families exist as an organized group, why were they interested in Dylan? Kelly speculates, "He was a leader in the Jewish community and he was taking everybody a different way. Great disruption...He was getting an awful lot of attention. They just wanted to know what he was planning...They saw him as a real political threat. Again, remember his political beginnings. That was natural for them to think that he had some political plan." Although they may have thought that he was planning to lead some new religious-political movement because of his 1960s Voice of a Generation reputation, Kelly points out the irony: "Dylan does *not* want to be a leader. I can tell you that. He doesn't want anyone to be looking to him to lead them."[81]

The strange goings-on in the hotel, limo, and restaurants occurred. But was the story told to Kelly by the old gentleman true? The coauthor who interviewed Kelly is familiar with power analyses and conspiracy theories but he has never heard of the Fifty-Five Families. In political science, there is something called the Elite Theory. First published in Italy in 1896, *The Ruling Class* by Gaetano Mosca points out that every society has two classes of people: "a class that rules and a class that is ruled." The relationship between the two is simple: "The first class, always the less numerous, performs all political functions, monopolizes power and enjoys the advantages that power brings, whereas the second, the more numerous class, is directed and controlled by the first."[82] Applying this assumption to the United States; looking beyond feel-good platitudes about democracy, equality, and social mobility; and examining the role of money and connections in politics, Elite Theory scholars argue that the nation is a plutocracy (rule by the wealthy few—specifically, by those connected with international investment banks and large transnational corporations).[83] This is a perspective shared by Dylan.

It is one thing for average Americans to feel that the system is rigged against them by the high and mighty, or for the Elite Theory to think that corporate wealth has disproportionate political power within a system that claims to be based on the popular sovereignty of "We the People." It is quite another thing for someone to say that Fifty-Five Families control the nation. This is more specific and seems less likely. Yet there have been a few books that might lend credence to such a possibility. Examples include *America's 60 Families* (1937) by financial journalist Ferdinand Lundberg, *Tragedy and Hope: A History of the World in Our Time* (1966) by Georgetown University historian Carroll Quigley, *America's Secret Establishment: An Introduction to the Order of Skull & Bones* (1983) by former Hoover Institution (Stanford University) scholar Antony Sutton, *American Dynasty: Aristocracy, Fortune, and the Politics of Deceit in the House of Bush* (2004) by political analyst Kevin Phillips, and *The Wise Men: Six Friends and the World They Made* (1986) by mainstream journalists Walter Isaacson and Evan Thomas.[84]

Whether the older gentleman was dishonest, delusional, or truthful, the story as recounted by Dave Kelly does indicate the level of cultural importance that some gave to Bob Dylan in 1979. This included his political potential as leader of a social movement. It is possible that "The Man" took notice of Dylan during this important time in his life.

The Politics of Bob Dylan

Where does all of this leave Bob Dylan? Is Dylan a Democrat? No. Is Dylan a Republican? No. Is Dylan an Independent? Maybe. Dylan does not seem to care about electoral politics. He will perform for a President Clinton or a President Obama but he is not partisan. (He would likely have played for a Republican president but was not asked.) Dylan's post-1978 ideology is what you would expect from a Christian whose first loyalty is to the Kingdom of God. It is a little of this, a little of that. No worldly ideology is a perfect match with Christian principles so Dylan is part liberal, part conservative, part populist, part libertarian, part communitarian. In relation to Christian anarchism, Dylan can be described as both a monarchist and an anarchist. If Christian anarchism says "All or Nothing—or Little," it has elements of monarchism and anarchism plus the Little translates into the ideologies of libertarianism (minarchism) and populism.

Dylan's affinity for Jeffersonian democracy has been mentioned from chapter 1 on. Thomas Jefferson's thought included both populism and libertarianism. Dylan's libertarianism is apparent from his lifelong tendencies toward individuality and freedom. In his nonapology to the ECLC after the Tom Paine Award brouhaha in December 1963, he wrote, "My life runs in a series of moods in private an in personal ways…I dont even claim to be normal by the standards set up…I do not apologize for being me nor any part of me." In 1986, Dylan told an interviewer, "I've always been just about being an individual, with an individual point of view. If I've been about anything, it's probably that, and to let some people know that it's possible to do the impossible." Dylan's mature self-summary is part "Maggie's Farm" and part "Something's Burning, Baby," or we could say part Patrick McGoohan and part Power of God.[85]

Decentralization of power is a natural fit for Dylan because he has always had a personal streak of freedom and diversity in the way that he views the world and lives his life. For instance, his visceral dislike of being pigeonholed has decentralist implications. Dylan does not use the language of subsidiarity or sphere sovereignty, partly because he is not a political theorist or theologian, and he has never invoked the Tenth Amendment of the Constitution in the context of the US political system, but a decentralist ethic is present.

One occasion on which Dylan specifically mentioned states' rights was during a discussion about slavery and the Civil War while being interviewed by *Rolling Stone* in 2012. In this instance, he did not sound like a social conservative who defends the Confederate States of America in opposition to "northern aggression" by Abraham Lincoln. Instead, his comment reflected his early 1960s persona as an advocate of equality, of civil rights, of liberty and justice for all. Dylan's antislavery stance was not only in line with his egalitarian progressive side but also with his individualistic libertarian side. It is hard to imagine anything less libertarian than slavery enforced by government.[86]

When asked about fears and propaganda of the southern elite on the eve of the Civil War, Dylan said, "There's a lot of that, too, about states' rights and loyalty to our state. But that didn't make any sense. The Southern states already had rights. Sometimes more than the Northern states. The North just wanted them to stop slavery, not even put an end to it—just stop exporting it."[87]

Dylan is correct. One example of southern states having more rights than northern states was the Fugitive Slave Act of 1850, which put the federal government on the side of slavery at the expense of (northern) states' rights. Wisconsin, Massachusetts, and other northern states used nullification to stop the federal government from forcing state and local officials to compel the return of escaped slaves to southern owners.[88] By using the rhetoric of states' rights in defense of slavery during and after the Civil War, Confederates and their apologists used an honorable means for a dishonorable end. Decentralization—selectively applied—was merely an opportunistic tool used by the wealthy white minority in the South to advance their economic and racial interests. They were never committed to the principle itself, as the Fugitive Slave Act proved.

President Lincoln, a conventional Hamiltonian, was, above all else, committed to preservation of the union, not emancipation of slaves. Was the Civil War primarily about slavery for the northern political and economic elite? No. But it was for their southern counterparts, for those in Dixie with power and money. The four southern states that publicly declared the causes of secession all identified opposition to their commitment to slavery as the main reason for leaving the union. In the four documents explaining secession by South Carolina, Mississippi, Georgia, and Texas, slavery was central in all four.

The Sony Pictures promotional website for Dylan's 2003 film *Masked and Anonymous* describes one scene: "Bob Dylan is handed a list of songs the network wants him to sing, and it's Revolution, Won't Get Fooled Again, Ohio and several other selections [including "Eve of Destruction"] from some VH1 or Mojo Magazine pick of The Top Ten Protest Songs. Dylan shrugs and pretends to consider it, and then picks up his guitar and plays a mournful version of Dixie. As if to say, You want rebel songs? Here's the all time number one."[89] Yet the movie also includes a scene of a young African American girl singing "The Times They Are A-Changin'" and a live Dylan audio version of "Blowin' in the Wind" closes out the movie. The performance of "Dixie" may have been intended as a dig at smug and shallow liberals. It was not a glorification of the Confederacy. It was not a romanticizing of the "Lost Cause" of the gallant South. It certainly was not a defense of slavery. The same can be said for Dylan's sublime performance of an original song, "Cross the Green Mountain," for the soundtrack of Ron Maxwell's Civil War film *Gods and Generals*. That movie was released the same year as *Masked and Anonymous* and was criticized for being pro-South.⁹⁰

American decentralism has often been linked to agrarianism because decentralized power includes a healthy dose of attachment to the land and to nature as a whole. Of course, it has made room for the benefits of urban life as well, in the context of neighborhood rather than metropolis. Ancient Jewish history is sometimes held up as a pastoral idyll. In addition to the Garden of Eden, examples include the comparison of God to a shepherd, the herdsman lifestyle, the decentralized or even anarchistic period described in the book of Judges, the Promised Land as a land of milk and honey, and the use of grapes and wine as spiritual metaphors. Even in an age of empires, the Jews lived in a preindustrial, precapitalist manner that was closer in proximity to the age of innocence.

Released in 1983, the Dylan songs "Jokerman" and "I and I" contain something of this Hebraic emphasis on nature. Ten years later, in the liner notes for *World Gone Wrong*, Dylan wrote, "Give me a thousand acres of tractable land & all the gang members that exist & you'll see the Authentic alternative lifestyle, the Agrarian one." Dylan's offhand remark at Live Aid about American small farmers in need inspired the creation of Farm Aid. He performed at the first Farm Aid benefit concert, in September 1985, backed by Tom Petty and the Heartbreakers. Dylan lived in rural Woodstock, New York, in the mid-to-late 1960s, and continues to have a farm in Minnesota that serves as a retreat from urban life and the concert road.⁹¹

Dylan criticized the space program, the pharmaceutical industry, and widespread computerization as dangerous folly during his 1984 interview with *Rolling Stone*. In his skepticism of the modern technological world, Dylan sounds like Wendell Berry. Ironically, when Berry declined to comment about Dylan for this book, he mentioned that he was not so fond of a dependence on electricity so he did not have much familiarity with Dylan's recordings. Sounding like an Amish farmer, Berry has more in common with Dylan than he may realize.⁹²

When Dylan's 1979–80 personal assistant Dave Kelly is asked if he recalls Dylan talking about specific politicians during that election season, Kelly says "No." Instead, he remembers Dylan's nonelectoral, ideology-transcendent populism:

> He was more interested in spiritual things. He was very into, I think, social issues. That's why I would say in his politics he probably straddles both parties, depending on what you're talking about. You know, I'd see him in the morning. Just outside the Warfield [Theater in San Francisco] there's a little café. I'd go down in the morning, wondering where he was.

And he's sittin' there talkin' to truck drivers and waitresses, just regular people. That was what he loved to do the most. Get away from all the people that knew him as the famous Bob Dylan and get back to being Robert Zimmerman and just being a regular guy. And none of the people knew who he was.

This love of interacting with the common people has a political dimension. It is called populism and is a type of ideology, although rarely discussed in modern America in comparison to the widely used but little-understood *liberal* and *conservative* labels.[93] When asked if Dylan's political way of thinking could be described as populism, Kelly says "Yes." Later in the interview, Kelly says of Dylan, "He's a rebel. And he favors the underdog. Like you said, a populist."[94]

This populist support for the underdog is linked to Dylan's reputation as a rebel. He is not rebelling against all authority but rather against unjust, illegitimate authority. At the end of a *Time* magazine article on Dylan in 1963, his politics were described: "He is an advocate of little men, and if he remains one himself, it only enriches the ring of his lyrics—as in his best song, *Blowin' in the Wind*, an anthem for the whole lost crowd he speaks for." A *Saturday Evening Post* lead story on Dylan in 1966 had a cover title of "Bob Dylan: Rebel King of Rock 'n' Roll."[95]

When asked about Dylan circa 1979, Dave Kelly says, "I don't think he trusted politicians across the board, by and large. [Prior to getting to know him,] I would have assumed that he was a Democrat... [because he had the] anti-The-Big-Man-owning-everything view that hippies had of businesses." Kelly sums up Dylan's politics as being "anti-The Man." In other words, anti-Establishment. During the Progressive Era, until 1913, Dylan might have been more comfortable being a Democrat, when the national party was led by William Jennings Bryan, enemy of Big Business and advocate of antitrust enforcement. Populism and dislike of monopoly capitalism long predated the hippies of the Counterculture. While growing up, Dylan probably absorbed these tendencies from a variety of sources—from Judaism, Iron Range laborers, pastoral and rebellious folk songs, down-home country music, honest blues singers, and democratic-minded Republican Party and Farmer-Labor Party politicians.

Kelly links Dylan's anti-The Man politics with his experiences in the music industry from a young age. (He was 20 years old when he signed his first recording contract with Columbia Records.) Kelly describes the culture that Dylan encountered with business managers, record producers, and label executives as a dictatorship, as a "fiefdom scenario," and as a "plantation mentality where he worked for The Man" who tried to totally control him.

When Kelly innocently asked one day why Dylan did not produce his own records, he received a look of "absolute contempt" as though he had asked "something incredibly stupid." As Kelly recalls the conversation, Dylan was basically saying, of his own situation, You're a slave. You can't produce your own. You're not in charge of your career. I work for The Man, you know. Kelly comments, "I'd say that colors everything he thinks, as far as authority and power in the world. He knows they've got the strength and he accepts it but he doesn't like it. He obviously fights against The Man all he can." Kelly concludes, "So that plantation mentality's existed in the music business for many decades and guys like Dylan came up thinking that that's how the politics really worked. These rich cats up in—you know, he hammers them all the time in his songs."[96]

Dylan's personal history with corporate-driven oppression found in the professional music world—so different from the freedom symbolized by the folk, blues, and gospel music traditions—may well be an important factor in his political outlook. As mentioned earlier, other likely influences are his Jewish heritage, his observation of economic imperialism at work in northeastern Minnesota, his state's tradition of populist major-party and third-party electoral politics, and his eventual embrace of a biblical, anarchistic type of Christianity.

Conclusion

Bob Dylan's life and career have been filled with seeming inconsistencies. Still, certain thematic constants have emerged, specifically as they apply to his political outlook. Since childhood, he has cared about liberty and justice, democracy and individuality, truth and morality. Dylan has exemplified freedom on personal, societal, and spiritual levels. His refusal to accept the legitimacy of human power structures reflects an anarchism that he brought with him when he converted to Christianity. Dylan has also consistently advocated justice, whether lending support for the legally dispossessed and economically downtrodden, or issuing moral directives urging people to reconcile with divine law.

Dylan's political worldview has remained essentially the same over six different decades and numerous private and public transformations. Whether he appeared as a New Left protest icon, rock music and Counterculture innovator, rural family man, Christian associated with the Jesus People, or cantankerous social critic distrustful of worldly leaders, Dylan's notions of freedom and justice, power and sin, have tied all of these roles together.

When music critic Nat Hentoff first interviewed Bob Dylan, in 1963, he could tell that the young singer was "very serious and very intelligent" and was "not revealing all he was."[97] Dylan the human being is a private person who has constructed "a strong mystery persona so he can hide behind it and then come off stage and be a normal person." As a shy, sensitive individual, Dylan "doesn't want anyone to be looking to him to lead them."[98] And yet he *is* a leader because he cares about important values. He has a genius for artistically pointing to those values, and therefore those he seeks to influence cannot help but notice the one who is doing the pointing. In his musical recordings, public comments, and personal conduct, Bob Dylan has served as an example of engagement with, and skepticism toward, a political world.

Notes

Preface

1. Ben Fong-Torres, "Knockin' on Bob Dylan's Door," *Rolling Stone*, February 14, 1974.
2. Interview with Dave Kelly by JT, November 1, 2014.
3. Ibid.
4. Conversation between Nat Hentoff and JT, June 9, 2014.

1 Bob Dylan's Roots and Traditional World

1. Colin Woodward, *American Nations: A History of the Eleven Rival Regional Cultures of North America* (New York: Penguin Books, 2011), 60.
2. Daniel Elazar, *Cities of the Prairie: The Metropolitan Frontier and American Politics* (New York: Basic Books, 1970), 262–64.
3. Daniel Elazar, *Minnesota Politics and Government* (Lincoln: University of Nebraska Press, 1999), xxv–xxvi.
4. Woodward, *American Nations*, 59.
5. Ibid., 62.
6. Steve Berg, "The Scratching of Heads in Hibbing," *Minneapolis Star Tribune*, December 7, 1979.
7. John Sirjamaki, "The People of the Mesabi Range," in Rhoda R. Gilman and June Drenning Holmquist, eds., *Selections from "Minnesota History": A Fiftieth Anniversary Anthology* (St. Paul: Minnesota Historical Society Press, 1965), 262.
8. Hyman Berman and Linda Mack Schloff, *Jews in Minnesota: The People of Minnesota* (St. Paul: Minnesota Historical Society, Press, 2002), 2.
9. Bruce M. White et al., *Minnesota Votes: Election Returns by County for Presidents, Senators, Congressmen, and Governors, 1857–1977* (St. Paul: Minnesota Historical Society, 1977), 15, 20.
10. Ibid., 191–196.
11. Aaron Brown, *Overburden: Modern Life on the Iron Range* (Duluth, MN: Red Step Press, 2008), 124.

12. White et al., *Minnesota Votes*, 29–30.
13. *Chicago Tribune*, July 31, 1988.
14. Mikal Gilmore, "Bob Dylan: The Rolling Stone Interview," *Rolling Stone*, September 27, 2012, 45; *60 Minutes*, CBS Network, December 5, 2004.
15. Brown, *Overburden*, 124.
16. "Mayfair Hotel Press Conference," May 3, 1966. Contained in: Carl Benson, ed., *The Bob Dylan Companion: Four Decades of Commentary* (New York: Schirmer Books, 1998), 81.
17. Brown, *Overburden*, 5.
18. Bob Dylan, *Chronicles, Volume One* (New York: Simon & Schuster, 2004), 271.
19. Toby Thompson, *Positively Main Street: Bob Dylan's Minnesota*, rev. ed. (Minneapolis: University of Minnesota Press, c1971, 2008), 136.
20. *A&E Biography: Bob Dylan*. A&E Television Networks, DVD, 2000.
21. Jules Siegel, "Well What Have We Here?" *Saturday Evening Post*, July 30, 1966, 34.
22. Joan Baez, *And a Voice to Sing With* (New York: Summit Books, 1987), 85.
23. Siegel, *Saturday Evening Post*, 34.
24. Dave Engel, *Just Like Bob Zimmerman's Blues: Dylan in Minnesota* (Rudolph, WI: River City Memoirs, 1997), 122.
25. Marvin G. Lamppa, *Minnesota's Iron Country: Rich Ore, Rich Lives* (Duluth, MN: Lake Superior Port Cities Inc., 2004), 217.
26. Anthony Scaduto, *Bob Dylan: An Intimate Biography* (New York: Signet, c1971, 1979), 11.
27. Berg, "The Scratching of Heads."
28. Ibid.
29. *Chicago Tribune*, July 31, 1988.
30. *60 Minutes*, December 5, 2004.
31. *Hibbing Daily Tribune*, July 29, 1964, and November 11, 1964.
32. *Chicago Tribune*, July 31, 1988.
33. "I Am My Words," *Newsweek*, November 4, 1963, 94–95.
34. *60 Minutes*, December 5, 2004.
35. Will Jones, "After Last Night," *Minneapolis Star Tribune*, May 24, 1964.
36. Bob Dylan, *Lyrics: 1962–1985* (New York: Knopf, 2004), 70–72, 106.
37. Paul J. Robbins, "Bob Dylan in His Own Words," originally *Los Angeles Free Press*, September 17 and 24, 1965. Contained in: *Bob Dylan Companion*, 54.
38. *60 Minutes*, December 5, 2004.
39. Pam Coyle, "Exclusive: An Interview with Bob Dylan," *Hibbing High Times*, Vol. 46, No. 2, October 18, 1978. Reprinted in *Hibbing Daily Times*.
40. Douglas Brinkley, "Bob Dylan's America," *Rolling Stone*, May 14, 2009, 49, 76.
41. Gilmore, "Bob Dylan" (2012), 45–46.
42. *No Direction Home*, DVD, directed by Martin Scorsese, Paramount Pictures, 2005.

43. Brown, *Overburden*, 125.
44. Lamppa, *Minnesota's Iron Country*, 204.
45. Ibid., 207–208.
46. Ibid., 211, 214–17.
47. Ibid., 210.
48. G. Theodore Mitau, "The Democratic-Farmer-Labor Party Schism of 1948," in Anne J. Aby, ed., *The North Star State: A Minnesota History Reader* (St. Paul: Minnesota History, 2002), 272–73.
49. Ibid., 273.
50. Lamppa, *Minnesota's Iron Country*, 222–23.
51. Ibid., 225–26, 240.
52. Chris Welles, "The Angry Young Folk Singer," *Life*, April 10, 1964, 114.
53. Dylan, *The Times They Are A-Changin'* (1964).
54. Ibid.
55. Lawrence W. Levine, *Defender of the Faith: William Jennings Bryan: The Last Decade, 1915–1925* (Cambridge, MA: Harvard University Press, 1987), 322.
56. Brown, *Overburden*, 183.
57. Ibid., 130.
58. Clinton Heylin, *Bob Dylan Behind the Shades Revisited* (New York: William Morrow, 2001), 553.
59. Dylan, *Infidels* (1983).
60. Kurt Loder, "The Bob Dylan Interview," *Rolling Stone*, June 21, 1984, 18.
61. Ibid.
62. Edna Gundersen, "Dylan on Dylan: Folk's Hero Faces the '90s in a Rare Interview," *USA Today*, September 21, 1989.
63. Dylan, *Infidels* (1983).
64. Sergei Petrov and Rene Fontaine, *Masked and Anonymous*, directed by Larry Charles (Culver City, CA: Sony Pictures Classics, 2003), DVD.
65. Robert Hilburn, "Bob Dylan: Still A-Changin'," originally *Los Angeles Times*, November 17, 1985. Contained in: *Bob Dylan Companion*, 206.
66. Dylan, *Saved* (1980).
67. Dylan, *Modern Times* (2006).
68. Ibid.
69. Jack A. Smith, "A World of His Own," *National Guardian*, August 22, 1963. Contained in: *Broadside* #31, September 1963, 7.
70. Dylan, *Lyrics: 1962–1985*, 68–69.
71. Dylan, *Blonde on Blonde* (1966).
72. Dylan, *Together Through Life* (2009).
73. Brinkley, "Bob Dylan's America," 47.
74. Brown, *Overburden*, 186–87.
75. Jon Bream, "Musical Maverick, Revisited," *Minneapolis Star Tribune*, October 31, 2002. Ethnic Jews—Rudy Boschwitz, Paul Wellstone, Norm Coleman, and Al Franken—have won this Senate seat in every election since 1978.

76. Laura E. Weber, "'Gentiles Preferred': Minneapolis Jews and Employment, 1920–1950," in Aby, *North Star State*, 397.
77. Ibid., 394–96.
78. Hasia R. Diner, *The Jews of the United States* (Berkeley: University of California Press, 2004), 238.
79. Jonathan Sarna, *American Judaism: A History* (New Haven: Yale University Press, 2004), 274.
80. Jerry Waldman (Major Gifts Officer, Herzl Camp), interviewed by Chad Israelson, November 13, 2014. Waldman also related a story about a role reversal day held in Herzl Camp, where the oldest campers would assume the duties of the counselors. Dylan became the music director for a day. Waldman also commented on the overwhelming support for Democratic candidates among the Jewish community in the Twin Cities.
81. Sarna, *American Judaism*, 296.
82. Jerry Waldman, interview.
83. Diner, *Jews of the United States*, 261–62.
84. Ibid., 265–66.
85. Ibid., 269.
86. Ron Rosenbaum, "The Playboy Interview, March 1978." Contained in: *Younger Than That Now: The Collected Interviews with Bob Dylan* (New York: Thunder's Mouth Press, 2004), 156.
87. Jerry Waldman, interview.
88. Berman and Schloff, *Jews in Minnesota*, 47.
89. Thompson, *Positively Main Street*, 66–67.
90. Dylan, *Lyrics: 1962–1985*, 163.
91. Dylan's Jewish heritage may have also influenced his interest in music. Referring to rabbinic Judaism, a theologian explains, "Intimately connected with the custom of reading and repeating aloud was the practice of reading the written Torah and repeating the oral with a rhythmical melody... In ancient Judaism the sacred texts were recited with cantillation [chant-singing], as is still done today in Jewish synagogues." Al Jolson (Asa Yoelson), the first Jewish American music superstar and a man whose talent is appreciated by Dylan, was the son of a cantor. Like Dylan's maternal grandparents, Jolson was born in Lithuania (Russian Empire). Jolson's movie *The Jazz Singer* (1927) was autobiographical.—Birger Gerhardsson, *Memory and Manuscript: Oral Tradition and Written Transmission in Rabbinic Judaism and Early Christianity* (Grand Rapids, MI: Eerdmans/ Livonia, MI: Dove Booksellers, c1961, 1998), 166; Dylan, *Biograph* (1985), interview with Cameron Crowe.
92. Fred Bernstein, *The Jewish Mother's Hall of Fame* (New York: Knopf Doubleday, 1986), 169.
93. Linda Mack Schloff, "Kosher with a Modern Tinge: Two Generations of Jewish Women in Virginia, Minnesota 1894–1945," in Annette Atkins and Deborah L. Miller, eds., *The State We're In: Reflections on Minnesota History* (St. Paul: Minnesota Historical Society Press), 105.

94. Engel, *Bob Zimmerman's Blues*, 88.
95. Berg, "The Scratching of Heads."
96. *No Direction Home*, DVD.
97. Thompson, *Positively Main Street*, 161; emphases in the original.
98. Kathleen Mackay, *Bob Dylan: Intimate Insights from Friends and Fellow Musicians* (New York: Omnibus Press, 2007), 13–14.
99. John Bream, "The Many Faces of Bob Dylan," *Minneapolis Star Tribune*, June 22, 1986.
100. Neil Hickey, "Bob Dylan," *TV Guide*, September 11, 1976, 5.
101. Stephen H. Webb, *Dylan Redeemed: From Highway 61 to Saved* (New York: Continuum, 2006), 35.
102. Dylan, *New Morning* (1970).
103. Numbers 6:24–26.
104. Dylan, *Slow Train Coming* (1979).
105. Jim Jerome, "Bob Dylan: A Myth Materializes with a New Protest Record and a New Tour," *People Weekly*, November 10, 1975, 26.
106. Ibid., 29.
107. Hickey, "Bob Dylan," 6.
108. Gilmore, "Bob Dylan" (2012), 51.
109. *60 Minutes*, December 5, 2004.
110. Abraham J. Heschel, *The Prophets* (New York: Harper & Row, 1962), xiv.
111. Ibid., xiv.
112. Allan Kozinn, "Sotheby's to Auction Bob Dylan Manuscripts," *New York Times*, May 1, 2014, C3; Michael Goldberg, "Audio: Manuscript Shows the Hard Truth about Bob Dylan's 'A Hard Rain's A-Gonna Fall,'" *Days Of The Crazy-Wild.com*, May 4, 2014, http://www.daysofthecrazy-wild.com/audio-the-hard-truth-about-bob-dylans-a-hard-rains-a-gonna-fall. Jeremiah 1:5 is often used by prolife advocates in arguing against abortion but that has mostly been in the post–*Roe v. Wade* (1973) context.
113. Dylan, *No Direction Home: The Bootleg Series Vol. 7* (2005).
114. Dylan, *The Freewheelin' Bob Dylan* (1963).
115. Heylin, *Behind the Shades Revisited*, 328.
116. Rosenbaum, "Interview," in *Younger Than That Now*, 154.
117. Ibid., 548–49.
118. Martin Keller, "Dylan Speaks," *US*, January 2, 1984, c1983, 59.
119. Heylin, *Behind the Shades Revisited*, 549.
120. *60 Minutes*, December 5, 2004.
121. Jeff Taylor, *Politics on a Human Scale: The American Tradition of Decentralism* (Lanham, MD: Lexington Press, 2013), 273.
122. Conversation between Robert Dean Lurie and JT, September 28, 2014.
123. Mark 6:4.
124. Greil Marcus, *Invisible Republic: Bob Dylan's Basement Tapes* (New York: Henry Holt, 1997); Michael Gray, *Song and Dance Man III: The Art of Bob Dylan* (London: Cassell, 2000).

125. Harry Smith, comp., *Anthology of American Folk Music* [sound recording] (Smithsonian Folkways Recordings, c1952, 1997).
126. Dylan, *Together Through Life* (2009).
127. *Bootleg Series 1–3*, booklet, 4.
128. Dylan, *Bringing It All Back Home* (1965).
129. Howard Sounes, *Down the Highway: The Life of Bob Dylan* (New York: Grove Press, 2001), 370–76. In the early 1960s, Dylan asked gospel-folk singer Mavis Staples to marry him. She declined but the two have remained friends.—Graham Rockingham, "Mavis Staples Recalls Her Lost Love," *The Hamilton Spectator*, January 21, 2012, http://www.thespec.com/whatson-story/2149883-mavis-staples-recalls-her-lost-love; Robert Love, "Bob Dylan Does the American Songbook His Way," *AARP The Magazine*, February/March 2015, 24, 26.
130. David Gates, "Dylan Revisited," *Newsweek*, October 6, 1997, 64; Robert Hilburn interview, West Berlin, June 1984. Contained in: Artur, *Every Mind Polluting Word: Assorted Bob Dylan Utterances* (Don't Ya Tell Henry Publications, 2006), http://content.yudu.com/Library/A1plqd/BobDylanEveryMindPol/resources/794.htm, 794; Dylan, *Biograph* (1985).
131. Clinton Heylin, *Bob Dylan: A Life in Stolen Moments, Day by Day: 1941–1995* (New York: Schirmer Books, 1996), 339; Robert Hilburn, "Rock's Enigmatic Poet Opens a Long-Private Door," *Los Angeles Times*, April 4, 2004.
132. Dylan, *Chronicles*, 109.
133. Ibid., 115.
134. Ibid., 89.
135. Mackay, *Intimate Insights*, 9.
136. Greil Marcus, "Self Portrait No. 25," *Rolling Stone*, July 23, 1970, 19.
137. Dylan, *Chronicles*, 34–35.
138. R. Gilbert, "Tomorrow's Top Twenty?" Scene No. 17, January 26, 1963. Contained in: *Bob Dylan Companion*, 16.
139. "Mayfair Hotel Press Conference," *Bob Dylan Companion*, 81.
140. Joseph Tirella, *Tomorrow-Land: The 1964–65 World's Fair and the Transformation of America* (New York: Lyons Press, 2014), 280.
141. Ralph Gleason, "A Folk Singing Social Critic," *San Francisco Chronicle*, February 24, 1964. Reprinted in *Broadside* #44, Late April 1964, 12.
142. Thomas Jefferson letter to William Branch Giles, December 26, 1825. Cited in: Charles A. Lindbergh [Sr.], *Why Is Your Country at War, and What Happens to You after the War, and Related Subjects* (Washington, DC: Lindbergh, 1917), 83.
143. Hickey, "Bob Dylan," 5. In comparison to fellow Founding Fathers, Franklin and Jefferson were more democratic (populist).—Vernon Louis Parrington, *Main Currents in American Literature: An Interpretation of American Literature from the Beginnings to 1920* (New York: Harcourt, Brace, c1927, 1930), 1:164–78, 342–56, 2:10–19.

144. Dylan, *Slow Train Coming* (1979).
145. Eric Foner, *The Story of American Freedom* (New York: W.W. Norton, 1998), 20.
146. Thompson, *Positively Main Street*, 159.
147. Brinkley, "Bob Dylan's America," 45.
148. Joel Porte, "Introduction: Representing America—the Emerson Legacy," and David Robinson, "Transcendentalism and Its Times," in Joel Porte and Sandra Morris, eds., *The Cambridge Companion to Ralph Waldo Emerson* (Cambridge: Cambridge University Press, 1999), 9, 13, 17.
149. Dylan, *Chronicles*, 86.
150. Ibid., 40.
151. Ibid., 283.
152. *No Direction Home*, DVD.
153. Christopher Lasch, *The Agony of the American Left* (New York: Alfred A Knopf, 1969), 6.
154. Gene Clanton, *Congressional Populism and the Crisis of the 1890s* (Lawrence: University of Kansas Press, 1998), 5.
155. Dylan, *Chronicles*, 86.
156. Gilmore, "Bob Dylan" (2012), 48.
157. Bill Kauffman, *Look Homeward, America: In Search of Reactionary Radicals and Front-Porch Anarchists* (Wilmington, DE: ISI Books, 2006), 167.
158. Dylan, *Love and Theft* (2001).
159. Ian Bell, *Once Upon a Time: The Lives of Bob Dylan* (New York: Pegasus Books, 2012), 117–18.
160. Dylan, *Chronicles*, 235.
161. Jann Wenner, "Country Tradition Goes to Heart of Dylan Songs," *Rolling Stone*, May 25, 1968, 14.
162. Marcus, "Self Portrait No. 25," *Rolling Stone*, July 23, 1970, 16.
163. Paul Williams, *Watching the River Flow: Observations on Bob Dylan's Art in Progress, 1966–1995* (New York: Omnibus Press, 1996), 102.
164. Bill Reed, "Bob Dylan's Nashville Skyline Sessions June 1969," *Rolling Stone*, April 16, 1970, 47.
165. David Gates, "Dylan Revisited," *Newsweek*, October 6, 1997, 65.
166. Bob Dylan, *Together Through Life* (2009).
167. Russell Kirk, *The Conservative Mind: From Burke to Eliot* (Chicago: Regnery, 1953); William F. Buckley Jr., *God and Man at Yale: The Superstitions of Academic Freedom* (Chicago: Regnery, 1951).
168. Ronald Radosh, *Prophets on the Right: Profiles of Conservative Critics of American Globalism* (New York: Free Life Editions, c1975, 1978), 128, 131, 135.
169. "The Sharon Statement." Contained in: Alexander Bloom and Wini Breines, eds., *Takin' It to the Streets: A Sixties Reader* (New York: Oxford University Press, 1995, 2003), 290.

170. Smith, "A World of His Own," reprinted in *Broadside* #31, 7.
171. Dylan, *Chronicles*, 283.
172. Robert Dean Lurie, "Unlike a Rolling Stone," *The American Conservative*, May/June 2014, 38. For an interesting book-length examination of Dylan from a conservative perspective, see Webb, *Dylan Redeemed*.
173. Ron Rosenbaum, "Interview." Contained in: *Younger Than That Now*, 152.
174. Barry Goldwater, "Acceptance Speech 1964 Republican National Convention." Contained in: *Takin' it to the Streets*, 291.
175. John A. Andrew III, *The Other Side of the Sixties: Young Americans for Freedom and the Rise of Conservative Politics* (New Brunswick, NJ: Rutgers University Press, 1997), 61.
176. This was precisely the critique of organized labor by C. Wright Mills, a father of the New Left. Rick Tilman, *C. Wright Mills: A Native Radical and His American Intellectual Roots* (University Park: Pennsylvania State University Press, 1984), 21–23.
177. *Broadside* #35, November 1963, 8.
178. Kauffman, *Look Homeward*, 134–35.
179. Smith, "A World of His Own," reprinted in *Broadside* #31, 7.
180. Ron Rosenbaum, "Interview," *Younger Than That Now*, 149.
181. Brinkley, "Bob Dylan's America," 47; and Gilmore, "Bob Dylan" (2012), 48.
182. David Yaffe, *Bob Dylan: Like a Complete Unknown* (New Haven: Yale University Press, 2011), 90.
183. Jon Bream, "Croaky Dylan Welcomes Winds of Change: Concert Review," *Minneapolis Star Tribune*, November 5, 2008.
184. Gilmore, "Bob Dylan" (2012), 48–49.
185. Mikal Gilmore, "Positively Dylan," *Rolling Stone*, July 17/31, 1986, 135; emphasis in the original.

2 Voice of a Generation

1. Gilmore, "Bob Dylan" (2012), 44–45.
2. Mackay, *Intimate Insights*, 69.
3. Dylan, *Chronicles*, 29.
4. Massimo Teodori, ed., *The New Left: A Documentary History* (New York: Bobbs-Merrill Company, 1969), 73.
5. Stuart Kallen, ed., *Sixties Counterculture* (San Diego: Greenhaven Press, 2001), 11.
6. Teodori, *New Left*, 36.
7. William L. O'Neill, *Coming Apart: An Informal History of America in the 1960s* (New York: Quadrangle Books), 1971.
8. Teodori, *New Left*, 23.
9. John Robert Greene, *America in the Sixties* (Syracuse: Syracuse University Press, 2010), 104.
10. "The Port Huron Statement." Contained in: Teodori, *New Left*, 163.

11. Ibid., 164.
12. Ibid., 165–66.
13. Greene, *America in the Sixties*, 104.
14. Ibid., 108–109.
15. SDS: "America and New Era." Contained in: Teodori, *New Left*, 180.
16. James J. Farrell, *The Spirit of the Sixties: The Making of Postwar Radicalism* (New York: Routledge, 1997), 6–9.
17. Teodori, *New Left*, 36–37.
18. Smith, "A World of His Own," reprinted in: *Broadside* #31, 7.
19. Mackay, *Intimate Insights*, 35.
20. Dylan, *Another Side of Bob Dylan* (1964).
21. Baez, *A Voice to Sing*, 95.
22. Victor Maymudes, *Another Side of Bob Dylan: A Personal History on the Road and off the Tracks*, ed. Jacob Maymudes (New York: St. Martin's Press, 2014), 253. Alberta Cooley participated in the third and final Selma to Montgomery March when she was a high school girl, in March 1965. She remembers Joan Baez and Peter, Paul and Mary, among others, singing Freedom Songs for the marchers on the last evening, and says that Dylan's music, including "Blowin' in the Wind," was "a big influence on the movement." Entering Montgomery the next day, on their way to the Alabama State Capitol, "thousands of people stood out along the street" to cheer on the marchers. Alberta recalls, "There was an old black woman in a wheelchair in front of her house, waving us on. She had no legs, with tears in her eyes, shouting, 'Go on! Go on!'" Today, Alberta Cooley McCrory is mayor of Hobson City, Alabama—the second-oldest incorporated black town in the United States. Alberta McCrory e-mails to JT, March 6–7, 2014.
23. Baez, *Voice to Sing*, 92–93.
24. Dave Moberg, "The Folk and the Rock," *Newsweek*, September 20, 1965, 88.
25. "The Port Huron Statement." Contained in: Teodori, *New Left*, 171.
26. Robert Shelton, "Songs a Weapon in Rights Battle," *New York Times*, August 20, 1962.
27. David King Dunaway and Molly Beer, *Singing Out: An Oral History of America's Folk Music Revival* (New York: Oxford University Press, 2010), 79.
28. Heylin, *Behind the Shades Revisited*, 91–92.
29. Joel Whitburn, *Billboard Hot 100 Charts: The Sixties* (Menomonee Falls, WI: Record Research Inc., 1990).
30. Baez, *Voice to Sing*, 84.
31. *Broadside* #1, February 1962, 1.
32. *Broadside* #5, May 1962, 4.
33. Ibid.
34. *Broadside* #1, February 1962, 3; *Broadside* #2, March 1962, 4.
35. *Broadside* #5, May 1962, 4.
36. Alan Haber, "Nonexclusionism: The New Left and the Democratic Left." Contained in: Teodori, *New Left*, 222.

37. Dylan, *Lyrics: 1962–1985*, 18–19. Dylan's song was funny but unfair. JBS founder Robert Welch was not an anti-Semite. He was a radical Taft Republican.
38. Brinkley, "Bob Dylan's America," 76.
39. Teodori, *New Left*, 22–23.
40. Dylan, *Chronicles*, 270–71.
41. *Broadside* #3, April 1962, 3; Bob Dylan, *Bootleg Series Volumes 1–3* (1991).
42. *Broadside* #4, mid-April 1962, 2.
43. Dylan, *Bootleg Series Volumes 1–3* (1991).
44. John Morton Blum, *Years of Discord: American Politics and Society 1961–74* (New York: W.W. Norton, 1991), 273.
45. Todd Gitlin, "Power and the Myth of Progress," *The New Republic*, 1966. Contained in: Teodori, *New Left*, 188; emphasis in the original.
46. Dylan, *Highway 61 Revisited* (1965).
47. Robert Hilburn, "I Learned That Jesus Is Real and I Wanted That," *Los Angeles Times*, November 23, 1980. Contained in: Benson, *Bob Dylan Companion*, 165.
48. Christopher Sykes interview, October 18, 1986; emphasis in the original. Reprinted in Bob Dylan 1988 Tour Program.
49. Baez, *Voice to Sing*, 95.
50. Dylan, *Lyrics: 1962–1985*, 46–47.
51. Nat Hentoff, "Joan Baez and Bob Dylan: The Voice Meets the Poet," *HiFi/Stereo Review*, November 1963. Reprinted in *Hootenanny* Volume 1, No. 2, March 1964, 11.
52. Welles, "Angry Young Singer," 114.
53. Engel, *Bob Zimmerman's Blues*, 30–31.
54. Dylan, *Chronicles*, 29–30.
55. Webb, *Dylan Redeemed*, 44.
56. Teodori, *New Left*, 14.
57. *Broadside* #3, April 1962, 2.
58. *Broadside* #17, December 1962, 2.
59. Scaduto, *Bob Dylan*, 171.
60. Nat Hentoff, "The Crackin', Shakin', Breakin' Sounds," *The New Yorker*, October 1964. Contained in: Benjamin Hedin, ed., *Studio A: The Bob Dylan Reader* (New York: W.W. Norton, 2004), 26.
61. *Broadside* #17, December 1962, 5.
62. *Broadside* #16, mid-November 1962, 4–7.
63. Dylan, *Lyrics: 1962–1985*, 24.
64. *Broadside* #16, mid-November 1962, 2.
65. *Broadside* # 20, February 1963, 2, 10; *Broadside* #31, September 1963, 8; Dylan, *Lyrics: 1962–1985*, 160.
66. Heylin, *Behind the Shades Revisited*, 93.
67. Nigel Williamson, *The Rough Guide to Bob Dylan*, 2nd ed. (London: Metro Books, 2006), 28–29.

68. *Broadside* #6, late May 1962, 2.
69. Whitburn, *Billboard Hot 100: Sixties*; Robert Shelton, "Freedom Songs Sweep North," *New York Times*, July 6, 1963.
70. Dylan, *The Freewheelin' Bob Dylan* (1963).
71. Hickey, "Bob Dylan," 6, 8.
72. Bell, *Once Upon a Time*, 223.
73. Baez, *Voice to Sing*, 91.
74. The chairman of the ECLC, Corliss Lamont, was an interesting figure. Son of first-tier Wall Street banker Thomas W. Lamont of J.P. Morgan & Co., he apparently played a role in his father's service as "Morgan's apostle to the Left." During his ECLC speech, Dylan identified Lee Oswald as the man who had shot President Kennedy three weeks earlier. But Dylan expressed ambiguity about Oswald being the assassin in his post-speech letter: "I was not speakin of his deed if it was his deed." Coincidentally, Corliss Lamont was author of a pamphlet handed out by Oswald on the streets of New Orleans in the summer of 1963 as part of the Fair Play for Cuba Committee. Oswald's one-person local chapter was apparently fake and CIA-backed. "Bob Dylan and the NECLC," *Corliss Lamont Website*, January 7, 2012, http://www.corliss-lamont.org/dylan.htm; Carroll Quigley, *Tragedy and Hope: A History of the World in Our Time* (New York: Macmillan, 1966), 945, 935–56.
75. Scaduto, *Bob Dylan*, 189; emphasis in the original.
76. Heylin, *Behind the Shades Revisited*, 138.
77. Lawrence Grobel, *Endangered Species: Writers Talk about Their Craft, Their Visions, Their Lives* (Cambridge, MA: Da Capo Press, 2001), 169.
78. Todd Gitlin, *The Sixties: Years of Hope, Days of Rage*, rev. ed. (New York: Bantam Books, 1993), 198.
79. Bell, *Once Upon a Time*, 308–10.
80. Dunaway and Beer, *Singing Out*, 121.
81. Dylan, *The Times They Are A-Changin'* (1964). One evening, during the 1965–66 period, the 14-year-old son of Governor George Wallace (D-AL) played the guitar and sang "The Times They Are A-Changin'" for his father. George Jr. believed that the line about standing in the doorway was a reference to his father "standing in the schoolhouse door," symbolically blocking the registration of two black students at the University of Alabama in June 1963. Dylan wrote the song a few months later. The young Wallace thought that he saw a look of regret in the eyes of the segregationist governor as he listened. George Wallace Jr., *Governor George Wallace: The Man You Never Knew* (Wallace Productions, 2011), xii–xiii.
82. Baez, *Voice to Sing*, 92.
83. Bob Dylan, "For Dave Glover," *Broadside* #35, late November 1963, 7–8.
84. Mackay, *Intimate Insights*, 23–24.
85. Dunaway and Beer, *Singing Out*, 134–35.
86. Welles, "Angry Young Singer," 109.

87. Daniel Mark Epstein, *The Ballad of Bob Dylan: A Portrait* (New York: Harper Collins, 2011), 76–77.
88. Thompson, *Positively Main Street*, 73.
89. Scaduto, *Bob Dylan*, 142.
90. Williamson, *Rough Guide*, 42.
91. Scaduto, *Bob Dylan*, 139.
92. Ibid., 187, 205.
93. Hentoff, "Crackin' Shakin' Breakin'"; emphasis in the original. Reprinted in: Hedin, *Studio A*, 27.
94. David Hajdu, *Positively 4th Street: The Lives and Times of Joan Baez, Bob Dylan, Mimi Baez Farina and Richard Farina* (New York: Farrar, Straus, Giroux, 2001), 210–11.
95. Paul J. Robbins, "Bob Dylan in His Own Words." Contained in: Benson, *Bob Dylan Companion*, 49.
96. Dylan, *Freewheelin' Bob Dylan* (1963).
97. Dylan, *Another Side of Bob Dylan* (1964).
98. Whitburn, *Billboard Hot 100: Sixties*.
99. Bob Dylan, "A Letter from Bob Dylan," *Broadside #38*, January 1964, 7–12.
100. Irwin Silber, "An Open Letter to Bob Dylan." Contained in: Craig McGregor, *Bob Dylan: The Early Years a Retrospective* (Cambridge, MA: De Capo Press: c1972, 1990), 67.
101. Robert Shelton, "Pop Singers and Song Writers Racing Down Bob Dylan's Road," *New York Times*, August 27, 1965.
102. Dunaway and Beer, *Singing Out*, 158.
103. John Orman, *The Politics of Rock Music* (Chicago: Nelson Hall, 1984), 62.
104. Farrell, *Spirit of the Sixties*, 70.
105. *No Direction Home*, DVD directed by Martin Scorsese, Paramount Pictures, 2005.
106. Thomas Meehan, "Public Writer No. 1?" *New York Times Magazine*, December 12, 1965, 134.
107. Mayfair Hotel Press Conference, London May 3, 1966. Contained in: *Bob Dylan Companion*, 78.
108. Robbins, "In His Own Words." Contained in: *Bob Dylan Companion*, 52.
109. Robert Shelton. *No Direction Home: The Life and Music of Bob Dylan* (New York: Beech Tree Books, 1986), 187.
110. Dylan, *Bringing It All Back Home* (1965).
111. Ibid.
112. Ibid.
113. Carl Oglesby, "Trapped in a System." Contained in: Teodori, *New Left*, 182.
114. Robert Shelton, "Dylan Conquers Unruly Audience," *New York Times*, August 30, 1965.
115. Meehan, "Public Writer," 136.
116. Ibid., 132.
117. Whitburn, *Billboard Hot 100: Sixties*.

118. Orman, *The Politics of Rock*, 62.
119. Meehan, "Public Writer," 132.
120. Blum, *Years of Discord*, 273.
121. "The Truth about Bob Dylan," *Rolling Stone*, November 23, 1967, 6.
122. "Beverley Hills Press Conference September 4, 1965." Contained in: *Bob Dylan Companion*, 59.
123. Greene, *America in the Sixties*, 138–39.
124. Dylan, *Highway 61 Revisited* (1965).
125. Laurie Henshaw, "Mr. Send Up," originally *Disc Weekly*, May 22, 1965. Contained in: *Bob Dylan Companion*, 63.
126. Gilmore, "Bob Dylan" (2012), 46.
127. Dylan, *Lyrics: 1962–1985*, 180.
128. Farrell, *Spirit of the Sixties*, 203.
129. Alice Echols, *Shaky Ground: The '60s and Its Aftershocks* (New York: Columbia University Press, 2002), 28.
130. O'Neill, *Coming Apart*, 298.
131. "Berkeley Barb: From the Haight." Contained in: Teodori, *New Left*, 362–63.
132. O'Neill, *Coming Apart*, 298.
133. Gitlin, *Days of Rage*, 344.
134. Greene, *America in the Sixties*, 141.
135. Nat Hentoff, "Interview," *Playboy*, March 1966. Contained in: Jonathan Cott, ed., *Bob Dylan: The Essential Interviews* (New York: Wenner Books, 2006), 108; emphasis in the original.
136. Jerome, "Myth Materializes," 30.
137. O'Neill, *Coming Apart*, 295–96.
138. Farrell, *Spirit of the Sixties*, 229.
139. "Berkeley Barb." Contained in: Teodori, *New Left*, 362.
140. Jerome, "Myth Materializes," 30.
141. Edna Gundersen, "Dylan on Dylan: Folk's Hero Faces the '90s in a Rare Interview," *USA Today*, September 21, 1989.
142. Jerome, "Myth Materializes," 30.
143. Alan Light, "Bob Dylan: At Ease," *Rolling Stone*, November 29, 1990, 30.
144. John Cohen and Happy Traum, "Interview" *Sing Out!*, October/November 1968. Contained in: Cott, *Bob Dylan*, 137.
145. Gitlin, *Days of Rage*, 417.
146. Christopher Lasch, *The Culture of Narcissism* (New York: W.W. Norton, 1978), 4.
147. Ed Ward, "Review of 'New Morning,'" *Rolling Stone*, November 26, 1970, 32.
148. Joel Whitburn, *Billboard Hot 100 Charts: The Seventies* (Menomonee Falls, WI: Record Research Inc., 1990).
149. "Bob Dylan at Old Nassau," *Rolling Stone*, July 9, 1970, 8.
150. Anthony Scaduto, "Won't You Listen to the Lambs, Bob Dylan?" *New York Times Magazine,* November 28, 1971, 35.

151. Jonathan Cott, "I Dreamed I Saw Bob Dylan," *Rolling Stone*, September 2, 1971.
152. Heylin, *Behind the Shades Revisited*, 367.
153. Scaduto, "Listen to the Lambs," 34–35.
154. Ibid., 50.
155. Ibid., 35
156. Ibid., 52.
157. Ibid., 36.
158. Ibid., 35–36.
159. Edward D. Berkowitz, *Something Happened: A Political and Cultural Overview of the Seventies* (New York: Columbia University Press, 2006), 6.
160. Ben Fong-Torres, "Knockin' on Dylan's Door," *Rolling Stone*, February 14, 1974, 38.
161. Dennis McDougal, *Bob Dylan: A Biography* (New York: Wiley, 2014), 245.
162. Larry "Ratso" Sloman, *On the Road With Bob Dylan* (New York: Three Rivers Press, 2002), 132.
163. Ralph Gleason, "The Bob Dylan/Richard Nixon Synchronicity," *Rolling Stone*, December 6, 1973, 13.
164. David Felton, "Bob Dylan Sells Out," *Rolling Stone*, January 3, 1974, 14.
165. Fong-Torres, "Knockin on Dylan's Door," 44.
166. Maureen Orth, "Dylan Rolling Again," *Newsweek*, January 14, 1974, 48.
167. Ibid., 49.
168. Christopher Lasch, *The Culture of Narcissism* (New York: W. W. Norton, 1978), 5.
169. John Crespino, "Civil Rights and the Religious Right." Contained in: Bruce J. Schulman and Julian E. Zelizer, eds., *Rightward Bound: Making America Conservative in the 1970s.* (Cambridge: Harvard University Press, 2008), 90; Grace Elizabeth Hale, *A Nation of Outsiders: How the White Middle Class Fell in Love with Rebellion in Postwar America* (New York: Oxford University Press, 2011), 255.
170. Hickey, "Bob Dylan," 4.
171. Orman, *Politics of Rock,* 19.
172. Robert W. Turner, ed., "I'll Never Lie to You," *Jimmy Carter in His Own Words* (New York: Ballantine Books, 1976), 95–96.
173. Rosenbaum, "Interview." Contained in: *Younger Than That*, 150.
174. Williams, *Watching the River Flow*, 105.
175. Ibid., 107.
176. Joel Whitburn, *The Billboard Albums* (Menomonee Falls, WI: Record Research Inc. 2006), 317.
177. Jann Wenner, "Bob Dylan and Our Times: The Slow Train Is Coming," *Rolling Stone*, September 20, 1979, 94–95.
178. Dylan, *Lyrics: 1962–1985*, 417.
179. Dylan, *Infidels* (1983).
180. Ibid.

181. Bernard Kleinman, "Dylan on Dylan," Westwood One (Radio Station Discs), November 17, 1984. Contained in: Benson, *Bob Dylan Companion*, 40.
182. Keller, "Dylan Speaks," 59.
183. Brown, *Overburden*, 190.
184. John Bream, "Has Rock Overdosed on Aid?" *Minneapolis Star Tribune*, October 12, 1986.
185. Mikal Gilmore, "Dylan at a Crossroads Once Again," originally *Los Angeles Herald-Examiner,* October 13, 1985. Contained in: Benson, *Bob Dylan Companion*, 181.
186. Heylin, *Behind the Shades Revisited*, 547, 580, 596. Epstein, *Ballad of Bob Dylan*, 239–40; Tim Riley, *Hard Rain: A Dylan Commentary*, updated ed. (New York: Da Capo Press, c1992, 1999), 278.
187. Light, "At Ease," 30.
188. Keller, "Dylan Speaks," 59.
189. Smith, "World of His Own," reprinted in *Broadside #31*, 7.
190. "OFFICIAL Chrysler and Bob Dylan Super Bowl Commercial 2014—America's Import," YouTube, February 2, 2014, http://www.youtube.com/watch?v=KlSn8Isv-3M.
191. Epstein, *Ballad of Bob Dylan*, 425.
192. This is exactly what happened to Peter, Paul and Mary as performers. They became a nostalgia act for aging Baby Boomers with personally pleasant but politically irrelevant appearances.
193. "Dylan," 20/20 Transcript (ABC News), October 10, 1985, 10.
194. Edna Gundersen, "Dylan on Dylan: 'Unplugged' and the Birth of a Song," *USA Today,* May 5–7, 1995. Contained in: Benson, *Dylan Companion*, 225.

3 Freedom and Justice

1. Norm Fruchter, "Mississippi: Notes on SNCC." Contained in: Teodori, *New Left*, 114.
2. "America and New Era." Contained in: Teodori, *New Left*, 172.
3. Raymond Mungro, "The Road to Liberation (A Letter to What Used to Be His Draft Board)." Contained in: Teodori, *New Left*, 349.
4. Hale, *A Nation of Outsiders*, 1.
5. Steven Ives director, *The American Experience: 1964* (Boston: WGBH PBS Video, 2014), DVD.
6. Farrell, *Spirit of the Sixties*, 17.
7. Ibid., 229.
8. Robert Shelton, "Bob Dylan Sings His Compositions," *New York Times*, April 13, 1963.
9. Liner Notes, Bob Dylan *Biograph*, Columbia Records 38830-LP, 1985.
10. Karl Jaspers, "Freedom" from *Philosophy Vol. 2* (trans. E. B. Ashton). Contained in: Robert C. Solomon, ed., *Existentialism* (New York: Random House, 1974), 149.

11. "Port Huron Statement." Contained in: Teodori, *New Left*, 166.
12. Henshaw, "Mr. Send Up." Contained in: Benson, *Bob Dylan Companion*, 64.
13. "I Am My Words," *Newsweek*, November 4, 1963, 95.
14. Hubert Saal, "Dylan Is Back," *Newsweek*, February 26, 1968.
15. Dylan, *Bringing It All Back Home* (1965).
16. Pete Seeger, *Pete Seeger in His Own Words*, eds. Rob Rosenthal and Sam Rosenthal (Boulder: Paradigm Publishers, 2012), 320.
17. Heylin, *Behind the Shades Revisited*, 89.
18. Shelton, *No Direction Home*, 1986, 131–32.
19. Mayor Alberta Cooley McCrory was six or seven years old when the story of Emmett Till appeared in *Jet* magazine. The black youth from Chicago was killed in Money, Mississippi, while visiting relatives in the summer of 1955. He was accused of whistling at a white woman at the store her husband operated. In the magazine, the picture of his face beaten and shot beyond recognition was next to one of a handsome boy neatly dressed, wearing a nice hat, and looking like he was on his way to a becoming a successful black man. Alberta recalls, "Mothers and fathers passed the magazine around in the community, making sure that everyone—particularly young boys—saw what evil white men had done to this little boy. It served as a reminder of what could happen to their sons. In spite of what happened black people kept going to church and kept believing that God would punish those who murdered Emmett Till and others because they were black." Alberta McCrory, e-mail to JT, September 23, 2013.
20. Dylan, *The Times They Are A-Changin'* (1964).
21. This view of power in the South was not found only among Marxists. Respected political scientist E. E. Schattschneider set forth the same analysis in 1960. E. E. Schattschneider, *The Semisovereign People: A Realist's View of Democracy in America* (Hinsdale, IL: Dryden Press, c1960, 1975), 70–80.
22. Six years later, Charles Evers was elected mayor of Fayette, Mississippi.
23. Suzanne Duscha was ten years old when she attended the March on Washington. She and her brothers were there, unaccompanied, as "part of a sea of people of all colors." She does not recall Bob Dylan singing "When the Ship Comes In" or "Only a Pawn in Their Game," but does remember the crowd singing "We Shall Overcome." Of that song, Suzanne writes, "Even as a young person, I was so moved there were tears in my eyes and chills running up and down my spine." Suzanne Duscha, e-mails to JT, July 25 and August 3, 2014.
24. Interview with Charles Evers by JT, June 30, 2014.
25. "The Spinsters' Ball," *Time*, February 22, 1963, 26.
26. Phil Ochs, "The Art of Bob Dylan's 'Hattie Carroll,'" *Broadside* #48, July 1964, 3.
27. *Broadside* #23, late March 1963, 5.
28. *Broadside* #29, July 1963, 2.
29. *Broadside* #31, September 1963, 4.

30. Dylan, *The Times They Are A-Changin'* (1964).
31. Carl Oglesby, "Trapped in a System." Contained in: Teodori, *New Left*, 184.
32. Gitlin, "Power and the Myth of Progress." Contained in: Teodori, *New Left*, 189.
33. Baez, *Voice to Sing*, 85.
34. Scaduto, *Bob Dylan*, 137.
35. *Sing Out!* Vol 12, No.4, October/November 1962, 9.
36. Engel, *Bob Zimmerman's Blues*, 203.
37. Dunaway and Beer, *Singing Out*, 69.
38. Dylan, *Bootleg Series Volumes 1–3* (1991).
39. Ibid.
40. Shelton, "Bob Dylan Sings."
41. *Broadside* #21, late February 1963, 7.
42. *Broadside* #29, July 1963, 4.
43. Webb, *Dylan Redeemed*, 52.
44. Ralph Gleason, "A Folk Singing Social Critic," *San Francisco Chronicle*, February 24, 1964. Reprinted in: *Broadside* #44, late April 1964, 12.
45. *Broadside* #25, late April 1963, 5.
46. Dylan, *Another Side of Bob Dylan* (1964).
47. Dylan, *Chronicles*, 115.
48. Robbins, "In His Own Words." Contained in: Benson, *Bob Dylan Companion*, 51.
49. C. Vann Woodward, "What Happened to the Civil Rights Movement?" *Harpers*, January 1967. Reprinted in: Katharine Whittemore, Ellen Rosenbush, and Jim Nelson, eds., *The Sixties: Recollections of the Decade from Harper's Magazine* (New York: Franklin Square Press), 79.
50. Dylan's criticism of respectability in the mainstream Civil Rights Movement—black and white—was also voiced in his 1963 speech to the ECLC. "Bob Dylan and the NECLC."
51. Robbins, "Dylan in His Own Words," Contained in: Benson, *Bob Dylan Companion*, 55.
52. Dylan, *Another Side of Bob Dylan* (1964).
53. Hickey, "Bob Dylan," 6.
54. Dylan, *Planet Waves* (1974).
55. Dylan, *Bringing It All Back Home* (1965).
56. Ibid.
57. Dylan, *Highway 61 Revisited* (1965).
58. Ibid.
59. Dylan, *Blonde on Blonde* (1966).
60. The Beatles, *Rubber Soul*. Capitol Records 0946 3 82418 2 9, 2009 compact disc. Originally released in 1965.
61. Bob Dylan, *Bringing It All Back Home* (1965).
62. This is a more positive echo of a negative verse in "Like a Rolling Stone."
63. Scaduto, "Listen to the Lambs," 43.

64. Bono, "Bob Dylan 100 Greatest Singers," *Rolling Stone*, November 27, 2008, 80.
65. Dylan, *John Wesley Harding* (1967).
66. Ibid.
67. Jean Strouse, "Bob Dylan's Gentle Anarchy," *Commonweal*, 1968. Contained in: Benson, *Bob Dylan Companion*, 89.
68. Bob Dylan, *Blonde on Blonde* (1966).
69. Dylan, *Nashville Skyline* (1969).
70. Bob Dylan, *Chronicles*, 115–16.
71. *Hartford Times*, April 13, 1969.
72. Dylan, *New Morning* (1970).
73. Greene, *America in the Sixties*, 139.
74. Dylan, *New Morning* (1970).
75. Bell, *Once Upon a Time*, 531–32.
76. Dylan, *Lyrics: 1962–1985*, 302.
77. "Ole Bob Dylan: Everybody Wants Me to Be Just Like Them," *Rolling Stone*, January 6, 1972, 10.
78. Scaduto "Listen to the Lambs," 52.
79. Joel Whitburn, *Billboard Hot 100 Charts: The Seventies* (Menomonee Falls, WI: Record Research Inc., 1990).
80. Scaduto, "Listen to the Lambs," 52.
81. Ibid.
82. Dylan, *Blood on the Tracks* (1975).
83. Sid Griffin, *Shelter from the Storm: Bob Dylan's Rolling Thunder Years* (London: Jawbone Press, 2010), 38–41.
84. Heylin, *Behind the Shades Revisited*, 398.
85. Nat Hentoff, "The Pilgrims Have Landed on Kerouac's Grave," *Rolling Stone*, January 15, 1976, 35.
86. Dylan, *Desire* (1976).
87. Dylan, *Infidels* (1983).
88. Jerome, "A Myth Materializes," 24.
89. Griffin, *Shelter from the Storm*, 45–48.
90. Bob Dylan, *Desire* (1975).
91. Benjamin Hedin, *Studio A: The Bob Dylan Reader* (New York: W.W. Norton, 2004), 220.
92. Dylan, *Bootleg Series Volume 5* (2002).
93. Jerome, "A Myth Materializes," 30.
94. Baez, *A Voice to Sing*, 92.
95. Dylan, *Street Legal* (1978).
96. Ibid.
97. Paul Williams, *Watching the River Flow: Observations on Bob Dylan's Art-in-Progress, 1966–1995* (New York: Omnibus Press), 103.
98. Hale, *Nation of Outsiders*, 1–3.
99. John 8:32; Romans 6:18; Galatians 5:1; II Corinthians 3:17.

100. Dylan, *Slow Train Coming* (1979).
101. Dylan, *Saved* (1980).
102. Bruce Heiman, "Radio Interview KMEX, Tuscon, Arizona," December 7, 1979. Contained in: Jonathan Cott, ed., *The Essential Interviews*, 272–73.
103. Robert Hilburn, "Forever Dylan: On the Never Ending Tour With Rock's Greatest Poet," *Los Angeles Times*, February 9, 1992. Contained in: Benson, *Bob Dylan Companion*, 222.
104. John Dolan, "A Midnight Chat with Bob Dylan," *Fort Lauderdale Sun Sentinel*, September 29, 1995. Contained in: Benson, *Bob Dylan Companion*, 229.
105. Robert Hilburn, "I Learned That Jesus Is Real and I Wanted That," *Los Angeles Times*, November 23, 1980. Contained in: Benson, *Bob Dylan Companion*, 163.
106. Keller, "Dylan Speaks," 59.
107. Who is Jokerman? Interpretations have included Dylan, the World, Jesus, and ethnic/spiritual Israel. The song apparently contains allusions to Abraham, possibly Jacob (aka Israel), and either Moses or David, in the context of apocalyptic references to the book of Revelation and an LP inner sleeve showing Dylan on the Mount of Olives outside of Jerusalem.
108. Dylan, *Infidels* (1983).
109. Ibid.
110. Ibid.; Exodus 21:24; Leviticus 24:20; Deuteronomy 19:21; Matthew 5:38–39.
111. Larry Yudelson, "Dylan: Tangled Up in Jews," *Washington Jewish Week*, 1991. Contained in: Benson, *Bob Dylan Companion*, 174.
112. Seth Rogovoy, *Bob Dylan: Prophet, Mystic, Poet* (New York: Scribner, 2007), 230.
113. C. I. Scofield was the father of American dispensationalism. It may not be a coincidence that Scofield's first notable publication was the booklet *Rightly Dividing the Word of Truth*, originally published in 1896. The title was taken from a phrase used by Paul in II Timothy 2:15. In "I and I," Dylan paraphrases the exact same verse in the line right before the passage in question. Gazing into heavenly Justice's face may have shown Dylan the inadequacy of eye-for-eye, tooth-for-tooth earthly justice. In other words, not seeing it as synonymous with Justice but rather seeing it for what it is (natural but flawed). It has been observed that Dylan stopped singing the line about Jesus not forgiving in "Masters of War" after he became a Christian. If this interpretation of "I and I" is correct, the stranger is likely a rabbi named Jesus rather than a Lubavitch rabbi. C. I. Scofield, *Rightly Dividing the Word of Truth: Ten Outline Studies of the More Important Divisions of Scripture* (Fincastle, VA: Scripture Truth Book Company, n.d.).
114. Dylan, *Oh Mercy* (1989).
115. Dylan, *Good As I Been To You* (1992).
116. Dylan, *Love and Theft* (2001).

117. Scaduto, "Listen to the Lambs," 46.
118. Sergei Petrov and Rene Fontaine, *Masked and Anonymous*, directed by Larry Charles (Culver City, CA: Sony Pictures Classics, 2003), DVD.
119. Brinkley, "Bob Dylan's America," 45.

4 Conversion and Culture

1. Robert Hilburn, "'I Learned That Jesus Was Real and I Wanted That,'" *Los Angeles Times*, November 23, 1980. Contained in: Benson, *Bob Dylan Companion*, 164; and in: Artur, *Every Mind Polluting Word*, 719, 720.
2. Clinton Heylin, *Bob Dylan Behind the Shades: A Biography* (New York: Summit Books, 1991), 315–23; Howard Sounes, *Down the Highway: The Life of Bob Dylan* (New York: Grove Press, 2001), 322–27; Scott M. Marshall, with Marcia Ford, *Restless Pilgrim: The Spiritual Journey of Bob Dylan* (Lake Mary, FL: Relevant Books, 2002), 21–33.
3. Artur, *Every Mind Polluting Word*, 712; Clinton Heylin, ed., *Saved!: The Gospel Speeches of Bob Dylan* (New York: Hanuman Books, 1990), 55. Concert raps in *Saved!* excerpted from Heylin, "Saved!: Bob Dylan's Conversion to Christianity," Parts 1–3, *The Telegraph* #28–30 (1987–88).
4. Morris Bishop, *Pascal: The Life of Genius* (New York: Reynal & Hitchcock, 1936), 172–80; Artur, *Every Mind Polluting Word*, 711. Dylan resembles another brilliant scientist, Isaac Newton, with his interest in End Times biblical prophecy, especially the books of Revelation and Daniel. Newton spent years studying prophecy and his book *Observations upon the Prophecies of Daniel and the Apocalypse of St. John* was published posthumously.
5. There were some secular exceptions to the dismay, including *Rolling Stone* publisher Jann Wenner, as noted in chapter 2. More than 20 years after the release of Dylan's gospel trilogy, Jesse Walker paid tribute to the albums, especially *Slow Train Coming* and *Saved*. Jesse Walker, "Highway to Heaven Revisited," *No Depression*, November–December 2003, http://archives.nodepression.com/2003/11/highway-to-heaven-revisited.
6. "The (New) Word According to Dylan," *Newsweek*, December 17, 1979, 90.
7. Interview with Dave Kelly by JT, November 1, 2014.
8. Kurt Loder, "Bob Dylan: The Rolling Stone Interview," *Rolling Stone*, June 21, 1984, 17; Revelation 17:1–6.
9. Portions of chapter 4 are adapted from: Jeff Taylor, "Bob Dylan and Antithetical Engagement with Culture," *Pro Rege* 41:4 (June 2013), 16–26.
10. David Biven, "How 'Yeshua' Became 'Jesus,'" *JesusisaJew.org*, http://jesusisajew.org/YESHUA.php; "Jesus Is a Jew," *JesusisaJew.org*, http://jesusisajew.org/Jesus_is_a_Jew.php.

11. Dan Wooding, "How Bob Dylan Found Christ," *ASSIST News Service*, October 2, 2008, http://www.assistnews.net/Stories/2008/s08100017.htm; Marshall, *Restless Pilgrim*, 30–31.
12. Heylin, *Life in Stolen Moments*, 238, 242, 243, 278; "THANK GOD—Chabad Telethon—1986," *Facebook*, May 19, 2011, https://www.facebook.com/video.php?v=10150257379840540.
13. Marshall, *Restless Pilgrim*, 62; Artur, *Every Mind Polluting Word*, 801.
14. Dylan, Infidels (1983); Acts 1:1–12; Zechariah 14:1–9.
15. Artur, *Every Mind Polluting Word*, 755.
16. Larry Norman's antioccult song "Forget Your Hexagram" was released by Capitol Records in 1969. Larry Norman, *Upon This Rock* [sound recording] (Capitol Records, 1969/Impact Records, 1970).
17. YahFollower, "The Truth of the Shield of David," *The Way of the Ancient Nazarene: Followers of the Mosshiac [Messiah]*, 2011, http://yahfollower.webs.com/thestarofdavid.htm. This website is Christian in the sense of recognizing Jesus as the Messiah, but it is theologically unorthodox. For example, contrary to the New Testament, it rejects the deity of Christ.
18. Robert Hilburn, "Bob Dylan at 42: Rolling Down Highway 61 Again," *Los Angeles Times*, October 30, 1983, U3–4. Contained in: Artur, *Every Mind Polluting Word*, 757, 758.
19. Matthew 7:14.
20. Heylin, *Life in Stolen Moments*, 302; Larry Yudelson, "Dylan: Tangled Up in Jews," *Washington Jewish Week*, 1991. Contained in: Benson, *Bob Dylan Companion*, 174–75; "Happy Pesach: Bob Dylan Performs 'Hava Nagila,'" *Media Funhouse*, March 25, 2010, http://mediafunhouse.blogspot.com/2010/03/happy-pesach-bob-dylan-performs-hava.html. In addition to Himmelman, actor Harry Dean Stanton played a second acoustic guitar. Stanton is a Dylan friend who appeared with him in *Pat Garrett & Billy the Kid* (1973), did some recording with him on *Planet Waves* (1974), and played a role in Dylan's film *Renaldo & Clara* (1975, 1978).
21. Manis Friedman, *Doesn't Anyone Blush Anymore?: Reclaiming Intimacy, Modesty, and Sexuality*, ed. J. S. Morris (New York: HarperCollins, 1990).
22. Bob Dylan, *New Morning* (1970).
23. At the same time, we do not want to take this too far. The Lubavitchers had no claim of affiliation, let alone ownership, in regard to Dylan. He had never been an Orthodox Jew and the group in Brooklyn was just one sect of that type of Judaism. There has probably been an element of self-promotion in their efforts to woo Dylan and make use of his name over the years. It might be said that Dylan disappointed the Jewish Community when he turned to Christ but the "Community" is mostly an abstraction. There are many different kinds of Jews. It is probable that most of Dylan's Jewish fans in America were secular-minded agnostics and atheists. The number of Orthodox Jewish fans would have been small. The Lubavitchers saw an opportunity, and they ran with it.

24. Interview with Dave Kelly by JT, November 1, 2014.
25. Dave Kelly e-mail to JT, November 19, 2014. Dylan appeared on the Chabad Telethon in 1991, saying "Give plenty of money to Chabad, it's my favorite organization in the whole world, really. They do nothing but good things with all the money." Artur, *Every Mind Polluting Word*, 1128.
26. Loder, "Bob Dylan," 17; Mikal Gilmore, "Bob Dylan: The Rolling Stone Interview," *Rolling Stone*, September 27, 2012, 51.
27. Loder, "Bob Dylan," 17.
28. Scott Cohen, "Don't Ask Me Nothin' about Nothin' I Might Just Tell You the Truth: Bob Dylan Revisited," *Spin*, December 1985, 81.
29. Ibid.
30. Bob Dylan, with Tom Petty and the Heartbreakers, *Hard to Handle* [videocassette] (CBS/FOX Video Music, 1986); Marshall, *Restless Pilgrim*, 89–90.
31. For concert set lists, see http://www.bjorner.com/still.htm. For book-length treatments of Dylan's spirituality, see Marshall, *Restless Pilgrim*; Don Williams, *Bob Dylan: The Man, the Music, the Message* (Old Tappan, NJ: Fleming H. Revell, 1985); Webb, *Dylan Redeemed*.
32. Interview with Dave Kelly by JT, November 1, 2014.
33. *New Musical Express*, August 6, 1983. Contained in: Artur, *Every Mind Polluting Word*, 754, 756, 803.
34. Luke 14:25–33; John 15:18–21, 17:14–16; II Corinthians 4:1–12; Dietrich Bonhoeffer, *The Cost of Discipleship*, rev. ed. (New York: Collier, c1937/49/59, 1963).
35. Hilburn, "Bob Dylan at 42." Contained in: Artur, *Every Mind Polluting Word*, 757, 760.
36. Loder, "Bob Dylan," 17; John 3:1–10; Artur, *Every Mind Polluting Word*, 712; Hilburn, "'I Learned That Jesus Was Real and I Wanted That.'" Contained in: Benson, *Bob Dylan Companion*, 164; and in: Artur, *Every Mind Polluting Word*, 719. Dylan's song "In the Garden" paraphrased the born-again part of Nicodemus' conversation. Bob Dylan, *Saved* (1980).
37. *Interview*, February 1986. Contained in: Artur, *Every Mind Polluting Word*, 873; Matthew 5:39; Romans 12:21, 6:23.
38. Bob Dylan, *Chronicles, Volume One* (New York: Simon & Schuster, 2004), 153; David Gates, "Dylan Revisited," *Newsweek*, October 6, 1997, 66. Dylan's 2001 interview with *Rolling Stone* featured this story as its opening paragraph. Mikal Gilmore, "Bob Dylan: The Rolling Stone Interview," *Rolling Stone*, November 22, 2001, 56; emphasis in the original.
39. Coauthor Jeff Taylor was surprised and honored to learn that the last book on Dylan by Paul Williams contained a single footnote: a half-page quotation of JT's e-mailed thoughts on Dylan's Locarno '87 experience. Paul Williams, *Bob Dylan, Performing Artist: 1986–1990 & Beyond, Mind Out of Time* (London: Omnibus Press, 2004), 91–92.
40. Yudelson, "Dylan: Tangled Up in Jews." Contained in: Benson, *Bob Dylan Companion*, 176.

41. Luke 8:30; Artur, *Every Mind Polluting Word*, 1097, 1098, 1098–99; Luke 12:7.
42. Heylin, *Life in Stolen Moments*, 351.
43. Gates, "Dylan Revisited," 64.
44. Caesar, a gospel singer, first recorded the song when it was new. Shirley Caesar, *Rejoice* [sound recording] (Myrrh Records, 1980).
45. Daniel 5; Genesis 1:1–2; Luke 22:44; Genesis 2–3; Psalm 118:24; Matthew 24:42–44; Romans 13:11–12; Revelation 16:15; Genesis 2:8–10; Revelation 22:1–3; John 20:11–16.
46. II Corinthians 5:17; Hebrews 12:1; Revelation 9:1.
47. "Bob Dylan Talks to Bill Flanagan about *Christmas in the Heart*," *RightWingBob.com*, November 24, 2009, http://www.rightwingbob.com/weblog/archives/7221.
48. Mikal Gilmore, "Bob Dylan on His Dark New LP," *Rolling Stone*, August 16, 2012, 15–16.
49. Revelation 17:1–6; Matthew 7:13–14; Exodus 16:1–3; Matthew 27:24; Daniel 5:5; Philippians 4:1, 5–6; Deuteronomy 8:3; Matthew 4:1–4; Luke 23:46.
50. Gilmore, "Bob Dylan" (2012), 48, 81.
51. In 2014, Dylan told an interviewer, "I'm drawn to spiritual songs. In 'Amazing Grace,' that line 'that saved a wretch like me'—isn't that something we could all say if we were honest enough?" Robert Love, "What I Learned From Bob," *AARP The Magazine*, February/March 2015, 4.
52. Hilburn, "Bob Dylan at 42." Contained in: Artur, *Every Mind Polluting Word*, 757, 760. Interview with Dave Kelly by JT, November 1, 2014.
53. H. Richard Niebuhr, *Christ and Culture* (New York: Harper Torchbooks, c1951, 1975), xliii–xlv, 82, 64–65.
54. Ibid., 102.
55. Ibid., 191.
56. Ibid., 45.
57. Ibid., 45–46; Heylin, *Saved!*, 53, 37, 38.
58. Olof Björner, "Still on the Road: 1980 Second Gospel Tour," *About Bob*, http://www.bjorner.com/DSN05347%201980%20Second%20Gospel%20Tour.htm#DSN05410; Heylin, *Saved!*, 47–48, 70–71; Dylan, *Blonde on Blonde* (1966); Dylan, *Saved* (1980); Dylan, *Highway 61 Revisited* (1965); Dylan, *Bringing It All Back Home* (1965).
59. Heylin, *Saved!*, 47, 12–13; Revelation 16:12–16, 19:11–21, 20:1–10; Dylan, *Times They Are A-Changin'* (1964); Dylan, *Freewheelin' Bob Dylan* (1963).
60. Tertullian, *Apologetic and Practical Treatises*, trans. C. Dodgson (Oxford: John Henry Parker, 1842) (Nabu Public Domain Reprint), 120–30; Niebuhr, *Christ and Culture*, 49, 51–55.
61. The word *ek* means "out of." The word *kaleo* means "to call."
62. John 17:6, 9, 14, 16.
63. Matthew 6:10; John 18:36.

64. I John 2:15; Romans 12:2; I Corinthians 7:31; James 1:27, 4:4.
65. Luke 4:5–8; John 12:31, 14:30, 16:11, 17:15; II Corinthians 4:3–4; Ephesians 2:1–2; II Thessalonians 2:9; Revelation 13:2, 7.
66. Matthew 5–7; Luke 6. For insightful commentary, see Bonhoeffer, *Cost of Discipleship*, 117–220.
67. Heylin, *Saved!*, 70, 23–24.
68. Abraham Kuyper, *Abraham Kuyper: A Centennial Reader*, ed. James D. Bratt (Grand Rapids, MI: Eerdmans, 1998), 22, 23, 67, 193, 211, 220. See also: James K. A. Smith, "The Temptations of Assimilation," *The Twelve*, December 21, 2011, http://the12.squarespace.com/james-ka-smith/2011/12/21/the-temptations-of-assimilation-schilder-our-bellow.html.
69. D. Williams, *Bob Dylan*, 144–45; *Wonder Boys: Music from the Motion Picture* [sound recording] (Sony Music Entertainment, 2000).
70. Paul Williams, *Dylan—What Happened?* (Glen Ellen, CA: Entwhistle Books, 1980), 86–89.
71. "Slow Train" and "When You Gonna Wake Up" on: Dylan, *Slow Train Coming*.
72. P. Williams, *Dylan*, 89, 90.
73. Heylin, *Saved!*, 35.
74. Cohen, "Don't Ask Me Nothin' about Nothin' I Might Just Tell You the Truth," 80, 81.
75. Bob Dylan, *Biograph* (1985), Side Four record sleeve ("Every Grain of Sand"), 28, 31; Ben Corbett, "Bob Dylan's Victoria's Secret Commercial: Dylan's Deal with the Devil," *About.com*, http://folkmusic.about.com/od/bobdylan/a/Bob-Dylan-Lingerie.htm.
76. C. I. Scofield, ed., *The Scofield Reference Bible* (New York: Oxford University Press, 1917), 1342.
77. Love, "Bob Dylan Does the American Songbook His Way," 28.
78. Gilmore, "Bob Dylan" (2012), 51; Kuyper, *Abraham Kuyper*, 165–201; Eleanor H. Porter, *Pollyanna* (1913); Voltaire, *Candide, or Optimism* (1759); Dylan, *Tempest* (2012).
79. Heylin, *Saved!*, 109, 110.

5 Christian Anarchism

1. The drummer cliché is a paraphrase of a passage by Henry David Thoreau in *Walden* (1854). Thoreau is also famous for the essay *Resistance to Civil Government* (aka *Civil Disobedience*) (1849).
2. Romans 13:1–7. Cf. I Peter 2:13–17.
3. Colossians 1:15–17; Revelation 1:5, 17:14; Acts 4:19–20, 5:29; Lewis Perry, *Radical Abolitionism: Anarchy and the Government of God in Antislavery Thought* (Ithaca, NY: Cornell University Press, 1973), x–xi.
4. Genesis 1:27; Joshua 24:15; Isaiah 1:18–20.

5. Genesis 3:16. Human government being a result of sin, being a post-Fall innovation, was the position of Augustine, Luther, Kuyper, Dooyeweerd, and Bushnell. William Ebenstein and Alan Ebenstein, *Great Political Thinkers: Plato to the Present*, 6th ed. (Belmont, CA: Thomson Wadsworth, 2000), 195 (Citing: Augustine, *The City of God*, "Liberty and Slavery"); Martin Luther, "Lectures on Genesis, Chapters 1–5," in *Luther's Works*, ed. Jaroslav Pelikan, trans. George V. Schick (St. Louis, MO: Concordia, 1958), 1:104; Martin Luther, *Martin Luther: Selections from His Writings*, ed. John Dillenberger (Garden City, NY: Anchor Books, 1961), 368–71 ("Secular Authority"); Abraham Kuyper, *Lectures on Calvinism* (New York: Cosimo Classics, c1931, 2007), 80–82 ("Calvinism and Politics"); Herman Dooyeweerd, *A New Critique of Theoretical Thought* (Phillipsburg, NJ: Presbyterian & Reformed Publishing, c1935, 1969), 3:423–24 (Chapter 3: "The Structural Principle of the State"); Jonathan Chaplin, *Herman Dooyeweerd: Christian Philosopher of State and Civil Society* (Notre Dame, IN: University of Notre Dame Press, 2011), 176–77; Katharine C. Bushnell, *God's Word to Women: One Hundred Bible Studies on Woman's Place in the Divine Economy* (North Collins, NY: Ray B. Munson, c1923, [1976]), 104, 124, 167.

6. Psalm 53:2–3; Ecclesiastes 7:20; Romans 3:9–12, 21–23; I Corinthians 15:21–22.

7. Matthew 12:36, 16:27; Romans 14:12; II Corinthians 5:10; Revelation 20:11–15.

8. Matthew 7:12; Galatians 5:13–23. See also Romans 6:12–23.

9. II Thessalonians 2:1–12; Wayne Blank, "Who is the Lawless One?" *Daily Bible Study*, September 24, 2003, http://www.keyway.ca/htm2003/20030924.htm. Different translations render II Thessalonians 2:3 as either "man of lawlessness" or "man of sin" because ancient manuscripts vary between the two. Given the context, *lawlessness* and *sin* mean the same thing. This also occurs in Matthew 24:12, where Jesus is describing the end of the age. There will be an increase in lawlessness/sin/iniquity/wickedness/evil/disregard of God's law (various translations). Dylan uses Paul's phrase "man of sin" in "Tin Angel" and mentions dedication to God's laws in "Pay in Blood." Matthew 24:12, *Bible Hub*, http://biblehub.com/matthew/24-12.htm; Dylan, *Tempest* (2012).

10. I Peter 1:17, 2:9; Galatians 2:6; James 2:1–4; Romans 12:16; I Corinthians 1:26–29; Galatians 3:28; Matthew 23:8–10; Luther, *Martin Luther*, 407–10 ("An Appeal to the Ruling Class of German Nationality" aka "To the Christian Nobility of the German Nation"), 345–50 ("The Pagan Servitude of the Church" aka "On the Babylonian Captivity of the Church"); 391–92 ("Secular Authority").

11. Matthew 23:27–28; Revelation 17:1–6.

12. Heylin, *Saved!*, 67–68; Matthew 11:25 (KJV).

13. Matthew 22:18–22; Genesis 1:26; I Corinthians 6:19–20.

14. Exodus 20:3–4; Francis A. Schaeffer, *The Church at the End of the 20th Century* (Downers Grove, IL: InterVarsity Press, 1970), 82–83; J. Budziszewski, *The Revenge of Conscience: Politics and the Fall of Man* (Dallas: Spence Publishing, 1999), 108. See also: James K. A. Smith, *Desiring the Kingdom: Worship, Worldview, and Cultural Formation* (Grand Rapids, MI: Baker Academic, 2009), 103–12.
15. In 312, Emperor Constantine I became the world's first political leader to embrace a pseudo-Christian version of "With God on Our Side." The linking of Christ and Caesar brought some short-term benefits to the church but the long-term harm was immense. The facilitation of war by the chaplains of power has been one sad effect.
16. Mikal Gilmore, "Positively Dylan," *Rolling Stone*, July 17/31, 1986, 135.
17. Isaiah 2:2–4, 9:6–7, 11:2–4, 6, 9–10, 32:1, 5, 35:6, 10; Jeremiah 23:5; Ezekiel 34:22–24, 37:21–22, 24; Hosea 2:18; Zechariah 9:9–10, 14:9, 16; Luke 1:30–33; Matthew 6:9–10; Revelation 19:11–12, 15–16, 20:1–3; Erich Sauer, *The Triumph of the Crucified: A Survey of Historical Revelation in the New Testament*, trans. G. H. Lang (Grand Rapids, MI: Eerdmans, c1951, 1977), 144; J. Dwight Pentecost, *Things to Come: A Study in Biblical Eschatology* (Grand Rapids, MI: Academie Books, 1964), 385–86, 390–91.
18. Because Satan is the prince or ruler of this world, the human rulers of the various nations are under his dominion and operate according to his "cosmic principles of force, greed, selfishness, ambition, and pleasure." Scofield, *Scofield Reference Bible*, 1342. See also Watchman Nee, *Love Not the World: A Prophetic Call to Holy Living* (Fort Washington, PA: CLC Publications, 2009).
19. Heylin, *Behind the Shades*, 321–23; Robert Shelton, *No Direction Home: The Life and Music of Bob Dylan* (New York: Ballantine Books, c1986, 1987), 570.
20. Dylan, *Biograph* (1985); Heylin, *Saved!*, 23–25, 44, 54, 63–65, 90, 102–03.
21. Matthew 5–7, 7:15–17, 22:36–40, 25:34–36, 40; James 1:27, 2:1–9, 5:1–6, 2:14–17; Galatians 5:22–23, 6:2. In his definition of pure religion, James balances this emphasis on active compassion and social justice with an exhortation to "keep oneself unstained from the world" (i.e., spiritual separation). This book was apparently written by the half-brother of Jesus.
22. The phrase does not come directly from Scripture but it is a biblical concept, with similar language being used by Jesus during his prayer at the Last Supper (John 17:6–20).
23. Douglas Gwyn, *Apocalypse of the Word: The Life and Message of George Fox (1624–1691)* (Richmond, IN: Friends United Press, 1986), xx, xxi, xiv, xv, 215; James K. A. Smith, "Naturalizing 'Shalom': Confessions of a Kuyperian Secularist," *Comment*, June 28, 2013, http://www.cardus.ca/comment/article/3993/naturalizing-shalom-confessions-of-a-kuyperian-secularist.
24. Ronald J. Sider, ed., *Cry Justice!: The Bible on Hunger and Poverty* (New York: Paulist Press, 1980).

25. Dylan, *Slow Train Coming* (1979); Bob Dylan, *Infidels* (1983); Bob Dylan, *Knocked Out Loaded* (1986).
26. Gilmore, "Positively Dylan," 135; emphasis in the original; Gilmore, "Bob Dylan," 48.
27. Gilmore, "Positively Dylan," 135; Matthew 19:24; Heylin, *Saved!*, 81–82; *Interview*, February 1986. Contained in: Artur, *Every Mind Polluting Word*, 871; Gilmore, "Positively Dylan," 135.
28. Dylan, *Another Side of Bob Dylan* (1964); Bob Dylan, *Oh Mercy* (1989); *Gotta Serve Somebody: The Gospel Songs of Bob Dylan* [sound recording] (Columbia Records, 2003); Bob Dylan, *Modern Times* (2006). After the first verse, Dylan's song seemingly leaves the subject of blue-collar economics behind as it focuses on battles of a personal and perhaps spiritual nature. It is likely, though, that the entire song is sung from the perspective of a working man.
29. Genesis 6:11–13; Exodus 20:13; I Chronicles 22:6–10; Isaiah 2:4; Matthew 5:9, 38–45.
30. Romans 12:17, 19; II Corinthians 10:3–5; Ephesians 6:11–12; James 4:1–3; I Thessalonians 5:2–3; Revelation 13:1–4, 7–8, 16–17, 16:13–16, 19:17–21; Dylan, "Are You Ready?" *Saved* (1980).
31. Dylan, *The Freewheelin' Bob Dylan* (1963); *Infidels* (1983).
32. Interview with Dave Kelly by JT, November 1, 2014.
33. Ronald M. Enroth, Edward E. Ericson Jr., and C. Breckinridge Peters, *The Jesus People: Old-Time Religion in the Age of Aquarius* (Grand Rapids, MI: Eerdmans, 1972), 168.
34. Sydney E. Ahlstrom, *A Religious History of the American People* (Garden City, NY: Image Books, c1972, 1975), 2:457, 608.
35. Charles P. Schmitt, *Root Out of a Dry Ground: A History of the Church* (Grand Rapids, MI: Fellowship Publications, 1979), 151; Glenn D. Kittler, *The Jesus Kids and Their Leaders* (New York: Warner Paperback Library, 1972), 45.
36. John L. Sherrill, *They Speak with Other Tongues* (New York: McGraw Hill, 1964).
37. Enroth et al., *The Jesus People*, 151, 195.
38. David Wilkerson, *David Wilkerson Speaks Out* (Minneapolis: Bethany Fellowship, 1973), 15–22; Peter E. Gillquist, *Let's Quit Fighting about the Holy Spirit* (Grand Rapids, MI: Zondervan, 1974); Chuck Smith, *Charisma vs. Charismania* (Eugene, OR: Harvest House, 1983); Enroth et al., *The Jesus People*, 199. Bob Dylan has apparently not made public reference to the spiritual gift of tongues. Despite his connection with Vineyard Fellowship in the late 1970s–early 1980s, he may not have self-identified as a charismatic. Artur, *Every Mind Polluting Word*, 709; Heylin, *Saved!*, 106, 9.
39. David Wilkerson, with John and Elizabeth Sherrill, *The Cross and the Switchblade* (New York: Pyramid, 1963); Kittler, *The Jesus Kids and Their Leaders*, 16, 140; Enroth et al., *The Jesus People*, 147. Dylan's spiritual and musical path crossed that of Green in 1980, as noted in the next chapter.

40. Enroth et al., *The Jesus People*, 84, 105, 175.
41. Wilkerson, *David Wilkerson Speaks Out*, 58; emphasis in the original.
42. Kittler, *The Jesus Kids and Their Leaders*, 32; Revelation 17–18; Enroth et al., *The Jesus People*, 183. The last verse of Dylan's song "Jokerman" refers to the convergence of evil political power (Antichrist) and evil religious power (Babylon). Dylan, *Infidels* (1983); Revelation 13:1, 17:1–6.
43. Dana Roberts, *Understanding Watchman Nee* (Plainfield, NJ: Haven Books, 1980), xi.
44. Enroth et al., *The Jesus People*, 143, 169–170; Larry Norman, "Let the Lions Come," *Bootleg* [sound recording] (One Way Records, 1971) [the details about Nee are largely inaccurate]; Gene Edwards, *How We Began/God's Eternal Purpose* (Santa Barbara, CA: Christians, n.d.), xv; Watchman Nee, *The Normal Christian Church Life* (Los Angeles: Stream Publishers, c1938, 1962). Imprisoned by the Chinese Communists for two decades, Nee died in prison in 1972.
45. Edwards's book *The Early Church* was a manifesto for church revolution (not reform). Gene Edwards, *The Early Church* (Goleta, CA: Christian Books, 1974). For Smith's influence on Gulliksen and, by extension, Dylan, see Paul Vitello, "Chuck Smith, Minister Who Preached to Flower Children, Dies at 86," *New York Times*, October 13, 2013. For the important role of Calvary Chapel and Vineyard Fellowship on the worship style of evangelical churches (e.g., praise choruses, guitars and drums, worship team), see Frank Viola, *Pagan Christianity: The Origins of Our Modern Church Practices* (Present Testimony Ministry, 2002), 209–11.
46. Revelation 22:20 (penultimate verse of the Bible). An Aramaic version of the word, found in I Corinthians 16:22, can be translated "Come, Lord!" or "Our Lord has come."
47. Enroth et al., *The Jesus People*, 179, 186; Kittler, *The Jesus Kids and Their Leaders*, 99–100.
48. Love Song, *Final Touch* [sound recording] (Good News Records, 1974); Love Song, *Feel the Love* [sound recording] (Good News Records, 1977); Heylin, *Saved!*, 12, 15–19, 20–21, 36, 46–47. The band was a ministry of Calvary Chapel. "Cossack Song" writers Tom Coomes and Tom Stipe were both affiliated with Calvary. Maranatha! Music, founded by Smith, produced influential albums of praise music in the late 1970s under the guidance of Coomes.
49. Hal Lindsey, with C. C. Carlson, *The Late Great Planet Earth* (Grand Rapids, MI: Zondervan, c1970, 1977), cover; Enroth et al., *The Jesus People*, 187. Lindsey's book influenced Dylan nine years after first publication.
50. C. I. Scofield was the grandfather of Dallas Theological Seminary, the world's leading seminary of dispensational fundamentalism. Ahlstrom, *Religious History of the American People*, 2:279.
51. Enroth et al., *The Jesus People*, 136–40, 139.
52. Ibid., 80.

53. Larry Norman, *Upon This Rock* (1969/1970); *Only Visiting This Planet* [sound recording] (MGM/Verve Records, 1972; Street Level Records, 1978); "Peace, Pollution, Revolution," UK single [sound recording] (MGM Records, 1972); *So Long Ago the Garden* [sound recording] (MGM Records, 1973; Phydeaux, 1980); *In Another Land* [sound recording] (Solid Rock Records, 1976). The version of "I Wish" on the classic OVTP album was recorded in George Martin's AIR Studios in London and includes John Wetton on bass guitar. Martin was, of course, the Beatles' producer. Wetton has been bassist for King Crimson, Uriah Heep, and Asia (and lead vocalist for Asia, best known for the hit "Heat of the Moment"). The recording engineer for the song (and album) was Bill Price, who later ran the sound board for albums by Mott the Hoople, the Clash, the Pretenders, and Pete Townshend. Price also coproduced the Sex Pistols' only studio album.
54. *A Thief in the Night* [motion picture] (Mark IV Productions, 1972); *Left Behind* [motion picture] (Stoney Lake Entertainment, 2014). Both films were produced by Christians. The first movie was a very low-budget production that was filmed in Iowa. Despite amateurish production values, it kicked off a series of End Times movies by Mark IV that were influential among fundamentalists, pentecostals, charismatics, and other evangelicals. The second movie was filmed in Hollywood and released in mainstream theaters but was low-budget by Hollywood standards and was almost universally derided by secular and religious critics alike.
55. Henry D. Thoreau, *Reform Papers*, ed. Wendell Glick (Princeton, NJ: Princeton University Press, 1973); Dwight Macdonald, *Memoirs of a Revolutionist: Essays in Political Criticism* (New York: Farrar, Straus and Cudahy, 1957); Dwight Macdonald, *Discriminations: Essays & Afterthoughts* (New York: Da Capo, c1974, 1985); C. Wright Mills, *The Power Elite* (New York: Oxford University Press, 1956); C. Wright Mills, *Power, Politics and People: The Collected Essays of C. Wright Mills*, ed. Irving Louis Horowitz (New York: Oxford University Press, 1963).
56. James Simon Kunen, *The Strawberry Statement: Notes of a College Revolutionary* (New York: Avon, 1970); Christopher R. Reaske and Robert F. Willson Jr., eds. *Student Voices/One: On Political Action, Culture, and the University* (New York: Random House, 1971); Ethel Grodzins, *The Open Conspiracy: What America's Angry Generation Is Saying* (Harrisburg, PA: Stackpole Books, 1970); Mitchell Goodman, comp., *The Movement toward a New America: The Beginnings of a Long Revolution* (Philadelphia: Pilgrim Press/New York: Knopf, 1970).
57. Robert Griffith, ed., *Major Problems in American History Since 1945: Documents and Essays* (Lexington, MA: D.C. Heath, 1992), 476, 491.
58. David E. Apter and James Joll, eds., *Anarchism Today* (Garden City, NY: Anchor Books, 1972), 41–69.
59. E. J. Dionne Jr., *Why Americans Hate Politics* (New York: Touchstone, c1991, 1992), 40–41.

60. Apter and Joll, *Anarchism Today*, 56.
61. Enroth et al., *The Jesus People*, 17.
62. Acts 2:44, 4:35; Enroth et al., *The Jesus People*, 211; Nee, *Love Not the World*, 17, 111, 112, 177; Kittler, *The Jesus Kids and Their Leaders*, 34.
63. Ibid., 135; Duane Pederson, with Bob Owen, *Jesus People* (Glendale, CA: Regal Books, 1971), 78.
64. Kittler, *The Jesus Kids and Their Leaders*, 99; emphasis in the original.
65. Norman, *Bootleg* (1971).
66. Larry Norman, *Street Level* [sound recording] (One Way Records, 1970–71); "Peace, Pollution, Revolution" UK single [sound recording] (MGM Records, 1972); Norman, *Only Visiting This Planet*; Larry Norman, "If God is My Father," Omaha concert, February 15, 1980. Norman's concert in Omaha occurred 20 days after Dylan appeared in the city (January 25).
67. Angus I. Kinnear, *Against the Tide: The Story of Watchman Nee* (Fort Washington, PA: Christian Literature Crusade, 1973), 117; Schaeffer, *Church at the End of the 20th Century*, 82–83; Enroth et al., *The Jesus People*, 77, 111.
68. Kittler, *The Jesus Kids and Their Leaders*, 231.
69. Ruben Ortega, comp., *The Jesus People Speak Out!* (Elgin, IL: David C. Cook Publishing, 1972), 66–74.

6 Dylan and the Jesus People

1. In January 1974, in Miami during his tour with the Band, Dylan happened upon a Christian rally led by Arthur Blessitt, a prominent Jesus Movement street preacher (the "Minister of Sunset Strip"). Afterward, Dylan approached Blessitt and spoke with him for about ten minutes. *Knockin' on Dylan's Door: On the Road in '74* (A Rolling Stone Book) (New York: Pocket Books, 1974), 57.
2. Heylin, *Behind the Shades*, 318–23; Vitello, "Chuck Smith, Minister Who Preached to Flower Children, Dies at 86"; Dan Wooding, "'Please Pray for Bob Dylan' Asks His Former Pastor," *ASSIST News Service*, April 25, 1999, http://www.assistnews.net/strategic/s0000027.htm.
3. Larry Norman, *Down Under But Not Out* [sound recording] (San Jose, CA: Phydeaux Records, 1986), "On Being" 10; Larry Norman, ed., *The "Blue Book"* [linked to *Home At Last* [sound recording] (Benson Records, 1989)] (Santa Cruz, CA: Phydeaux, 1989), special Phydeaux insert.
4. Kittler, *The Jesus Kids and Their Leaders*, 119–23.
5. Ibid., 121.
6. Bob Dylan, *Shot of Love* (1981); Heylin, *Behind the Shades*, 354; D. Williams, *Bob Dylan*. Some readers of the *Shot of Love* sleeve may have assumed that Dylan was thanking Don Williams the country singer when he was actually thanking Don Williams the Christian minister. Williams was one of only three individuals thanked.

7. Marshall, *Restless Pilgrim*, 24–25. In 1979, Roger McGuinn said, "There are guys out there working for Satan and they're blatant about it. I'm working for Jesus and I'm not a closet Christian." Other prominent folk-rock converts to born-again Christianity by the late 1970s included Arlo Guthrie (son of Woody); Maria Muldaur; Noel Paul Stookey of Peter, Paul and Mary; Richie Furay of Buffalo Springfield and Poco; and Dan Peek of America. Furay became pastor of a Calvary Chapel church in Colorado in the early 1980s. His excellent album *I've Got a Reason* (1976)—with Christian lyrics on a secular label—was a forerunner of Dylan's *Slow Train Coming* (1979). T-Bone Burnett was on the fringe of the CCM industry in the 1980s. Davin Seay, "Rock & Roll Believers," *Current* [Maranatha! Music of Calvary Chapel], vol. 1, no. 1, Fall 1979, 14, 15 (Alpha Band: 17–18); Richie Furay Band, *I've Got a Reason* [sound recording] (Asylum Records, 1976); Joseph Farah, "I'm Not Stupid Enough to Want to Be Famous," *Contemporary Christian Music*, February 1983, 39.
8. Heylin, *Behind the Shades*, 315–23.
9. In connection with her May 1980 interview with Dylan, in Dayton, Karen Hughes wrote, "Whether on or off the road, Dylan worships whenever he can at the Assembly of God, a fundamentalist, pentecostal, evangelical denomination that believe[s] in the literal Bible and speaking in tongues." If Dylan attended Assemblies of God churches while on tour—at this time, Vineyard churches were not found outside of southern California—he was following in the footsteps of AG alums Elvis Presley and Jerry Lee Lewis. When asked if Dylan was interested in miraculous gifts of the Spirit such as tongues, his 1979–80 personal assistant Dave Kelly says, "I never saw any of the pentecostal kind of attitude out of Dylan but I saw lots of the prophet, End Times kind of attitude." The Vineyard contained "a whole mish-mash" of more charismatic and more prophetic believers. Artur, *Every Mind Polluting Word*, 712; Interview with Dave Kelly by JT, November 1, 2014.
10. Heylin, *Behind the Shades*, 321, 321–23. Dave Kelly of Ark, personal assistant to Dylan in 1979–80, had earlier been baptized by Lindsey. Referring to Vineyard understanding of Bible prophecy at this time, Kelly says of Lindsey, "He was the authority." Interview with Dave Kelly by JT, November 1, 2014.
11. Paul Baker, *Why Should the Devil Have All the Good Music?: Jesus Music—Where It Began, Where It Is, and Where It Is Going* (Waco, TX: Word Books, 1979); Stephen J. Nichols, *Jesus Made in America: A Cultural History from the Puritans to The Passion of the Christ* (Downers Grove, IL: IVP Academic, 2008), 122–45; "The Original Christian Street Rocker: Larry Norman," *Contemporary Christian Music*, March 1981, 8–11, 25; T-Bone Burnett, "Cross Over Music," *Contemporary Christian Music*, March 1981, 13.
12. Michael Gray, *The Bob Dylan Encyclopedia* (New York: Continuum, 2006), 275–76, 439.

13. Melody Green, with David Hazard, *No Compromise: The Life Story of Keith Green*, Legacy ed. (updated and expanded) (Nashville, TN: Thomas Nelson, c1989, 2008), 8, 112–14, 116, 125–26, 132, 136, 191. Norman apparently also played a role in Green's conversion. Norman, ed., *"Blue Book,"* special Phydeaux insert; "The Gospel Music Hall of Fame Biography," *LarryNorman.uk.com*, http://www.larrynorman.uk.com/bio.htm.
14. Keith Green, *So You Wanna Go Back to Egypt*... (Lindale, TX: Pretty Good Records, 1980); Green, *No Compromise*, 339–41.
15. Ibid., 340; 2nd Chapter of Acts, *The Roar of Love* [sound recording] (Sparrow Records, 1980); 2nd Chapter of Acts, *Mansion Builder* [sound recording] (Sparrow Records, 1978); Heylin, *Life in Stolen Moments*, 220, 228. Heylin's book gives two different years for "Mansion Builder" as a possible concert song so it is unclear whether it was under consideration for fall 1980, summer 1981, or fall 1981.
16. Norman, *Upon This Rock* (c1969/70, 2002), liner notes.
17. Barry McGuire, *Seeds* [sound recording] (Myrrh Records, 1973). "Eve of Destruction" was a folk-rock protest song. In the 1960s, McGuire was viewed by critics as a second-rate Dylan. In the 1970s, he was a pioneer CCM artist.
18. Dallas Holm and Praise, *Live* [sound recording] (Greentree Records, 1977); Dallas Holm, *His Last Days* [sound recording] (Greentree Records, 1979); Heylin, *Life in Stolen Moments*, 223, 228, 229, 351; Bob Dylan, *A Musical Retrospective* [sound recording] (Doberman/Scorpio/Gold Standard, 2000). The bootleg CD *A Musical Retrospective* contains two 1980 versions of "Rise Again" (both duets of Dylan and Clydie King): one with only piano in San Francisco on November 18 and a stunning full-band version in Portland on December 3.
19. "Best Selling Inspirational LPs," *Billboard*, September 20, 1980, 41. By this time, *Saved* had already peaked on the pop music charts. It failed to make the Top 10, instead stalling at #24.
20. The Richie Furay Band, which released the aforementioned *I've Got a Reason* album in 1976, consisted of Furay, Jay Truax and John Mehler (former members of pioneer Christian rock band Love Song, associated with Calvary Chapel) and Tom Stipe (Calvary Chapel pastor, cofounder of Maranatha! Music, and a Vineyard Fellowship leader—at various times). Al Perkins also played guitar on the album. Perkins also played on Love Song's final studio album (*Final Touch*, 1974). Another Love Song veteran, Chuck Girard, had a successful solo career as a CCM artist. Phil Keaggy, a popular CCM artist in the late 1970s, was briefly a member of Love Song.
21. Ark, *The Angels Come* [sound recording] (Spirit Records, 1979).
22. The Beatles, *Let It Be* [sound recording] (Apple Records, 1970).
23. Bruce Adolph, "Dave Kelly: The Resilient Musician," *Christian Musician*, November/December 2013, 21–22.
24. Tony Cummings, "Dave Kelly: The Jesus Music Veteran with the Bob Dylan Connection," *Cross Rhythms*, February 15, 2012, http://www.crossrhythms.

co.uk/articles/print.php?Article_ID=47253; Heylin, *Behind the Shades*, 330 41. One Kelly memory of the tour that did not make it into the book: continual death threats directed at Dylan because of his Christian testimony. The mutual friend at Vineyard was Mike Canfield. Strangely enough, Canfield was also a friend of A. J. Weberman and the two had earlier collaborated on a JFK assassination book. "Who's Dylan? Garbologist Can Tell You" (Knight-Ridder wire story), [Montreal] *Gazette*, July 3, 1980, 50.
25. Cummings, "Dave Kelly."
26. Dave Kelly, *Crowning of a Simple Man* [sound recording] (Pilgrim America, 1980); "About," *The Christian Badfinger* (Facebook), 2011, https://www.facebook.com/thechristianbadfinger/info.
27. P. Williams, *Dylan*, 87.
28. Enroth et al., *The Jesus People*, 80.
29. *Variety*, February 28, 1973.
30. Baker, *Why Should the Devil Have All the Good Music?*.
31. "The Best Contemporary Christian Albums of All Time," *Contemporary Christian Music*, June 1988, 58, 61; Randy Stonehill, *Welcome to Paradise* [sound recording] (Solid Rock, 1976). The Top 20 also included albums by 2nd Chapter of Acts, Love Song, Keith Green, Phil Keaggy, Mark Heard, Leslie Phillips, U2, and T-Bone Burnett.
32. Norman, *Only Visiting This Planet* (1972); Dylan, *The Freewheelin' Bob Dylan* (1963); Dylan, *The Times They Are A-Changin'* (1964); Dylan, *Bringing It All Back Home* (1965); Norman, *So Long Ago the Garden* (1973); Dylan, *Highway 61 Revisited* (1965); Dylan, *Blonde on Blonde* (1966); Norman, *In Another Land* (1976); Larry Norman, *Something New Under the Son* [sound recording] (Solid Rock Records, 1981).
33. "The White House," *LarryNorman.com*, November 18, 2014, http://www.larrynorman.com/blog/the-white-house.
34. Larry Norman, *Barking at the Ants* [sound recording] (Solid Rock Records, 1981); *Rock, Scissors et Papier* [sound recording] (Solid Rock Records, 2003); *Copper Wires* [sound recording] (Solid Rock Records, 1998).
35. Larry Norman, *"Why Should the Devil Have All the Good Music"* [songbook] (Hollywood: One Way Publications, n.d.), 4. He was also friends with Barry McGuire (9). This interesting songbook, which includes an interview and photographs, was apparently published in 1973 ("Inside Track," *Billboard*, July 7, 1973, 66). The logo for MGM Records appears on the first page.
36. Suzy Spencer, "Born-Again Bob Dylan Sings the Gospel in His New LP," *People*, September 10, 1979; Michael Gross, *Bob Dylan: An Illustrated History*, rev. ed. (New York: Tempo Books, 1980), 203–04; Heylin, *Life in Stolen Moments*, 206; Debby Boone, *With My Song* [sound recording] (Lamb & Lion Records, 1980); Dylan, *Saved* (1980). Debby Boone was a Vineyard member in LA.
37. Norman, *In Another Land* (1976), interview. Norman was describing his involvement with Vineyard three or four years before Dylan's conversion so

he cannot be accused of exaggerating his role in order to gain reflected glory through Dylan.

38. Wooding, "'Please Pray for Bob Dylan' Asks His Former Pastor"; Larry Norman, "Note from Larry sent by Bill," *jesusmusic.org* chatroom, April 13, 1999, http://www.thetruthaboutlarrynorman.com/wp-content/uploads/jmorgresponse1.pdf. Although Dave Kelly is not an admirer of Norman, he confirms some of what Norman wrote in the 1970s and 1990s: when the Vineyard began, under Gulliksen's leadership, it did not have its own building; it was "very small" and was "mostly actors and musicians." Interview with Dave Kelly by JT, November 1, 2014.

39. Norman, *Bootleg* (1972); Norman, *Only Visiting This Planet* (1972); Norman, *In Another Land* (1976); Dylan, *Slow Train Coming* (1979); Allen Flemming e-mail to JT, October 10, 2014. It is an interesting possibility: an MGM single/album track influencing, seven years later, a Columbia single/album track. Two of the three producers of OVTP were Rod Edwards and Roger Hand, who as a musical duo (Edwards Hand) had been thrice produced by George Martin (1968–71). Martin worked on their first album during a break on the Beatles' *White Album*. Production of STC was by famed producer Jerry Wexler and Muscle Shoals Studio cofounder Barry Beckett. The US and UK single releases of "Righteous Rocker, Holy Roller" (aka "Without Love") credit production of the song to Larry Norman and Carol Hunter.

40. Allen Flemming e-mail to JT, October 25, 2014.

41. Ibid.; Dylan, *Freewheelin' Bob Dylan* (1963); Norman, *Bootleg* (1972), *Only Visiting This Planet* (1972), *In Another Land* (1976); Dylan, *Saved* (1980).

42. Dylan, *Empire Burlesque* (1985); Dylan, *"Love and Theft"* (2001); Dylan, *Modern Times* (2006).

43. The "Without Love You Are Nothing" / "Gotta Serve Somebody" possible connection is a thought of Allen Flemming. Right or wrong, the "Great American Novel" / "Slow Train" possible connection is my idea (coauthor Jeff Taylor).

44. Dylan, *Infidels* (1983); Loder, "Bob Dylan," 18; Heylin, *Life in Stolen Moments*, 269.

45. Some have speculated that Norman's oddness and inability to match the quality of his earlier musical work can be attributed to brain damage from drug abuse. Others have seen his strange behavior as an artistic affectation. Norman himself eventually pointed to an accident aboard a commercial airplane in 1978 that caused brain injury and/or depression from the collapse of his marriage (separated in 1978). This might have been around the time that Kelly met Norman (the Ark album was recorded in 1978). Coauthor Jeff Taylor saw Norman in concert in 1980 and a couple times afterward. Norman seemed normal enough on stage although he had a serious demeanor with humor of the dry sort. Musically, he was focused and talented.

46. Interview with Dave Kelly by JT, November 1, 2014.

47. Martin Wroe, "The Height of Norman Wisdom," *Strait*, October 1984, http://www.larrynorman.uk.com/word31.htm.
48. Norman, *"Blue Book."*
49. Ibid.; Interview with Charles Norman by JT, December 10, 2014.
50. Norman, *"Why Should the Devil Have All the Good Music"* [songbook], 7, 9; People, *People* [sound recording] (Capitol Records, 1968).
51. *Jesus Sound Explosion* [sound recording] (CCC/Strawberry Creek Productions, 1972). Although Cash and Norman had both expressed disapproval of the Vietnam War by this time through song, the young evangelicals who attended the music festival were conservative in their politics. It was an election year and the Explo '72 crowd was overwhelmingly pro-Nixon. Only 11 percent expressed support for McGovern. With the festival being created by Campus Crusade and Billy Graham, this was not the Jesus People demographic. Daniel K. Williams, *God's Own Party: The Making of the Christian Right* (New York: Oxford University Press, 2010), 101, 97.
52. Larry Norman, "Johnny Cash, the Man in Black: Johnny, We Hardly Knew Ye," 2003.
53. Bono, The Edge, Adam Clayton, and Larry Mullen Jr., with Neil McCormick, *U2 By U2* (New York: HarperCollins, 2006), 20, 59–60.
54. Cliff Richard, *Small Corners* [sound recording] (EMI, 1978); "Larry in the UK," *LarryNormanUK.com*, 2004, http://www.larrynorman.uk.com/inuk.htm.
55. Interview with Charles Norman by JT, December 10, 2014.
56. Allen Flemming e-mail to JT, October 12, 2014.
57. Allen Flemming e-mail to JT, October 10, 2014.
58. "U2, Linda Ronstadt Albums to be Preserved by Library of Congress," *Associated Press*, April 2, 2014, http://www.billboard.com/articles/news/6029550/u2-linda-ronstadt-albums-to-be-preserved-by-library-of-congress.
59. David Cooper, "Pure and Undefiled Religion: Why Bono May Be a Better Christian Than You," *The Alexis De Tocqueville Society*, November 15, 2004, http://atsociety.blogspot.com/2004/11/pure-and-undefiled-religion-why-bono.html; Hank Bordowitz, ed., *The U2 Reader: A Quarter Century of Commentary, Criticism, and Reviews* (Milwaukee: Hal Leonard, 2003), 30, 32.
60. Niall Stokes, *Into the Heart: The Stories behind Every U2 Song* (New York: Thunder's Mouth Press, c1996, 1998), 43.
61. Adam Block, "Bono Bites Back," *MotherJones.com*, May 1, 1989 (updated February 2001), http://www.motherjones.com/media/1989/05/bono-bites-back.
62. Steve Stockman, *Walk On: The Spiritual Journey of U2* (Lake Mary, FL: Relevant Books, 2001), 25–34; Bono et al., *U2 By U2*, 117–19; Bono, *Bono in Conversation with Michka Assayas* (New York: Riverhead Books, 2005), 122.
63. U2, *October* [sound recording] (Island Records, 1981).
64. Block, "Bono Bites Back."

65. Stockman, *Walk On*, 40; U2, *War* [sound recording] (Island Records, 1983).
66. Bordowitz, *U2 Reader*, 171.
67. Bono, *Bono in Conversation with Michka Assayas*, 123–24.
68. U2, *Rattle and Hum*; U2, *Zooropa* [sound recording] (Island Records, 1993); Bono, *Bono in Conversation with Michka Assayas*, 242; Bob Dylan, *Down in the Groove* (1988).
69. Wooding, "'Please Pray for Bob Dylan' Asks His Former Pastor."
70. Noam Chomsky, *Radical Priorities*, ed. Carlos P. Otero (Montréal: Black Rose Books, 1984), 247.
71. Hickey, "Bob Dylan," 5; Dylan, "Slow Train," *Slow Train Coming* (1979).
72. Heylin, *Saved!*, 13, 21–22, 23, 26–27, 36–37, 47, 51–52. In 1974, Dylan told a reporter, "I like monarchies, kings, and queens," as opposed to the American two-party system, but this statement may have been more playful than serious. *Knockin' on Dylan's Door*, 58.
73. Plato, *Statesman*, ed. Martin Ostwald, trans. J. B. Skemp (Indianapolis: Bobbs-Merrill, 1957), 29, 32–33, 66, 72, 78.
74. Scofield, *Scofield Reference Bible*, 1342. The New Testament teaches that Satan is the supreme ruler of this world during the present age even as it recognizes the ultimate sovereignty of God over the whole universe (past, present, and future). For the Devil as prince or god of this world, see Luke 4:5–8; John 12:31, 14:30, 16:11, 17:15; II Corinthians 4:3–4; Ephesians 2:1–2; II Thessalonians 2:9; Revelation 13:2, 7.
75. Plato, *Statesman*, 83.
76. Ibid.
77. Revelation 11:15.
78. John 18:36; Luke 17:20–21; Matthew 24:29, 30, 25:31, 34; Revelation 19:11, 15, 16, 20:4, 6.
79. Matthew 6:10; Revelation 22:20. Bono of U2 made this point about the Lord's Prayer in 1988. Stockman, *Walk On*, 46.
80. Stephen J. Whitfield, *A Critical American: The Politics of Dwight Macdonald* (Hamden, CT: Archon Books, 1984), 105.
81. Ibid., 70.
82. Hilburn, "'I Learned That Jesus Was Real and I Wanted That.'" Quotation also found in: "Dylan Tells Story of Christian Conversion," *Contemporary Christian Music*, February 1981, 22; Benson, *Bob Dylan Companion*, 167.
83. Heylin, *Saved!*, 95, 81; emphasis in the original.
84. Ibid., 65, 91, 92–93, 43.
85. Artur, *Every Mind Polluting Word*, 754.
86. Loder, "Bob Dylan," 17.
87. Interview with Mick Brown, June 1984. Contained in: Artur, *Every Mind Polluting Word*, 800.
88. Cohen, "Don't Ask Me Nothin' about Nothin' I Might Just Tell You the Truth," 81.
89. Gilmore, "Positively Dylan," 135. Dylan made the same point about there being no left and no right 23 years earlier during his Tom Paine Award

speech. Methodist theologians Hauerwas and Willimon have echoed Dylan the Christian, saying that the political choice is not between liberal and conservative but between "truth and lies." "Bob Dylan and the NECLC"; Stanley Hauerwas and William H. Willimon, *Resident Aliens: Life in the Christian Colony* (Nashville: Abingdon Press, 1989), 156, 160.
90. Robert Hilburn, "How Does It Feel? Don't Ask," *Los Angeles Times*, September 16, 2001.
91. Gilmore, "Bob Dylan" (2012), 48, 49.
92. "Not Dolly Parton's *Jolene*: Part Two of Bob Dylan Talking to Bill Flanagan," *RightWingBob.com*, March 23, 2009, http://www.rightwingbob.com/weblog/archives/4643; "Bob Dylan Talks to Bill Flanagan About *Christmas in the Heart*."
93. Dylan, *Slow Train Coming* (1979); Dylan, *Shot of Love* (1981).
94. Dylan, *Infidels* (1983). Boswell, biographer of Samuel Johnson, tells us that he made this verbal observation on April 7, 1775. In *The City of God*, Augustine recounts a conversation between Alexander the Great and a pirate (Book IV, Chapter 4: "Justice being taken away, then, what are kingdoms but great robberies?"). For modern application of Augustine's example, see Noam Chomsky, *Pirates and Emperors, Old and New: International Terrorism in the Real World* (Cambridge, MA: South End Press, c1986, 2002).
95. Dylan, *Oh Mercy* (1989); Dylan, *World Gone Wrong* (1993).
96. Romans 12:2.

7 Dylanesque Politics in the Real World

1. Interview with Karen Hughes. Contained in: Artur, *Every Mind Polluting Word*, 711.
2. For evaluations of Bush and Carter, see Jeff Taylor, *Where Did the Party Go?: William Jennings Bryan, Hubert Humphrey, and the Jeffersonian Legacy* (Columbia: University of Missouri Press, 2006), 245–55, 264–65.
3. Dylan's grandparents emigrated to the United States from Ukraine and Lithuania (both in the Russian Empire). Wellstone's parents were from Ukraine. One set of Feingold's grandparents were from Russia.
4. Although La Follette (liberal) and Taft (conservative) could be seen as representing opposite tendencies within the GOP, they had much in common. A line of ideological descent can be made from La Follette to Taft given their shared opposition to Wall Street and imperialism. See Jeff Taylor, "Fighting Bob vs. Silent Cal: The Conservative Tradition from La Follette to Taft and Beyond," *Modern Age* 50 (2008): 295–305.
5. Bill Kauffman, *Ain't My America: The Long, Noble History of Antiwar Conservatism and Middle-American Anti-Imperialism* (New York: Metropolitan Books, 2008), 125–26, 112–15. Howard Buffett was the father of billionaire investor Warren Buffett.

6. In the mid-1970s, Governor Brown's girlfriend was country-rock singer Linda Ronstadt. Ronstadt covered Dylan's song "I'll Be Your Baby Tonight" on her debut solo album. Linda Ronstadt, *Hand Sown...Home Grown* [sound recording] (Capitol Records, 1969).
7. Interview with Karen Hughes. Contained in: Artur, *Every Mind Polluting Word*, 712; Revelation 12–18; Larry Norman, Omaha concert, February 15, 1980.
8. John Nichols, "The Lone Dissenter," *The Progressive*, November 2001, 28.
9. Dylan, *Chronicles, Volume One*, 283.
10. Robert Sam Anson, *McGovern: A Biography* (New York: Holt, Rinehart and Winston, 1972), 287.
11. Karl Hess, "An Open Letter to Barry Goldwater," *Ramparts*, August 1969, 28–29. Quoted in: Kauffman, *Ain't My America*, 140.
12. Harold E. Hughes with Dick Schneider, *The Man From Ida Grove: A Senator's Personal Story* (Lincoln, VA: Chosen Books, 1979), 299; Mike Glover, "Former Iowa Governor and Senator Harold Hughes Dead at 74," *Associated Press*, October 24, 1996.
13. Hilburn, "'I Learned That Jesus Was Real and I Wanted That.'"
14. Dylan, *Slow Train Coming* (1979).
15. "Kissinger Confirmed, 78–7, as Secretary of State" in: *CQ Almanac 1973* (Washington, DC: Congressional Quarterly, 1974), 858–61.
16. Juli Loesch, "Abortion and the Left," *Religious Socialism*, Spring 1981. Reprinted in: Gail Grenier Sweet, ed., *Pro-Life Feminism: Different Voices* (Toronto: Life Cycle Books, 1985), 75; "When Does Life Begin?" *Congressional Record* (Senate), May 31, 1973, 17559–60, 17565.
17. Historically, abortion had little to do with women's rights, individual liberty, or Democratic Party liberalism. Its roots were in the eugenics/population control movement and the *Playboy* philosophy before it was adopted by feminists, at the urging of Betty Friedan, in the late 1960s.
18. Dylan, *Slow Train Coming* (1979); Dylan, *Shot of Love* (1981); Dylan, *Bootleg Series, Volumes 1–3* (1991); Loder, "Bob Dylan," 24, 78.
19. Leonard Verduin, *The Reformers and Their Stepchildren* (Grand Rapids, MI: Eerdmans, 1964).
20. Mark Hatfield, *Between a Rock and a Hard Place* (Waco, TX: Word Books, 1976), 219–24.
21. Ibid., 94–95, 96–101.
22. "Bob Dylan and the NECLC," *Corliss Lamont Website*, http://www.corliss-lamont.org/dylan.htm; Ben Corbett, "Bob Dylan's Breaks from Politics: The 1963 ECLC Speech," *About.com*, http://folkmusic.about.com/od/bobdylan/a/Bob-Dylan-Quits-Politics.htm.
23. "Nixon Tapes Transcripts: Wednesday, February 21, 1973–8:10pm–8:30pm" (043–161), *Presidential Recordings Program*, http://whitehousetapes.net/transcript/nixon/043-161. Years later, Graham regretted his naive association with Nixon. D. K. Williams, *God's Own Party*, 94–103. In his book, Hatfield describes Hughes as his "closest friend within the Senate" by the early 1970s

(25). Their spiritual bond as Christian brothers transcended the partisan labels of "R" and "D."
24. Hatfield, *Between a Rock and a Hard Place*, 142–43.
25. Ibid., 143; Interview with Martin Keller. Contained in: Artur, *Every Mind Polluting Word*, 755.
26. Hatfield, *Between a Rock and a Hard Place*, 175.
27. Kauffman, *Ain't My America*, 127, 136, 151.
28. Jesse Walker, "Mark O. Hatfield RIP," *Reason.com*, August 8, 2011, http://reason.com/blog/2011/08/08/mark-o-hatfield-rip; Murray Rothbard, "Hatfield for President?" *The Libertarian Forum*, August 1970, 1, 4, http://mises.org/journals/lf/1970/1970_08.pdf. In a fascinating 1986 analysis of ideology, New Left thinker Noam Chomsky links Taft of the 1940s–1950s to Hatfield of the 1970s–1980s. It also includes an astounding statement in which Chomsky the radical leftist calls himself a true modern conservative. Noam Chomsky, *Language and Politics*, ed. C. P. Otero (Montréal: Black Rose Books, 1988), 656.
29. Tor Egil Førland, "Bringing It All Back Home *or* Another Side of Bob Dylan: Midwestern Isolationist," *Journal of American Studies* 26 (December 1992): 339. Congressman Lindbergh (R-MN), father of the famous aviator, was a member of the US House from 1907 to 1917. He opposed both the Federal Reserve System and World War I, partly because he saw them as projects of the Eastern Establishment centered on Wall Street. In his later years, Lindbergh was a candidate for US senator and Minnesota governor. Senator Shipstead (R-MN) was a member of the US Senate from 1923 to 1947. He opposed US participation in the League of Nations, World Court, World War II, and United Nations. He also opposed imperialistic US intervention in the Caribbean and Latin America. Lindbergh and Shipstead were progressive Republicans in the La Follette tradition but were also, at times, nominees of the populist Minnesota Farmer-Labor Party. Senator Robert Taft (R-OH), leader of the conservative wing of the GOP in the 1940s and early 1950s, shared the foreign policy of La Follette, Lindbergh, and Shipstead.
30. Kauffman, *Ain't My America*; Murray Polner and Thomas E. Woods Jr., eds., *We Who Dared to Say No to War: American Antiwar Writing from 1812 to Now* (New York: Basic Books, 2008).
31. Bob Dylan, *The Freewheelin' Bob Dylan* (1963); Bob Dylan, *The Times They Are A-Changin'* (1964); Bob Dylan, *Empire Burlesque* (1985); Dylan, *Knocked Out Loaded* (1986); Bob Dylan, *World Gone Wrong* (1993); Hilburn, "'I Learned That Jesus Was Real and I Wanted That.'" Contained in: Benson, *Bob Dylan Companion*, 165.
32. Dylan, *Infidels* (1983); Dylan, *Biograph* (1985), Side Four record sleeve ("Every Grain of Sand"), 22.
33. Gilmore, "Positively Dylan," 135; Dylan, *Oh Mercy* (1989).
34. Dylan, *World Gone Wrong* (1993), liner notes 7. The essence of capitalism is the lending of money (capital) at a rate of interest. Usury (lending of money

at interest) is most often handled by banks. For usury, see also: C. S. Lewis, *Mere Christianity* (New York: Macmillan, c1943, 1960), 80–81. While the parable of the talents can be interpreted as a pro-usury passage (Matt. 25:14–30), most Bible passages speak of usury/banking in disparaging ways (e.g., Deut. 23:19–20, Neh. 5:1–13, Pro. 28:8, Ezek. 18:10–13, Lk. 6:32–36, Jn 2:13–17).

35. Gilmore, "Bob Dylan" (2012), 48.
36. Hilburn, "How Does It Feel?"; Gilmore, "Bob Dylan" (2001), 63.
37. Hilburn, "How Does It Feel?"
38. *Masked and Anonymous* [motion picture] (Sony Pictures, 2003).
39. Ralph Nader, *The Seventeen Traditions* (New York: HarperCollins, 2007).
40. Ralph Nader, *Unstoppable: The Emerging Left-Right Alliance to Dismantle the Corporate State* (New York: Nation Books, 2014).
41. Ralph Nader, "Business is Deserting America," *American Mercury*, March 1960, 25–28.
42. Ralph Nader, "U.S. Companies Should Pledge Allegiance," *Washington Times*, June 4, 1996; Ralph Nader, *The Ralph Nader Reader* (New York: Seven Stories Press, 2000), 57–59; Patrick J. Buchanan, "Patriotism in the Boardroom," June 30, 1998, http://www.chuckbaldwinlive.com/board.html. September 17, 2014
43. For Berry's sociopolitical thought, see, for example: Wendell Berry, *Sex, Economy, Freedom & Community: Eight Essays* (New York: Pantheon, 1993). Nader and Berry both declined to comment on Dylan's political legacy when asked by coauthor Jeff Taylor. Matthew Zawisky (Nader aide) e-mail to JT, September 17, 2014; Conversation between Berry and JT, September 27, 2014.
44. Dylan, *Freewheelin' Bob Dylan* (1963); *Broadside Ballads, Vol. 1* [sound recording] (Folkways Records, 1963) [song released under pseudonym Blind Boy Grunt]; Dylan, *Bootleg Series, Volumes 1–3* (1991); Dylan, *Times They Are A-Changin'* (1964).
45. The same can be said for the Christian statesman William Jennings Bryan from a century ago. Sometimes Bryan's patriotism trumped his pacifism, but he was a very peace-minded politician in comparison to most of his peers on the national stage. Bryan was directly influenced by the Christian anarchist/pacifist Leo Tolstoy, who hosted Bryan at his home in Russia in 1903.
46. William Jennings Bryan, ed., *The Second Battle, or, The New Declaration of Independence, 1776–1900: An Account of the Struggle of 1900* (Chicago: W.B. Conkey, 1900); William Jennings Bryan, *Speeches of William Jennings Bryan* (New York: Funk & Wagnalls, 1909), 2:6–49; I Kings 21; Revelation 13.
47. Heylin, *Saved!*, 44, 46; Nee, *Love Not the World*; Gilmore, "Positively Dylan," 135.
48. Dylan, *Slow Train Coming* (1979); P. Williams, *Dylan*, 86; Noel Paul Stookey, "Bob Dylan Finds His Source," *Christianity Today*, January 4, 1980, 32.

49. Artur, *Every Mind Polluting Word*, 754.
50. Cohen, "Don't Ask Me Nothin' About Nothin' I Might Just Tell You the Truth," 81; Gilmore, "Positively Dylan," 135.
51. Charles Callan Tansill, *America Goes to War* (Boston: Little, Brown, 1938).
52. Robert S. Maxwell, ed., *La Follette* (Englewood Cliffs, NJ: Prentice-Hall, 1969), 75, 76; H. C. Engelbrecht and F. C. Hanighen, *Merchants of Death: A Study of the International Armament Industry* (New York: Dodd, Mead, 1934).
53. Wayne S. Cole, *Senator Gerald P. Nye and American Foreign Relations* (Minneapolis: University of Minnesota Press, 1962).
54. Smedley D. Butler, *War Is a Racket* (Los Angeles: Feral House, c1935, 2003), 35; Dylan, *Times They Are A-Changin'* (1964). For attempted sanctification of World War I, see also: Ray H. Abrams, *Preachers Present Arms* (New York: Round Table Press, 1933). Two years later, Round Table Press published the first edition of Butler's *War Is a Racket*.
55. Hans Schmidt, *Maverick Marine: General Smedley D. Butler and the Contradictions of American Military History* (Lexington: University Press of Kentucky, 1987), vi, 231; Butler, *War Is a Racket*, 10.
56. "The Iran-Contra Affair 20 Years On" (National Security Archive Electronic Briefing Book No. 210), *The National Security Archive* (George Washington University), November 24, 2006, http://www2.gwu.edu/~nsarchiv/NSAEBB/NSAEBB210/index.htm.
57. Cole, *Senator Gerald P. Nye and American Foreign Relations*, 63.
58. Radosh, *Prophets on the Right*, 128, 131, 135, 140–42; Michael W. Miles, *The Odyssey of the American Right* (New York: Oxford University Press, 1980), 83; Radosh, *Prophets on the Right*, 161–62, 167–68.
59. Ibid., 174, 192–93; Bill Kauffman, *America First!: Its History, Culture, and Politics* (Amherst, NY: Prometheus Books, 1995), 171–72.
60. Justin Peligri, "Jesse Ventura: Military Doesn't 'Fight for Our Freedom,'" *CNN.com*, November 11, 2014, http://www.cnn.com/2014/11/11/politics/jesse-ventura-veterans-day.
61. Hilburn, "How Does It Feel?" (2001). Referring to his new song "Union Sundown," in 1983, Dylan said, "I don't think the enemy is going to conquer America with atom bombs or missiles. I think they are just going to buy America or steal America and sell it back to them." Robert Hilburn, "Bob Dylan at 42: Rolling Down Highway 61 Again," *Los Angeles Times*, October 30, 1983, U3–4. Contained in: Artur, *Every Mind Polluting Word*, 758.
62. Dylan, *Infidels* (1983); Loder, "Bob Dylan," 18; emphasis in the original.
63. Revelation 18:2–3.
64. Loder, "Bob Dylan," 18; emphasis in the original. Dylan later wrote a song about Hibbing and Iron Range economic colonialism: "Under the Red Sky." Dylan, *Under the Red Sky* (1990); Heylin, *Behind the Shades*, 417.
65. Cole, *Senator Gerald P. Nye and American Foreign Relations*, 234. Cole's book was published by the University of Minnesota Press two years after Dylan was

a student at the U of M. Cole was born and raised in Iowa and received his PhD from the University of Wisconsin—states that border Dylan's Minnesota. Nye's North Dakota also borders Minnesota. In 1963, after the Tom Paine Award controversy, Dylan wrote, "My country is the Minnesota-North Dakota territory" and "contrary to rumors, I am very proud of where I'm from." Samantha Raphelson, "Wayne S. Cole, 90, Dies; Scholar of America's pre-WWII Isolationist Movement," *Washington Post*, October 10, 2013; "Bob Dylan and the NECLC."

66. Robert Love, "Bob Dylan Does the American Songbook His Way," *AARP The Magazine*, February/March 2015, 30.
67. Dylan, *Infidels* (1983); Loder, "Bob Dylan," 17. Dave Kelly confirms that Dylan was not interested in political Zionism after his conversion. His interest in Jewish identity was biblical and spiritual. Interview with Dave Kelly by JT, November 1, 2014.
68. Norman, "Nightmare," *So Long Ago the Garden* (1973); Norman, *"Why Should the Devil Have All the Good Music,"* 5.
69. Loder, "Bob Dylan," 24, 78.
70. Ibid., 24.
71. Heylin, *Life in Stolen Moments*, 214, 218; Heylin, *Saved!*, 77–78.
72. Loder, "Bob Dylan," 24; emphasis in the original.
73. Dylan, "Gonna Change My Way of Thinking" and "When You Gonna Wake Up," *Slow Train Coming* (1979); Dylan, "Trouble in Mind" (B-side of "Gotta Serve Somebody" single, 1979); Heylin, *Saved!*, 58.
74. Friedman, *Doesn't Anyone Blush Anymore?*.
75. P. Williams, *Dylan*, 92.
76. Loder, "Bob Dylan," 17; emphasis in the original.
77. P. Williams, *Dylan*, 86, 89, 86–87.
78. Hilburn, "'I Learned That Jesus Was Real and I Wanted That.'" Contained in: Benson, *Bob Dylan Companion*, 163. Evangelical philosopher Francis Schaeffer, an intellectual father of the Moral Majority, quoted Dylan's "When You Gonna Wake Up" in his influential book *A Christian Manifesto*. Francis A. Schaeffer, *A Christian Manifesto* (Westchester, IL: Crossway Books, 1981), 105.
79. Interview with Dave Kelly by JT, November 1, 2014. Kelly could not remember the man's name. He used "Mr. Gordon" a couple of times as a hypothetical name.
80. During the interview, Kelly said Jupiter Beach but he probably meant Jupiter Island. The island town is very small but the people are very rich. According to Wikipedia, "Some of the wealthiest people in the United States live in Jupiter Island; it has the highest per capita income of any inhabited place in the country." Kelly could not remember the exact location of the second possibility. He thought it was North Carolina, somewhere in the hills. As this book was being written, a reference to William C. Whitney having an estate in Aiken, South Carolina, led to a new possibility. Aiken

is in the foothills of the Appalachian Mountains (Piedmont region). As Wikipedia notes, in the late 1800s and early 1900s, "Aiken served as a winter playground for many of the country's wealthiest families such as the Vanderbilts, Bostwicks, and the Whitneys." The Astors were also part of the community. It is likely that at least one of the rich families still owned a mansion in the area in 1979. When asked about Aiken, Kelly replied, "Yes, it does sound like the place he was talking about." By the 1940s, grandchildren of Whitney, including John Hay "Jock" Whitney, were among the part-time residents of Jupiter Island (as were members of the Bush, Harriman, and Mellon families). W. C. Whitney's mother was a Collins and she was descended from William Bradford, who arrived on the Mayflower and became Governor of Plymouth Colony. Whitney's paternal line settled in Massachusetts in the 1630s. Many of the WASP members of Yale University's Order of Skull and Bones came from Puritan families who emigrated from England at that time (e.g., Phelps, Perkins, Wadsworth, Bundy, Lord, Stimson, Whitney, Gilman families). Dave Kelly e-mail to JT, November 21, 2014; Antony C. Sutton, *America's Secret Establishment: An Introduction to the Order of Skull & Bones* (Billings, MT: Liberty House Press, c1983, 1986), 17–20.

81. Interview with Dave Kelly by JT, November 1, 2014.
82. Gaetano Mosca, *The Ruling Class*, trans. Hannah D. Kahn, ed. Arthur Livingston (New York: McGraw-Hill, 1939), 50.
83. Mills, *Power Elite*; Dan Smoot, *The Invisible Government* (Dallas: Dan Smoot Report, 1962); G. William Domhoff, *Who Rules America?* (Englewood Cliffs, NJ: Prentice-Hall, 1967); Gary Allen with Larry Abraham, *None Dare Call It Conspiracy* (Rossmoor, CA: Concord Press, 1972); Kenneth Prewitt and Alan Stone, *The Ruling Elites: Elite Theory, Power, and American Democracy* (New York: Harper & Row, 1973); Michael Parenti, *Democracy for the Few* (New York: St. Martin's Press, 1974); Thomas R. Dye, *Who's Running America?: Institutional Leadership in the United States* (Englewood Cliffs, NJ: Prentice-Hall, 1976); G. David Garson, *Power and Politics in the United States: A Political Economy Approach* (Lexington, MA: D.C. Heath, 1977); Philip H. Burch Jr., *Elites in American History*, 3 vols. (New York: Holmes & Meier, 1980–81).
84. Ferdinand Lundberg, *America's 60 Families* (New York: Halcyon House, c1937, 1939); Quigley, *Tragedy and Hope*; Sutton, *America's Secret Establishment*; Kevin Phillips, *American Dynasty: Aristocracy, Fortune, and the Politics of Deceit in the House of Bush* (New York: Viking, 2004); Walter Isaacson and Evan Thomas, *The Wise Men: Six Friends and the World They Made* (New York: Touchstone/Simon & Schuster, c1986, 1988). A less-reputable source—by two Lyndon LaRouche–affiliated writers—gives some interesting details about Jupiter Island. Webster Griffin Tarpley and Anton Chaitkin, *George Bush: The Unauthorized Biography* (Leesburg, VA: Executive Intelligence Review, 1991), http://tarpley.net/online-books

/george-bush-the-unauthorized-biography/chapter-4-the-center-of-power-is-in-washington.

85. "Bob Dylan and the NECLC"; Gilmore, "Positively Dylan," 136; Dylan, *Another Side of Bob Dylan* (1964), *Empire Burlesque* (1985). McGoohan was creator and star of *The Prisoner*, a countercultural television series in the United Kingdom that influenced the Beatles, among others, in 1967–68. Dylan's reference to doing the impossible is less positive thinking and more divine empowering. The Beatles, *The Beatles Anthology* (San Francisco: Chronicle Books, 2000), 234, 272; Luke 1:37; Matthew 19:26.
86. David Beito and Charles Nuckolls, "Wrong Song of the South," *Reason.com*, July 19, 2004, http://reason.com/archives/2004/07/19/wrong-song-of-the-south.
87. Gilmore, "Bob Dylan" (2012), 48.
88. Taylor, *Politics on a Human Scale*, 67–68; Thomas E. Woods Jr., *Nullification: How to Resist Federal Tyranny in the 21st Century* (Washington, DC: Regnery, 2010), 77–83.
89. "About the Movie," *Masked and Anonymous* (Sony Pictures Classics), 2003, http://www.sonyclassics.com/masked/about.html.
90. *Masked and Anonymous* [motion picture]; *Masked and Anonymous: Music from the Motion Picture* [sound recording] (Columbia Records, 2003); Bob Dylan, *Tell Tale Signs* (The Bootleg Series, Vol. 8) (2008).
91. Dylan, *World Gone Wrong* (1993), liner notes 4; Artur, *Every Mind Polluting Word*, 801; Taylor, *Politics on a Human Scale*, 6, 17–53.
92. Loder, "Bob Dylan," 18; Conversation between Wendell Berry and JT, September 27, 2014.
93. Populism is the ideology that supports the rights, aspirations, and power of the people. In other words, it supports democracy. The Latin word *populus* means "people." The Greek word *demos* also means "people." Taylor, *Politics on a Human Scale*, 424.
94. Referring to establishment hostility toward 1950s rock 'n' roll because it was biracial, Dylan has said, "There must have been some elitist power that had to get rid of all these guys." Love, "Bob Dylan Does the American Songbook His Way," 26. For an analysis of underdog politics and its relation to the Democratic Party, see Karl G. Trautman, *The Underdog in American Politics: The Democratic Party and Liberal Values* (New York: Palgrave Macmillan, 2010).
95. "Folk Singers: Let Us Now Praise Little Men," *Time*, May 31, 1963, 40; Jules Siegel, "Well, What Have We Here?" *Saturday Evening Post*, July 30, 1966.
96. Interview with Dave Kelly by JT, November 1, 2014.
97. Conversation between Nat Hentoff and JT, June 9, 2014. Hentoff adds that Dylan has been, at other times, quite direct and revealing. He includes his *New Yorker* interview with Dylan (1964) and Dylan's *Chronicles* memoir (2004) in this category. Conversation between Nat Hentoff and JT, January 8, 2015.

98. Interview with Dave Kelly by JT, November 1, 2014; "The Groom's Still Waiting at the Altar," *Shot of Love* (1981, rev. 1985). In the mid-1960s, the great French novelist François Mauriac wrote, "The writer who bears our name represents us in the outside world. We see him as he is, showered with praise and decorations—sometimes insults. The letters overflowing with admiration and affection and sometimes loathing are addressed to him, not to this creature of flesh and blood whose solitude here on his rock is intensified the more that 'personage' is talked about as someone of importance in the world of men." François Mauriac, *The Inner Presence: Recollections of My Spiritual Life*, trans. Herma Briffault (Indianapolis: Bobbs-Merrill, c1965, 1968), 19–20.

Selected Bibliography

Aby, Anne J. *The North Star State: A Minnesota History Reader.* St. Paul: Minnesota Historical Society Press, 2002.
Artur, ed. *Every Mind Polluting Word: Assorted Bob Dylan Utterances* (Don't Ya Tell Henry Publications, 2006), http://content.yudu.com/Library/A1plqd/BobDylanEveryMindPol/resources/755.htm.
Baez, Joan. *And a Voice to Sing With.* New York: Summit Books, 1987.
Baker, Paul. *Why Should the Devil Have All the Good Music?: Jesus Music—Where It Began, Where It Is, and Where It Is Going.* Waco, TX: Word Books, 1979.
Bell, Ian. *Once Upon a Time: The Lives of Bob Dylan.* New York: Pegasus Books, 2012.
Benson, Carl, ed. *The Bob Dylan Companion: Four Decades of Commentary.* New York: Schirmer Books, 1998.
Berg, Steve. "The Scratching of Heads in Hibbing." *Minneapolis Star Tribune,* December 7, 1979.
Berman, Hyman, and Linda Mack Schloff. *Jews in Minnesota: The People of Minnesota.* St. Paul: Minnesota Historical Society Press, 2002.
Bloom, Alexander, and Wini Breines, eds. *"Takin' It to the Streets" A Sixties Reader.* 2nd ed. New York: Oxford University Press, 2003.
Blum, John Morton. *Years of Discord: American Politics and Society 1961–74.* New York: W.W. Norton, 1991.
"Bob Dylan and the NECLC." *Corliss Lamont Website,* January 7, 2012, http://www.corliss-lamont.org/dylan.htm.
Boucher, David, and Gary Browning, eds. *The Political Art of Bob Dylan.* New York: Palgrave Macmillan, 2004.
Brinkley, Douglas. "Bob Dylan's America." *Rolling Stone,* May 14, 2009.
Broadside [folk music magazine]. 1962–64.
Brown, Aaron. *Overburden: Modern Life on the Iron Range.* Duluth, MN: Red Step Press, 2008.
Cohen, Scott. "Don't Ask Me Nothin' about Nothin' I Might Just Tell You the Truth: Bob Dylan Revisited." *Spin,* December 1985, 36–41, 80–81.
Cole, Wayne S. *Senator Gerald P. Nye and American Foreign Relations.* Minneapolis: University of Minnesota Press, 1962.

Diner, Hasia R. *The Jews of the United States*. Berkeley: University of California Press, 2004.

Dunaway, David King, and Molly Beer. *Singing Out: An Oral History of America's Folk Music Revivals*. New York: Oxford University Press, 2010.

Dylan, Bob. *Chronicles, Volume One*. New York: Simon & Schuster, 2004.

———. *The Lyrics*. Ed. Christopher Ricks, Lisa Nemrow, and Julie Nemrow. New York: Simon & Schuster, 2014.

———. *Lyrics: 1962–2001*. New York: Simon & Schuster, 2004.

———. *A Musical Retrospective* [sound recording]. Doberman/Scorpio/Gold Standard, 2000.

———. *Younger Than That Now: The Collected Interviews with Bob Dylan*. New York: Thunder's Mouth Press, 2004.

Dylan, Bob, with Tom Petty and the Heartbreakers. *Hard to Handle* [videocassette]. CBS/FOX Video Music, 1986.

Elazar, Daniel J. *Cities of the Prairie: The Metropolitan Frontier and American Politics*. New York: Basic Books, 1970.

Elazar, Daniel J., Virginia Gray, and Wyman Spano. *Minnesota Politics and Government*. Lincoln: University of Nebraska Press, 1999.

Eller, Vernard. *Christian Anarchy: Jesus' Primacy Over the Powers*. Grand Rapids, MI: Eerdmans, 1987.

Ellul, Jacques. *Anarchy and Christianity*. Trans. Geoffrey W. Bromiley. Grand Rapids, MI: Eerdmans, c1988, 1991.

———. *The Subversion of Christianity*. Trans. Geoffrey W. Bromiley. Grand Rapids, MI: Eerdmans, c1984, 1986.

Engel, Dave. *Just Like Bob Zimmerman's Blues: Dylan in Minnesota*. Rudolph, WI: River City Memoirs—Mesabi, 1997.

Enroth, Ronald M., Edward E. Ericson Jr., and C. Breckinridge Peters. *The Jesus People: Old-Time Religion in the Age of Aquarius*. Grand Rapids, MI: Eerdmans, 1972.

Epstein, Daniel Mark. *The Ballad of Bob Dylan: A Portrait*. New York: Harper Collins, 2011.

Farrell, James J. *The Spirit of the Sixties: The Making of Postwar Radicalism*. New York: Routledge, 1997.

Fischer, David Hackett. *Albion's Seed: Four British Folkways in America*. New York: Oxford University Press, 1989.

Foner, Eric. *The Story of American Freedom*. New York: W.W. Norton, 1998.

Fong-Torres, Ben. "Knockin' on Bob Dylan's Door." *Rolling Stone*, February 14, 1974.

Førland, Tor Egil. "Bringing It All Back Home *or* Another Side of Bob Dylan: Midwestern Isolationist." *Journal of American Studies* 26 (December 1992): 339.

Gilman, Rhoda R., and June Drenning Holmquist, eds. *Selections from "Minnesota History": A Fiftieth Anniversary Anthology*. St. Paul: Minnesota Historical Society Press, 1965.

Gilmore, Mikal. "Bob Dylan: The Rolling Stone Interview." *Rolling Stone*, September 27, 2012, 42–51, 80–81.

———. "Bob Dylan: The Rolling Stone Interview." *Rolling Stone*, November 22, 2001, 56–69.

———. "Positively Dylan." *Rolling Stone*, July 17/31, 1986, 30–34, 135–36.

Gitlin, Todd. *The Sixties: Years of Hope, Days of Rage*. Rev. trade ed. New York: Bantam Books, 1993.

Gotta Serve Somebody: The Gospel Songs of Bob Dylan [sound recording]. Columbia Records, 2003.

Gray, Michael. *The Bob Dylan Encyclopedia*. New York: Continuum, 2006.

———. *Song and Dance Man III: The Art of Bob Dylan*. London: Cassell, 2000.

Greene, John Robert. *America in the Sixties*. Syracuse: Syracuse University Press, 2010.

Griffin, Sid. *Shelter from the Storm: Bob Dylan's Rolling Thunder Years*. London: Jawbone Press, 2010.

Gross, Michael. *Bob Dylan: An Illustrated History*. Rev. ed. New York: Tempo Books, 1980.

Hajdu, David. *Positively 4th Street: The Lives and Times of Joan Baez, Bob Dylan, Mimi Baez Farina and Richard Farina*. New York: Farrar, Straus, Giroux, 2001.

Hale, Grace Elizabeth. *A Nation of Outsiders: How the White Middle Class Fell in Love with Rebellion in Postwar America*. New York: Oxford University Press, 2011.

Hatfield, Mark. *Between a Rock and a Hard Place*. Waco, TX: Word Books, 1976.

Hedin, Benjamin, ed. *Studio A: The Bob Dylan Reader*. New York: W.W. Norton & Company, 2004.

Heschel, Abraham J. *The Prophets*. New York: Harper & Row, 1962.

Heylin, Clinton. *Bob Dylan Behind the Shades: A Biography*. New York: Summit Books, 1991.

———. *Bob Dylan Behind the Shades Revisited*. New York: William Morrow, 2001.

———. *Bob Dylan: A Life in Stolen Moments, Day by Day: 1941–1995*. New York: Schirmer Books, 1996.

———. *Bob Dylan: The Recording Sessions, 1960–1994*. New York: St. Martin's Griffin, c1995, 1996.

———, ed. *Saved!: The Gospel Speeches of Bob Dylan*. New York: Hanuman Books, 1990.

Hickey, Neil. "Bob Dylan." *TV Guide*, September 11, 1976.

Hilburn, Robert. "Bob Dylan at 42: Rolling Down Highway 61 Again." *Los Angeles Times*, October 30, 1983, U3–4. Contained in: Artur, *Every Mind Polluting Word*.

———. "How Does It Feel? Don't Ask." *Los Angeles Times*, September 16, 2001.

———. "'I Learned That Jesus Was Real and I Wanted That.'" *Los Angeles Times*, November 23, 1980. Contained in: Benson, *Bob Dylan Companion*.

Holmquist, June Drenning, ed. *They Chose Minnesota: A Survey of the State's Ethnic Groups*. St. Paul: Minnesota Historical Society Press, 1981.
Jerome, Jim. "Bob Dylan: A Myth Materializes with a New Protest Record and a New Tour." *People Weekly*, November 10, 1975.
Kauffman, Bill. *Ain't My America: The Long, Noble History of Antiwar Conservatism and Middle-American Anti-Imperialism*. New York: Metropolitan Books, 2008.
———. *Look Homeward, America: In Search of Reactionary Radicals and Front-Porch Anarchists*. Wilmington, DE: ISI Books, 2006.
Keller, Martin. "Dylan Speaks." *Us*, January 2, 1984.
Kierkegaard, Søren. *Attack upon "Christendom," 1854–1855*. Trans. Walter Lowrie. Princeton, NJ: Princeton University Press, 1968.
———. *Provocations: Spiritual Writings of Kierkegaard*. Comp. Charles E. Moore. Farmington, PA: Plough Publishing House, 1999.
Kittler, Glenn D. *The Jesus Kids and Their Leaders*. New York: Warner Paperback Library, 1972.
Knockin' on Dylan's Door: On the Road in '74 (A Rolling Stone Book). New York: Pocket Books, 1974.
Lamppa, Marvin G. *Minnesota's Iron Country: Rich Ore, Rich Lives*. Duluth: Lake Superior Port Cities Inc., 2004.
Lasch, Christopher. *The Culture of Narcissism*. New York: W.W. Norton, 1978.
Lindbergh [Sr.], Charles A. *Why Is Your Country at War, and What Happens to You after the War, and Related Subjects*. Washington, DC: Lindbergh, 1917.
Lindsey, Hal, with C.C. Carlson. *The Late Great Planet Earth*. Grand Rapids, MI: Zondervan, c1970, 1977.
Loder, Kurt. "Bob Dylan: The Rolling Stone Interview." *Rolling Stone*, June 21, 1984, 14–24, 78.
Love, Robert. "Bob Dylan Does the American Songbook His Way." *AARP The Magazine*, February/March 2015, 22–30.
Mackay, Kathleen. *Bob Dylan: Intimate Insights from Friends and Fellow Musicians*. New York: Omnibus Press, 2007.
Marcus, Greil. *Invisible Republic: Bob Dylan's Basement Tapes*. New York: Henry Holt, 1997.
Marqusee, Mike. *Chimes of Freedom: The Politics of Bob Dylan's Art*. New York: New Press, 2003.
Marshall, Scott M., with Marcia Ford. *Restless Pilgrim: The Spiritual Journey of Bob Dylan*. Lake Mary, FL: Relevant Books, 2002.
Masked and Anonymous [motion picture]. Sony Pictures, 2003.
Masked and Anonymous: Music from the Motion Picture [sound recording]. Columbia Records, 2003.
Maymudes, Victor. *Another Side of Bob Dylan: A Personal History on the Road and off the Tracks*. Ed. Jacob Maymudes. New York: St. Martin's Press, 2014.
McGregor, Craig. *Bob Dylan: The Early Years: A Retrospective*. New York: Da Capo Press, c1972, 1990.
Mills, C. Wright. *The Power Elite*. New York: Oxford University Press, 1956.

Nee, Watchman. *Love Not the World: A Prophetic Call to Holy Living.* Fort Washington, PA: CLC Publications, 2009.

Niebuhr, H. Richard. *Christ and Culture.* New York: Harper Torchbooks, c1951, 1975.

No Direction Home [documentary]. Martin Scorsese director, Paramount Pictures, 2005.

Norman, Larry, ed. *The "Blue Book."* (Linked to *Home at Last* [sound recording], Benson Records, 1989.) Santa Cruz, CA: Phydeaux, 1989.

———. *Bootleg* [sound recording]. One Way Records, 1971.

———. *In Another Land* [sound recording]. Solid Rock Records, 1976.

———. *Only Visiting This Planet* [sound recording]. MGM/Verve Records, 1972; Street Level Records, 1978.

———. *So Long Ago the Garden* [sound recording]. MGM Records, 1973; Phydeaux, 1980.

———. *Street Level* [sound recording]. One Way Records, 1970–71.

———. *Upon This Rock* [sound recording]. Capitol Records, 1969; Impact Records, 1970.

———. "Why Should the Devil Have All the Good Music" [songbook]. Hollywood: One Way Publications, n.d.

The Old and the New Testaments of the Holy Bible: Revised Standard Version. Camden, NJ: Thomas Nelson, c1946/52.

O'Neill, William L. *Coming Apart: An Informal History of America in the 1960s.* New York: Quadrangle Books Inc., 1971.

Orman, John. *The Politics of Rock Music.* Chicago: Nelson Hall, 1984.

Pederson, Duane, with Bob Owen. *Jesus People.* Glendale, CA: Regal Books, 1971.

Perlstein, Rick. *Before the Storm: Barry Goldwater and the Unmaking of the American Consensus.* New York: Nation Books, 2009.

Pichaske, David. *Song of the North Country: A Midwest Framework to the Songs of Bob Dylan.* New York: Continuum, 2010.

Quigley, Carroll. *Tragedy and Hope: A History of the World in Our Time.* New York: Macmillan, 1966.

Radosh, Ronald. *Prophets on the Right: Profiles of Conservative Critics of American Globalism.* New York: Free Life Editions, c1975, 1978.

Rogovoy, Seth. *Bob Dylan: Prophet, Mystic, Poet.* New York: Scribner, 2007.

Sarna, Jonathan D. *American Judaism: A History.* New Haven: Yale University Press, 2004.

Scaduto, Anthony. *Bob Dylan: An Intimate Biography.* New York: Signet, c1971, 1979.

———. "Won't You Listen to the Lambs, Bob Dylan?" *New York Times Magazine*, November 28, 1971.

Schaeffer, Francis A. *The Church at the End of the 20th Century.* Downers Grove, IL: InterVarsity Press, 1970.

Scofield, C. I., ed. *The Scofield Reference Bible.* New York: Oxford University Press, 1917.

Seeger Pete. *Pete Seeger in His Own Words*. Ed. Rob Rosenthal and Sam Rosenthal. Boulder: Paradigm, 2012.

Shelton, Robert. "Bob Dylan Sings." *New York Times*, April 13, 1963.

———. *No Direction Home: The Life and Music of Bob Dylan*. New York: Ballantine Books, c1986, 1987.

Sloman, Larry "Ratso." *On the Road with Bob Dylan*. New York: Three Rivers Press, 2002.

Smith, Harry, comp. *Anthology of American Folk Music* [sound recording]. Smithsonian Folkways Recordings, c1952, 1997.

Smith, Larry David. *Writing Dylan: The Songs of a Lonesome Traveler*. Westport, CT: Praeger, 2005.

Sounes, Howard. *Down the Highway: The Life of Bob Dylan*. New York: Grove Press, 2001.

Spitz, Bob. *Dylan: A Biography*. New York: McGraw-Hill, 1989.

Taylor, Jeff. "Fighting Bob vs. Silent Cal: The Conservative Tradition from La Follette to Taft and Beyond." *Modern Age* 50 (2008): 295–305.

———. *Politics on a Human Scale: The American Tradition of Decentralism*. Lanham, MD: Lexington Press, 2013.

———. *Where Did the Party Go?: William Jennings Bryan, Hubert Humphrey, and the Jeffersonian Legacy*. Columbia: University of Missouri Press, 2006.

Teodori, Massimo, ed. *The New Left: A Documentary History*. Indianapolis: Bobbs-Merrill Company, 1969.

Thompson, Toby. *Positively Main Street: Bob Dylan's Minnesota*. Rev. ed. Minneapolis: University of Minnesota Press, 1971, 2008.

Trager, Oliver. *Keys to the Rain: The Definitive Bob Dylan Encyclopedia*. New York: Billboard Books, 2004.

Verduin, Leonard. *The Anatomy of a Hybrid: A Study in Church-State Relationships*. Grand Rapids, MI: Eerdmans, 1976.

———. *The Reformers and Their Stepchildren*. Grand Rapids, MI: Eerdmans, 1964.

Webb, Stephen H. *Dylan Redeemed: From Highway 61 to Saved*. New York: Continuum, 2006.

Welles, Chris. "The Angry Young Folk Singer." *Life*, April 10, 1964.

White, Bruce M., et al., eds. *Minnesota Votes: Election Returns by County for Presidents, Senators, Congressmen, and Governors, 1857–1977*. St. Paul: Minnesota Historical Society, 1977.

Whittemore, Katharine, Ellen Rosenbush, and Jim Nelson, eds. *The Sixties: Recollections of the Decade from Harper's Magazine*. New York: Franklin Square Press, 1995.

Wilentz, Sean. *Bob Dylan in America*. New York: Doubleday, 2010.

Williams, Daniel K. *God's Own Party: The Making of the Christian Right*. New York: Oxford University Press, 2010.

Williams, Don. *Bob Dylan: The Man, the Music, the Message*. Old Tappan, NJ: Fleming H. Revell, 1985.

Williams, Paul. *Bob Dylan, Performing Artist: 1986–1990 & Beyond, Mind Out of Time.* London: Omnibus Press, 2004.

———. *Dylan — What Happened?* Glen Ellen, CA: Entwhistle Books, 1980.

Williamson, Nigel. *Bob Dylan Rough Guide.* London: Metro Books, 2006.

Woodward, Colin. *American Nations: A History of the Eleven Rival Regional Cultures of North America.* New York: Penguin Books, 2011.

Wonder Boys: Music from the Motion Picture [sound recording]. Sony Music Entertainment, 2000.

Selected Bob Dylan Albums

The Freewheelin' Bob Dylan (1963)
The Times They Are A-Changin' (1964)
Another Side of Bob Dylan (1964)
Bringing It All Back Home (1965)
Highway 61 Revisited (1965)
Blonde on Blonde (1966)
John Wesley Harding (1967)
Nashville Skyline (1969)
Self Portrait (1970)
New Morning (1970)
Planet Waves (1974)*
Blood on the Tracks (1975)
Desire (1976)
Street Legal (1978)
Slow Train Coming (1979)
Saved (1980)
Shot of Love (1981)
Infidels (1983)
Empire Burlesque (1985)
Biograph (1985)
Knocked Out Loaded (1986)
Down in the Groove (1988)
Oh Mercy (1989)
Under the Red Sky (1990)
Rare and Unreleased: Bootleg Series Vols. 1–3 (1991)
Good As I Been to You (1992)
World Gone Wrong (1993)
"Love and Theft" (2001)
Live 1975: The Bootleg Series Vol. 5 (2002)
No Direction Home: The Bootleg Series Vol. 7 (2005)
Modern Times (2006)
Tell Tale Signs: The Bootleg Series Vol. 8 (2008)
Together Through Life (2009)

The Witmark Demos: 1962–1964: The Bootleg Series Vol. 9 (2010)
Tempest (2012)
*Originally released by Asylum Records. All others by Columbia Records.

Conversations

Conversations between Nat Hentoff and JT, June 9, 2014; January 8, 2015. Telephone.
Conversation between Wendell Berry and JT, September 27, 2014. University of Louisville (KY), Front Porch Republic Conference.
Conversation between Robert Dean Lurie and JT, September 28, 2014. Louisville International Airport.
Conversation between Rabbi Michelle Werner and CI, October 15, 2014. B'nai Israel Synagogue, Rochester, MN.

Interviews

Interview with Charles Evers by JT, June 30, 2014. Telephone.
Interview with Dave Kelly by JT, November 1, 2014. Telephone.
Interview with Jerry Waldman by CI, November 13, 2014. Telephone.
Interview with Charles Norman by JT, December 10, 2014. Telephone.

E-Mails

Alberta McCrory e-mails to JT, September 23, 2013; March 6–7, 2014.
Suzanne Duscha e-mails to JT, July 25 and August 3, 2014.
Matthew Zawisky (Ralph Nader aide) e-mail to JT, September 17, 2014.
Allen Flemming e-mails to JT, October 10, 12, and 25, 2014.
Dave Kelly e-mails to JT, November 19 and 21, 2014.

Index

2nd Chapter of Acts (band), 175–6, 177, 184, 266n15, 267n31

Abel, 20
abortion, 40, 85–6, 176, 179, 199, 203, 207, 207–8, 222, 239n112, 272n17
Abourezk, James, 204
Abraham (patriarch), 20, 154, 161, 253n107
Academy Awards, 140
Acheson, Dean, 228
Acuff, Roy, 140
Adams, John Quincy, 211
Afghanistan War, 204, 213
African Americans, 19, 22, 26–8, 39, 45, 46, 48, 55–9, 61, 93, 96–101, 108, 119–20, 162, 199, 212–13, 229–31, 243n22, 250n19, 250n23, 251n50, 278n94
agnosticism, 137, 255–6n23
agrarianism, 32, 33, 75–6, 80, 88, 114, 116, 191, 215, 231
Ali, Muhammad, 94
Alpert, Herb, 70
Alpha Band, 174
Amash, Justin, 204
America (band), 265n7
American Friends Service Committee, 160
Amish, 142–3, 208
Amnesty International, 88

Anabaptists, 142–3, 153–4, 161, 208
anarchism, 11, 29, 39–40, 46–7, 66, 74–8, 108, 109–15, 123, 125, 128, 139, 143, 150, 151–72, 173, 179, 180, 189, 185, 190–2, 194–9, 201–11, 216, 225, 229, 233, 234, 274n45
Anderson, John, 5
The Animals, 67, 70
animals, treatment of, 199
Antichrist, 135, 137, 156, 164, 204, 216, 220, 259n9, 262n42
anti-Semitism, 17–18, 244n37
Apocalypse Now (film), 86
apocalyptic theology. *See* eschatology
Aquinas, Thomas, 209
aristocracy. *See* The Establishment
Ark (band), 177–8, 184, 185, 265n10, 268n45
Artes, Mary Alice, 22, 128, 174
Ashbrook, John, 203
Asia (band), 263n53
Assemblies of God, 166, 265n9
Astor family, 277n80
astrology, vii, 140–1
atheism, vii, 122, 133, 136, 140–1, 141–2, 160, 224, 255–6n23
Augustine of Hippo, 20, 198, 209, 259n5, 271n94

Baby Boomers, 44, 85–6, 88–9, 125, 249n192
Babylon the Great, 130, 156, 167, 204, 207, 220, 262n42
Badfinger, 178
Baez, Joan, 7, 47–8, 49, 53, 54, 58, 61, 62–3, 68, 80, 88, 90, 102–3, 119, 120–1, 243n22
Bakunin, Mikhail, 169
Ball, David, 139
The Band, viii, 75, 81, 264n1
Bangladesh, Concert for, 79
Bangs, Lester, 120
Baptists, 203, 208
Barnett, Ross, 56
Barrett, Syd, 185
Barth, Karl, 142
Batista, Fulgencio, 217
The Beach Boys, 65, 67
The Beatles, 44, 61, 65, 67, 71, 75, 80, 85, 112, 116, 177, 178, 180, 188, 263n53, 268n39, 278n85
Beats (writers), 66, 67, 69, 73, 93, 111, 219, 223
Beckett, Barry, 268n39
Bell, Ian, 34, 59
Berg, Peter, 74
Berkeley Free Speech Movement, 46, 61, 63, 76, 93
Beron, Jim, 103–4
Berry, Wendell, 215, 231, 274n43
Bible prophecy. *See* eschatology
big business. *See* The Establishment
big government. *See* decentralism; libertarianism; statism
Bikel, Theodore, 48
Billy Jack (film), 116–17
birth control pill, 222
Björner, Olof, 256n31
Black, Frank, 181
Black Americans. *See* African Americans
Black Panthers, 79, 85
Black Sabbath, 128
Blessitt, Arthur, 264n1

Blow, Kurtis, 34
blues music, 8, 12–13, 16, 26–8, 33, 34, 39, 50, 65–9, 90, 103, 110, 111, 136, 144, 146, 163, 177, 181, 183, 185, 232, 233
Blum, John Morton, 71
B'nai B'rith, 19
Bogart, Humphrey, 184–5
Bohlen, Charles, 228
Bolin, Tommy, 177
bomb shelters, 51–2, 57
Bonhoeffer, Dietrich, 258n66
Bonior, David, 203
Bonnie and Clyde (film), 117
Bono, 114, 188, 189–90, 270n79
Boone, Debby, 177, 182
Boone, Pat, 129, 176, 181, 182
Born on the Fourth of July (film), 86
Boschwitz, Rudy, 237n75
Bostwick family, 277n80
Boswell, James, 271n94
boxing, 94, 105–6, 118, 119
Bradford, William, 277n80
Bradley, Ed, 8, 26
Brethren, Church of the, 208
Bretton Woods Agreements, 219
Brinkley, Douglas, 31
Broonzy, Big Bill, 28
Brown, Aaron, 13
Brown, Jerry, 204, 206, 272n6
Brown, Mick, 131–2
Bruce, Lenny, 102, 156, 198, 207
Bryan, William Jennings, 13, 205, 214, 216, 217, 224, 232, 274n45
Bryant, Anita, 223
Bryant, Roy, 97
Buchanan, Pat, 215
Bucklen, John, 7, 21
Buckley, William F., Jr., 36–7
Buddhism, 140–1, 204, 224
Budziszewski, J., 260n14
Buffalo Springfield, 177, 265n7
Buffett, Howard, 203, 271n5
Buffett, Warren, 271n5
Bundy family, 277n80

Burnett, T-Bone, 174, 265n7, 267n31
Burton, Richard, 206
Bush, George H. W., 202, 203, 218–19, 228
Bush, George W., 41, 91, 196, 197, 202, 204, 228, 271n2
Bush, Prescott, 202, 219, 228
Bushnell, Katharine, 259n5
Butler, Smedley, 218, 275n54
Butterfield Blues Band, Paul, 27
The Byrds, 70, 174

Cadoux, Cecil John, 208
Caesar, Shirley, 139, 257n44
Cage, Nicolas, 169
Cain, 20
Calvary Chapel, 162–3, 168, 171, 191, 262n45, 262n48, 265n7, 266n20
Calvin, John, 161
Campus Crusade for Christ, 168, 188, 269n51
Canfield, Mike, 267n24
Carey, James, 71
Carmichael, Stokely, 108
Carnegie, Andrew, 10
Carroll, Hattie, 56, 66, 83, 97, 99–101, 106, 114, 115, 118, 119
Carter, Jimmy, 82–3, 180, 182, 202, 271n2
Carter, Rubin "Hurricane," 79, 105, 118–21, 162
Carter Family (band), 28
Cash, Johnny, 35, 103, 115, 183, 188, 269n51
Catholic Workers, 84, 161, 179
Catholics. *See* Roman Catholics
Center, ideological. *See* The Establishment
Central America Free Trade Agreement, 220
Central Intelligence Agency, 218, 245n74
Chabad sect. *See* Lubavitch sect
Chaitkin, Anton, 277n84
Chaney, James, 63

Chaplin, Charlie, 16
Chapman, Tracy, 88
charismatics, Christian, 162–3, 165–6, 174, 180, 189, 261n38, 265n9
Child, Francis James, 26
Chomsky, Noam, 153, 191, 271n94, 273n28
Christ. *See* Dylan, Bob: and Christianity
Christian anarchism, 151–72
Christian rock. *See* Contemporary Christian Music
Christian World Liberation Front, 166–7, 170–1
church, definition of, 146–7, 257n61
Church, Frank, 204
civil rights. *See* Dylan, Bob: and civil rights
Civil Rights Act, 39
Civil War, 32, 33, 82, 162, 212–13, 227, 229–31
Clancy, Liam, 62
The Clash, 263n53
Clay, Henry, 205
Clayton, Adam, 189
Cleaver, Eldridge, 85
Clinton, Bill, 41, 88, 91, 228
Coburn, Tom, 203
Cockburn, Bruce, 183
Cohen, John, 77
Cohen, Scott, 138, 163
Cold War, 40–1, 47, 49–55, 109, 206, 219
Cole, Wayne, 221, 275–6n65
Coleman, Norm, 237n75
Collins family, 277n80
Collyard, Dewey, 7–8
Coming Home (film), 86
commercial culture. *See* Dylan, Bob: and commercial culture
common grace, 149–50
communism, 5, 6, 11, 12, 14, 36, 37, 39, 40–1, 47, 49, 49–51, 51, 57, 71–2, 108, 262n44
communitarianism, 2–3, 201–11, 229

Congress for Racial Equality (CORE), 56, 96–7
conservatism, 29–36, 36–41, 229
conservatism, social. *See* moralism
Constantine I (emperor), 260n15
Constitution, 39, 60, 62, 203, 207, 213, 214, 229
Contemporary Christian Music, 141, 174–89
Coolidge, Calvin, 5, 219
Coomes, Tom, 262n48
Copeland, Gloria, 180
Copeland, Kenneth, 180
corporate America. *See* The Establishment
Cott, Jonathan, 79, 128
Counterculture, vii, 43, 47, 59–86, 106–15, 116, 164, 169–70, 180, 195, 199, 205, 224, 232, 233
country life. *See* agrarianism
country music, 26–8, 29–30, 34–5, 75, 80, 83, 103, 114, 115, 144, 177, 232
Crosby, Stills, Nash & Young, 78–9, 230
Crowe, Cameron, 148–9
Cuban Missile Crisis, 24

Dallas Theological Seminary, 168, 262n50
Daltrey, Roger, 90
Daniel (prophet), 138–9
David (king), 132, 158, 163–4, 194, 253n107
Davis, Clive, 72
Davis, John, 5
Day, Dorothy, 162, 179
De La Beckwith, Byron, 97–8, 100
Dean, James, 102
Deborah (judge), 132
Debs, Eugene, 4
decentralism, 14–15, 30–1, 39–40, 75–6, 152, 190–2, 193–4, 201–11, 229–31
Declaration of Independence, 31, 213
The Deer Hunter (film), 86

DeMint, Jim, 203
democracy. *See* populism
Democratic Party, 1, 5–6, 13, 15, 18, 33, 40, 50–1, 76, 77, 82–3, 88, 171, 179, 201–11, 226, 228, 232, 270n72, 272n17, 278n94
Dennis, Carolyn, 28
Depression Era. *See* Great Depression
Devil. *See* Satan
Diggers, 74
Dionne, E. J., 169–70
Dirty Harry (film), 116
disco music, 83
Disney, 27
dispensationalism, Christian, 124, 161, 168, 192, 222, 253n113, 262n50, 265n10
see also eschatology
Donatus, 153
Donnelly, Ignatius, 4
The Doors, 113
Dooyeweerd, Herman, 259n5
Dove Awards, 175
drug companies, 189, 222, 231
drugs, illegal, 72, 75, 78, 87, 111–12, 113, 131, 170, 195, 268n45
Duncan, Jimmy, 204
Duscha, Suzanne, 250n23
Dworkin, Andrea, 223
Dylan, Bob
  in 1960s, vii, ix, 24, 27, 43–78, 93–116, 126, 128, 139, 144, 146, 149, 149–50, 155, 156, 162, 163, 164, 173, 181–2, 184–5, 195, 205, 206, 208–9, 211–12, 215, 227, 229, 231, 232, 233–4, 240n129, 266n17, 278–9n98
  in 1970s, vii, ix–x, 44, 78–85, 86, 110, 116–23, 127–50, 159, 173–99, 228
  in 1980s, viii, x, 44, 85–8, 91, 94–5, 123–5, 127–50, 151, 159, 173–99, 212, 264n66
  in 1990s, x, 3, 28, 36, 53, 76–7, 78, 88–90, 91, 103, 104–5, 120, 123,

125, 133, 138, 139–40, 159, 177, 190–1, 198, 199, 211, 212, 223
in 2000s, vii, x, 8, 9, 9–10, 15, 16, 17, 23, 26, 28, 33–4, 36, 50, 90, 116, 125–6, 140, 147, 149, 159, 163, 184–5, 196–8, 199, 213–14, 230, 278–9n98
in 2010s, x, 17, 27, 33, 36, 39, 41, 43, 57, 86, 90, 125, 126, 140, 141, 149, 162, 197, 199, 212–13, 221, 229, 257n51, 259n9, 278n94
and Christianity, vii–x, 22–3, 25–6, 40, 41, 52, 83–5, 95, 121–3, 124, 127–50, 151, 173–99, 211, 216, 233, 253n113, 257n51
and civil rights, 39, 48, 55–9, 96–101, 108, 162, 229, 243n22, 250n23, 251n50, 278n94
and commercial culture, 26, 27, 58, 62–9, 85–7, 89–90, 100, 107, 123, 125–6, 148–9, 175, 208, 221, 223
and conversion to Christ, 41, 84–5, 95, 122–3, 127–50
as family man, 22, 29–36, 44, 74–6, 114–16, 118, 131–2, 133, 139, 233
as folk singer, 1–2, 8–9, 26–8, 43–67, 91, 93–110, 128, 144, 146, 148, 151, 157, 181, 195, 233, 266n17
and freedom, viii–ix, 94–5, 107–15, 125, 126, 155–6
and going electric, 27, 30, 35, 43, 61, 65, 84, 89, 109, 112, 114, 116, 141, 195
and international relations, 31, 49–55, 90, 157, 191, 195, 204, 211–22
and Judaism, vii, 4, 17–26, 26, 33, 75, 98, 124, 128, 130–6, 139, 140–1, 144, 154, 159, 161, 163–4, 202, 211, 223, 227, 231, 232, 233, 237n75, 238n80, 238n91, 244n37, 253n107, 253n113, 255n23, 256n25

and justice, viii–ix, 46–7, 94–5, 96–106, 126, 156–7, 157, 158, 159–64, 169, 192, 199, 201–11, 214, 216, 229, 233, 259n9
and peace, x, 16, 49–55, 64, 72, 76–7, 79, 86–7, 88, 89, 125, 157, 158, 163–4, 179, 195, 199, 201–11, 211–22, 220, 273n29, 274n45
and politicians, 38–40, 40, 41, 47, 63, 77, 83, 91, 109, 126, 196–7, 201–21, 228
and poverty, viii, 104–6
and power, viii–ix, x, 2–4, 6, 12–16, 26, 28, 40, 46, 51, 59, 60, 68, 85, 90, 94–102, 105, 110–19, 121–3, 134, 137, 141, 148, 152–8, 163, 164, 191–8, 201, 204–9, 213–14, 216, 220, 226–8, 229, 233, 262n42, 278n94
as rock star, 65, 67–71, 110–14, 128, 144, 145–6, 195, 197, 226, 233
and tradition, 1–41, 43, 94, 103, 120, 124, 133, 144, 146, 161, 164, 199, 203, 205, 210, 211–17, 223–4, 233
and truth, viii, x, 37, 38–9, 40, 46, 122, 124, 138, 147, 148–9, 196, 204, 208–9, 214, 233, 253n113, 271n89
as voice of generation, 23, 41, 43–91, 227
and wealth, 3, 32, 85, 90, 100, 141–2, 148, 155, 161, 162, 162–3, 164, 180, 196, 204, 211, 212, 228
Dylan, Jesse, 131–2
Dylan, Maria, 133
Dylan, Samuel, 131
Dylan, Sara, 118, 131–2
Dylanesque politics in real world, 201–34

The Eagles, 177–8, 180
Eastern Establishment. *See* The Establishment

Index

Eastern Orthodox, 153, 204
Economic Research Action Project, 60
Eden, Garden of, 154, 158, 192, 231, 259n5
Edge, 189
Edwards, Gene, 168, 262n45
Edwards, Rod, 268n39
Eisenberg, Marilyn, 56
Eisenhower, Dwight, 52, 210, 213, 218, 219
Elazar, Daniel, 2–4
Electric Light Orchestra, 179
Elijah (prophet), 132
Elite Theory, 191, 227–8
elitism. *See* The Establishment
Elliott, Ramblin' Jack, 26
Emergency Civil Liberties Committee, 60–1, 103, 115, 208–9, 229, 245n74, 251n50, 270–1n89, 276n65
Emerson, Ralph Waldo, 32
Empire, American. *See* imperialism
End Times. *See* eschatology
Energy Crisis, 81, 121
Engelbrecht, H. C., x, 217–18
environmentalism, 78
Episcopalians, 165–6
Epstein, Daniel Mark, 91
Equal Rights Amendment, 40
equality. *See* justice, social; populism
eschatology, x, 124, 130, 135–6, 138–9, 140, 142, 145–6, 157, 158–9, 160–1, 164, 168, 174, 191, 192–4, 216, 217, 220, 222, 226, 253n107, 262n42, 262n49, 265n9
Esmond, Paul, 25
The Establishment, 30–1, 37, 87, 88, 101, 191, 202, 207, 214–20, 225–8, 232–3, 271n4, 273n29, 276–7n80, 277n80, 277n84, 278n94
Esther (queen), 132
ethics, social. *See* moralism
eugenics, 272n17

Evers, Charles, 98–9, 250n22
Evers, Medgar, 56, 94, 97–101, 119
Fabares, Shelley, 49
Fair Play for Cuba Committee, 245n74
Falwell, Jerry, 223, 224
Farm Aid, 88, 163, 231
Farmer-Labor Party (Minnesota), 5, 18, 232, 273n29
farming. *See* agrarianism
Farrell, James, 94
Federal Reserve System, 273n29
Feingold, Russell, 202, 271n3
feminism, 31–2, 78, 114–15, 170, 199, 222–3, 272n17
Fidler, Linda, 7
Fifty-Five Families, 225–8
Fischer, David Hackett, 2
Fischer, John, 175
Flanagan, Bill, 140, 197–8
Fleetwood Mac, 177
Flemming, Allen, 183–4, 188–9, 268n43
Ford, Gerald, 82–3
foreign policy. *See* Dylan, Bob: and international relations
Førland, Tor Egil, 211
Fortenberry, Jeff, 203
Four Seasons, 70
Fox, George, 142–3, 153–4, 160
Francis, Connie, 49
Francis of Assisi, 153
Franken, Al, 237n75
Franklin, Benjamin, 31, 240n143
freedom. *See* Dylan, Bob: and freedom; libertarianism
Friedan, Betty, 272n17
Friesen, Agnes, 51
Fromm, Erich, 208
Fruchter, Norm, 93
Fugitive Slave Act, 230
Furay, Richie, 177, 265n7, 266n20

Gaebelein, Arno C., 161
Gallo, Joey, 119–20
Gandhi, Mohandas, 162, 208
Garnier, Tony, 196–7
gay rights. *See* homosexuality
General Agreement on Tariffs and Trade, 220
Gideon (judge), 132
Gilbert, Ronnie, 107
Gilman family, 277n80
Gilmore, Mikal, 41, 140, 141, 213
Ginsberg, Allen, 60, 73, 223
Girard, Chuck, 175, 266n20
Gitlin, Todd, 52, 102
Gleason, Ralph, 30, 81, 106
globalism (political). *See* imperialism
globalization, 13–15, 90, 162, 163, 164, 211–20, 220–1, 228, 275n61
The Godfather (film), 117
Gods and Generals (film), 33, 230–1
Goldwater, Barry, 38–40, 61, 109, 205–6, 214
Goode, Virgil, 204
Goodman, Andrew, 19, 63
Goodman, John, 15
Gore, Al, 196
gospel music, 16, 26–8, 34, 84, 89, 98, 122, 130–40, 163, 174, 175, 176, 180, 181, 187, 233, 240n129, 254n5, 257n44
Gospel Music Association, 175
Graham, Bill, 225
Graham, Billy, 208–9, 269n51, 272n23
Grammy Awards, vii, 53, 139, 203, 212
Granger, Ken, 71–2
Grassley, Charles, 203
Grateful Dead, 140
Gray, Michael, 27
Great Depression, 5, 12, 18, 36, 70, 104, 114
Grebel, Conrad, 153
Green, Keith, 131, 166, 175–7, 177, 184, 185, 261n39, 266n13, 267n31

Green, Peter, 177
Green Party, 179
Greenbelt Festival, 188
Greenblath, Gene, 57
Greisen, Nelly, 176
Grogan, Emmett, 74
Guinness, Os, 180
Gulf of Tonkin Resolution, 203
Gulliksen, Kenn, 136, 168, 174, 182–3, 190–1, 262n45, 268n38
Guthrie, Arlo, 104, 265n7
Guthrie, Woody, x, 1, 26, 28, 58, 96, 104, 121, 265n7
Gwyn, Douglas, 160

Haber, Alan, 50
Hadassah, 19
Haggard, Merle, 16
Hale, Grace Elizabeth, 93
Hall, Gus, 5
Hamilton, Alexander, 30–1, 230
Hammond, John, 71–2
Hand, Roger, 268n39
Hanighen, F. C., x, 217–18
Hardin, John Wesley, 114, 120
Harold and Maude (film), 116
Harriman, W. Averell, 228
Harriman family, 277n80
Harrison, Benjamin, 4
Harrison, George, 79, 179
Hasidic Jews. *See* Lubavitch sect
Hatfield, Mark, 202–3, 206–11, 224, 272–3n23, 273n28
Hauerwas, Stanley, 271n89
Hayden, Tom, 45
Haymarket Riot, 82
Heard, Mark, 267n31
Hefner, Hugh, 272n17
Helms, Jesse, 190, 203, 206
Helstrom, Echo, 7, 20, 62
Hendrix, Jimi, 112
Henry, Aaron, 98
Hentoff, Nat, x, 56, 75, 233–4, 278–9n98

Herring, Annie, 176
Herzl Camp, 19–20, 238n80
Heschel, Abraham, 19, 23
Hess, Karl, 39, 205–6
Heylin, Clinton, 178, 266n15
Hibbing (Minnesota), 5, 6–21, 33, 51, 56, 87, 106, 110, 275n64
Hilburn, Robert, 28, 52, 132, 138, 141, 213
Hilliard, David, 79
Hillman, Chris, 177
Himmelman, Peter, 133, 255n20
Hinduism, 140–1
hippies. *See* Counterculture
Hispanics, 121
Hiss, Alger, 60
Hoffman, Abbie, 79
Hollywood Presbyterian Church, 174
Holm, Dallas, 139, 176–7, 184, 266n18
Holocaust, 18–19, 55
homosexuality, 40, 78, 85–6, 113, 179, 198–9, 223
Hooker, John Lee, 28
Hoover Institution, 228
Hopkins, Nicky, 179
Horton, T., 71
House Un-American Activities Committee, 46
Hughes, Harold, 202–3, 206–7, 209, 211, 224, 272–3n23
Hughes, Karen, 128–9, 137, 265n9
Humphrey, Hubert, 40
Hunter, Carol, 268n39
Hunter, Robert, 17, 140
Hutterites, 208

identity politics, 196
Illuminati, 227
imperialism, 13–15, 50–1, 54–5, 210, 211–21, 217, 219, 233, 271n4, 275n64
Indians, American, 33, 54, 162
Industrial Workers of the World (IWW), 11

international relations. *See* Dylan, Bob: and international relations
internationalism. *See* imperialism
Iron Range (Minnesota), 1, 3–21, 38, 87, 220–1, 232, 275n64
Isaac (patriarch), 20
Isaacson, Walter, 228
Isaiah (prophet), x, 132, 158
Israel (ancient). *See* Dylan, Bob: and Judaism
Israel (modern). *See* Zionism

J.C. Light and Power House, 168
Jackson, Andrew, 14–15, 33
Jackson, Bruce, 57
Jackson, George, 80, 117–18, 120, 162
Jackson, Mahalia, 98
Jackson, Thomas "Stonewall," 33
Jacob (patriarch), 132, 253n107
Jagger, Mick, 90
James (brother of Jesus), 156, 199, 260n21
Jaspers, Karl, 95
jazz music, 34, 116
The Jazz Singer (film), 238n91
Jefferson, Thomas, 14–15, 30–1, 33, 40, 191, 205, 206, 211, 214, 229, 240n143
Jeffery, Derek, 177
Jeremiah (prophet), 2, 24–5, 131, 132, 158, 176, 239n112
Jesus. *See* Dylan, Bob: and Christianity
Jesus music. *See* Contemporary Christian Music
Jesus People, 84, 122, 142–5, 153–4, 161, 164–72, 172, 173–91, 216, 222, 225, 233, 261n38, 261n39, 262n45, 262n49
Jews. *See* Dylan, Bob: and Judaism
John (apostle), 142
John Birch Society, 37, 39, 49, 50, 244n37
John the Baptist, 20, 132
Johns, Andy, 180, 186
Johns, Glyn, 180

Johnson, Lyndon, 38, 40, 47, 61, 69, 73, 81, 83, 104, 108
Johnson, Robert, 34
Johnson, Samuel, 157, 198, 271n94
Jolson, Al, 238n91
Jones, Charles, 48
Jones, Mother, 11
Jones, Rufus, 160
Jones, Walter, 204
Joplin, Janis, 113, 184
Joseph (patriarch), 132
Joyce, James, 66
Judaism. *See* Dylan, Bob: and Judaism
Judas Iscariot, 55, 141
justice. *See* Dylan, Bob: and justice

Kaptur, Marcy, 203
Kasha, Al, 131
Kasich, John, 203
Kastel, Kasriel, 25
Kauffman, Bill, 33, 39
Keaggy, Phil, 266n20, 267n31
Keller, Martin, 87, 132, 137
Kelly, Dave, viii, 129–30, 133–5, 136, 141, 164, 177–9, 185–6, 225–8, 231–3, 265n9, 265n10, 265n9, 267n24, 268n38, 268n45, 276n67, 276n79, 276–7n80
Keltner, Jim, 178–9
Kennan, George, 228
Kennedy, John, 40, 41, 47, 50–1, 56, 60, 61, 63, 80, 83, 245n74, 267n24
Kennedy, Robert, 77
Kent State University, 78–9
Kerouac, Jack, 73, 219
Kesey, Ken, 109
Kierkegaard, Søren, 142–3
Kilmer, Val, 15, 90
King, Clydie, 266n18
King, Martin Luther, Jr., 19, 48, 77, 98, 162
King Crimson, 263n53
The Kinks, 65, 113, 179
Kirk, Russell, 36, 39

Kissinger, Henry, 154, 207
Kittler, Glenn, 165
Kovic, Ron, 86
Kristofferson, Kris, 23, 113, 162
Kronos, myth of, 192
Ku Klux Klan, 18, 37, 97
Kucinich, Dennis, 203–4
Kuyper, Abraham, 144–5, 147, 149, 259n5

La Follette, Robert, 5, 203, 214, 217, 219, 221, 224, 271n4, 273n29
labor unions, 10–17, 37, 39, 51, 242n176
Lamont, Corliss, 245n74
Lamont, Thomas W., 245n74
Lamppa, Marvin, 11
LaRouche, Lyndon, 277n84
Lasch, Christopher, 78
Last Days Ministries, 175
Latin America, military intervention in, 53, 195, 212, 217, 218, 273n29
Leadbelly (Huddie Ledbetter), 28
League of Nations, 273n29
Learsi, Rufus, 19
Leary, Timothy, 75
Led Zeppelin, 180
Lee, Barbara, 204
Left Behind (books and films), 168–9, 263n54
Lennon, John, 59, 79, 85, 112, 149, 178, 179, 188, 230
Lerner, Michael, 169
Levy, Jacques, 119
Lewis, C. S., 175–6, 274n34
Lewis, Jerry Lee, 265n9
Lewis, Sinclair, 9
liberalism, 10–17, 45–82, 229
libertarianism, 75–6, 152, 201–11, 210–11, 223, 229–31, 233, 272n17
  see also decentralism; Dylan, Bob: and freedom
Libya, bombing of, 212

Lincoln, Abraham, 33, 212–13, 229–30, 230
Lindbergh, Charles, 273n29
Lindbergh, Charles, Sr., 211, 273n29
Lindsay, John, 210
Lindsey, Hal, 145, 159, 168, 174, 180, 222, 226, 262n49, 265n10
Little Richard (Penniman), 28
Live Aid, 88, 163, 231
Living Theater, 73
Locke, John, 122
Loder, Kurt, 14, 137, 220
Lord family, 277n80
Louvin Brothers, 140
Love Song (band), 168, 262n48, 266n20, 267n31
Lovett, Robert, 228
Lubavitch sect, 25, 131–5, 223, 253n113, 255n23, 256n25
Lundberg, Ferdinand, 228
Lurie, Robert Dean, 26, 38
Luther, Martin, 259n10, 259n5
Lutherans, 143, 165–6

Macdonald, Dwight, 169, 194–5
MacKinnon, Catharine, 223
The Man. *See* The Establishment
Manassas (band), 177–8
Mansfield, David, 174
Maranatha! Music, 262n48, 266n20
March on Washington, 98, 250n23
Marcus, Greil, 27, 29–30, 34, 35
Marcuse, Herbert, 35
Marshall, Scott, 256n31
Marshall Plan, 214–15, 219
Martin, Dean, 70
Martin, George, 186, 263n53, 268n39
Marx, Karl, 14, 154, 250n21
Mary (mother of Jesus), 199
Masked and Anonymous (film), 15, 53, 88, 90, 125, 213, 230–1
Massie, Thomas, 204
Mauriac, François, 279n99
Maurin, Peter, 162, 179
Maxwell, Ronald, 33, 230–1

Maymudes, Victor, 48
McCain, John, 197
McCarthy, Eugene, 207
McCarthy, Joseph, 12
McCartney, Paul, 59, 83, 112, 178, 188
McCloy, John, 228
McCrary and siblings, Regina, 175
McCrory, Alberta Cooley, 243n22, 250n19
McDonald, Larry, 203
McGinn, Matt, 57
McGoohan, Patrick, 229, 278n85
McGovern, George, 5, 205, 207, 269n51
McGuinn, Roger, 174, 265n7
McGuire, Barry, 66, 70, 176, 230, 266n17, 267n35
McKinney, Cynthia, 203–4
McTell, Blind Willie, 33, 34, 176
Mehler, John, 266n20
Meissner, Linda, 166
Mellencamp, John, 157
Mellon family, 277n80
Mennonites, 142–3, 153–4, 208
Meredith, James, 56–7
Merry Pranksters, 74, 109
Merton, Thomas, 208
Mestak, Pat, 8
Methodists, 161, 165, 165–6, 203, 205, 271n89
Mexican migrant workers, 121
Mexican-American War, 32
Milam, J. W., 97
military-industrial complex, x, 16, 52, 72, 89, 164, 203, 211–18
Millennium. *See* eschatology
Miller, Charles, 8
Miller, Jody, 70
Miller, Roger, 70–1
Mills, C. Wright, x, 45, 169, 242n176
Minnesota Farmer-Labor Party. *See* Farmer-Labor Party (Minnesota)
Mintz, Eliot, 139
Mitau, G. Theodore, 11
Mitchell Trio, Chad, 50

Modern Times (film), 16
modernism, theological, 143
monarchism, 192–4, 229, 270n72
Monroe, Bill, 28
Montanists, 153
Moore, Davey, 105–6
Moral Majority, 123, 148, 223, 224–5, 276n78
moralism, 2–6, 23, 84, 123, 128, 141–2, 147, 148, 155–6, 159–64, 166, 169, 179, 180, 201–11, 222–5, 233, 259n9, 276n78
Morgan, J. P., Jr., 218, 245n74
Morrison, Jim, 113
Morrison, Van, 28
Morse, Wayne, 203
Mosca, Gaetano, 228
Moses (patriarch), 20, 132, 136, 156, 253n107
Motown, 65
Mott the Hoople, 263n53
MTV, 53, 86, 137
Muggeridge, Malcolm, 180
Muldaur, Maria, 43, 265n7
Mullen, Larry, 189
multiculturalism, 196, 213–14
multinational corporations. *See* globalization
Mungro, Raymond, 93
Muslims, Black, 98
Muste, A. J., 215
mysticism, Christian, 142, 154, 160, 161, 165, 190

NAACP, 56, 97, 98
Nader, Ralph, 5, 214–15, 274n43
National Council of Churches, 161–2, 167
National Recording Registry, 186, 189
Nee, Watchman, 167–8, 171, 189–90, 216, 262n44
Nelson, Willie, 88
New Christy Minstrels, 176
New Left, 43, 45–9, 49–55, 57, 61–7, 68, 72–8, 86, 87, 91, 93, 164,

169–70, 191, 194–5, 196, 205, 205–6, 214, 224, 233, 273n28
New Right, 36–41, 47, 93–4
Newport Folk Festival, 57, 61–2, 65, 107, 110
Newton, Huey, 79
Newton, Isaac, 254n4
Nicholson, Jack, vii
Nicodemus, 137, 184, 256n36
Niebuhr, H. Richard, 127, 142–9, 153, 165, 208
Niebuhr, Reinhold, 83, 142
Nirvana, 181
Nixon, Richard, 5, 35, 37, 41, 61, 77–81, 207, 208–9, 269n51, 272n23
Nonpartisan League, 5
Norman, Charles, 187–8, 188
Norman, Larry, 145, 168–75, 179–89, 204, 255n16, 263n53, 264n66, 266n13, 267n35, 267–8n37, 268n38, 268n39, 268n43, 268n45, 269n51
North American Free Trade Agreement, 220
North Atlantic Treaty Organization, 219
Norton, Andrews, 32
nullification, 230
Nye, Gerald, 217–18, 219, 221, 275–6n65

Obama, Barack, 41, 91, 125, 196–7, 228
Ochs, Phil, 54, 57, 60–1, 63, 66, 79, 100, 101, 106
Oglesby, Carl, 69, 101
Oklahoma City bombing, 91
Old Right. *See* Taft, Robert
Olson, Floyd, 18
Osteen, Joel, 180
Osteen, John, 180
Oswald, Lee Harvey, 60, 245n74
Ovid, 184–5

Paine, Thomas, 114–15
Pascal, Blaise, 129

patriotism, 29–36, 86–7, 114–15, 120, 151, 157, 164, 171–2, 198, 199, 213–15, 271n94, 274n45
Patton, Charley, 34
Paul (apostle), 122, 138, 153, 155, 164, 253n113, 259n9
Paul, Rand, 204–5
Paul, Ron, 204, 220
Paxton, Tom, 50, 101
peace. *See* Dylan, Bob: and peace
Peck, Richard, 57
Pederson, Duane, 170–1
Peek, Dan, 265n7
Pentagon Papers, 80
pentecostals, 165–6, 265n9
People (band), 186, 188
People's ("Populist") Party, 4, 33, 205
Perkins, Al, 177–8, 266n20
Perkins family, 277n80
Perot, Ross, 5
Perpich, Rudy, 3
Persian Gulf War, 53, 212
personalism, 46–7, 94, 162, 170, 189, 191
Peter, Paul and Mary, 58, 217, 243n22, 249n192, 265n7
Petty, Tom, 131, 138, 231
Pharisees, 160
Phelps family, 277n80
Phillips, Kevin, 228
Phillips, Leslie, 267n31
Picasso, Pablo, 66, 96
Pilgrims, 120, 226, 277n80
Pink Floyd, 178, 185
The Pixies, 181
Plato, 192–3
Pledge of Allegiance, 215
plutocracy. *See* The Establishment
Plymouth Brethren, 167
Poco, 177, 265n7
The Point (film), 116
population control, 272n17
populism, 1, 3, 4, 7, 10–17, 21, 30–3, 104–6, 114–15, 164, 190–2, 192–4, 201–11, 214, 215, 219, 229, 231–3, 233, 240n143, 261n28, 273n29, 278n93, 278n94
pornography, 148, 223
poverty. *See* Dylan, Bob: and poverty
power. *See* Dylan, Bob: and power
power elite. *See* The Establishment
praise music, 262n45, 262n48, 266n20
premillennial dispensationalism. *See* dispensationalism, Christian
Presbyterians, 174, 204
Presley, Elvis, 23, 49, 265n9
The Pretenders, 263n53
Price, Bill, 263n53
Prinz, Joachim, 19
Progressive Era, 33, 104, 232
Progressive Party (1912), 4, 33
Progressive Party (1924), 5, 33
Prosperity Gospel, 162–3, 180
Proxmire, William, 203
Puritans, 2–3, 31, 120, 122, 226, 277n80

Quakers, 2, 142–3, 153–4, 160
Quigley, Carroll, 228

R.E.M., 88
Radiohead, 181
Rambo II (film), 86
Reagan, Ronald, 13, 38, 40–1, 85–6, 87, 195–6, 218–19
Red Scare (1940s–50s), 49, 50
Red Wing (reform school), 103–4
Reed, Bill, 35
Reed, Lou, 113
Reform Party, 5
Religious Right. *See* Moral Majority
Renaldo & Clara (film), 255n20
Republican Party, 4–5, 15, 32, 36–41, 82–3, 179–80, 201–11, 213, 219, 221, 226, 228, 232, 244n37, 270n72
Reuben (patriarch), 132
Revelation, Book of. *See* eschatology
Revolutionary Youth Movement, 75
Reynolds, Malvina, 50

Richard, Cliff, 188
Robbins, Paul, 107, 108
Robertson, Robbie, viii
Robinson, Jackie, 99
Rockefeller, David, 202
Rockefeller, John D., 10
Rockefeller, Nelson, 210
Rockefeller family, 143, 217
Rodgers, Jimmie, 28
Rogovoy, Seth, 124
The Rolling Stones, 65, 67, 71, 80, 83, 90, 112, 177–8, 180, 190
Roman Catholics, 4, 18, 46–7, 84–5, 153, 161, 165, 165–6, 179, 203–4, 204, 209
Ronstadt, Linda, 272n6
Roosevelt, Franklin D., 18, 36, 104, 218, 219
Roosevelt, Theodore, 4
Rosenbaum, Ron, 19
Rosenberg, Ethel, 40–1
Rosenberg, Julius, 40–1
Roszak, Theodore, 72
Rothbard, Murray, 210–11
Rotolo, Suze, 97
Rousseau, Jean Jacques, 122
Rubin, Jerry, 79, 85
rural life. *See* agrarianism
Russian Revolution, 82

Saga, Junichi, 184–5
Salt Company Coffeehouse, 174
Salzman, Ben, 79
Samson (judge), 132
SANE (committee), 51, 215
Sarna, Jonathan, 18
Satan, 130, 137, 139, 147, 149, 154–9, 191–6, 212, 216, 220, 260n18, 270n74
Saul (king), 132
Scaduto, Anthony, 80, 117
Schaeffer, Francis, 171, 180, 260n14, 276n78
Schattschneider, E. E., 250n21
Schmidt, Helmut, 85

Schmitt, Charles, 168
Schneerson, Menachem, 133
Schumacher, E. F., 208
Schweitzer, Albert, 159, 160, 162
Schwerner, Michael, 19, 63
Scofield, C. I., 253n113, 262n50
Second Coming of Christ. *See* eschatology
Second Great Awakening, 31
Seeger, Pete, 47, 50, 57, 58, 96
Selective Service Act (1940), 219
Selma to Montgomery March, 243n22
Sesame Street, 116
Sex Pistols, 263n53
sexuality, vii, 72, 74, 102, 113, 128, 133, 148, 179, 198–9, 208, 222–5, 274n43
Shah of Iran, 148
Shalom Fellowship, 189–90
Shangri-Las, 70
Sharon Statement, 37
Shelton, Robert, 56, 69–70, 94, 105
Sherrill, John, 166
Shipstead, Henrik, 211, 273n29
Silber, Irwin, 65
Siler, Eugene, 203
Silver Shirts, 18
Simons, Menno, 153–4
Simpson, Louis, 70
Skull and Bones, Order of, 228, 277n80
Slater, Christian, 15
slavery, 14, 22, 26, 31, 32, 33, 57, 69, 95, 110–15, 118–19, 122, 156, 162, 197, 212–13, 220–1, 229–31, 232–3
Sloan, P. F., 66
Sly and the Family Stone, 116
Smith, Chris, 204
Smith, Chuck, 162–3, 168, 171, 183, 262n45, 262n48
Smith, Harry, 27
Smith, James K. A., 161, 258n68, 260n14
SNACK, 79

Social Gospel, 161
social justice. *See* Dylan, Bob: and justice
Socialist Party, 4, 14, 33
Soles, Steven, 174
Solomon (king), 132
Somoza, Anastasio, 217, 218
Souther, J. D., 177
Southern Baptists, 203
southern music, 26–8
space program, 185, 231
Spector, Phil, 178, 180
Spivey, Victoria, 56
Springsteen, Bruce, 15, 87, 139, 157
Stanley, Ralph, 140
Stanley Brothers, 28, 139
Stanton, Harry Dean, 255n20
Staples, Mavis, 163, 240n129
Stark, Margaret, 6
Starr, Edwin, 79
statism, 14, 205, 210, 214
Stein, Carl, 57
Stevens, Cat, 116
Stevens, Thaddeus, 32
Stewart, Rod, 83
Stills, Stephen, 177–8
Stimson family, 277n80
The Sting (film), 117
Stipe, Tom, 262n48, 266n20
Stonehill, Randy, 175, 177, 181
Stookey, Noel Paul, 21–2, 29, 58, 217, 243n22, 249n192, 265n7
Streisand, Barbra, 133
Strouse, Jean, 115
Student Nonviolent Coordinating Committee (SNCC), 45, 46, 56, 108
Student Peace Union, 45, 51
Students for a Democratic Society (SDS), 37, 39–40, 45–50, 60, 68, 74, 75, 93, 102, 169, 191
Sullivan, Ed, 50
Summer of Love (1967), 74
Sutton, Antony, 228
Swiss Brethren, 153

Sykes, Christopher, 53
The System. *See* The Establishment

Taft, Robert, 36–7, 203, 205–6, 210, 214, 219, 244n37, 271n4, 273n28, 273n29
Taft, William Howard, 4, 217, 219
Tarpley, Webster Griffin, 277n84
Taylor, Elizabeth, 206
Teodori, Massimo, 55
terrorism, 204, 213, 271n94
Terry, Sonny, 28
Tertullian, 142, 146, 153
Tester, Jon, 204
Thatcher, Margaret, 85
A Thief in the Night (film), 168–9, 263n54
Thomas, Evan, 228
Thomas, Marlo, 116
Thoreau, Henry David, 32, 169, 191, 258n1
Three Dog Night, 59
Till, Emmett, 97, 118, 250n19
Timrod, Henry, 184–5
Titanic, 27
Tolstoy, Leo, 142–3, 151, 159, 169, 199, 208, 215, 274n45
Tom Paine Award. *See* Emergency Civil Liberties Committee
Townshend, Pete, 90, 263n53
tradition. *See* Dylan, Bob: and tradition
Transcendentalists, 31–2
transnational corporations. *See* globalization
Traum, Happy, 62, 77
Trautman, Karl, 278n94
The Traveling Wilburys, 89
Trilateral Commission, 202
Truax, Jay, 266n20
Truman, Harry, 36, 38
truth. *See* Dylan, Bob: and truth
Truth About Civil Turmoil, 71–2

U2, 114, 183, 188–9, 189–90, 267n31, 270n79
underdogs. *See* populism

Union Theological Seminary, 142
unions. *See* labor unions
United Nations, 219, 273n29
Uriah Heep, 263n53
USA for Africa, 88, 163
usury, 212, 273–4n34

Van Ronk, Dave, 32, 62, 97, 98
Vanderbilt family, 277n80
Vega, Suzanne, 88
Velvet Underground, 113
Ventura, Jesse, 5, 219–20
Vietnam War, 50, 51, 69, 73, 76–81, 86–7, 116, 121, 203, 207–9, 213, 219, 269n51
Vineyard Christian Fellowship, 25, 128, 131, 134–5, 145, 159, 162–3, 168, 173–4, 177, 178, 182–7, 191, 261n38, 262n45, 265n10, 265n9, 266n20, 267n24, 267–8n37, 268n38
Virgil House Christian Communal, 174

Wadsworth family, 277n80
Waldman, Jerry, 18, 19–20, 238n80
Walker, Jesse, 254n5
Wall Street. *See* The Establishment
Wallace, George, 39, 245n81
Wallace, George, Jr., 245n81
Walsh, Sheila, 188
war. *See specific wars*; Dylan, Bob: and peace
Ward, Matthew, 176
Warhol, Andy, 73
Washington, George, 211
Watergate, 80, 81, 121, 202
Waters, Muddy, 28
wealth. *See* Dylan, Bob: and wealth
Weathermen, 68, 75, 76
Weaver, James, 4
Weaver, Richard, 39
The Weavers, 107
Webb, James, 204
Webb, Stephen, 55, 242n172, 256n31

Weberman, A. J., 118, 267n24
Weezer, 181
Weinberg, Jack, 76
Welch, Robert, 37, 244n37
Wellstone, Paul, 17, 202, 237n75, 271n3
Wenner, Jann, 34–5, 85, 254n5
Wesley, John, 161, 165, 205
West, Don, 83, 101
Western Federation of Miners, 11
Wetton, John, 263n53
Wexler, Jerry, 268n39
Whiskey Rebellion, 35
White, Donald, 103, 104, 106, 117, 120
Whitney, John Hay "Jock," 277n80
Whitney, William C., 276–7n80
The Who, 65, 90, 180, 230
Wilkerson, David, 166, 167, 176
Williams, Don, 174, 256n31, 264n6
Williams, Hank, 28, 131, 132–3, 139
Williams, Paul, 84, 122, 179, 223–4, 256n39
Willimon, William, 271n89
Wilson, Tom, 63
Wilson, Woodrow, 217, 218
Wimber, John, 168
women's rights. *See* feminism
Wonder, Stevie, 59, 177
Woodward, C. Vann, 107
Woolman, John, 142–3
Worker Student Alliance, 75
World Council of Churches, 161–2, 167
World Court, 273n29
World War I, 33, 54, 54–5, 142, 217–18, 218, 273n29, 275n54
World War II, 12, 18, 19, 34, 36, 44, 54–5, 55, 219, 273n29
Worrell, Denise, 138
Wright, Frank Lloyd, 66

Yale Divinity School, 142
Yankees (New England). *See* Puritans
Yippies, 67, 74, 85
Yoder, John Howard, 208
Young, Izzy, 63–4
Young, Neil, 78–9, 88, 230
Young Americans for Freedom, 37, 93
Yudelson, Larry, 124

Zantzinger, William, 99–100, 111, 112
Zimmerman, Abraham, 7, 8
Zimmerman, Beatty, 8, 21, 31, 131–2, 133, 134
Zimmerman, Maurice, 7
Zimmerman, Paul, 7
Zionism, 19–20, 132, 134, 140–1, 179, 217, 220, 221–2, 276n67

CPSIA information can be obtained
at www.ICGtesting.com
Printed in the USA
LVOW04*1940300616
494773LV00011B/147/P